ALSO BY LIONEL TRILLING

LIFE IN
CULTURE

LIFE IN CULTURE

SELECTED LETTERS OF
LIONEL TRILLING

EDITED BY ADAM KIRSCH

FARRAR, STRAUS AND GIROUX

NEW YORK

Farrar, Straus and Giroux
175 Varick Street, New York 10014

Printed in the United States of America
First edition, 2018

Library of Congress Cataloging-in-Publication Data
Names: Trilling, Lionel, 1905–1975, author. | Kirsch, Adam,
    1976– editor.
Title: Life in culture : selected letters of Lionel Trilling /
    edited by Adam Kirsch.
Description: First edition. | New York : Farrar, Straus and Giroux, 2018. |
    Includes index.
Identifiers: LCCN 2018000146 | ISBN 9780374185152 (hardcover)
Classification: LCC PS3539.R56 Z48 2018 | DDC 813/.54 [B]—dc23
LC record available at https://lccn.loc.gov/2018000146

Designed by Jonathan D. Lippincott

Our books may be purchased in bulk for promotional, educational, or business use.
Please contact your local bookseller or the Macmillan Corporate and Premium Sales
Department at 1-800-221-7945, extension 5442, or by e-mail at
MacmillanSpecialMarkets@macmillan.com.

www.fsgbooks.com
www.twitter.com/fsgbooks • www.facebook.com/fsgbooks

1   3   5   7   9   10   8   6   4   2

CONTENTS

INTRODUCTION
LIONEL TRILLING'S LIFE IN CULTURE

It is rare for a literary critic to remain alive for readers decades after his death—even rarer than for a novelist or a poet. Lionel Trilling (1905–1975) belonged to what Randall Jarrell called "the age of criticism," a time when the analysis and judgment of texts had a prestige that is hard to imagine today. Many of the leading figures of that golden age appear in the correspondence collected in this volume, as Trilling's friends, colleagues, or antagonists. But only a few of them are still in print today, and fewer still have the ability to inspire devotion or argument.

If Trilling is the exception, it is because his own position in the age of criticism was exceptional, even anomalous. He was not, like the New Critics Allen Tate and John Crowe Ransom, a close analyst of textual strategies—one reason why he seldom wrote about poetry. He was not a journalist-critic like Edmund Wilson and Alfred Kazin, helping to shape the public's taste for new books and writers. Nor was he, after his first book, a literary historian like Newton Arvin or Leon Edel.

Perhaps to describe Trilling as a literary critic at all, though inevitable, is somewhat misleading. (When the philosopher Etienne Gilson told him that he "wasn't really a literary critic," Trilling responded with delight.) Really, he belonged to a different, though related, species: he was an intellectual, a thinker about society, politics, and ideas, who used literature as the medium of his investigations. Yet here, too, Trilling stands out from his contemporaries. Without a doubt, he was a charter member of the group known as the New York intellectuals—the writers, mostly first-generation American Jews, whose work filled the pages of *Partisan Review* and *Commentary*. He shared the eclectic approach of this group, as described by Irving Howe: "The kind of essay they wrote was likely to be wide-ranging in reference, melding notions about literature and politics, sometimes announcing itself as a study of a writer or literary group but usually taut with a pressure to 'go beyond' its subject, toward some encompassing moral or social observation."

Trilling, too, writes at what he famously called "the bloody crossroads" of literature and politics. When he discusses Orwell's honesty, or Keats's affirmativeness, or Forster's rejection of greatness, he is describing literary qualities that are at the same time visions of life and society. Yet what Howe goes on to say about the prose style of the New York intellectuals—that it was "nervous, strewn with knotty or flashy phrases, impatient with transitions and other concessions to dullness, calling attention to itself as a form or at least an outcry"— does not at all describe Trilling's work. Rather, his style is grave or elaborately ironic, impersonal, and authoritative, owing much to the Victorian sages who were the subject of his early academic study.

One way of describing Trilling's distinctive quality as a thinker and writer is to say that he was a hybrid of the twentieth-century radical intellectual and the nineteenth-century liberal moralist. This is why he was so acutely aware of the tensions that arose when liberalism evolved into radicalism, as it did for many American intellectuals in the 1930s and 1940s. Trilling's only published novel, *The Middle of the Journey*, published in 1947, was a dramatization of this confrontation; his essay collection *The Liberal Imagination*, which followed three years later, analyzed the same issue, in texts ranging from Henry James's *The Princess Casamassima* to the Kinsey Report.

Trilling's correspondence shows that the publication of these books marked a watershed in his life and career. Before them, he was a junior professor at Columbia and a respected member of the New York intelligentsia; after them, he became an intellectual celebrity and an academic grandee, with a national and international reputation. The last twenty-five years of his life saw him accumulate numerous honors, as he emerged as a kind of emblem of the life of the mind. When Trilling died, his obituary was on the front page of *The New*

York Times, and it spoke of him in reverential terms: his "criticism was a moral function, a search for those qualities by which every age in its turn measured the virtuous man and the virtuous society."

It is in this large and profound sense that Lionel Trilling's life can be described as a "life in culture." It is not simply that Trilling was "in culture" as a field, the way other people are "in business" or "in medicine," though it is true that he worked in several areas of the culture industry, not just as a teacher and writer, but as a participant in radio and TV discussions and as the editor of a subscription book club. Rather, his thought was an exploration of what it means to live in culture—as a set of assumptions and values governing individual life, and a set of transactions in which human potentialities are gained and lost.

This is the tragic, Freudian sense in which Trilling used the phrase in his essay "Art and Neurosis": "We come then to a remarkable paradox: we are all ill, but we are ill in the service of health, or ill in the service of life, or, at the very least, ill in the service of life-in-culture." To be cultured, or civilized, or humane, is for Trilling an ambiguous proposition. He admires the energy of modern literature as a destructive, antinomian force. "These structures," he writes of the modernist masterpieces in "On the Teaching of Modern Literature," "were not pyramids or triumphal arches, they were manifestly contrived not to be static and commemorative but mobile and aggressive, and one does not describe a quinquereme or a howitzer or a tank without estimating how much *damage* it can do."

Yet Trilling is also aware that civilization cannot be damaged without cost. Many of his best essays attempt to measure what is gained and lost when we become "modern" in literature and thought. When Trilling wonders why readers do not enjoy *Mansfield Park* as much as *Emma*, or when he compares the "wise passiveness" of Wordsworth with the spiritual sensibility of rabbinic Judaism, he is not asking strictly literary questions; rather, he is inviting the reader to reflect on the decline of traditional systems of ethics and values. "My own interests," he wrote, "lead me to see literary situations as cultural situations, and cultural situations as great elaborate fights about moral issues, and moral issues as having something to do with gratuitously chosen images of personal being."

As this suggests, Trilling's exploration of literary and cultural questions would not be so dramatic and compelling if they were not questions he asked himself as well. He was acutely aware of the irony involved in becoming an icon of culture, because he knew well that life in culture comes at a cost. In his own life, he experienced this cost as the sacrifice of creative work for critical writing, and of personal experience for respectability and achievement. Indeed, Trilling's life was seldom outwardly dramatic. Born in New York in 1905, he lived in the city for his entire life, with the exception of an early year spent teaching at the University of Wisconsin and a few later years at Oxford. His life in New York revolved around a single institution, Columbia University, where he was an undergraduate in the early 1920s, a graduate student in the 1930s, and a teacher for four decades, until he retired with the highest rank of University Professor. He was married to Diana Trilling in 1929 and remained married to her until his death in 1975. His days were filled with teaching, reading, thinking, and writing   quiet, sometimes invisible activities.

Yet the life in culture he led during these decades was as active as could be. The great value of his correspondence is that it shows him involved in constant inquiry about literature and public life, and about his own proper place in each. From the young radical issuing demands to the New York police commissioner, to the committed anti-Stalinist challenging the pro-Soviet policy of *The Nation*, to the senior professor reckoning with student rebels in 1968, Trilling remained engaged in American culture and its battles. Some writers, as Trilling says in his essay "Reality in America," are "repositories of the dialectic of their times—they contained both the yes and the no of their culture, and by that token were prophetic of the future." Trilling himself was one such writer, and he lived the tensions he wrote about: between activity and quiescence, self-assertion and humility, creation and criticism, revolution and respectability.

As Trilling noted in a 1961 memorandum, his business and professional correspondence was enormous—he estimated that he wrote at least six hundred letters a year—and his archives attest to the diligence with which he answered invitations, provided evaluations and recommendations, and shared information with inquiring strangers.

For this volume, I have selected what seem to me the letters of greatest biographical, intellectual, and historical interest. Annotations and identifications are offered where necessary, but they are usually brief, on the principle that in the age of the Internet it is easy to find fuller information about people, books, and events than any footnotes could usefully provide. (I have not attempted to annotate the many canonical books and authors that appear in the letters.) Omissions are indicated by [. . .]; I have only omitted material that I believed would be of no interest to the reader, such as scheduling arrangements, pleasantries, or details of business. Some early letters are undated or have an approximate date added later by another hand, usually that of Diana Trilling; in these cases, I have indicated the likely date in brackets. Throughout, Trilling's original spelling has been retained, though other features of the text, such as punctuation, have been standardized, and minor errors have been corrected.

These letters will shed new light on Trilling's life and relationships, as well as on the overlapping worlds in which he lived—the worlds of American letters, left-wing politics, academic scholarship, and New York intellectual debate. My hope is that Trilling's correspondence will help readers to better appreciate the "variousness, possibility, complexity and difficulty" to use his own phrase—of this important and inspiring thinker.

Adam Kirsch

SELECTED LETTERS OF
LIONEL TRILLING

1. TO ELLIOT COHEN[1]

October 23, 1924

Dear Mr. Cohen—

This is the story of which I told you; it is, as I also told you, not very good. Essentially, it deals with the same matter as "Impediments"[2] but it does so indirectly, ramblingly, and without much intensity or passion; it lacks all the compact "lyric" qualities that a short story should have. The people in it are very obvious and simple and not very clever. I would not so malign your alma mater as to suggest that these people are as they are merely because they are in and about Yale, nor so exalt my own as to imply that the "Impediments" people are interesting only because they went to Columbia.

Quite honestly, now that the thing is written and finished I do not consider the bare situation around which it is built to be good material for a story. As a pig's ear it does well enough, but as a silk purse it is not too admirable.—However, I am not sending it to you as a story but as a Human Document or as a tract. In that character perhaps you can find some use for it. If the title is the only thing that annoys you, you will find me entirely agreeable to any change you may suggest.

Sincerely,

Lionel M. Trilling

1. Elliot Cohen (1899–1959) was the editor of *The Menorah Journal*, a magazine of Jewish opinion, where Trilling would publish his earliest stories and essays. Cohen would go on to serve as the founding editor of *Commentary* in 1945.
2. "Impediments," Trilling's first published story, appeared in *The Menorah Journal* in 1925.

2. TO ELSA GROSSMAN[1]

September 28 [1926]
The University Club
Madison, Wisconsin

Dear Evelyn Elsa:

Please, and at once, send me your picture. It is not that I would recall you to distinctness but that I would crown your image with laurel and vine, or whatever grateful foliage this place affords. Whatever dark vagueness surrounds you is fitting, for the messengers of the gods move in a darkness and you are surely one. I refer in this manner to your letter which was a large delight. It was, apart from the unending stream from home, the first answer I have received from any of mine and it contained something of the essence of New York. I think that essence was betrayed by your irritation with the city and with people. No one here is ever irritated. There are times when someone will become annoyed—humorously and forgivingly—but never so irritated as to become—as I have known myself to become—passionately irritated. Even I, with that capacity for irritation become lifted to a burning flame—find myself sitting calmly through the most inconceivable departmental meetings with only a faint and unemotional consciousness of circumambient stupidity.—And that essence is also made up of boredom. There is no boredom here. Sometimes there is nothing to do, but actual, high-spirited boredom is not known. These things I fled from, thinking them unbearable, and these things I miss.—Truly, I am not yet maudlin about New York, nor would I return—though I have the feeling of having been here years—but in time I shall woo irritation and boredom. I think I implied a slight yearning for them in my last letters—I have heard that sudden insanity among sheepherders is very frequent. To me, that is easily believable. I have watched the herd stumbling of the immense freshman class here and I have stood before them and felt their trusting, stupid faces thrust out for orders and I can understand sudden insanity. One of the subjects for their test themes was "Qualities a Teacher Should Have." The number who demanded "faith in human nature"

---

1. Elsa Grossman, wife of James Grossman, Trilling's Columbia classmate; both would be lifelong friends.

was surprising and pathetic. It is a curious cant phrase and one that I only half understand, but I think I know what they mean by it. I think that if they were articulate—and more sensate—this hackneyed phrase would become a terribly pitiful cry of weakness, ignorance, and helplessness, much the same cry that may be heard in any good novel if it is listened to closely enough. But in the novel the cry is sometimes expressed and in the writing of the novel something is being done; in the boredom and irritation of my clever and cleverish New York friends there is something that changes the quality of the cry and gives it a sort of meaning and validity. These people here in their dumbness are rather awful—like the great mills of Gary, Indiana, which, when I saw them, passing through, had no sign of human life to give them significance. And the tiny proportion of the effectual and semi-effectual people of the East who deal torturedly with ideas is wrapped around by the immensity of those silent and pernicious folks in a way that I could never conceive. Out here, they (the New Yorkers) seem to me as well nonexistent for all the part they play in actuality—actuality being that thing which is largest and most imminent.—But I have yawped on in my usual incoherence and have made something out of nothing at all. Though that, after all, is my business, isn't it? Like God's

The man with the guts left for another university. People are taking form, however, and I am taking form for them, so that a loose sort of society is becoming apparent. That is some relief, for, as I may have explained to you, I need some sort of fairly tight social group to function properly in.—You, I imagine, do not. Indeed, I cannot imagine you easy in one, nor would you talk at all—or would you?   in a crowd.—The Society here must necessarily continue a loose one; there is so little prospect of women being added to it. The lady members of the staff are the strangest things imaginable. Evidently they are chosen much in the same way that dormitory chambermaids are chosen: to protect the morals of the men. If they are not startling in their ugliness, they twitter. I cannot reproduce it on paper, but if you'd try to twitter through a sentence or two you may yet have a notion what it is to be twittered at. It resolves itself into a very chaste and pedagogical coquettishness, the basis and foundation of a schoolmarm's charming ideas. It is not very nice—rather obscene.

Do you suppose you could really send me a photo? I'm asking for it rather sooner than I said and thought I would, but I should like to crown it before all the leaves here become sere.

Lionel

3. TO ELSA GROSSMAN

March [1927]
The University Club
Madison, Wisconsin

This, Evelyn Elsa, is the concluding—and only—couplet from one of the poems in my volume of Unwritten Works, from "Song for Late Winter":

Sit on this stone and watch this field dip West—
Nor love nor logic gives to man his rest.

You know, you, like most nice people, are a little stupid about the composition of your niceness. You, like most of them, try to conjure with that word "happy." There is only one use such people as you should make of the word: "a happy phrase," you may say, or "a happy thought," etc. But why don't you learn that the other uses are of no power at all? That the word is a low, bourgeois one, and that Aristotle is, ethically, a low, bourgeois man and philosopher. (Using "bourgeois" contemptuously drags me back untold years. I haven't used it so since high school.) Casting out the word "happy," I have found that I exist in these states: defense, when I mingle with people and do not want to be touched by them; irritation, when I mingle with them too long or when I teach; inertia, when I have indigestion of the soul and need to be drunk; anger, but seldom and for too short a time; scientific interest, usually concerned in meditating on the soul of women (men's being pretty apparent); and bliss near to frenzy, from three causes (a) from no cause at all, (b) a slow sort from doing what I like and working at it with the feeling reserved that if I wanted to I could work harder and do it better, (c) from hearing what I have done thoughtfully praised.—I suppose there are others, but these clamor most at present. Now go and see what that silly word has to do with any of these. Perhaps you will say it is the result of a proper proportioning of these. Probably not. You, I think, have not lost nostalgia. It is my greatest amazement that I have. If I see myself correctly, I am getting to be very much a son of this earth; the Platonic overtones are pretty well unheard. Which doesn't mean that I don't want things of the spirit; it means, though, that I want them, not desire them. Wanting is less graceful than desiring but one murmurs less.

I am at present immured with a cold (bad company) and hoping that I will not be well enough to go out to teach this afternoon but well enough this evening to hear Leon Kreisler. Instead of the Kant and Nietzsche I should be reading, my thick head is a good excuse for reading Yeats's *Autobiography*. When I get *so* thickheaded and miserable that I cannot read even that, I reread a letter wherein Rosenthal[1] writes about my story in terms of a spring day, and get amused when he tells me that he and another friend quarreled over its technique, because I never knew there was anything so awesome in it.— But then I get disgusted because I sit over one story like a hen, and do nothing about any others.

If you live with a large collection of heterogeneous souls, you are terribly torn between a disgusted hatred of them and a disgusted pitying love. You begin to have an interest in and a wonder about, and a deep concern for the nation and a despair and a hope in education. If I were simpler minded and had no other plans I should stay here and try to do something—if I knew what I wanted to do. But I have too much of the novelist to think in the flattened terms of the educator: people are too clear and tortuously stubborn for me, and besides, I haven't any clear set of values.

I begin to long now (or I have a memory [of] longing before my cold, I have now no mind or emotions) for the New York people again. I am heartily weary of seeing the iceboats go by under my window. They were thrilling at first, all white sail and speed, but now I furtively pray that they may go through the ice. But a south wind is blowing and the willow tree is getting its sprays yellower and yellower and everybody says—Just wait till spring.—But spring is not this year as pure and ultimate a good, it is mixed up with the clipping of the wheels of

_____

1. Henry Rosenthal, Trilling's Columbia classmate and friend; see page 9.

the Twentieth Century (for whatever the cost, I am coming home with as much pageantry as possible) and the rail-side brush closing together and opening wide as one looks from the observation car.

Reading back, I see that it is possible that in the couplet, you will read "stove" for "stone." Do not. I hate Browning now and more and more.

Lionel

4. TO JACQUES BARZUN[1]

March 26, 1927
University of Wisconsin, Madison

Dear Jacques:

There are certain limits of rudeness that tend to fade into nothingness: if one waits long enough they do fade (I hope) and one can begin again as though nothing had happened. That is, there are aberrations so large that they cannot be noticed. There are certain things that a man can do in a drawing room so terrible that he may be sure that they will never be mentioned, never thought about, even. Probably my rudeness is of such sort. If it is, there can be no apologies for it, of course. It must be stared at stonily as though it did not exist. I beg that you will stare.

About this time of year, I learn from other pedagogic exiles from New York, one settles down into a prolonged dogged effort of patience until one falls gasping into the arms of final exams, packing, and return.—Madison is a funny town. I try to understand it and do, a little, but it still retains its droll incomprehensibility for me. It has a code and civil equation of its own, fairly sophisticated and rather presentable, but subtly and rigidly its own. It would need a novel, of course, to explain it.

And teaching is a funny business. One feels somehow like a jack-in-the-box behind the platformed desk. I don't much like it but that is largely because the people are so stupid and undocile. Always: be

---

1. Jacques Barzun (1907–2012), historian, biographer, and essayist. Trilling and Barzun met as undergraduates and would remain lifelong friends; as colleagues at Columbia, they taught a seminar together for many years.

grateful for Columbia. When I remember it I am almost moved to send the Alumni Committee a check. For all its faults, it is an astonishing place and one realizes that only after one has seen others.

Thank you very much for the *Varsitys*. I think they are a decided improvement over last year but as a *Morningside* man can I speak undiluted good of *Varsity*?[1] Nevertheless, its faults are not due to anything you have control over and if you can't get the desired grade of writing from your people, you just can't. But the improved *tone* is something to be remarked and praised.—By the way, a perusal of the last few Wisconsin *Cardinals* (the daily paper) might be interesting. We are awful damned liberal here. They are in [the] *Spec* office, aren't they?

Please give my regards to all worthy persons known to me in the dear, dead days.—I should like to ask how *Morningside* is, and request you to ask the editor to send me some, but I fear to. Can I expect *Varsity* to continue coming? And will you write again?

Sincerely,

Lionel

P.S. Please excuse the sleazy envelope. I have no swell ones.

5. TO HENRY ROSENTHAL[2]

August 8 [1927]

Dear Henry—

This is chiefly to commemorate the completion of *Daniel Deronda*. "Herculean" might possibly be the word. If I had not been forced to intersperse the last four chapters with Charmides, Lysis, and Laches, I might say "Lindberghian."[3]

Vacuity continues, I fear, but I do my best not to get jumpy and hysterical. Find it almost impossible to talk and generally content myself with grimaces. Perhaps I shall evolve a new art of communica-

---

1. *Morningside* and *Varsity*, Columbia student publications.
2. Henry Rosenthal, rabbi and later professor at Hunter College, was a close college friend of Trilling's and officiated at his wedding in 1929. Their friendship ended in the early 1930s.
3. Charles Lindbergh made his solo flight across the Atlantic Ocean in May 1927.

tion. Marjorie Johnson gave me the only good evening in a very long memory. There is something more believable in her (for all her incredibility) than in most actual people.

Wyndham Lewis says Gertrude Stein reverses the Shakespearean line: she is the Monument on Patience. In his review, *The Enemy* (of which I own a copy now worth $15 I am told), he has some things to say about Joyce that seem quite thick. But he is a clever man.

Growth, we know, is cyclic. I felt in Madison at the end of the year that the growth of that period was over. Returned, I wonder what growth there was, though I think there was some; I cannot discover it, for the year seems a Xmas vacation. And here I am now with a dry skin about me ready to be shed and no new one yet grown. And if I cast a [word unclear] eye over people and activity I get only a sense of dryness and brittleness. If this present (very real and not at all romantic) hopelessness had hit me a year or more ago, I should have been pretty well knocked out. Jimmy[1] has always had this, hasn't he? It's very important, I guess. It seems to demand the immediate investigation of what I expect and should expect—what a good book or a bad book should mean to one, what a pretty leg or a fine breast, what human despicability and human virtue, what an emotion, what a sensation, etc. etc. When that is arrived at, I may be static and old in a bad sense and ahead of time, but with a point of view and the ability to write a book.

Next summer I mean to go to Germany if I have to mortgage my teeth.

Say Hello to Rachel for me. Write again.

Yours

Li

P.S. I read *The Sacred Wood*. It is remarkable criticism but I do not understand the hymns you made to it. I think I shall write to England for a copy. No doubt you will want one, so I shall try for two. It ought to be available in London. [. . .]

---

1. James Grossman.

6. TO HENRY ROSENTHAL

July 10 [1928]

Dear Henry,

Oddly, I had been planning to tell you of a dream. I am very proud of mine because I made a bon mot in it, an extraordinary occurrence certainly. I was so impressed in the dream that I should be witty in a dream that, a pencil and paper being by my bed, I awoke and set down the sentence. It was there and plausible when I awoke in the morning. The circumstance was that Rachel,[1] another person, and I were in a room and I wanted to tell something to the other person which I did not want Rachel to know. So I spoke in French. "Sshh," said the other person. "She understands French." "Don't worry," I said, "she can't understand *my* French."—And again oddly, last night I dreamed of *The Nation*. Somebody had inserted an ad in the form of a letter urging liberals to support Prohibition whether or not they believed in it. "Why? Because 10 cents of everyone will then go for bacon and so the rabbis will be defeated."

There has been purpose and a deep lesson for us, in Rachel's illness for you and in my own for me. Or perhaps you had no need of it. But I had. "Look" runs the meaning of the gentle tap we have got "just look what can be done to you. You didn't quite believe in such things, did you?" Well, I for one didn't, and now I do and it scares me. I understand why my mother declares all her plans with "With the help of God." A necessary lesson maybe. The doctor tells me to "concentrate on my health" this summer and I actually want to do just that. I want to be as well as hell. Now I feel lousy: not sick of course but quite squeezed and despising myself for it. I sit up a few hours a day. I am irritable and find myself constantly fretting and worrying. About twice a week for the last three weeks I have been getting quite black fits at night with lots of real despair and shocking fear. They have usually taken the artistic form of long unwritten letters to you. I expect they will stop soon. However, I am at present very flat. There is nobody whom I actively want to see save you, whom I have been missing; your letters were very useful. I am very sick of women. I seem to be and to have been actively surrounded by women

---

1. Rachel Rosenthal, wife of Henry Rosenthal.

all year at every turn. I should like to spend a month in the company of quiet men. The strain of women loving, needing, tending, wanting, resenting is a great one, culminating as it has in the present tyranny of a mother and a nurse. Don't tell Rachel of this; she will certainly break me into twenty-two pieces for it, though she is probably the only woman I should now like to see.

There are lots of other things quite cockeyed about me but I shall not burden you with the listening nor myself with the recital. Simply, I don't feel good and I insist upon feeling good. There are two ways, I have discovered, of wearing despair. One is over all your clothes, a great vestment hanging well over your shoes and liable to trip you; the other is to tie it about your middle like a Cordelier's rope—only under your pants—to make you keep your belly in.

Had you heard that I have a mustache? I don't much like it.

Allowed only three cigarettes a day, I have taken to English Virginians, very delicious.

Everybody was amazingly nice to me. I received no end of flowers and presents, including a suit of orange, white, and black pajamas. Thank you for *The Possessed*. I didn't read it, *The Magic Mountain* did quite enough to me. It is a great book, but misses somewhere. I am too lazy to find where.

I had the strangest love affair (as my quite keen and very nice nurse discovered for me) with a flower.[1] Someone sent me some roses unlike any I had ever seen—colored red and yellow. One of them opened into one of the very few perfect things I have ever seen. It was flawless in shape and the colors blended to look like some transcendent flesh. I could look at it for hours and it was funny to see how the nurse fell into the idiom of teasing one uses to a man who has actually fallen in love. I felt like a Greek myth.

[...]

Love

Lionel

---

1. A similar experience would be given to John Laskell in *The Middle of the Journey*.

7. TO DIANA TRILLING[1]

Dearest,

It has been a mean little January day, very suited and comfortable to be in bed in, and passing very quickly and unnoticed. I am not going out tonight to teach having run two degrees of fever, but I feel far better than last night. At present I smell like a tongue sandwich, having just had a mustard plaster. Did you arrive safely? And I hope you are settled and comfortable by now. Is it nice country?

I puttered at my story. There are some things in it still weak and unresolved but tomorrow if my nose does not attempt to imitate the glacier descending North America I shall adjust them and type it. Tentatively I call it "Round Trip" from these lines of Hardy:[2]

> I travel on by barren farms,
> And gulls glint out like silver flecks
> Against a cloud that speaks of wrecks,
> And bellies down with black alarms.
> I say: "Thus from my lady's arms
> I go; those arms I love the best!"
> The wind replies from dip and rise,
> "Nay; toward her arms thou journeyest."

I should like to give you the end of the story which for some reason I like though I do not find it exceptional.

. . . "He felt not happy, not eager, not sternly strong, but complete. He was complete not as a story is complete that a writer sends to the printer, but as the idea for that story becomes complete in the mind of the writer over many months; for the idea will come to the writer perhaps as a bald little sentence or a mere static situation, and as it rests in his mind it begins to take on little additions of significance, of which it drops some and cultivates others, growing and

---

1. Trilling and Diana Rubin met on Christmas Eve 1927 and were married on June 12, 1929. As Diana Trilling, she would become a prominent critic and essayist and a central figure in New York intellectual life. Her memoir, *The Beginning of the Journey* (1993), offers the fullest available account of Trilling's early life and career.
2. From Thomas Hardy's poem "The Wind's Prophecy."

forming itself until the writer finds it sufficiently full to begin to translate upon paper. But as the writer sits down to the paper, he knows and is afraid that, however complete and promising seemed the idea, words will perhaps betray it, will probably expose it cruelly, will certainly change it, and so he writes with the probability of failure on his pencil. But as he sits down, though he is not elated, nor happy, nor has he time for any posture of heroism in the face of this fear, he knows that his thus sitting down and beginning his first paragraph is the only thing he can do and the best moment of his life."

There is something like an inaccuracy here for "he" becomes both the "idea" and the "writer," but perhaps you will not have noticed it. I did not notice it until just now and perhaps it will have to be changed but I think not. But do you *like* it?

I have been wondering for a good part of the day why I find so much satisfaction in your being away: when I woke at ten this morning and remembered that you were gone I was very pleased, immediately. And I think I have the reason. It is that for a few weeks now we have not been alone but have been submitting to company, to scrutiny, to appraisal. This submission I can find necessities for, even interesting necessities, but this does not lessen my resentment. I resent even such a thing as Henry's or Rachel's approval of us and their liking for you. Now that it has largely gone I find our first secrecy precious for it seemed to conserve us in a dark strange way. Your being away removes you again and makes you again solitary and complete. Perhaps subconsciously that is why I wanted you to go away. Had I not so thick a head now I could tell you more of this; and I will, later, if you care to know. But now I am so completely loggish, and the thing is delicate, interesting, and, I think, important.

Today I read in D. H. Lawrence and was strangely encouraged by myself. For there are, for me, four transcendently great novelists: Dostoevski, Proust, Cervantes, and Dickens. (I omit Rabelais for his book is perhaps not rightly a novel.) Dostoevski has always depressed me by seeming to be scarcely human; Middleton Murry[1] says, rather preciously, that by several tests he does not write novels but some-

1. John Middleton Murry (1889–1957), English literary critic.

thing beyond. At present Dostoevski has no applicable meaning for me and I do not read him, but his power I remember as something never again to be attained by anyone and as making effort futile, for somehow, though temporarily I have rejected him, his seems the greatest sort of thing to do. Proust I can see at work; I understand him pretty completely and so can control my feelings about him; but he, in fertility and strength, can too discourage me. (We never understand enough the tremendous originality and courage of his method.)

As for Cervantes and the great parts of Dickens, they are primal, from the very beginning; they just are, and allow no comparison or categorizing. But Lawrence is pretty great, I am sure; he is not Dostoevski, but there is as much validity in him if not so much terrible greatness; and by being great as he deals with the things of this world and not of some other—and more important—world which is Dostoevski's and which I cannot conceivably touch, he allows in me the presumption that I, too, etc.—In short, he assures me that by using what good methods are at hand and by seeing clearly and deeply at eye level I may do something first-rate. I think if that is so it cannot happen for some time yet—not until I get blasted free: I am a good river, I think, but I am frozen down my length if not at my source, and I need that blasting.—Well, is this not a laying bare? Are you bored with this so-spontaneous confession of the young man's shy hopes? I think you perhaps are not but that you are furiously angry that I asked if you were. Oh, darling, I love you so.

Coleridge wrote a sonnet to Linley upon the singing of some of Purcell's music. I have just remembered it, and as I remember it, it says that almost he does not want to hear this music which can make him forget the bleeding and suffering of man while he himself is young, happy, loved, and safe; he wishes that it could be saved for when he himself is old, friendless, and at the point of death. It sounds flat so, I guess, but I will find it for you.—Have you ever sung Purcell? Did he write *Dido and Aeneas*?

I love writing to you. I knew I would and I do. Even though I am perforce illegible and prosy. It is nice being ill and having nothing to do save to think of you, and of you quite alone (or with only that nice girl, Bettina, to whom my greetings) and to write to you, being quite

Diana, entirely Diana, so lovely a thing to be.—Write me soon, beloved. I send you all my love. It is a great deal.

Lionel

A Voice has come to visit my mother. Ah, but a voice! You should be vibrating in a constant shudder. There is nothing in words; it is all voice. A sensitive novelist therefore can never do "types"—or not with a surety of success or without a tremendous amount of explanation. But I love you anyway, Diana dearest, dearest, Diana beloved.

8. TO DIANA TRILLING

[1928]

Darling,

[. . .]

Got up early this morning. Headache gone, though I am still looking for the piece of skull it took off last night.

You can't imagine how much I love you. I get a sentimental pleasure from contemplating the fact that I have only to stop and think about you to understand that I do it (love you) in a romantic, excited way and not calmly and evenly out of mutual "adjustment" and companionship which I had feared childishly would happen, just as when I see you from a distance I never say There's Diana but There's a good-looking girl; could I make her?—Have been reading *New Grub Street*, which is literary life in the '80s, and there's a writer's wife in it, not very nice, so I've also been lost in admiration of your moral charm and wondering if there ever was another girl like you. And knowing there wasn't.

[. . .]

I bet you think I'm writing now just to do a "screw-letter" but no. But it would be nice to have you back before incapacitation.

See you soon, Beloved—

Lionel

9. TO DIANA TRILLING

[December 1928]

Dearest Diana,

I am writing to you for quite no reason at all save that thinking of you half an hour ago—and for all the half hour, and now, of course— I was so strangely joyous that I wanted to make sure of your reality by reaching out to touch you, and this is the nearest I can come to doing it. Often I want to make a big literary gesture to you, a superb piling up of the best and truest words I know: someday maybe I shall be able to do that, to let all the splendid words come out as they want to, and give them to you. But now I am glad to say almost any words, so long as you are glad to receive them, and satisfied to say only "dearest" and "Diana."—It is funny, it is superbly and terrifyingly curious how you seem to be a stiffening to all the tenuity and the necessary weakness of every sort of book.—Probably this will come to you by the morning's first mail: and that, for no reason that I can discern, gives me pleasure.

Lionel

10. TO DIANA TRILLING

[1929]

Darling,

I had meant to write and send this last night but I had been seeing people every minute of the day and the last one, Jimmie, did not leave until 3:30 this morning.

Kip[1] spent the afternoon here. He read the story and seemed to like it very much, finding it less good and significant in some places than in others but on the whole interesting and meaningful and somewhat important. Henry, who finished it last night, seemed rather moved by it and thinks it beyond anything I have done. He said some swell things. Kip's professional and technical approval, and Henry's emotionally critical reaction very much relieved the feeling left by Jim's and Elsa's comment and attitude. Perhaps you will wonder why

---

1. Clifton "Kip" Fadiman (1904–1999), writer, editor, radio and television host, was another of Trilling's friends from college.

I should be so much affected by these. Well, Jim used to be an important critic, and a careful and assiduous one, for me; and Elsa is an intelligent girl who has liked some of my work. My story—it is not rightly a story but something more and less—had, I thought, a great many implications. Purposely, I kept many of its significances veiled so that the reader, trying to find the meanings, might be free to find whatever he wanted to. For instance, the story is divided into three parts, though it all takes place in an hour—two incidents, and an incident-essay on a man's attitude to Jewishness. Seemingly there is only the faintest relation to be seen linking the three, but I intended a very deep one. And all that Jim and Elsa could see was that it was a disjointed story with an essay on Judaism to sell it to the *Menorah*. This judgment reduced the MS to blank blue lines on blank white paper: it killed all my potency and I was quite certain I should never be able to convey another meaning in my life. It took Kip's and Henry's praise to restore the story to life. It is an emotion I never feel but I was what is called "hurt"—what Henry would call "betrayed." I was devastated that I would have to show this blank blue-and-whiteness to you and that all my life I would teach freshman composition. It was really quite horrible. I am sorry to have bored you with this but I had to get rid of it somehow.

Kip was here yesterday for a long time. We spoke of you, he with high terms of apt admiration, and I—well. He spoke nicely and practically—as he would—of us. He conceives a most tortuous relationship between you and him: that you despise him, that he is angered and injured by your despite, that he scorns it, and some more: all this quite casually, of course. He seems to have been once infatuated (his word) by you. He so often assures me that there has been nothing between you that I must ask—but in parentheses—(What in hell *was* there between you?) (Do you mind if I write closer? I shall not have enough stamps at this rate.) He spoke of him and Polly[1]—hopelessly but without much dramatization—and I told him what I have always wanted to, that it would help him and spare his friends not to jar publicly. It is all horrible, I guess. He spoke of his talent with the

1. Pauline "Polly" Fadiman, Clifton Fadiman's first wife, was a high school classmate of Diana Trilling's.

same awful hopelessness, made me ill by envying me my talent and my use and development of it—he could be twice as good as me if he wanted—and refusal to be comforted. I am no good at argument, especially with a man's devils, so I was of little help—not that he wanted any. But it was all—not shocking for we know it all—but tragic as tragedy must, I suppose, now be understood.

I felt much as Kip used probably to feel when he acted confessor to most of the college, for in the evening Rachel gave me the copies of some tremendous and affected letters which she and Henry wrote to try to adjust their relationship to Henry's sister, and later Jim came to talk about Elsa. New Year's Eve was, by the way, the first he knew of her California plans, he at the same time with the rest of us, a circumstance that, at least, implies culpable stupidity. I feel that somehow I am mixed up in that thing, though how I do not know. She is bitterly angry, I am told, that I never see her, and Jim wants me to go because she thinks I do not think well of her, and (according to Jim) she thinks then that she is really not much and that Jim's opinion of her is not important but is merely the opinion of one who, not having known many women, is not fitted to judge. What people!

Yesterday and the day before I felt astonishingly weak but today I am quite well. It is not possible to express the irritated chagrin I have been feeling at not being able to get up to you. Did it rain there immensely as it did here?

Night before last, I fussed around and found your letter to me from Rio. How delightfully you write! Darling, I love you for your literary skill. That is reason 27 I think or more. Hey—I want to see you. You have not truly been away weeks, have you? Did you get the book and the letter? I love you, Diana, and I love you.

Lionel

11. TO DIANA TRILLING

[1929]

Dearest,

There is in me so much confusion, so much that is like shame and humiliation, so much of a nervelessness that is yet endlessly sensitive, and so much of unreasoning despair, that I hesitate to write to you. And yet I must write to you and the reason for my hesitation is the same for my writing. I think you have never seen me so: I have never exhibited it to you and indeed, though I sometimes—often— get so, all this year I have been untouched, and because of you, I know. Were I now to see you, it would be certain to disappear, this quite absurd state, and it would not have to be mentioned to be exorcised. But though I thought to call you at your teacher's to try to see you again today, I find it is too late. So that write to you I must (though I think you will not like the gesture) partly because it seems sometimes natural to some to make a gift in love of their own misery (I shall not do it often) and partly because the feeling came when I left you after our few minutes today and because I cannot help tracing it to that few minutes. I met you, I fear, rather ready for misery, with a weakness in my thoughts and that strange internal hand that sometimes closes ever so lightly on my vitals, not at all heavily but ready and warning to grasp and constrict and take from me all power. This you could not know (and why should you?) and you could not know that casually and lightly you made the hand come tighter, much too tight. I am sure that it was nothing essential in your manner, nothing important, that gradually began to touch me hurtfully; probably it was only the usual playful brusquerie that we like (am I not absurd!), perhaps it was that I wanted to be deeply noticed and that I wanted you to know that I was on the edge of misery, and was frustrated that I could not tell you. Whatever it was (and oh my dear, it was no fault of yours!) I desired, when I left you, to see my body dissolve on the pavement. All the world in this false and terrible weather was (trite word but here true) a mockery, and every shopping woman and every perambulated child was a denial and a wickedly comic disease.—Let me go further, Diana my beloved, and perhaps when I have done I shall have quite overpassed this mean malaise which I thought I had forever done with, and if anything I have said or say annoys or disgusts, you will forgive me, please, and quite forget about it for it is certainly but momentary. And I think that what I would say is that now for several days I have been feeling—dimly, most of the time— that somehow, in some quite indefinable way, I have been losing— not importance, nor meaning—but (shall we say?) figure and form for you: that I was losing sharpness and acquiring typicality and a conventionality. More than probably this is not any thing in you (if it be true at all) but in me: and another and simpler way of saying it is that I have been dull, and affected you only in old molds of impression. If this is true, my dear, please do not be too impatient of it. Certainly it will pass. True, it frightens me a little, for because of it I think I feel you combating and resenting something in me.

Diana, whom I so much love, has this letter tried and annoyed you very much? I love you so and I have my love for you at present so much wrapped about with unhappiness that I am everlastingly frightened for our love, and when I offer you mine it is too likely to be still stuck with the unhappiness enclosing it. Oh my love, believe again, completely again and at once, that I love you well and you will forgive this letter and not find it too much lacking in that dignity you prize. It has been good to write you, even in this way, and it has made me happier. Goodbye, dear, and love me.

Lionel

12. TO DIANA TRILLING

[1929]

My beloved,

Your letter was—is, will always be—so good, and so dear and important to me. It is—but this is almost fatuous because of the sweet things about me in it—so wise: it has so much the grace of wisdom everywhere about it. It is too bad that I am now abysmally and absurdly tired—I think it is my shoes: I shall not be the same until I get back from the cobbler my proper shoes—and cannot tell you as I would how deeply I received it. But when I see you.

I am glad that you found something to jib at. I hope to write an article on Jewish fiction—which can be made a more subtle subject than it sounds—and if I may I should like to quote your objection to the fact and logic which I do not explain that lies in the idea "Jew." I am sorry I did not get the letter this morning so that we could talk of it. Now I shall not explain why I do not make the intellectual clinch, though I shall explain in the article, but I am not hedging when I say that I allowed the omission purposely. I did not want to define the concept "Jew": I was sure that there would be enough meaning for everyone in the word of a sort that would make clear its effect in the story. But more when I see you.

Of course you "may" point out the bad sentences. I regretted, giving you the story, that you did not yourself write so that you could have that vision into the functional structure of every sentence which writing alone, I guess, gives: just as I have always been afraid to press you to sing for me because I might completely miss the significance of each of your different efforts and find importance only in the effect, and miss often the true effect: simply, our technical snobbism, but I am tired and have got the sentence confused.—Bettina would triumph and gloat at this but our sentences have very analogous rhythms.

I want this to go by the last collection but I cannot help quoting this from a swell book I have just discovered, Coleridge's *Table Talk*:

"The best way to bring a clever young man, who has become skeptical and unsettled, to reason, is to make him *feel* something in any way. Love, if sincere and unworldly, will in nine instances out of ten, bring him to *a sense and assurance of something real and actual* [italics mine]; and that sense alone will make him *think* [italics the author's] to a sound purpose instead of dreaming that he is thinking." Which I said something like to you before, I think; in particular, if the story is the best thing I have done etc.—And therein lies the truth about Kip and a great man said it.

I kiss you goodnight.

Lionel

Forgive the envelope it is the only one in my desk.

13. TO DIANA TRILLING

[1929]

Beloved,

I am so ill! I am all a whimper and a snivel. I am not fit to write you a letter; but I have been trying to name the strange physical warmth and strength that has been girding my waist (almost I could put my finger and say "there it begins and there it ends"). I get from you the feeling often; as though I had been buttoned up warmly and lightly. It is not as though some woman had so buttoned me up so comfortably—some mother, or maternal aunt, or a wife—but as though an old general should say to a young soldier, "Here, wear this—so. You will find it good." Do you at all follow what I mean, Diana, for I am not sure I do entirely? But I think I do.

I am always trying to find words for my love for you, and you know I cannot. Perhaps that is just as well, because if I could it would become crystallized and controllable. I do not want to be able to control it. I want it to control me, and I am willing always to stammer about it. But you must know about it as maybe you do, with all generosity guessing it.—I cannot get the word for it but sometimes I get pictures of us. Just now I do not see us together, but each of us grasping hard to either end of a stout rope. Do you remember how children do that, lean backward, and then move in great circles with scarcely any effort? I see us leaning back so, moving so, at either end of the rope, and on the tight-stretched rope are hung the particles of the world. So long as each keeps the rope tight, we move with ease, and the particles of the world stay in alignment. But if the rope is let slacken, they jumble; and at least one of us falls down.

But that is but one picture. My dear, you have so grown into me—so organically become a part of me. I wonder if you still resent and fear this, as you once did? I think perhaps you do. But you need not. It is scarcely a demand upon you, and not at all a weakening of me.—Darling, and I have not said anything to you!

Two little girls have finished their exams and are acting like a pair in *The Wild Party*.[1] They should live so long!—in the jungle where I spent my youth learning to look lean, mean, keen. One is black-haired and one yellow, and the yellow one is called Weinrib, Miss Weinrib. Dear, two spiritually snotty girls can get a great deal of low fun watching their instructor being actually and materially snotty.

Didy darling, please feel well and eat a big breakfast. I'll see you soon.

    Lionel

---

1. Narrative poem by Joseph Moncure March, published in 1928.

14. TO RACHEL ROSENTHAL

[1929]

Dear Rachel,

You will, I know, forgive me for having waited so long to write. To use a phrase much current in my family, "after what I have been through"—which implies, though it is never said: "Just nothing must be expected of me." However, it was not nearly so bad as I expected it to be. I sailed through with considerable composure, sufficient to convince that there was nothing to be done about the crime I was committing, and after a few days the idea became for them quite bearable. Now, as Henry predicted, it is even exciting. A family dinner went off well enough and save for the annoyance of wedding discussions from which Diana suffers a lot, everything is smooth. All the sensible unsentimental people have been at mother saying not only that it is *not* an intolerable thing, but, either charmed by Diana herself when they have met her or by the report of her and the idea of a rich girl giving up having breakfast in bed to marry a poor writer when they have not met her, have actually been convincing mother that it is a good thing. Harriet[1] has been behaving quite well: indeed, in a far better way than I expected. She is undoubtedly hurt by it, and scarcely romantically excited, yet she is being most sensible and strong, and not unintelligent.—All this has been a very grateful release from the tension of secrecy and waiting.

Yet everything is not quite adjusted, nor, I suppose, will it be until June—and perhaps for several months after June. The situation is creating emotional consequences in me (I will not speak of Di) and requires emotional adjustments such as, of course, I have never had before. In themselves I do not resent them too much and my rather full consciousness of them gives me a control over them that is actively reassuring, and yet they are painful.—The primary reason for them—the fertilizer of them, rather—is, of course, the absurdly anomalous position we are in. Had we not to shudder up into ourselves to resist the interference and handling that we must get and did not that resistance carry over often to each other, I think there would be nothing at all painful. But in taking reality from all

---

1. Trilling's sister, Harriet (later Harriet Schwartz).

other things in defense, we are likely to become a little abstract to each other. This, I think, is true of both of us, but for me there is also the worry that comes from a complete loss of the sense of any power. Partly, it is from the business of family again: I get the sense that I have delivered Diana over to them, and they, very kindly, have allowed me to have her. Too, there is the necessary humiliation of having to be "sonny dear" when Di is present, the little boy who so precociously and so poetically is taking a woman. To this situation, the annoyance and sterility of my teaching job contributes; and far from unimportant is my status as a student which I hate and resent, a feeling intensified by an academic disappointment recently; at the present time the unbenevolent paternalism of my professors is detestable and harmful, but this I foretold long ago, and it was one of the reasons I did not want to marry before I had passed my examination. But perhaps the most important and the most interesting factor of all is the result of the very relationship between Di and me. Now, as, more than ever, I begin to love her more and more every day, with a frightening depth and completeness, and as I acquire a painful sensitivity to her, an almost complete consciousness of her (though still a little stopped and hindered by past habits of thought and feeling), I find asserting itself subconsciously a resentment against myself for many things in our curious past relationship. That she felt importantly about me before I did about her, that I was once casual about her and clumsy, that perhaps I hurt her a little, and that once there was a relationship between us in which I was a dolt and a close-eyed and vulgar dolt, not seeing half of what I should have seen, gives me a sense of guilt, not conscious in the least until it is sought for, and a not-conscious desire to take punishment for it.— All this is driving me to a sense of weakness and incompetence, absurd but sometimes agonizing: to a devastating fear of myself, to worry about Diana and our relationship, actually to a chaotic and nameless jealousy. And as I seem to shrink, Diana seems to grow, so that there sometimes seems to me an intolerable disparity between us which I fear she will at any moment recognize. This fear her admiration for strength intensifies, so that last night I had, after I left her, partly when awake, partly when asleep and in a dream, a most terrible time—from a picture! It is almost too neat, like a story. We had come from my house and walked down the park to take Di home. I suggested going in to see Henry and we did and had a good hour talking. As we left I saw a book I had lent him which had in it a picture I had wanted Di for a long time to see. It was a photo of a statue of a Samnite warrior, of an art I did not know—early inhabitants of Italy I presume—and one of the most beautiful things in the world. It is hard to describe here: a terrible face composed in beautiful linear masses, a body all clean lines, the armor part of the body, the mightiest arm from great shoulders, long gleaming legs in stride. It is very sophisticated for all its primitiveness—it has the *craft* of strength—and as a composition, abstractly, astounding—at once bizarre and classic. We admired it and talked about it for some time. Even while talking I felt somehow beaten by it and I could dream of nothing but Diana and this thing together.

Of course, all this state is completely subjective in me. Di sees manifestations of it, resents them, and has interpreted them cleverly but incorrectly. That it will pass I have no doubt, but it must pass soon.

But four pages is quite enough for my neurosis. No one ever taught me that life was easy and uncomplicated, yet I am always surprised when it is not. Diana grows lovelier every day in strange ways. She is tired and irritated by all the absurd adjuncts to getting married. I wish she could go to sleep until June.

[. . .]

Yours, with love,
Lionel

15. TO HENRY ROSENTHAL

[1929]

c/o Rorty, R.D. 1, Westport, Connecticut

Dear Henry,

Save this letter be inordinately long and detailed it must necessarily be false. But I must risk falsity—extenuated by my knowledge of it and relieved by your sense and intuition—and forgo length and detail.—I am very happy. It is a happiness that I have so completely taken into myself that unless I stop for a moment to look at myself and find it interfused with me, or unless it comes suddenly apparent out of some word one of us has said, I scarcely remember it. I only know that at almost every moment I am in a lovely ease.—We acted like a pair of dopes when we got here. Some top layer of empty romanticism which I fear we both have, dictated to us to try to act like any honeymoon couple. We kept this up for a couple of days, the strain wearing us both into an internal annoyance until I pointed out what we were doing. Di agreed, and we stopped. Then we became elaborately phlegmatic until Di explained that, and we stopped. We had then no more postures to go through and I had got over a slight physical indigestion and febrility, and the several weeks' madness I had been entertaining (of which I think you do not know but sometime I will tell you), and so we eased into ourselves and into happiness and have stayed there. Marriage in its reality I find more pressing and complex and more exhilarating than I had guessed it. We are "making adjustments" and I like it; as an exploration and an import it is a more beautiful adventure than I could have supposed. I have to walk like a cat, but with the certainty that I cannot slip. There are many things that must happen to me; I think they will and I am glad.— Every day she gets lovelier. She had been doing that a long time, but now in a new way, so that I fear she will bust or I will bust, or something, with her loveliness.

I wish you could come to us here, but I suppose you cannot. It is infinitely peaceful and quiet. All morning I sit out in the sun and read while Diana sings in the house and curses and breaks things when it goes wrong. But when it goes right it is amazing. I have become a startling plumber and mechanic. I feel and look splendid. Di seems better but not so well as she should. But she is drinking milk.—Today she went to the city for a lesson, something having happened to her diaphramic psychology, and has had to stay the night; it is horribly lonely. We get eggs and milk and strawberries from a farmer out of Robert Frost. There are plenty of New Englanders round about, and pleasant folk in reality. We are very far from almost anyone save our communist landlord, so Diana goes about in shorts and bare legs, which is good for her but she gets bitten, she lives in constant and mortal fear of ants in the food.

What is this momentous gossip about Elliot's marriage and your performance of it? I was delighted with it—was I right to be, do you think?—and with the whole situation of it. No doubt you will write me about it.

Why was everybody so sad at our wedding? I do not mean the conventional sadness of the older people, but of the younger. Yourself we could understand, but so many of the others not. Diana's friends, most of them. And why Kip, sadder than the rest—very sad. What did you say to each other that made you say to me, "This man is harmless?" I did not speak to him, nor to you all evening. I was scarcely existent.—By the way, the girl who sat next you at dinner—Diana's sister-in-law—was in fear all evening of a miscarriage as a result of her accident; she was plucky, I think.

Di was deeply touched by your ceremony and by you and so was I and we thank you very much.

[. . .]

I want to get—somewhere; to work, I think, in the world, among people, as soon as this time of peace and seclusion is over. This year and Diana have overset me. I seem to have divested myself of a great deal, of good things perhaps as well as bad, and I feel very naked—a little quintessential and impalpable. I need some new attitudes, some new affirmations and denials. Nakedness for too long is not good for me or for me-and-Diana. But it is all right now.

What is the last word on Jim and Elsa? When I saw them at the wedding they seemed foreign and unreal—very much more so than usual. I must get hold of Jim again, or try. But Elsa? I thought to have them here for a weekend but Diana fears madness from Elsa.

Write to me soon. What are you doing with your summer days? Nothing I hope.

Diana has a plot for a high-comedy Jewish story, a swell one. She wants me to write it but I insist that she do, though I eye it enviously. I should like to do a piece of comic writing and this is good solid fundamental stuff; a chastened Meredith style would be good for it.—Write soon; but I've said that. Are you doing maybe a leeddle bit creation?—Diana sends her love with mine to you and to Rachel.

Lionel

16. TO ALICE FAY

July 25, 1929

Dear Miss Fay:

Some time ago Mr. Gassner requested that, if possible, I review your book, *Our America*, in the *New York Evening Post*. The editors of the *Post* received the book but from reasons either of space or of taste decided not to have it reviewed. Though I was willing to accommodate my friend Mr. Gassner, I did not feel that I need push the matter beyond the decision the editors had made.

Your offer of $100 to review the book and have the review printed in the *Post* embarrasses me and, I hope, yourself. Were I a publicity agent the offer would be a legitimate and welcome business item. Unfortunately I attempt to be a critic. Were I to review your book and praise it I should lay myself under the implication (even to myself) of having been venally influenced. Were I to dispraise the book (and I fear that I could not like a poem containing the line "Dream with the stars, America, one constellation lighting the world" or containing the idea or the phrases that one can find in America "Palaces—alabaster walls, bordered with purple grapes and passion flowers") I could not but feel that I was cheating you.

I regret to have to disappoint you but I fear I must

Sincerely,

17. TO ELLIOT COHEN

December 2, 1929

Dear Elliot:

What you have written me about the [Menorah] *Journal's* situation is very frightening, yet I can be almost grateful for the opportunity it gives me to express what I feel about the *Journal*.

What I feel can best be said and explained by a few paragraphs of autobiography. I shall not make the usual apology for introducing the personal, both because what I have to say is inescapably personal and because I am sure that it is also very typical and that it contains very important general implications. These implications are so important, I feel, that if they are ignored—that is, if the *Journal* is abandoned—Judaism will be making not only a great spiritual mistake, but also a great practical mistake: perhaps an ultimate and fatal one. Does this sound extravagant and melodramatic? I am sure it is not.

I first saw the *Journal* when I was a senior at college—about four years ago. My family is orthodox, with a pretty sound tradition of learning and piety behind it. But, like most families with such a tradition and with sincere and not unintelligent intentions of continuing it, it was losing out. I see its Jewish gestures as the swing of the clapper of a bell: while the clapper hung in the bell it was intended for, it struck the sides and gave forth a sound. But now the clapper had been hung in a bell that was too big for it. It swung but it could never reach the side of the new environment. No sound came.

So, except sentimentally, my parents' gestures could not touch me at all. I need not go through for you the rationalizations of a young man who was bored and unattracted by the whole business.

At college I was one of the clever young men. I need not explain this, either. At the time, it was, I believe and you perhaps will remember, taken for granted that a clever young man was a completely free spirit. This, too, you will understand. I suppose that the characteristic thing about our intelligent society was its assumption that religion (I use the word with a little Ruskinian machinery: "religious" "binding" of any sort) was not a valid thing.

With two environments such as this I was pretty divorced from Jewish life or thought of any sort. I cannot remember that I made any extravagant flutterings or uttered cries of despair at being [word missing]. I was comfortable enough. On the one hand, I never received any personal manifestations of anti-Semitism, and on the other, I found that I simply preferred my Jewish to my Gentile friends. I was not rebelling, I was merely ignoring. Implicit in my feeling about Judaism was that it was not unpoetic, but quite empty of meaning now and inclined to manifest itself stupidly.

When I first saw the *Journal*, my emotions were naive but not, I think, difficult to explain or unworthy. I was first struck by its handsomeness: I had never seen a modern Jewish publication that was not shoddy and disgusting. Here I found no touch of clumsiness or vulgarity—believe me: this was perhaps the first public Jewish manifestation of which I could say that. I suppose my naive apprehension of this acted as a sort of catalyst to whatever vestigial Jewish feeling

I had. I saw that this Jewish manifestation was careful, considered, intelligent. I had heard no rabbi to be these things, though I had heard many rabbis. I saw Judaism taken as an accepted and legitimate thing; no apology was being made.

It seems to me that I could stop this letter here. It seems that if the *Journal* could mean and do the things it did then, to me, its existence is not merely justified but utterly necessary. But I want to say more because there is more to say.

I had in my drawer a story I had written about two Jewish students. I do not usually remember the things I write with much affection, but as I remember that story it still seems a pretty good story. It exploited a situation between two Jews; but I had not said they were Jews; and I tried to hint it but not say it by giving the characters names that might or might not be Jewish. This evasion did not make the story dishonest. It had truth—general truth. But when, before sending the story to the *Journal*, I indicated unmistakably that they were Jews it gained more truth. Not only did it contain particular truth; by the gain of particular truth it made a gain in general truth. It became a better story. It could have been printed nowhere save in *The Menorah Journal*.

The implications of this I shall not develop, save to say that, in one way or another, this situation is repeated about twenty times a month, in every piece of writing the *Journal* publishes. Nowhere else can these pieces appear, and for each one that will not be able to appear, a lie will have been told because the truth has not. I myself am chiefly interested in the fictional representation of the Jew; and remembering the fiction which exploits the Jew, as it is published by the established houses, I know that the Jew is written about carefully, fearlessly, without easy "sympathy" *nowhere* but in the *Journal*, nowhere else as a human being and not as a problem. And I know that this is a terribly important thing to have done.

But I fear I must return to myself. With the publication of my story I was caught. I could not escape thinking about Jews. I was not obsessed with Jewishness. I did not get religion. I did not, I think, make romantic and compensatory gestures. But I accepted the fact of Jewishness as an important thing. I accepted it as part of my individuality and it functioned like a personal characteristic—I could talk of it as "mine" as one talks of a person's honesty, weakness, strength, selfishness. I wasn't very sure what it was, but it helped direct my life. When I began to conceive a story, some element of Jewishness entered into it. I used to be told that this Jewishness was extraneous, that the story would have a more "universal" appeal without it. This may have been true, though I think not, but certainly the story always took on more life for me, more clarity, more point, if it contained Jewishness.

I have been personal at so great length because, as I said, I think my situation is not untypical. Nowadays, as you know, young men do not say, "I will not be a Jew," and immediately gulp an oyster. What they do is to forget quietly. If they get a sock in the eye from anti-Semitism they say words like "race," "habits," "personal appearance," "manners," "solution." The old explanation for the young man when he left Judaism was that he was "ashamed" of his heritage and that he wanted "to get on" in "the larger world." But neither of these is any longer valid. The young man only *seems* to leave Judaism most of the time; often Judaism has really left him. If he is "ashamed" of his heritage it is only after the separation has been made and he looks across the distance.

It seems to me that there is but one thing which must be done for Judaism today. Content must be given it. Meaning must be given it. And content and meaning must be given it in a form as fine, as dignified, as effective as possible. I think that the only thing in Jewish life that could have done that for me was *The Menorah Journal*. There are thousands of young men for whom it can do the same thing, and it alone can do this thing. These are young men earnest, trained, perhaps talented, whom Judaism loses only with a terrible effect on itself.

The *Journal* has attracted to itself many young men who are thinking and writing about Judaism from many different aspects and with many degrees of intensity—but all of them doing so simply and naturally. All the young men in the Jewish world will not be writing for the *Journal* if the *Journal* has opportunity to exercise its function, but very many because of the *Journal* will be living with the consciousness, which they will gladly accept, of being Jews. They will not be orthodox Jews, or only Jews—if either of these two things mean anything anymore—just as they will not all be writing for the *Journal*. But they will be Jews in a good, simple, positive sense, if the proper method is used to *allow* them to be that.

I have been trying hard to understand the reason which would, of all Jewish activities, first abandon the *Journal*. I can only see such an action as to the last degree illogical. It seems to me that the whole purpose of practical Jewish endeavor is to create a community that can read *The Menorah Journal*. More exactly, of course, what I mean is that this purpose is to construct a society that can consider its own life from a calm, intelligent, dignified point of view; take delight in its own arts, its own thoughts, the vagaries of its own being. It may be argued, of course, that the *Journal* does not do these things. But granted that it does, it is performing an essential function in the Jewish body. And if it does these things, it is a madness to cut it out from the Jewish body.

If the situation of the Jews were suddenly made perfect, if there were no longer struggle and heartbreak, many forces in present Jewish life would be stranded and made useless. But *The Menorah Journal* would not. In a perfect Jewish world, the *Journal*, with very little change, would still be valid and useful. It is not often that a thing can be both a means and an end. Perhaps only the best things are both—creation, love, truth.

I have tried to think why the *Journal* must of all things in Jewish life be first sacrificed. I cannot discover why. I can only see the sacrifice as a terrible *waste*. As for how the Intercollegiate Menorah Society can be justified without the *Journal*, I simply cannot conceive it. The Society's purpose is cultural, is it not?—the purpose of Jewish life is cultural, is it not? Have we then so much learning, have we then so much spiritual fertility, have we so much intelligence in Jewish life that we can afford to chuck a good deal of it very casually over the side? Nobody can think that we have. A good Jewish book, a fine Jewish thought is rare enough, God knows. You bet He knows. And He knows that all the ewes are blemished, that the column of smoke rises crooked as a corkscrew, that unclean accidents happen to the priests, that the sanctuary buzzes with flies.

You asked me what I thought of the *Journal* and I have taken a long time to say it, and I could say more. But let me atone for all these words by a sentence of very few, which will say all that I have said, all very simple things: If the *Journal* is chucked, then Judaism has also to be chucked and made over into a Benevolent Association.

And then a man could decently make up his mind whether he wanted to join that bunch or the Elks.

Yours,

Lionel Trilling

18. TO W. BARRETT BROWN[1]

December 8, 1929
1 Bank Street

Dear Mr. Brown,

It was kind of Mr. Williams to suggest my name for membership in the Columbia Club and of you to write me. Thank you very much, and may I ask you to convey my thanks to Mr. Williams?

I am sorry that I cannot consider membership in the Club. My primary reason for this is that difficulty was made for an intimate friend of mine—and, I hear, for not a few other applicants—on the ground of race. I suppose that the Club's attitude in this matter has not changed, for another friend, a member of the club, tells me that your letter to me was something of an "honor" because "the club does not usually take Jews." Under such a circumstance, you will surely perceive, I cannot decently stand for membership.

Truly yours,

Lionel Trilling

19. TO GROVER WHALEN[2]

March 7, 1930

My dear Mr. Whalen:

In the *New York Telegram* account of Thursday's disturbances in Union Square, I find the following sentences: "Whalen ordered talkie cameras removed from the vicinity of the stands. 'I don't think there will be anything edifying to record in this kind of speeches,' he ex-

---

1. Chairman of the membership committee of the Columbia Club.
2. New York City police commissioner.

plained." I wonder if you will be kind enough to answer the following questions.

1. Did you order the removal of the talkie cameras and did you offer as explanation of this order [that] there would be nothing edifying in the speeches?

2. If you did give this order for the reason quoted, what statutory or implied power were you exercising to prevent the dissemination, by a common and legitimate means, of utterances which, since they had been permitted by the City's license, were as legal as a speech delivered by the president of the United States or by yourself to an honest taxicab driver?

I shall indeed be very grateful for your answer.

Yours truly,
    Lionel Trilling

20. TO RACHEL AND HENRY ROSENTHAL

June 23, 1930
Hotel Somerset, Boston, Mass.

Dear Rachel and Henry:

A few weeks after Henry left, Diana was found to be much sicker than she had ever been—about twice as sick numerically—and after a few consultations it was decided that an operation was the best course. There was the alternative of trying to treat her by complete seclusion in a hospital for many weeks, rest, diet, and medication, but though this treatment would have produced an undoubted beneficial effect there was no telling when merely normal activity would produce the same condition, though probably in an aggravated form. So we came to Boston yesterday to have Lahey, the best surgeon for thyroid in America, operate. Di went to the hospital today. She will have to rest and be observed for about eight days before the operation can be performed. She is not at all disturbed by the prospect of the operation itself. I gather that it is a simple one, almost sure to be successful—though cutting at glands cannot but be frightening to me, they are so mystical. They don't give ether, but oxygen gas—to avoid the pain to the throat from vomiting, I guess. The scar, if the cut is skillfully made, heals quickly and in the soft skin of the neck becomes scarcely visible I am told. One possibility we simply do not consider—all the New York doctors said that it was sure that the vocal cords are not affected but the men here were specific that they would not be responsible for any change in Di's singing voice. They said that there was no necessity that any harm would be done to it but they refused to give us any assurance on that point, though they said that the cords are not usually affected. Di seems to be very sensible about it; after all, the threat of invalidism was much more certain.

She had the nurse bob her hair in the hospital and she looks like a child. She has all the nurses by the ears and they do not know what to make of us. They are nice little Boston Baptists—the hospital is the New England Baptist Hospital.

I am moving out to Cambridge. I have a great deal of work to do to finish my lectures for the Menorah School. I have two in notes and seven more to do in three weeks. Living is cheap in Cambridge. I have engaged a fine room for $6 a week near the Library. Cambridge is a lovely town, though fairly far from the hospital. One cannot imagine the self-consciousness of Boston and especially of Cambridge. Everybody seems to be always feeling, "I am a Bostonian," and in the natural course of events every woman over forty-five looks as though she has something on all the world. These people see life as history— really a serious condition. The place is plastered with stones which read to this effect:

> On this very spot
> (The day being hot)
> General Prescott
> Took off his waistcoat.

But Harvard has more real charm than any other university I have seen. We visited Di's old hangouts and I could not help feeling that I did not quite exist—a feeling which Proust, being always the reminiscer, could never explore.

I saw Irwin[1] before we left. He had been to take us out to dinner a few weeks ago, talked a great deal and wanted to know about marriage. We were very priggish about our marriage and were probably a

---

1. Irwin Edman (1896–1954), professor of philosophy at Columbia.

little offensive. I talked hard about sex. We tried to convince him that he ought to marry, but the way he put the case—"we have no common vocabulary to disagree in"—made it impossible to go ahead. He left for his year abroad last week. I saw him for a while, one of those terrible whiles, and he seemed to indicate, though he did not say, that it was off. (Mike Schapiro[1] tells me that she is a very intelligent and handsome girl.) But the point of our while together was not his marriage but that he made me very mad. I smiled to him while I was there, but I cursed when I came away, and I have gotten increasingly angry since. I have a funny sort of anger, I guess. He referred to my review of Lawrence in *The Freeman* and praised it very highly (everybody, by the way, likes it and talks about it almost extravagantly; I have almost got a reputation out of it; it is very bewildering for I thought it good but commonplace and still do; Henry read it in MS). Then he said: "I want to tell you two things about your writing. I know you won't mind. First, why are you being so much influenced by Lawrence? You seem to be making so much of sex lately." He referred to the review, which scarcely mentioned sex, and to another one in *The Nation* of Amiel's *Philine* which was newly published sections from the *Journal* dealing with Amiel's sexual difficulties almost exclusively—very much like Irwin's they were too. "Sex," he continued, "is very important, of course. We all know how important it is. But there are many other things important too. As Woodbridge once said to me, 'Irwin, I've discovered what is wrong with the younger generation. At sixteen they discover that they have sexual organs and they never get over it.'" I made some deprecatory gesture and he went on, "And the other thing—why are you writing with so much exacerbation? Amiel was not a great man but he was not an unrespectable man and you should not be irritated with him. But not only in this review—all your writing is marked by this perturbation. Someone whose opinion you probably respect (Who?—Babette Deutsch[2]) said the same thing. It seems to be a new note. Can you find a reason for it in yourself?" So I told him the reasons because I happened to know them. I told him that my marriage had made me

---

1. Meyer Schapiro (1904–1996), art historian, was another of Trilling's college friends.
2. Babette Deutsch (1895–1982), poet and critic.

aware and vulnerable and that I felt much closer with the world and much more responsible for it and that a few years ago I had become afraid of death and that my marriage had intensified that fear. I said that I was very angry at things and that I was getting angrier all the time and that I was in a fair way to become some sort of revolutionary. He said that he too saw things he did not like and spoke of his serenity in the face of them. He said things were not so bad as to be worth all that anger. All *my* anger! Oh God and oh the years that bring the philosophic mind. So I smiled and was very mild and vague with him. He thinks I am some vague filial dope by the way I act with him (essentially he thinks the same of Henry and all his old students) but I promise myself the luxury of bullying the pants off him when he returns next year. I am even thinking of writing him a letter about the interview, which may read trivial but which was very bad when it happened.

[. . .]

Diana and I send our best love to you both. We miss you very much.

Lionel

21. TO DIANA TRILLING

[1930]

Diana darling,

Your gift was so lovely. It was tangible; I could feel it all day. Thank you, beloved. You give me many gifts.

I wish I could be with you. You are very miserable, aren't you? The nurse doesn't fool me when she says your condition is good. But I'll be out with you soon.

Aiken[1] wrote me this morning and I went to see him. He's a nice man, fortyish, quiet, not unlike myself, I imagine. These indistinguishable American writers. He and Kreymborg[2] had quarreled! They haven't spoken for two years: result of living in the same house for

---

1. Conrad Aiken (1889–1973), poet.
2. Alfred Kreymborg (1883–1966), avant-garde poet and editor.

the summer. He leaves town for the holiday but we are to play tennis Tuesday.

So they cut my review. I am not sore for the review, I had no special love for it, but the principle of the thing does bother me.

Are the nurses good? Can you eat at all? Do you like the flowers? Do you think I love you?

Lionel

22. TO RACHEL AND HENRY ROSENTHAL

July 7, 1930
Cambridge, Massachusetts

Cheris,

It was lovely of you to cable. The operation was successful and Diana is now feeling very well and cheerful. Evidently, however, the business was not so simple as it was made out to be. I gather that the night of the operation they were working desperately on her, pumping water into her to wash out the toxins that had been released. She was unspeakably close to death; for a while, too, they feared for her reason—the toxins sometimes act that way. I heard of this only several days later. It had no meaning then and the meaning is now just beginning to seep into me with a nightmare unreality. But she is really well now, though pretty deeply scared by what happened. She has been beautifully plucky; the morning of the operation she never batted an eyelash and might have been going to have her hair shampooed. I shall never forget that surgeon's face when he spoke to me after the operation: I thought he was being cold to me as he told me her condition was fine—he was just scared. Unfortunately, this operation was not complete. Another one will have to be performed in six weeks. This procedure is very common and they tell us there will be none of the danger, delay, and discomfort of the first. After that several months of very strict rest and a year of going slow and lots of sleep. Di frets that her singing will be put off for six months but there is nothing for it.

A few days before the operation my mother was taken very ill and for a while she too was in danger, but she recovered and is now feeling pretty well.

Conrad Aiken lives in Cambridge and I forced myself on him, he being about the only writer in America I have admiration for. We had an hour and a half together, neither very good nor very bad.

Diana was very touched by the cable and so was I. She sends her love with mine.

How are you both? You must have had a grand time in Rome. Does Rachel continue to improve? What are your plans now?

Love,

Li

23. TO HENRY HURWITZ[1]

August 16, 1930

Dear Henry:

I am sure you know that there are few people who understand your position better than I do. It has always been a source of very real wonder to me how you have managed to do what you have done—which is so much. Quite apart from any stake in the thing which I have I am hoping like the dickens for your continued success with an impossibility. I wish there were something I could do to help.

The news of your letter was, I confess, rather a blow. I think I can manage to borrow for the expenses of our stay here and of our next trip to Boston, perhaps up to the limit of the advance we agreed on for the articles. Beyond my personal credit, I haven't a cent of resource until October, and my borrowing must be done from literary people who cannot spare it for long. I mention this only because it may be that in the back of your mind is the notion that Diana and I have rich connections who can be touched. We simply haven't: we have been taking considerable sums for doctors etc. and there just isn't any more to take. So, even if we manage to pick up the cash for our immediate wants, your check will be very avidly welcomed. Meanwhile, if you can manage any smaller amounts, such as $25, we shall be very grateful.

You cannot imagine how it grieves me to have to add my troubles

---

1. Henry Hurwitz (1886–1961), founder of *The Menorah Journal* and its sponsor, the Intercollegiate Menorah Association.

to the carnage of your desk. But I hope it will be all over soon—yours together with mine.

Diana sends her best greetings and her thanks for your good wishes.

24. TO DR. HOWARD M. CLUTE

September 3, 1930
18 Sumner Road
Cambridge, Massachusetts

My dear Dr. Clute:

If, by addressing you on a financial matter, I am committing a breach of etiquette, I am sure you will forgive me, especially since what I have to say applies not merely to myself but to a whole class of people. I am sure, too, that you will forgive me for introducing details which should, perhaps, be relevant only to myself; but they are essential to the case.

Both Mrs. Trilling and myself come from parents of "the comfortable middle class." Brought up in this class, neither Mrs. Trilling nor myself now belong to it. At the time of our marriage, Mrs. Trilling was training for the career of a professional singer and working at a part-time position; I was studying for my Ph.D. degree at Columbia, earning my living at a part-time job as assistant editor of a magazine and by reviews and critical articles. At the beginning of our marriage, our combined incomes promised to total about $3,500 a year, a sum sufficient to keep us quite comfortable. It is difficult to say without sounding priggish, but neither of us was much interested in making money and we were far more concerned with perfecting ourselves in our arts than in securing ourselves financially.

Mrs. Trilling's illness, which began in the winter, of course made it impossible for her to work. We supplied the resultant deficit in our income by using wedding gifts of money, intended for a year of study abroad, and by borrowing. The necessity of an operation, while it encouraged us for Mrs. Trilling's health, was financially a very serious matter; however, we felt sure that the sliding scale of charges which we knew to prevail at the Clinic would make the expenses reasonable. The successful results of the first operation have delighted us beyond words, and we feel sure that the second will secure Mrs. Trilling's complete health.

It was, however, no small shock when, in conference with Mrs. Strand, I was told that the cost of the operations would be $1,000, a sum which, together with examination fees, anesthetist's fee, etc., was exactly a third of our last year's income—or rather, of the cost of our last year's living, for the income of $3,500 which we had every reason to expect, did not materialize because of Mrs. Trilling's illness.

I was told that the reason I had been charged so large a fee (after a second conference it was reduced by $50 an operation) was that I had provided a private room and nurses for Mrs. Trilling. Mrs. Strand characterized these provisions as inessential luxuries. True, had I known at the time I engaged the room that the Clinic's charges would depend entirely on the cost of it, I should certainly have engaged a less expensive one; unfortunately I did not know. I cannot help feeling strongly that Mrs. Strand's characterization is mistaken. I have been told that had it not been for the skill and experience of Mrs. Trilling's first night-nurse, a Miss Vends, it is doubtful if she would have survived the first operation.

As for the need of a private room, I am sure that, for a sensitive person, trained all her life to cherish privacy, the lack of it for nearly five weeks would have been very real torture.

It is not easy to justify our position simply. We are people, as I have said, trained to one class, now living in another. Certain appurtenances of the former class unfortunately remain with us as necessities. It is as impossible for us to take charity as it is for us to pay large prices. This position is obviously a terrible one to be in.[1] I can scarcely think it just for the Clinic to penalize that position.

I shall be deeply grateful should this letter cause you to have reconsidered the bill that is being sent to me; I shall be much gratified if it throws any light on the situation of people in the same position as myself.

In closing, may I thank you personally and the Clinic through you for the good that has been done for Mrs. Trilling? I should be deeply

---

1. In Trilling's carbon, the words from "I am sure that" to this point are crossed out.

sorry if this letter implied to you anything less than gratitude on my part for your work.

> Sincerely yours,
> Lionel Trilling[1]

25. TO HENRY ROSENTHAL

[1931]
Yaddo

Dear Henry—

So. An enormous mansion built circ. 1880 but planned in an interesting style. Woods, a great Oxfordian lawn, great formal gardens, a tennis court. Our bedroom huge and a private bath. Adjoining is Diana's studio, very comfortable. Above is mine in a tower from which I can see miles, into Vermont. Well, the swallows nested in the chimney and made so much noise I couldn't work, swarms of them. So they are chasing the swallows away from me. The food delicious and Diana, who is smoothing out like a fresh sheet, is getting fat and beautiful. One can work marvelously and I am beginning to. Diana is as industrious as a beetle and doing very well indeed with a play and a story. The people are, of course, people, some good, some bad, some strange, some talented—about a dozen of them. But on the whole they are a good sort of crowd, mostly young, mostly Jewish. There is much chitchat which now gets on the nerves and no talk. But one gets the comforting sense of fairly decent people around one and no great tax on one. Emanuel Eisenberg—strange, mad, mixed-up boy and very touching in his craziness and very sweet—has been getting himself into scrapes and out again and in again and out. He is very trying but one likes him. He has done some fine pictures of Diana and a silly one of me.

Mrs. Ames[2] has been very kind and charming to both of us.

---

1. According to Natalie Robins's *The Untold Journey: The Life of Diana Trilling*, "The Trillings would spend decades trying to pay off the bills until the hospital forgave the debt."
2. Elizabeth Ames, longtime director of Yaddo, the artists' colony in Saratoga Springs, New York.

She seems to like Diana, is trying to have her stay through July, though what this will mean about August is not clear.

The insurance on our robbery is still pending. They got away, when we had made final count, with about $600 worth of stuff including some things that are irreplaceable—the antique Russian earrings and rings that my father gave Di. They got my typewriter and I have had to buy a new one.—While the agent was around I took out life insurance.

The Arnold[1] begins to take shape, and to present some of its difficulties and some of its interest. When it gets cleaner I shall write you about it. But how I wish I were through it. I begin to worry about myself. I feel often that the power of writing is gone from me. I took some mornings off to try a story and I was sterile as a stone. And even if this is not permanent I am losing material that now presents itself to me as good and which would be good if taken now but which in a year I will be beyond. It is felt among some of the creative interests here that I am of the "smug professorial type," and though I recognize the snobbism of the thing, I begin to worry if much that I have been doing and living has not entered into my blood and done me harm. I haven't got that animal faith in myself that I should have. Well, one year more and then we shall see and maybe it will have been for the best.

[. . .]

One becomes so removed here from reality. It was a little startling for a few days and uncomfortable. Human relationships are dissolved by the space of the rooms and the country but after a while it becomes acceptable and one begins to catch a sense of one's self that is pleasant.

There is much material here for novels—a novel, rather. That is, of course, obvious enough but when one gets here one sees just how much it is true and tempting. The background of the place, the history of the people who built it and lived in it, and their tradition, and the contrast of the people now visiting it summers would have sent Henry James into fits of delight.

---

1. Trilling's doctoral dissertation would become his first published book, *Matthew Arnold.*

[. . .]

Write soon. I shall be getting my bearings by then and shall be having something maybe to say. Just now I am in one of those Proustian new-place wobbles of the spirit I usually experience whenever I change my seat.

Tell Rachel I send my best love and that Diana sends hers to both of you.

Yours

Lionel

26. TO HENRY ROSENTHAL

July 21, 1931
Yaddo

Dear Henry:

Your letter was good to get. I would have answered sooner but that for the last bunch of days I have been writing and this took my time and I wanted to send you what I had done before a letter. I have finished but I shall not send it for a day or two because there are one or two soft spots still on the child's head and these I want to ossify before it gets banged around in the mails. Diana raves, which is very gratifying and indeed the whole business has been a source of the greatest happiness to me. Not that it was not managed, trying to break myself of old habits of style and approach which clung irrelevantly from my stories of years ago. But I found myself fertile and in control; the old subconscious was working fine and it was a great joy. I simply *had* to take time out to do it; I had no great hopes for it but I had to do it or bust; and whether or not it is all Diana says it is, it is enough to hold me for a while in the confidence that I have not yet gone to seed. I wish you would consider it severely and in detail, watching for breaks in mood or style. You might think of a title. Ecclesiastes is always a good source for striking, nonexplanatory titles.

I was happy and more than that to hear from Di that you were at last started on a novel. It does not matter that only four lines have come (more by now I hope). I speak from the recent experience that it takes a lot of friction to produce the orgasm. It is important to take large chunks of time and to make a beginning. It is sure to come. My best and most expensive blessing on it.

We will have to let the dynamite go and thank the good Joyce and all the other gods that we have prose and pray to use it well. I have here with me one of the best revolutionary dialecticians in the country to tell me that. This is Sidney Hook,[1] who is here. He is the only philosophical mind that I have been attracted to in the flesh. A little Jew-boy with an enormous love for and facility at logic and metaphysics which he turns on actuality in an exciting way. A scholar on Marx (there is an article by him in the current *Symposium*) the Communists here won't have him. He is a passionate fellow, naive, romantic, gentle, and warm but as trenchant as a cutting machine. I should like you to meet him in the fall; his antireligious bent might be mitigated for you by his glow and his lust for poetry. I showed him my story in an incomplete version and he was impressed by it. Now he is warning me to keep out of "politics" and to cultivate for the good of the cause what he calls my "forte," which, he discovers, is not ideas but emotions! I take this as the Moscow dispensation and am comforted. Just where our statues will be placed when the postrevolutionary monuments are built is, of course, questionable if we do not handle dynamite. But let that pass. I believe that one can weave into the most delicate and personal emotions that people are concerned with the emotion of straight direct hatred of injustice and evil and a direct awareness of it. I believe this can be done only by interweaving it with and not by isolating it from these emotions—so that (as you implied in your dialogue) a man will be conscious of it while he is screwing his wife. A literature that does this can have splendid effect and be, in conception at least, greater than the best of what is recently passed. Something of this I tried to do in my story.

Of my Arnold there is not much at present to say. I am going back to it today much refreshed by the little excursus. I still have respect for my conception of the book. By the way, Harcourt, Brace have written me to ask for a look at it; it's a very sound house intellectually and I should much like them to take it. If you should have the time this summer, I should be very grateful if you would skim through Arnold's

---

1. Sidney Hook (1902–1989), philosopher.

St. Paul and Protestantism. There are Arnold's dicta on Judaism that I should like to ask you about.

Speaking of Joyce as I was a way back, Diana did a very clever thing. In my story I had him always in mind, not for style or method but for the *distance* that he keeps from his stories. He probably was not out of my mind for a moment, yet nothing of his actual writing, I am sure, crept in. But when I asked Diana if she could find any obtrusive influences she said no—except that she felt Joyce somewhere about. In the actual writing I was chiefly afraid of Lawrence.

There is a very good book that I am reading: *Pelle the Conqueror* by a Swede named Nexø.[1] It is rather enormously long but very delightful. If Rachel is away in the country it is just the thing for her to have—lazy, loping, objective, moving, intelligent: it is the only delicate (for all its size) book that has real social awareness that I know. Diana tells me that Rachel's health is not satisfactory. That is very painful to hear. But perhaps the summer rest will accelerate improvement. Will you give her my love when you write? I should like to have her opinion on my story. Will you undertake to forward it to her?

Despite the fact that I have grown a mustache, this place has been doing me good in various ways. I like the meeting with new and different people. It has freshened me up considerably and it has given me a scheme for a novel that I have great faith in. I should like to stay as long as possible but if Di has to leave earlier than I hope for I shall go with her.

It is amusing what you say about the sex chapters of Irwin's book being a counter to my articles on Lawrence. I am to do the Aldous Huxley biography for *The Nation* and I intend making a review of all the asinine estimates and "refutations" that have appeared. It is strange how sickening they can be and how much a touchstone of people Lawrence can be.

Thanks for the offer of the loan, but I doubt very much if the European trip will come through. However, I look forward to a good year and would with more confidence if both sets of parents weren't broke and ill. But I have come enormously more alive in the past few

---

1. *Pelle the Conqueror* (1906–1910), a novel in four volumes by Martin Andersen Nexø.

months and if I can hold to the sense of that I shall be happier than last year.

Write soon and tell me, if you can, about the book. I am excited to see its first chapters. This year you must determine to save three or four hours out of every day for it. A great deal can be done that way if it is done regularly and one should be able to write regularly after a little practice. I am sure the power to turn oneself on like a tap becomes possible after a while. But let me hear about it.

With love,
Lionel

27. TO DIANA TRILLING

[1931]
Yaddo

Belovedest—

Your book just came and I cannot possibly thank you for it and for the telegram yesterday which was so sweet. I am delighted with the book, which is very hot-making, I really wanted it. But the telegram message was so dear and charming.—We *shall* have a good year, believe me. We are in so much better case than we were last year at this time in Boston.—My birthday was really rather pleasant. Twenty-six suddenly seemed very young and the fact of a new number didn't bother me at all. Mrs. Ames was really very charming. The note I enclose was on my breakfast tray and when I saw her she took my hand in both hers and patted it. At lunch I had a birthday cake with a candle and Woolworth gifts from Miss Scarborough and cigarettes from Miss Gard. In the evening I made myself very happy by writing a little, about six pages which I think will stand. *Perhaps* I may have something to show you when you return—I wanted you here to kiss me, and missed you very much.—Received a telegram from your folks.—Harriet sent one from mine; it was a facetious Fourth of July oration, something like "Today the flags are flying and the cannon booming and our hearts beating high. Man and boy we have watched your progress for twenty-six years etc." It was read over the phone and the man positively orated it, using all the "expression" he could muster to do justice to the sentiments. It was terribly funny.

Played a lot of tennis in the afternoon and late in the evening some of us walked to town. So at least yesterday, I got enough exercise to please you. But I am really in rather good shape. We play tennis now without shirts. [. . .]

I miss you always but in a sense I am glad that we are away from each other for a while. You see, I have been in a bad state and now that I am alone I am beginning to cure myself of it. There was some sort of disintegration taking place in me and now it is ceasing. I do not know surely what caused it. Perhaps it was a lot of subtle subconscious reasons but it is profitless to think in those terms. One reason I can assign is that, quite apart from my love for you, I have the deep-rooted knowledge of your admirability. I feel of you—and this is not the language of love-flattery—that you are the finest and best-judging person I know. This, of course, I feel almost transcendentally, but also very simply and practically and with full knowledge of where you have been mistaken and unsure: I mean it is not an abstract mythological notion without reason and criticism. And as you are the person I admire most, as well as loving most, it is your admiration that I most want. And by admiration I mean (in my case, it is different when I use the word of you) approval of what I do. I know that I have your approval for a large part of what I am, but I have a burning, adolescent need for the other thing, simply, of course, because I am a person who has committed himself to doing something, to being something by doing. And I have done nothing. This in itself is simple enough that in finding this need for your approval, I have, as it were, put my "center" outside myself. To use an outworn terminology I have given my soul into your keeping, put my pride with you, and all my desires. What the reason for doing that is, what quirk of temperament it is, I do not know. Perhaps it is the culmination of the process begun long ago of losing my wit and swagger. (I do not think you could have read any reproach of you in what I have written: the idea that you may have worries me because we are always feeling "reproached" by the other's confusion or unhappiness and get "hurt." But certainly there is no jot of fault of yours in this. I think I allowed a bad thing to happen in allowing what I have just described and I know that the fault of it was mine and that you had nothing to do with it.) But I feel that much of our unhappiness—which has not in itself been overwhelming or even large but which need not have been at all—is the result of this situation in me. I have been thinking about it and the recognition of it is beginning to resolve it. When I used the word "disintegration" I used it literally—loss of integration, the result of some bad by-process in loving you. But I have been examining myself carefully and feeling around my insides and I am rearranging myself as carefully as I can. The technique of this cannot easily be described. Of this you can be sure: that you, dearest, did not figure at all in the rearrangement: I did not move to touch either my love of you nor that admiration of you which is the loveliest thing I feel—that sense of your grace and justice which touches the whole world for me and makes me love living. I think I have in the past tried to tamper with those things: it was cowardly and mean and no doubt it was what caused those occasional dead nodes in our happiness. I am glad this is happening; it is making me very happy. I hope you followed what I very confusedly, no doubt, tried to describe. If you do not follow it, I am sure that you will sense what I mean very accurately.—Do you remember how we used to tell each other "I love you more than ever" every week and how we said it so often, and meant it, that we began to wonder how we had dared to marry on so little love because we felt sure that if our love had grown so much it must have begun very small and that the present size of it was the only decent size for lovers to have? And here I am still saying it.—It seems to be getting richer and brighter: and that cloaked curse that people are always gently putting on love, "Of course, it gets calmer and less intense, though just as strong," doesn't come true: it seems to get subtler and subtler and we have only to be away to revive all the fresh silliness we sometimes miss.—So you see I have a strong fixation on my sex object.

Writing again was a great delight. I promise myself a few hours every day. That is no way, of course, for genius to dole out itself but it will do for now. I managed what I did with some small authority and dash: did about a thousand words in an hour and a quarter: which is to say almost fifteen words a minute. I think it is presentable. But no more of this until I see what happens. How is your work getting on? Will the story be finished soon? I suppose the holiday was too riotous for work. Write soon and everything.—Must stop if this is to get to you, beloved.—Again, thank you for the book, the telegram, and your dear love.—I love you.

Lionel

28. TO DIANA TRILLING

July 11, 1931

12:30

I have been trying to sleep for two hours and cannot because I want you so. I want to kiss you all over—your neck and your shoulders and the hollows beside your shoulders: your breasts, your nipples, between your breasts and under your breasts, your belly and the place above your hips, and the little hollows beside your hips; and your thighs and your feet and your cunt (but you wouldn't let me). And to see you open your thighs, surely the most beautiful gesture in the world, and to slip into you and lie on your rich sweet body; and to have my hands under your buttocks and to feel your hands on mine and touching my balls. It is terrible not to have done that for so long. I am so hungry for you. Now that you are coming so soon it is much harder to wait. I love you terribly and it is sour sleeping alone and so pointless. Even so stupid a thing as really going to sleep you make beautiful—Do you think we'll fit as we used to or have we lost the knack. The thought of you sleeping with your thigh thrown over me almost makes me weep. I want so much to kiss you. Good night, Diana beloved.

Lionel

29. TO MEYER SCHAPIRO

December 1, 1931

Dear Meyer:

I have been, since Sunday, going through the tortures of a Proustian social situation. For I was not able then to remember whether or not I had *asked* you to bring me a Daumier, could not discover whether you were executing a commission, which, indeed, would have been kind enough, or making me a gift, and, though I am not usually so "delicate," was somehow prevented from asking. Will you somewhat help me out of my embarrassment—which might eventually have a terrible effect on the length of my sentences and might eventually even make me contract asthma—by accepting the copy of Mac-Mahon's book which I am sending you and which you said you wanted to read? This is a clumsy way of getting out my situation but it will help. I could wish that the book were better for several reasons; it is obviously not a fair exchange of gifts.

Diana and I had a delightful time with you and Lillian. I hope that we will see you soon again.

Lionel

30. TO MEYER AND LILLIAN SCHAPIRO

[Spring 1932]
160 Claremont Avenue

Dear Meyer and Lillian,

Diana and I have volunteered to help raise money to bail out the nineteen miners, relief workers, and writers who are being held in the county jails of Harlan, Pineville, and Middlesboro, Kentucky, on charges of "criminal syndicalism." We are writing to you among others, because we think you will be as deeply moved by this cause as we are.

I know I do not need to tell you of the conditions in the Kentucky coalfields. But perhaps you do not know of the case of these jailed people. Their only crime, of course, is courage and high-mindedness. Their jail conditions are indescribable. Their cells are mere closets. Their floors are often under inches of water. Their food is meager and filthy and they are sick and weak from it. One girl, a classmate of Diana's, recently had pneumonia; she was taken to a hospital but returned to jail immediately she was convalescent.

Bail for these people has been set at $10,000 each. Arrangements have been made here by labor organizations for real-estate bail. This will, however, cost $1,250 and the treasuries of the labor groups, depleted by a winter of great demands, cannot find that sum. It is necessary, therefore, to raise it elsewhere.

The bail for each of the nineteen persons is $66 and Di and I are trying to raise enough to release two or at least one. We have given as much as we can. Will you? Our sum was not very large and I know yours cannot be but I hope you are able to send something. If you do, the check can be made to me.

Two more things: Could you answer by return mail? Immediate action seems necessary because there is real danger that some of the men may be lynched. And, second, if there are people whom you yourselves might approach and who might be moved to contribute, will you not speak to them?

Yours,

Lionel

31. TO HERMAN JACOBS[1]

August 3, 1932
160 Claremont Avenue

Dear Herman Jacobs:

I am sorry that I have had to delay beyond the time I promised to send you the tentative plan for my lectures. Here it is, very tentative still and subject to a possible complete revision. I want to make this clear because as yet I have not been able to conceive a course that is actually a *unit* course such as I gave last year: that had a definite coherence but so far I have not been able to discover a suitable unity for the course of this year. One will turn up, however; I will send you a fuller and more detailed outline of what I shall try to do when I am clearer about it.

I want to give one lecture on "Psychology and Literature"—that is, to attempt, after a simple statement of the dominant schools of modern psychology, to show the effect, conscious or unconscious, of these schools on the writing of fiction and poetry, and on both content and form. I touched on this in a few sentences in one of my lectures last year and it aroused considerable interest.

I spoke to you of a lecture on "The Jew in Fiction." This subject is the good old warhorse of the literary hacks of the Anglo-Jewish press but I have gone into the subject pretty closely: spent several months of research on it, gave a course of lectures on it, and have written on it. The approach will be a sociological one, showing how, as the social and political virtues and vices changed, the portraiture of the Jew

---

1. Of the 92nd Street YMHA in New York City.

changed to accommodate him to his position of scapegoat, in very much the literal biblical sense. The lecture will range from Chaucer through modern times when, with greater subtlety and, perhaps, civilization, the Jew is seen rather as the intensification of general human characteristics of the time (as in Joyce and Proust) than as the crude scapegoat.

I think I should also like to return to a subject that used to occupy me a great deal and which I should like to consider again—the "Jew as Creator" in the occidental literatures. This would be both historical (beginning with the unfortunate Amy Levy[1] perhaps) and critical, tracing the changing view of the Jewish writer of his role and trying to discover for him a position. The possibility of isolating peculiar Jewish literary qualities or themes will be considered, how far these are traditional, etc. Beside American and English novels, French and German will also be considered.

The fourth lecture is still vague and uncertain in my mind but I shall want it not to have a specifically Jewish content. I will let you know as soon as I get it formulated.

Sincerely yours,
    Lionel Trilling

32. TO HENRY HURWITZ

September 3, 1932
160 Claremont Avenue

Dear Henry

I am sorry that I have not been able to write you sooner.

I am afraid that I shall have to refuse your suggestion that I write for the *Journal* again. When I spoke to you I gave three reasons why I thought it unlikely that I should do so. The first was a reason of personal loyalty toward Elliot—not merely a blind loyalty but a reasoned one: I feel that he was in the right in the matter of last year, if not in every detail at least in most details and certainly in essentials.

The second reason was that to do my best work I must find myself in some degree of accord with the policy of the organ for which

---

1. Amy Levy (1861–1889), Anglo-Jewish writer, died by suicide.

I am writing. This accord I cannot find with the *Journal*. When I said this to you you made the natural reply: that I should write for the *Journal* as a free mind, without regard to policy. But I have been too intimately connected with the *Journal* to do that. You would not say that it had no policy, and whether or not its policy has changed since my active connection with the magazine, I feel too strongly and personally about the policy which I once recognized as belonging to it and which I helped to further, to write as a "free mind." Even if we leave opinion apart from the question, I should feel personally impeded and cold writing now for the *Journal*.

The third reason I gave you was that I am this year too pressed by money matters to undertake unpaid work. But this is only true in part. In sincerity I should say that I *would* undertake unpaid work if it afforded me the opportunity to write something that I thought needed to be said and that I wanted very much to say. Frankly and simply, I do not feel that the *Journal* is likely to impel me to such an effort.

Although I outlined all this to you at our meeting, I gave you no definite decision. That was because—weakly, I suppose—I could not entirely avoid allowing my feeling of friendliness to you to obscure my present sentiments about the *Journal*. That feeling of friendliness makes me regret now after reflection that there is nothing I can do but to say no to your suggestion and to wish you luck in your work even though I cannot any longer give it my personal support.

Sincerely,

33. TO LOUIS COLEMAN[1]

April 11, 1933
160 Claremont Avenue

Dear Coleman:

I have been told that, at a meeting of the Writers' Committee of the John Reed Club, when my name was proposed as a participant in a symposium, you opposed it and said by way of explanation, "He is our enemy." Since I have no connection with the John Reed Club,

---

1. Head of International Labor Defense, a legal advocacy group affiliated with the Communist Party USA.

I suppose that, if the remark was actually made, "our enemy" meant "an enemy of the working-class movement."

Will you please tell me (1) whether or no you made the remark and (2) if you did make it, on what basis you made it.

Sincerely yours,
Lionel Trilling

34. TO ADDISON T. CUTLER

December 11, 1933

Dear Cutler:

After a great deal of thought on the matter, I find that I must change my answers to questions 3 and 4 of the questionnaire which was sent by the committee to request the cancellation of the invitation extended by the University to Hans Luther, ambassador from Germany.[1]

I do not think that the third question can be answered with a simple "Yes" or "No." There is no doubt that the invitation to Dr. Luther is likely to have unfortunate inferences drawn from it. I would have preferred that the University had not put itself in a position to have itself misinterpreted or that, having put itself in that position, it had denied the inferences. (The reception I conclude to be a deplorable but nonofficial function which need not be considered under the same head as the invitation to lecture.)

The inferences that might be drawn from the University's invitation were foremost in my mind when I answered question 4 in the affirmative. My concern with them led me to minimize and even to deny that the situation involved the question of free speech.

I feel now that I was mistaken. The principle of free speech, once the invitation had been extended, does enter into the situation, and this principle I conceive to be a formal and absolute one. There is no doubt that the principle of free speech sometimes entails anomalies— its invocation in behalf of the representative of the Nazi regime is an obvious one. Yet I believe that it is wiser for the University to adhere

1. The invitation to Luther, the ambassador to the United States from Nazi Germany, to speak at Columbia sparked student and faculty protests.

to the principle of free speech on all occasions with all its possible anomalies than to reject the principle of free speech on any occasion because of any of its anomalies.

I suppose that by now the request to Dr. Butler to cancel the invitation has already been sent, with my name included. If it has not, will you please omit my name? If it has, I should like you nevertheless to know my more fully considered opinion in the matter.

Sincerely,

35. TO MEYER SCHAPIRO

December 14, 1933
15 East 77th Street

Dear Meyer:

I have been told that, in conversation with Bettina Sinclair and Bernhard Stern, you ascribed my doubts and hesitations in political questions to a fear of losing my job, and that, when this statement was challenged by Mrs. Sinclair, you went on to defend and develop it at some length.

It would seem that your excellent powers of inference fail when they concern themselves with me. The motive you ascribe to my political thought is as little existent as the baby you recently conceived for me.

Your statement and its circumstances automatically abrogate any friendship between us, so that beyond the mere denial of the truth of your statement I need not go. I should like to point out, however, that at any time when I shall feel it necessary to refrain from political action for personal-practical reasons I shall do so, and I shall state my reasons quite openly to the person who solicits me for the action. I have already done this, with a sense of deprivation but no sense of guilt. This may assure you that any doubts and hesitations of mine that you may hear of in the future will be quite purely intellectual.

I cannot help adding that if you really believe, as you seem to, that there are no two ways of thinking about the particular form which my protest against Luther took, if you can really believe that only practical-personal considerations would make one hesitate to sign it, you are, to say the least, walking a very dangerous political path.

I wish you would show this letter to Jerry Kline. I recall that, in a phone conversation on Monday, he misinterpreted a phrase of mine in a way that I understand better since I have heard of your statement about me. I recall, too, that, some months ago, I had a conversation with him about financial insecurity which may possibly have created some misunderstanding which this letter might help to correct.

Sincerely,

36. TO MALCOLM COWLEY[1]

May 5, 1935
417 West 114th Street

Dear Malcolm:

I have just been reading in the *New Masses* the paper you presented at the Writers' Congress. I was very much surprised to see you use that old misconception about Wordsworth in support of the spiritual efficacy to the writer of revolutionary sympathies and activities. Your point does not stand or fall by your example, but the perpetuation of the erroneous idea by revolutionary critics lays them open to a disproportionately effective counterattack by the merest pedants. For the very reverse of your statement about Wordsworth seems to be true and very obviously true.

How the error got under way in the first place I don't know, not being anything of a Wordsworth scholar. Nor am I enough of a Wordsworth scholar to have all the facts at hand to prove the statement—which, however, you may depend on, that Wordsworth was writing very poor poetry during the time of his revolutionary sympathies and very good poetry when he gave them up.

I guess Wordsworth didn't write a line of memorable poetry until 1798. This gives him nearly ten years of revolution in which he might have proved that he was the kind of person that revolutionary ideals stimulate to great production. By 1798—the year, you will remember, of Coleridge's recantation of revolutionary ideals in "France: An

---

1. Malcolm Cowley (1898–1989), writer and editor, was the literary editor of *The New Republic*.

Ode"—Wordsworth had been worked on by the Terror (he had been a Girondist and many of his friends had died under Robespierre), by the invasion of Switzerland, by Napoleon, by patriotic feelings after England declared war, to feel pretty remote from the Revolution. I don't know if we can entirely blame him if he felt that the Revolution had deserted him, not he the Revolution. Not, of course, that this justifies his later reactionary political philosophy.

But it must be noted that this same reactionary political philosophy was largely instrumental in producing the poetry of his great period. Because his effectiveness came only after his rejection of the rationalism which had been one of the components of his revolutionary sympathy. He took up instead a mystical point of view, in many ways not unlike Burke's: the conjunction of whose name with W.'s poetry is usually enlightening. I seem to remember that W. says somewhere that he intended the *Lyrical Ballads* of 1798 to help people who had been disillusioned by the French Revolution to reach a new and consoling and positive philosophy.

The diminution of Wordsworth's genius—I really do not think it had vanished utterly, as you say—must be explained on other grounds than the simple political ones. The Marxian critic has to face the fact that something like philosophical Idealism with all its reactionary implications was Wordsworth's conscious doctrine as a great poet. I think the Marxian critic may have many things to say about this that would save Wordsworth from being cast into the outer darkness. He must remember that the bourgeois character of the Revolution had appeared—and the fact is that Wordsworth, though suspicious of the proletariat, knew something of the character of the bourgeoisie and disliked it. He must remember too that when Wordsworth was a revolutionary sympathizer, he took up, along with his passion for mankind, a pretty shoddy philosophy. It was in part a radical philosophy but we wouldn't want a poet to subscribe to it. Godwinian rationalism, if really felt—and Wordsworth felt it—is pretty bad stuff for poets; it denies all the springs of life that a poet (and also a revolutionary thinker in the modern sense) lives by and relies on and works with. His political philosophy, his whole philosophy, was the result of a wise revulsion from this.

Sincerely,

37. TO JACQUES BARZUN

July 26, 1935
417 West 114th Street

Dear Jacques:

You are the prince of epistolarians. I had been meaning to write you momentarily when your letter came to shame me. I am no longer what my doctor calls below par—feel fine, in fact, and am back at work.

Your notebooks and your confidence in them fascinate me. When you return you must explain the system. I have been planning notebooks for years now but have never managed anything save the scrawniest attempt. And I need something to take the place of a memory. Card files are but morgues. Gail Kennedy spent a long evening here last night and we spent hours commiserating with each other on our faulty memories, pointing out that we lost two-thirds of what we ever had known and that we would never get on in the world. But you have a splendid memory and it is unfair for you to have notebooks too: which have for me, too, by the way, the aesthetic appeal of being the symbols of an orderly and decent life.

[. . .]

As for our official titles, standings, recognitions, melon cuts, and perquisites—well, I am inclined to agree with [you] just now: not, perhaps, Emersonianly but simply because I find in myself a huge distaste—which, unfortunately, I may not have when the academy opens again—thinking of myself in that fixed and dependent relation to *others* in their institutions, hierarchies, and selves, which thinking about an academic career involves. In a sense, it sounds silly to sweep aside so large a group—but really I don't think there are ten men in the university who have the right to pass on us. I don't think that is arrogance. I am sure there are scores who surpass me intellectually and hundreds in knowledge but I think that they are *wrong*—wrong and desiccated and liars and fatheads. Fighting them is useless—for me anyway—and all I want to do is to learn not to smile at them affably when they exhibit their lack of grace but to look at them very gravely and discomfit them. And for the rest, to do my own particular job—which I guess is to explain and exhibit their miserable condition: a little (but not too much) as Henry James would. But still it makes me sore that they aren't lusting and hanging out their tongues to make you a professor.

[. . .]

The actions of the Communist International—which, of course, I expected—make me despair of revolutionary action on the part of the Communist Party. They really have become the modern Second International of 1914. Their intellectual publications are reaching here a lower and lower level. The mood that this starts is not new but newly and forcibly confirmed. As for the Trotskyist point of view—I think it is utterly correct, but in point of power it is so submerged that I, being essentially a nonpolitical man in point of view of activity, see little hope for it. To insist that we must not fight in support of *any* imperialist war is the only sensible insistence and the Trotskyites make it. But I have small hope just now of its making any headway. And so for a time I feel justified in retiring from thinking that I ought to have any place in the active Left.—But when the book is finished I want to learn Marxism. Partly because I think we cannot teach our best students—mostly Marxists—until we know a great deal more than they do about their religious conversions. And I know very little.

Diana sends her most cordial greetings. She is a great admirer of yours, citing especially your intellectual and emotional tolerance—to which word she gives a special meaning.

If you should not be moved to write so that I will get a letter before we leave on the third, I will drop you a card giving you our new address.

Yours in affection and in the life of splendid isolation—
    Lionel

38. TO ALAN BROWN[1]

August 26, 1936
254 Richmond Avenue, Amityville

Dear Alan:

Believe it or not, even before your letter came I had planned to write you today for I had promised to write you without your answer,

1. Trilling's colleague in the Columbia English Department.

thinking you might not be allowed much correspondence and grateful for the prohibition. So you have been on *my* conscience and I am sorry that I have been on yours. But your X-ray news gives me a double pleasure—in your improving health and in the expectation of letters from you. I am really terribly glad everything is going so well. Make it continue. I am relieved that the Saranac people treat you drastically. I am a great believer in medical drasticness (drasticity?) and I always fear—from experience of friends—the comparative desultoriness of N.Y. treatment of tuberculosis.

Is it likely that you will stay at Saranac now? I really don't think the winter will be as bad as you anticipated, though the West might be more interesting. Your letter made me quite nostalgic: I spent so many summers at Saranac, camping on the lake—Eagle Island, you can see it from the head of the lake—and I know how exciting the air and the country are this time of the year. We have our first touch of fall today so yours must have come some time ago.

A letter isn't any place to talk about the Russian business;[1] it needs a novel or an autobiography. Everybody I know is very confused and dejected; I know that, though for long my feelings about Russia have been mixed enough to make me try to be philosophical, I feel now that I must completely overhaul all my ideas and my whole character. But there are a few objective things that one can say.

First—there is the political significance of the event. You will remember that at the Kiroff trial[2] some of these fellows admitted to a "moral" or "logical" guilt of Kiroff's death. General feeling is that they were coerced to this. Now why the sudden revival of the whole business with the attack on Stalin Almighty included? We must remember that the Trotskyist party in Spain is very powerful and its influence very wide. According to some, it is the spearhead of the radical forces. In France the Trotskyists, though numerically small, are rather influential. At any rate, they are the militant group of the proletariat and they feel that the Popular Front is going to end up as a betrayal of the working class. Their agitation has been met by police suppression by

---

1. The show trial of the former Bolshevik leaders Gregory Zinoviev and Lev Kamenev began on August 19.
2. The Bolshevik leader Sergei Kirov was assassinated in 1934, likely on Stalin's orders.

the Blum government—at the instigation of the Stalinists. In short, Russia fears Trotskyist revolution; it fears revolution in any form, of course, but especially the Trotskyist power that may emerge. The Russian trials are an attempt to discredit Trotskyism. In effect, it is a sabotage of the revolutionary movement. There is also the possibility, claimed by some, that the Trotskyist—or some dissident—movement is strong in Russia itself.

Second: Most of the people involved in the trial have either repudiated Trotsky or have been repudiated by him. I myself do not believe in Trotsky's complicity. I am not entirely sure how far the mutual repudiation went, however, for I get this at second hand.

So much for objective fact or what may be fact. We may then imagine coercion at work to produce the kind of hideous spectacle [of] the trial. As you say, it is inconceivable that these old Bolsheviks should not thunder out their political reasons when they had the opportunity. But would the opportunity have been given to them if the officials were not sure that there would be no thunder? We can imagine threats of reprisal to families unless this particular show were gone through, implicating Trotsky and blessing Stalin; even with death a certainty, these men would knuckle under to protect wives and children.

On the other hand, there is, as you say, religious hysteria. When it becomes not only a crime but a sin to be in opposition—I mean not counterrevolution but just political opposition, say, about the rule of collectivization—then I suppose men may possibly get the horrible emotions of the defendants forced on them.

Well, all this settles nothing for me: except to convince me that I must always have a reservation of faith in anything. The revolutionary heroes—and they certainly were that—were disgusting; Russia was disgusting. Perhaps every revolution must betray itself. Perhaps every good thing and every good man has the seeds of degeneration in it or him. And life—he said, with that self-deprecating air of badinage with which he delivered always his finest bits of wisdom—is a perpetual struggle. Never a being, always a becoming.

Which leads me to report that the book now moves along and I hope before school opens to have a major portion in the hands of a publisher. I should like to have it accepted for publication before I submit it to the university committee.

Jacques Barzun has gotten himself married.

I dipped into the Huxley book[1]—and, like you, fell and had to finish before I could work. Beatrice is right: it isn't as good as PCP[2] but only in a literary sense does it fail. I found it an extremely moving and respectable failure. Is there any other man who writes for grown-up people! He doesn't solve his problem and he even doesn't pose it too well. But there the problem is, the problem of human virtue. And I find it funny how distressed people are by the book, how they only want to talk about its literary weakness and dismiss the problem with a flip word, embarrassed. I have an essay I want to do on liberal and radical faith: it will use Ibsen as a springboard.

We are getting tired of this place and will probably abandon it after Labor Day. We are going to live in the same apartment, proud because we are the only tenants in the house whose rent hasn't been raised, on the ground that we were such desirable tenants! It makes us feel like two fat and middle-aged people in a story by de Maupassant.

I haven't read *Gone with the Wind* and damned if I will lose any more time on novels.

[. . .]

Are you allowed movies? *We Went to College* might have been a swell comedy but it fizzled. Hugh Herbert delivering a lecture on Adam Smith opens the picture and that's grand and then he plays the cello in a concert at a faculty tea and that's fine but thereafter it falls away. However, Una Merkel gives an excellent performance as a faculty wife which pleased Diana very much and we both said Beatrice would like it.

Keep getting well even more rapidly; Diana joins me in this exhortation and we both send our best greetings to Beatrice.

Yours,
Lionel

---

1. Probably Aldous Huxley's *Eyeless in Gaza* (1936).
2. Aldous Huxley's *Point Counter Point* (1928).

39. TO LEWIS MUMFORD[1]

November 28, 1936
Columbia University

Dear Mr. Mumford:

Thank you very much for your letter. I am, naturally, very pleased at your description of the present good situation in the city colleges.

But I feel that perhaps now I should explain to you more fully why I wrote to you as I did. The assumptions on which I wrote were not based on "reports"; they were conclusions of my own experience. It was, for instance, only a very few years ago that I was told—at a place which I shan't name—that I had an excellent chance for an appointment were it not that "there is now a Trustee's candidate ahead of you." This was said so simply and with such admirable candor that I could only conclude that it was part of the routine. This conclusion was confirmed by another conversation, with a person of even greater authority.

When I asked your help as I did, I of course had this experience in mind. I felt, however, that the fact that we were in the same general field and that you probably had some professional opinion of me, would, subjectively at least, eliminate some of the taint of wire-pulling for both of us. For I assumed that anything you might do on my behalf, not being motivated by personal or "political" friendship, would be motivated by your opinion that I might be useful to the college.

But though I suppose that, realistically considered, the harm of "influence" is its disregard for the fitness of the man for the job, the whole thing is at best a bad business and I am sincerely glad that the situation has been changed. I shall certainly see the head of department at Brooklyn as soon as possible.

Sincerely yours,

---

1. Lewis Mumford (1895–1990), writer and urbanist.

40. TO THE EDITORS OF *THE NATION*

April 4, 1937
620 West 116th Street

Dear Sirs:

As a contributor to *The Nation* and—more important—as someone who believes in truth as *The Nation* has fought for it, I am profoundly disturbed by your treatment of the Trotsky-Malraux exchange of statements.[1] I am, to be sure, a member of the Trotsky Defense Committee;[2] but I am not writing at this time to further that defense but rather to defend *The Nation* against itself, for I feel that in its handling of the controversy *The Nation* has betrayed its own best principles.

Is it, first, a mere technicality to request that a magazine like *The Nation* check its material before publishing it? By now you no doubt are aware that the Trotsky "statement" of March 8, as sent out by the United Press, dangerously garbled Trotsky's actual words, a transcription of which I have before me as I write. I am told that you were warned that the UP dispatch was not to be trusted and that you were asked to withhold publication of the "exchange" until you had the opportunity to see Trotsky's original statement. You yourselves hint in your editorial paragraph at the possibility of inaccurate quotation but go on, nevertheless, to make your adverse judgment in spite of your doubt. Why did you not wait to check this doubted accuracy? Is a good story ever so pressing that it cannot wait on truth? By representing Trotsky to have said, "In 1926 Malraux was serving the Comintern and the Kuomintang in China and is *the one* who carries the responsibility for the strangulation of the Chinese revolution," you not only made Trotsky appear shrewd and disingenuous but you also set up a question of straw which his opponent could demolish with great éclat. What Trotsky actually said was, "In 1926 Malraux was in China in the service of the Comintern-Kuomintang, and is *one of those* who carry the responsibility for the strangulation of the

---

1. In *The Nation*, March 27, 1937.
2. The American Committee for the Defense of Leon Trotsky, made up of American writers and intellectuals under the chairmanship of John Dewey, undertook to rebut the charges of subversion made against Trotsky in the Moscow Trials.

Chinese revolution." This is indeed something very different and it forces Malraux not to a deprecation of his personal role in the Chinese revolution (to which he devotes so much of his reply) but to a political defense of the policy of the Comintern—and by obvious implication to a defense of the policy of the Comintern in Spain today. Nor is it only by the inaccuracy of this one sentence that the whole intent of Trotsky's statement is misrepresented for readers of *The Nation*. Only by publication of Trotsky's entire statement—as, rightly, you published Malraux's entire statement—could you make that intent plain and conform to the elementary procedure of liberalism in conducting a controversy.

But even more disturbing to me are the implications of your editorial paragraph on the dispute. You say, "Leon Trotsky was no doubt stirred into making his press statement against Malraux . . . by Malraux's failure to comment on Trotsky's assertion that Malraux had visited him in southern France at the time he was accused of meeting Romm in Paris. While we may understand Trotsky's resentment, his gratuitous attack can only arouse indignation." I presume that you used the word "gratuitous" only of the garbled sentence I corrected above and I feel sure that a reading of the whole actual statement will seem to you, in its full political context, very far from "gratuitous," whether or not you agree with it. But I cannot so easily explain your attitude toward what you supposed to be Malraux's act which "stirred" Trotsky to his press statement. To be sure, there seems to be some confusion here, for I do not believe that Trotsky needs a comment from Malraux on his visit in southern France—I understand that the incident is established by an article which Malraux published in Paris and reprinted in this country in *The Modern Monthly*. However, your assumption seems to be that Malraux is willfully holding back information which might help Trotsky clear himself of the charges made against him. Perhaps you are being as unfair to Malraux as to Trotsky, but if you really do believe that Malraux is withholding information which might establish Trotsky's innocence of meeting Romm, your quiet—can it be cynical?—acceptance of the moral implications of Malraux's supposed silence in such circumstances is more than disturbing. Malraux has publicly declared his anti-Trotskyist position and that is certainly his right. Is it conceivably the right of *The Nation* to veil the fact of that partisanship and to dismiss as something merely to be "resented"—and "resented" by Trotsky alone—a crime of omission motivated by this partisanship which would be thoroughly reprehensible if Malraux had committed it—as *The Nation* assumes he did?

Let me be trite: liberals serve no good end at all when they cease to look for truth and, in the name of "action"—even in the name of the immediacy of the Spanish situation or in the name of a much wished-for unity—substitute wish thinking and rationalization for the functions of the critical intellect. These are times which try our minds even more than our emotions and if we cannot look to liberal organs like *The Nation* for an honest effort toward intellectual clarity we are in a sad case indeed.

Lionel Trilling

41. TO JACQUES BARZUN

June 24, 1937

Dear Jacques:

I have delayed writing because I wanted to include the check which I have been led to expect momently. The firm wishes to express its appreciation of your long years of service and tenders you as a token of its esteem this guaranteed solid-gold seventeen-jeweled Swiss-movement combined watch and cigar cutter. The check for $1 is for your Gibbs scientific essays; I think I have replaced all the other massacred books you brought to what we shouldn't call a holocaust. (Nero: he raised the holocaust of living.) I believe you now have duplicates of some via humanities largesse, but you can make an exchange at the bookstore when you return.

It now looks as if I shan't be able to send you any more book[1] before you sail. I am particularly sorry because the next chapter touches on r-ce [*sic*]. But I will, unless you offer some more practical or spiritual objection, mail you some c/o Thos Cook. By spiritual objection I mean maybe you don't want to be followed over Europe by somebody else's intellect, which I could very well understand. If you want a

---

1. The manuscript of *Matthew Arnold*.

really complete rest, please speak. Jim and Elsa Grossman read the book with intense and vociferous enthusiasm, all any writer could ask. Do not be alarmed by my failure to produce more; it is only that I move ahead faster than I go back to revise and I prefer to keep this proportion.

A few days ago when I intended to write you I had a lot of very fine observations to make but the observatory mind has vanished now. There were some observations especially about Henry James, whose *Washington Square* I have just read. Go—analyze for me the emanation that emanates from that man. There are few people to whom my heart goes out as it does to him. I wonder why I delayed so long getting to him. Is it a kind of learning humility that he has? Did you see Cantwell's article in *The New Republic*? A crass piece of work, which, if I had the time, I would undertake to answer. It is factually misleading too, I gather. Cantwell writes a kind of polite vulgar Marxism which goes down with intellectual liberals so easy and which I conceive it my job in the future to destroy. I find no intellectual position more grateful to me than that of trying to keep the walls of the Right and the Left from moving together to squash me, like the Poe story. If you want to see the complete degeneration of official Marxist thought—Stalinist—read a certain Osborn's *Marx and Freud*.[1] This is a juxtaposition I have long wanted to make. The outcome of O.'s thought, approved by John Strachey,[2] is that Freud is very useful, he teaches Communists how to make their leader into a Father Image to whom the masses will devote themselves in the fascist fashion. Doesn't this perfectly reflect the horrible and depressing news from Russia?

The Leonard translation of Lucretius has the look of a starched collar wilted. Try to say the third line: "Makest to teem the many-voyaged main." The Loeb is a good trans. I have a worser job than you: to frame (with mats) 150 questions on Mockus; Or, Really Is.[3]

Are you going to buy any books in France? If you are and if you can confirm the report that the French have a very good classical or

---

1. Reuben Osborn's *Freud and Marx: A Dialectical Study* (1937).
2. John Strachey (1901–1963), left-wing British writer and politician.
3. That is, Marcus Aurelius.

mythological dictionary, would you get it for me?—if it isn't a chore. About $3 is all I'd want to spend.

This carries best wishes for a happy trip.

Yours,

Lionel

You probably won't have time to write before you sail but will you advise me of the safe arrival of the check?

42. TO EDMUND WILSON[1]

July 16, 1937
620 West 116th Street

Dear Mr. Wilson:

I don't know why we feel freer to remark on things we differ with than on things we admire. When I read your essay on More I thought it was so superb that I wanted to sit down at once and write to you— but I hesitated to intrude my praise. Yet now that I differ with your characterization of Matthew Arnold in your last piece on the origins of Socialism, I feel quite free to intrude a difference of opinion!

You speak of Arnold as one of a group of thinkers who insisted "more and more on individual liberty" and you go on to say of this group as exemplified by Taine that it insisted "that individual conscience and the private operation of industry should be free from interference by the State." Arnold is a terribly slippery fellow, of course—as I've found to my cost in writing about him: you never know where to have him because he uses what might loosely be called a dialectical method—what he calls "criticism" is really that and the dialectical idea is embodied in "Culture"—and he was constantly changing his emphasis to meet the occasion. But one thing is clear about him: he took no stock at any time in individual liberty as an ideal and he worked always toward the formulation of the State's right to interfere. So far as I remember, he didn't touch explicitly on the interference of the State in the operation of industry, and that, of course, is one of his weaknesses, but I think he was working toward

---

1. Edmund Wilson (1895–1972), critic and man of letters.

the idea; certainly it is perfectly consistent with his hatred of vulgar Liberalism and with his rejection of the "right" of private property. He thought of himself as a continuator of the French Revolution and though that seems laughable at first I think he really was what he thought he was, in a very complicated way, despite all the unctuous overtones of religion and all the counsels of moderation.

I hope you don't mind me leaping out at you this way from the dark of my "special field." I think that by this time I feel a kind of family responsibility for Arnold—he's been with me so long.

Sincerely yours,
Lionel Trilling

43. TO DR. NATHANIEL ROSS[1]

July 23, 1937
620 West 116th Street

Dear Nat:

I have kept removed from Harriet's psychoanalytical plans because I thought it best that way, and so, though she has told me something about the situation, I am a little confused. But I learn that there is still some possibility that you may decide to take her yourself and it occurs to me that there are one or two things I ought to tell you that may help you in your decision.

It may be pertinent for you to know that Harriet does not know, from anything Diana and I have said, that either Diana or I were treated by you. I doubt if she knows that I have had psychoanalytical treatment at all, and though she probably guesses that Diana has, she does not know, probably, that it was with you.

It seems to me too that this would be a good time for me to tell you about the effects of the analysis on me. I have often wanted to, during the past year, as a matter of gratitude and for your informa-tion and satisfaction. Now it may be relevant to you in the question of analyzing a person you know before treatment. The results of the analysis have been most marked and beneficial. I will not say that I have no more of the old depressions, but when they are intense they

---

1. Nathaniel Ross (1904–1986), Trilling's friend and sometime psychoanalyst.

are of short duration and these are *very* rare, and when they are of any extended time they are perhaps no more than temperamental. At any rate, I can no longer think of them as a problem. Indeed, for a full year now I have been almost impossibly cheerful, very energetic, very concentrated in my work. In part, perhaps, this is the result of good material luck but after all we know what *that* means! My writing has improved a great deal, I consider—and so, I gather, do others; my teaching has gone up; I was able to fight the university to reinstatement, and even to an admitted reversal of opinion and a raise. I was even able to ask a fantastically high price for a hack job and get it! So, if you remember the whole situation, you will see I have come a long way; and that I owe you a lot.

I speak of this, as I say, because I know you'll be glad to hear it but also because it may have some bearing on Harriet's case. The success with me despite the personal relationship should, I think, indicate that perhaps the slighter relationship with Harriet and the disparity of age might make your treatment of her be even more practicable. In my own case I'll be frank to say this: that I sometimes think the treatment would have been perhaps even more decisive had there been a greater dissimilarity of temperament and outlook between us which would have pushed me into conflict with you. But similarity, of course, is not present in the case of Harriet.

As you may imagine, I'm very anxious to have you take her and so is Diana. But we urged her to see you (indirectly through her husband; we did not discuss the matter with her) even though we thought it possible you might not want to take the case, knowing that you would send her to the best possible person if you yourself wouldn't undertake it.

I hope—for two reasons—that we'll be able to see you soon.

Yours,

Lionel

As I read this it sounds rather as though I were importuning you to take Harriet's case. Of course, you will understand that I really am not. It's just that I wanted to clear up anything at this end. By the way, Harriet's husband knows as little as Harriet about our analytical pasts.

44. TO SIDNEY HOOK

December 10, 1937
620 West 116th Street

Dear Sidney:

I've just read your splendid review of Huxley[1] and I'm writing to thank you for keeping my reason from tottering. I haven't read the book yet but I know enough about its main idea to get scared at the opinions, in print and out, of the intellectuals who have ganged up to show that Huxley is nothing but a pious monkey and that the problem he presents is no problem at all but only a piece of escapist sentimentality. The superbly single-minded commitment of the intellectual to an ethics of power is really quite a spectacle to watch. And that goes, it seems, not only for literary Stalinists but for our intelligent Trotskyist friends as well. The publication of Wilson's piece in the same issue with your review was fortunate—and by a coincidence I finished Lyons's book[2] the day I read both. So maybe there's a chance that what you call the basic moral problem of our time—or *any* moral problem—will yet be forced upon our intellectuals.

Sincerely,
Lionel Trilling

45. TO CORLISS LAMONT[3]

February 1, 1938
620 West 116th Street

Dear Mr. Lamont:

Thank you for sending me John D. Littlepage's article "Red Wreckers in Russia."[4] I am sorry that a great press of work has prevented me from answering your note before this.

I presume that when you send me the article because I am a member of the American Committee for the Defense of Leon Trotsky

---

1. Hook's review of Aldous Huxley's *Ends and Means* appeared in *The Nation*, December 11, 1937.
2. Eugene Lyons's *Assignment in Utopia*, a memoir of his years as a newspaper correspondent in the Soviet Union.
3. Corliss Lamont (1902–1995), pro-Soviet activist and longtime civil libertarian.
4. *Saturday Evening Post*, January 1, 1938.

and when you call my attention to Mr. Littlepage's "specific data about the sabotage of the defendant Yuri Pyatakov," you wish to convince me that Pyatakov did commit sabotage and, by implication, that the findings of the Commission on Trotsky's innocence and on the nature of the trials are baseless.

But I fear that you are under a misapprehension. The Commission in no way undertook to judge whether or not the late Pyatakov was guilty of sabotage. It undertook only to pass on the guilt or innocence of Trotsky—among other things, on the truth of the allegation that Trotsky had relations with Pyatakov, that Pyatakov made an airplane visit to Trotsky, etc. On the point of these alleged relations, the findings of the Commission seem to me conclusive. I think they must convince any fair-minded person that the alleged relations never existed, that the "proofs" offered at trial were false and fraudulent, and that the trials themselves were indeed a political frame-up.

Like the Commission, I have no opinion on the actual guilt of sabotage of Pyatakov himself. But any opinion formed on this matter should surely use Mr. Littlepage's evidence only with the greatest caution. I have no doubt that the gentleman is, as you say, "an engineer of high standing." But I have no doubt, too, that he is a man whose political views are of a kind not likely to lead him to objectivity. In the article you sent me, he writes, ". . . sabotage is a familiar Communist weapon in every country; industrial sabotage in the United States can usually be traced to Communists or to people who think like Communists." Now, I do not believe this; I'm sure you don't believe it. And, frankly, I am surprised not only that you should use the testimony of a man who intends such a statement to be open Red-baiting, but that you should use as evidence of anything the words of a man who speaks so loosely.

Sincerely yours,
Lionel Trilling

46. TO SIDNEY HOOK

May 28, 1938
620 West 116th Street

Dear Sidney:

I sent you yesterday by American Express a copy of my manuscript. It's really very kind of you to engage to go through its bulk and I'm grateful.

As I think I told you, the book has been greeted with unexpected enthusiasm at Columbia. This is very gratifying—professionally. But intellectually it does not wholly reassure me. Among all the academic readers I know of none who shares my political point of view and the fact that no one has quarreled with it, or with my religious analysis, makes me a little uneasy that, in my effort to be flexible with my rather complicated subject, I may have been too "understanding"— to the point of causing myself to be misunderstood. I think you know my point of view well enough to pass on whether or not I have in any way falsified it: you know that I don't set up to be an avowed, professional-philosophical Marxist. You probably know that I am in solution about a lot of Marxist doctrine. At the same time you know what my "direction" is and can tell me whether I have explicitly or implicitly departed from it. (But I don't mean to confine you to a "nihil obstat". tell me what you think of the whole job.)

Little, Brown—or the Atlantic Monthly Press— shows considerable interest in the book for early publication but tells me it must await decision from the head man.

I'm leaving Sunday for a month's trip west. When you write you'd better address me here at home: the letter will be held.

Have a good summer. And, again, thank you.

Sincerely,

Lionel

P.S. Will you hold the MS until I send you word?

47. TO JACQUES BARZUN

June 15, 1938
Mar Monte Hotel, Santa Barbara, California

Dear Jacques:

This is what Life is like: you are walking down the main street of Santa Barbara and you hear "Why Lionel Trilling" and it is Richmond B. Williams, '25 C, who gives an imitation for half an hour of two old ladies at a sewing circle. Meditate on this.

Our trip has been delightful but aside from the scheduled events uneventful. Traveling, I find on my first real venture into it, is a *pure* pleasure—the sense of movement, of distance, of one's conveyance, the problems of one's identity are all more interesting than anything one sees. The Rockies in Canada are fine but only when one is moving through them; a mission is best seen from a train. It's a fine country to see but on the whole I think it should be seen incidentally, on business; it is not really meant for tourism. There are a few experiences—seeing the barrier of the Rockies rise out of the plain, the look of the San Francisco hills in the sun, the really astonishing beauty of the California landscape on the way south—but the real pleasure is just in *going*. Travel is the opiate of the intellectual and I love it.

I write from a nearly empty head, then. A few sessions of the Am. Psychiatric Association have provided me with nearly all the fodder I have. It was much as you would expect—profoundly unphilosophical, uncritical, even unscientific, though I could never tell whether what disturbed me was the skips in the thinking or the hiatuses in the exposition—perhaps they understand their intentions better than I do. But the excuse should not be made. Schilder, in the little I heard him, was exceptional, for he knows what philosophy is, knows what an idea is, respects the mind, and this makes his analysis commonsensical and incisive. I feel that the man who undertakes a sympathetic but critical consideration of psychoanalysis will be doing one of the real jobs of the generation. [. . .]

Yours,
Lionel

48. TO THE EDITOR OF *THE NEW REPUBLIC*

[1938]

Sir: Short of making a complete analysis of the *Partisan Review*'s contents for the past year, I cannot attempt to *prove* the injustice of Malcolm Cowley's attack upon it.[1] The most I can do is to put on record an opinion counter to Mr. Cowley's. In my estimation, then, the *Partisan Review* is one of the few good critical magazines in the country and the only organ of the Left to take culture seriously. If some part of its outlook is political, that is because it is following its own program and because there is (still) a deep, though not a simple, connection between literature and politics. If it is anti-Stalinist that is because the politics of such organs as the *New Masses* have made their cultural manifestations (as Mr. Cowley so convincingly says) second- and third-rate. Second- and third-rateness may be accepted as a neutral thing; or it may be understood as an active and dangerous thing, as both a symptom and a source of intellectual infection. The *Partisan Review* has taken the latter attitude. That it is not the "irresponsible" Little Magazine that Mr. Cowley wants it to be seems to me a virtue. That its tone is sneering and superficial has never been true. That its appearance in a green cover would make it resemble *The American Mercury* is also not true; I have seen it in a green cover.

I may be exempted from suspicion of personal pique by Mr. Cowley's generous praise of my own contribution to the *Partisan Review*. I have no connection with the review's editorial staff; I am barely acquainted with its members. Although my contempt for the cultural attitudes of the *New Masses* is perhaps even greater than Mr. Cowley's, I am not a Trotskyist.

Lionel Trilling

49. TO HARRIET TRILLING SCHWARTZ

February 21, 1939
620 West 116th Street

Dear Harriet:

Now that my book is out of the way and I have a chance to get some parts of my life in order again, I very much want to take up with

---

1. In *The New Republic*, October 19, 1938.

you a matter that has been disturbing me for a very long time. This is a practical matter in large part; but in larger part it is an emotional matter; and it is the latter that I want to speak to you about first and chiefly.

And I think that now is a good time to speak of it because you and Rolly[1] are coming to dinner on Thursday evening after a long period in which we have not seen each other. It seems to me very possible that the length of that period has raised in your mind and Rolly's certain misconceptions and these I want to clear up. For it seems to me that you may have misinterpreted this long interval as the result, for example, of our not enjoying your company or of our not liking Rolly. In point of fact the very opposite is the case and perhaps this is exactly what complicates matters. For our affection for you both has made it very difficult for me to say what was constantly in my mind and what has acted as a barrier between us. Yet with this barrier present I found that I experienced emotions in your company which made me unhappy and uncomfortable.

Of course you know what causes that barrier between you and me—it is your relation to Mother and Father. And if I feel resentment about that I think you will admit that I have justification. It is now eight years, more or less, that I have been carrying the chief support of Mother and Father. During the latter part of that time you also were included in that responsibility. In that time I have made that responsibility my chief financial concern—to the extent that the rent of Mother and Father was frequently paid when my own rent was not. Often enough I have had to borrow money to meet this obligation; indeed, I think that since I first undertook it I have not been wholly out of debt; nor am I now. During all [that] time I have not, I think you will admit, put any great pressure upon you to share this responsibility. In this I now think I was wrong—I mean wrong to you as well as to myself. I, and Diana with me, have constantly made excuses for your lack of action in the matter and we have spoken to each other of periods of adjustment which you had to go through and so on. But the upshot has been that you have pretty completely abrogated your responsibility.

---

1. Harriet Trilling was married to Roland Schwartz.

I know that you do not believe that you have done so. I know that frequently you must have great worry about the situation. But in *actual fact* you *have* abrogated responsibility. Let me be very realistic and even harsh for a moment. You have done equivalent things in other matters. I know, for example, that you believe that the Lows have treated you shabbily. But on the contrary: you have treated them shabbily. For however little the actual sum that you borrowed from them may mean in their total wealth, the fact is that when Sol lent you the money he thought he was entering into a realistic arrangement with you: but you treated it as though it were a kind of symbolic relationship that you could conjure away by a certain attitude. Your neglect of that debt was, in effect to Sol, an insult to the arrangement he made with you and an insult to his intentions. And again: you have let your debt to Charles Friedberg run for what is now many years, somehow on the assumption (what else can one conclude?) that he would forget it. But he has never forgotten it—not out of any meanness but because he feels, inevitably, that he has been put upon. He has frequently mentioned it to me. And he is right not to forget it when by the smallest possible payments over all these years you might have shown him that you valued the services he had rendered. But you have presumably proceeded on the principle that time and good intentions would take care of the situation.

And in a sense I feel much the same way that I have supposed the Lows and Charles to feel. By now, I cannot help thinking, I should have the right to expect three things of you: 1. that you help reduce my contribution to Mother and Father; 2. that you help in some small way to augment their way of living; 3. that I have someone to rely on to share with me the *sense* of responsibility, the merely emotional burden which, so far, I have had to carry alone.

Now I do not think that *all* these things are in your power—or have been. But some of them have been—and are, I am sure. A very small monthly sum could do at least two of these things—could help Mother and Father and could give me the feeling that I am not alone in responsibility for them.

And any one of these things would remove the very strong feeling which I have and which I have received from what conversation I have held with you and Rolly: that you believe that *I* have been during these years doing a very *foolish* thing and that *you* are now doing a *wise* one. In short, I have had the same sense of insult about my part in the whole business which I before ascribed to Sol Low and Charles Friedberg.

The mention of Rolly's name just now should not be taken by you as meaning that I think Rolly is directly concerned in this. I do not think so. The concern is wholly yours and the matter is between you and me. I will not say that I do not think that Rolly has indirectly concerned himself in the matter, I take it that he conceives that it is a "healthy" thing psychologically for you to put the matter out of your mind as an immediate issue. In this I believe that his notion is directed to what he thinks is your good—your emotional independence. But I think he is wrong. For so long as you have—as you must have—the sense of a duty unfulfilled you cannot achieve independence of your family in any real sense. Indeed, the very opposite is true.

Need I ask you to project yourself into my place and to imagine what your emotions would be if the roles were reversed and if, through this long period, I had allowed the obligation to Mother and Father to be wholly yours, if I undertook to do less and less and said nothing to you about the whole subject? And no matter what you *feel* about the subject, this, in actual fact, is what you have *done*.

Now, be sure that I understand very well what your difficulties are and have been—your difficulties of finance and of emotion. And be sure too that when I speak of your assuming responsibilities I do not prescribe what these should be. But it does seem to me that over all these years you could have staked out for yourself *some* realm of obligation and fulfilled its demands. After all, nothing is ever accomplished if one waits for the complete and perfect adjustment of circumstances, and just as you might by now have largely discharged your debt to Sol and Charles by the most insignificant payments, so by now you could have performed a great deal in this other responsibility.

As I said, I am not now talking about *amounts*. What I am talking about is your failure to face the problem fully, your failure to make it part of your life. It seems to me that you have put it off—with the best intentions in the world, I am sure—until some time when your life should be perfectly adjusted.

And it is *only* because you have not, in my opinion, made this problem part of your life—I take as exemplifying this that you have never discussed it with me but have in our relationship acted as though there were no problem—that the barrier between us has arisen. You have in effect dismissed the whole problem and in doing that you have, in emotional effect, denigrated whatever I have done for Mother and Father and for yourself while you were with them, and this, you can see, is not pleasant for me to contemplate.

It seems to me that there has been between us too long a history of strong affection for this situation to continue. I am sure that the barrier I speak of you are conscious of, and that it has caused you as much sorrow as it has me. And perhaps, misinterpreting the reason, you have felt resentment at me too. And the reason I am writing this letter is not to try to force you to give Mother and Father money (that, after all, isn't in my power) but because as long as you do not face your responsibility squarely with me our relationship is bound to be affected and I want you to know what I feel and where I stand.

So before we meet again on Thursday evening I want you to know all this so that there need be no more restraint and embarrassment between us. Perhaps you have thoughts and feelings on the subject that you too want to make clear; I suggest that you come up to see me in the late afternoon on Thursday if you feel that the matter needs discussion. In any case, we'll see you both at dinner.

 With love

  Lionel

50. TO NEWTON ARVIN[1]

March 19, 1939
620 West 116th Street

Dear Arvin:

I'm terribly sorry that your trouble continues so long and so heavy. I do hope it will soon pass.

It was good of you, things being as they are, to write at all. I'm delighted that you like the book so well. That you do take issue with it is, in a way, an added pleasure, for I did have in mind the propaga-

---

1. Newton Arvin (1900–1963), literary critic and biographer.

tion of a certain attitude, and your disagreement is, as you say, a sign that my intention was not missed.

Yet I wish I had your agreement. You see, I do not think that a criticism of "delicate lights and shades" is the luxury you call it. Indeed, I feel sure it is a necessity. I do not believe, of course, that such a criticism is possible as a basis of popular action (isn't that what's wrong with popular action?) but it should be, I believe, still maintained by those few who have been trained to exercise it. I do not think that it necessarily prevents even those few from acting; but I think it is their terribly difficult job, even when they must act, to keep their criticism going and not hang it up on the wall until they finish acting.

Of course, as Arnold himself says, human affairs must be carried on by anomalous actions, but that is no reason why we—intellectuals, I mean—have to say that the anomalies are anything *but* anomalies.

Thought, obviously, always implies action but I find terrifying these days the willingness of intellectuals to say that we must for a while stop thinking in order to put action first, that we should create myths and put aside carping realisms and stop being Hamlet-like and stuffy.

I find this attitude creeping—walking boldly, rather—into so much of the writing of the once-liberal wing. It seems to me always to bring with it an acceptance of things which we once all rejected. Liberals (I mean radicals too, of course) are now allying themselves with these once-rejected forces as if in the belief that they can use these forces as cat's-paws for their ultimate good aims, and that then, when they have got what they want, they can make the cat meekly retire into the corner.

I don't know that criticism of the kind you suspect can make things better. I guess it can't in any immediate way. But at least it keeps us, it seems to me, from what is maybe the worst of modern sins, self-deception, and helps us not to forward things we will eventually regret.

Well, this isn't a matter to be settled or clarified by letter; but maybe someday we'll be able to talk about it. Meanwhile I do hope things clear for you very soon; and believe me very grateful for your kind note.

Sincerely,
Lionel Trilling

51. TO SIDNEY HOOK

December 8, 1939
620 West 116th Street

Dear Sidney:

Some weeks ago a copy of your book[1] came to me from your publishers. I sat down to it at once, determined to read it before writing to thank you for it. But a mass of things descended on me before I had got very far along and I was unable to return to it until recently. But now I have finished it and I want to thank you for it and tell you how useful I have found it. I say "useful" advisedly; it will palliate my delay in writing to you if I tell you that one of the things that interrupted me was some reading of Dewey himself, *The Quest for Certainty*, to which I turned for help in the problem which an essay I was writing presented. Actually, I read little enough; I seem to be a Deweyan at heart or by osmosis and I got fairly quickly the confirmation I wanted for my idea. You see how the literary mind works; you can judge the result in an essay called "Parrington, Mr. Smith, and Reality,"[2] which is coming out in the next issue of the *Partisan Review*. But I don't think I could have got so quickly from Dewey what I needed if your book hadn't laid out the ground so beautifully. You've done a brilliant job of exposition and you've engaged the mind and feelings of at least one reader very thoroughly. Whether it was your book or my development or a conjunction of the two that did, I find myself very much committed to going on with Dewey. I'm really very grateful for your having the book sent to me.

I hope that we can get to meet sometime soon. Whether it is History or my disinclination from political meetings these days, we never seem to see each other even in passing.

Sincerely,
Lionel

---

1. Hook's *John Dewey: An Intellectual Portrait* (1939).
2. *Partisan Review* (January–February 1940); later included in the essay "Reality in America," in *The Liberal Imagination*.

January 14, 1940
Columbia University

Dear Mrs. Thayer:

I hope that my delay in answering your inquiry about Jim[1] has not caused you any concern. It seemed to me that before writing to you I should talk with him; and then I wanted to be sure that I could effect the plan for him that I had in mind.

Perhaps I should say first that there is, in my opinion, nothing in Jim's present state that should cause his parents to worry. If Jim is depressed, or bored with his work, there is nothing unusual in that for a young man of his kind—that is, the very best kind. He is in many ways very mature and I suspect that, as you say, [he is] facing some of the problems of his life a little ahead of schedule. Perhaps you know that Jim has what I consider a very remarkable talent for writing; I do not think I have had a student with so much present ability and so much future promise. And gifts of this kind can be a heavy burden; the possessor of them cannot be sure that he really has them and that must make him all at loose ends; he does not quite know what to do with them and they sit upon him uneasily. But, too, he is well enough aware of them to find them more important than anything else in his intellectual life, and sometimes (and I think this may be happening in Jim's case) they run ahead of his general intellectual development.

So far as his midterm grades here, Jim has been doing pretty good work in his courses, but he *has* been fairly bored by them. I have therefore invited him into a special course in which I am one of the instructors. Normally the course is limited to senior students but it seems to me that Jim's abilities and his needs make it right for him to come into it now. The course is a more or less informal one, designed to allow the student to pursue, under direction, the kind of work in literature in which he is most interested. Jim will go ahead with his fiction writing (which gets better and better, by the way) and in addition he will do a considerable amount of reading under my guidance. I hope that this will bring his strongest interest into his college curriculum; at best, it may help make his other work seem

---

1. A student of Trilling's at Columbia.

more relevant to him; at least it will give a sanction to the thing he likes most. He seemed truly pleased by the invitation; I think it ought to have a good effect and I look forward to working with him. I have also suggested a minor change in his program for next term, and I will try to see that for the year after he takes courses that will challenge his interest.

In short, as you can see, I think there is no need for you to be alarmed over Jim's state of mind. I suspect that he has great powers for living; that means, we must suppose, stumbling into difficulties and confusions as well as overcoming them.

Thank you very much for your kind congratulations on my promotion.

Sincerely yours,
Lionel Trilling

53. TO JACQUES BARZUN

June 28, 1940
620 West 116th Street

Dear Jacques:

The little piece is wholly admirable and there is very little in it that I can object to. There is, however, one major point. In a sense you cover it in your last paragraph but that is a little too late. This is the difficulty as I see it: you do not early enough separate culture in the fine-arts and way-of-living sense from the wider sense of the word that legitimately includes politics. I don't know in what direction your own explanation of the French defeat[1] goes, but to me it's fairly clear that an important part of any explanation must be political; that is, I suspect in the past government and its class base a rift so deep as to be conceivably treasonable. Now, that this condition should prevail is, in the second sense of the word culture, a cultural failure.

What I should like to see, then, is for you to make, early in the piece, the separation of politics-culture from culture-culture (I haven't gone native). It is true, of course, that a culture (in one sense)

---

1. France capitulated to Nazi Germany on June 22, 1940.

of a very high kind can be topped by a politics of the worst kind: insofar as we want to see a connection between the two we can blame culture-culture for "permitting" the bad politics. But if you, by definition, take culture to mean kinds of art and ways of living etc. it is perfectly permissible to absolve it from the sins of the politics which lives symbiotically (or however) with it. But I think you must *make* the definition.

With this distinction made clear, there ought to be nothing for you to worry about. Except that I would have you reconsider the paragraph on page 3 beginning "Lastly—." Here you face the issue of *Success* as the criterion of a culture—that is, businessman success—and it is an important point. Now of course you don't take the view that this success is what marks a good culture (in the Lincoln Steffens way: "I have seen the future and it works"[1]). But then, on the other hand, your paragraph *seems* to be asserting the opposite view—that what *we* would call a good culture *must* fail and collapse, that it *cannot* be strong enough to defend itself. Maybe this is empirically true; but it need not be true in principle, as somehow you seem to be saying. At least, if it is true in principle, more demonstration is needed than you give. To use as symbols the *reputations* of Sparta and Athens after their falls seems to involve you in a kind of absolute defeatism which I'm sure you don't want and which really negates your whole essay. This is, perhaps, an even more important point than the other one.

Corollary to this is my objection to the question (p. 3) Where are the Spartans now? I don't think that is a fair question, nor one likely to be relevant to the average person's politico-cultural thinking. Where is anyone ancient now? Shouldn't you rather say Where were the Spartans in fifty or a hundred years? (Where were they, by the way?)

In every respect the piece *ought* to be acceptable to *The Nation*. It is *very* well written indeed and very well shaped. I hear, however, that Freda Kirchwey[2] (of Kinder—Kuche—and Kirchwey) is rather

---

1. Lincoln Steffens (1866–1936), muckraking journalist, made this statement after visiting Soviet Russia in 1919.
2. Freda Kirchwey (1893–1976), editor of *The Nation* from 1933 to 1955.

hysterical about the war and is not inclined to reasonable views. But I may be doing her an injustice; I myself seldom see *The Nation* these days.

[. . .]

Yours,

Lionel

54. TO NEWTON ARVIN

December 29, 1940
Columbia University

Dear Arvin:

It was kind, and like you, to send me that generous word about my work. It came in very good season, for I have not been feeling entirely happy about my writing. Not that I would want to reject what I've done, but I felt that the vein of the last few years is now a little played out and that a new one must be dug. My sense about the *Kenyon* piece is that it was written on the impetus of earlier things— that instead of dealing with the problem immediately and in its own terms, I asked myself, "What would a man who has written what I have written say about this matter?" This is a form of insincerity which is, I believe, one of the virulent literary diseases. It's probably salutary to be aware of this and to begin working up a new head of steam, and all in the course of literary living. But the stoking-up period is a good time for doubt to come in, and when one gets a note so cheering as yours it's truly a great help.

This year I'm trying to stay away from criticism as much as possible in order to get back to fiction, from which I've been away a very long time; everything goes slowly and resistantly but not discouragingly. What critical writing I shall do I want to be in the English romantic movement. When my book was finished I was thoroughly sick of nineteenth-century England and wanted to turn to America. But I had to take on a nineteenth-century course at college and the time this took and the ignorance it discovered made me decide to find out what that revolutionary effort meant and is worth. I have in mind a short critical book on Byron. But someday I will say my say about my two best American friends, Hawthorne and Henry James.

The job you have in mind sounds like just what is needed. I know so little about books about American culture that I cannot judge, but it seems to me that there is a large hole which needs to be filled. I had, when *The Flowering of New England* came out, a burst of enthusiasm for Brooks,[1] but that is now turned quite sour. You could do such a very good job. As for the pain and paralysis such a plan always generates, you know that, even with them, living with a book is superior to living with MLA articles and *New Rep.* reviews. When you come down in March we must be *sure* to meet; I want to know more about the book and other things.

[. . .]

Sincerely,

Lionel Trilling

55. TO JACQUES BARZUN

August 12, 1941

620 West 116th Street

Dear Jacques:

I have just sent you a copy of my Wordsworth paper.[2] It is in the form in which it will be published, if publication is decided upon, which is likely. For reading purposes at the meeting it will have to be cut down to be contained in thirty minutes; I should guess that this means reduction by a quarter or a third. As you read, will you look out for the best places to condense or omit? That will be a great help. Then let me have your very stringent opinion of the paper as a whole. First tell me what you think of it as a kind of criticism and as an example of my critical writing. Then, apart from this, tell me what you think of it in a "political" sense, in its academic setting. That is what worries me chiefly. Diana, who likes the piece, cannot say what it might mean for people who are professionally interested in poetry and who know the *Ode* very well; and I, who think the piece has *some* merit, am concerned that it may seem much too obvious to these people. In part my worry is the usual feeling one has after one has

---

1. Van Wyck Brooks (1886–1963), literary critic and historian; *The Flowering of New England, 1815–1865* was published in 1936.
2. "The Immortality Ode," included in *The Liberal Imagination*.

spent a time in exploring a subject: everyone must know at first glance what I have learned after labor. This feeling was enhanced by Emery Neff's[1] comment; I gave him the MS yesterday and he returned it this morning telling me (in Italian!) that he had enjoyed my discourse very much; he went on to say (in English) that he had only the fault to find that he did not resist my exposition enough, he never having thought otherwise of the poem. He somewhat reduced my concern by saying that he never read the critics and so was not aware of other interpretations. Of course one should not show things to Emery, even out of a desire to be friendly, but you can see how his response *would* be disturbing. So tell me very sharply what you think the piece is worth; I want it to be good and there is still time to better it. . . . You will see in the first section some reflection of your own attitudes and ideas. . . . I'd like very much to have your notes and comments on the manuscript by Friday, when, most likely, I will be leaving town; if on the whole you are satisfied with the piece send me a note by airmail and the MS can return at leisure with the stampage I have put on the return envelope; but if you have a good many corrections to make, then will you double the stamps and send the package by airmail. (By the way, doesn't our running account leave me in your debt for various odds and ends?) I'll be most grateful for your trouble and speed.

This is being written on my new Rerl typewriter. I had not planned to get it for some months, but the old one was disintegrating so rapidly after twelve years of fidelity and it began so to look that personal machines would not be available that I plunged and bought now. It is a nice machine but as you can see from the page it and I are not entirely good friends yet.

[. . .]

Yesterday I received a letter from Bruce Bliven of *The New Republic* asking—all contributors to the *NR* are being asked—for my opinion on whether we ought to declare war immediately on the Axis. For my "convenience" the arguments for and against the declaration were summarized and I felt that if this was politics and if this was the mind of a great liberal journal we are in a very sad way. There were reasons which had to do with uniting the American people, heartening the warring nations, not taking the low moral ground of

---

1. Trilling's doctoral adviser and then his longtime Columbia colleague.

letting others fight our battles; but the question of what an actual declaration of war has to do with the American political future, or with the aims of war, was not even suggested. I do not think that a declaration of war is the worst thing that could happen now—if we aren't at war, what are we at? And it's done good—but how can people with responsibilities go on thinking about things in the piddling, sideline Boy-scoutism of the *New Republic*? I think of myself as a political ignoramus but this letter, which I will save for you, makes me feel like Machiavelli.

I have not yet read the Tate book; in leafing through it I saw some poetical analysis and did not want to come under the influence; as it was, my eye lighted on some business with *finesse* and *geometrie* which I had written about the day before in my own piece. And I felt suddenly that that had become a cliché and maybe not so good a distinction after all. But now I intend to get at it. . . . Did I ever tell you that months ago in sifting through the book I came on and was delighted by your comment on Carl Becker's *Heavenly City*: you call it a work of sophomoric intelligence; we never happened to speak about that book and so I thought I was alone and perverse in thinking that it was intellectually inadequate, it is a great pleasure to find you with me. What a comment on the judgment of the academic world that this is the example of the "creative" scholarship.

[. . .]

There is no news, except that my tennis improves. I write you that every summer and by now you must be expecting me to turn up on a Center Court. . . . I like it that you have both landlord and tenant trouble: it seems the perfect situation for a critic and a philosopher. What a homily (homily and molasses of course) could be made on the theme: Marcus Aurelius, probably. In this world each man is both a tenant and a landlord, a tenant of the great house of Nature and a landlord of those qualities within him. And as a tenant the day of moving is before his eyes, wherefore then should he bother to hang up his pictures and look after the property, and plant his rhododendrons and set great store by his lawns, for the van is at the door even now. And as landlord must he be wary to evict those qualities in himself that are concupiscent or play the radio all night and reduce the value of the property for it is a part of the great neighborhood or residential development of Nature. But actually it must be Montaigne. It gives us pause to remember that he who as a tenant is indignant that repairs are not made is as a landlord aston-ished that repairs should be thought necessary and who that is one shall properly conceive the justice of the other.

Enough. Let me hear from you soon and that you are well.

Yours,

Lionel

56. TO NEWTON ARVIN

[1941]

620 West 116th Street

Dear Newton:

How very nice to hear from you again! And how good to know that you are again well. I was much disturbed by your mention in your let-ters of a while back that you weren't in top form. Do see to it that you continue in your recovered state and that one of the first fruits of it will be a long enough visit down here for us to meet as we have so of-ten planned. I know you hate the city but it isn't so bad. Though it gets one into a kind of weary involvement with it that about this time of year makes one suffer from a kind of unresilience: you throw yourself at things and you don't bounce. It seems that for the present I shall be here: I've been classified as having dependents and have been deferred in the drafts, how long that status will stand I can't know, though it would be a pretty bad situation if it is changed. I keep going pretty much at the old routine: a first impulse to get out of it, to take advan-tage of general social unsettlement to unsettle myself, has passed, and I no longer think about trying to get into some government bureau. I'm preparing to study bombs in order to pass on some (no doubt rule of thumb) information to the air raid wardens, but that is the full extent of my change of way of life. Perhaps events will carry me further but I'm not pushing them. Things are quiet at the college: there is very little inflated talk and we go [on] with our jobs without any consciousness of their being useless or foolish and that is very heart-ening. Of course the pressure exists and there are bound to be changes in organization. For instance, the graduate schools fall off in attendance and the professors there begin to eye the college with a new enthusi-asm for undergraduate education and that threatens the younger and less rooted men.

I'll be curious to know what you'll think of my review after you've read the Agee book[1] through. Some people tell me I was too generous: they feel more strongly than I do about Agee's twisting and turning and self-conscious announcement of his inadequacy to his subject and his certainty of failure; they think it a weakness in him deeper than the one he declares and theoretically a bad attitude. And I suppose they are right but I was quite overpowered by what over and above these things emerges in sensibility and good writing. And I'll be curious to know too what you make of a piece of mine coming out in the next *Kenyon*. I finished it with great trouble a few days ago and sent it off with some uncertainty about what I'd actually said. It's about E. M. Forster and about our generation of thought: there were more things, both statements and modifications, that I wanted to say and I'm not sure that I said what I really intended. I'd be really grateful if you'd tell me what you find.

Are you writing on anything now? Month to month I keep meaning to get to reading Hawthorne again (he comes up for a moment in my Forster piece) for he—or rather my old memory of him—comes up to haunt me, and then to read your book about him, which I never have read and which I came across yesterday in revising some bibliography. Does he still mean a good deal to you?

It was such a great pleasure to get your letter; do let us continue now to keep in touch. These days, I think, we need all the lines of communication we can have.

Yours,
Lionel

57. TO NEWTON ARVIN

May 10, 1942
620 West 116th Street

Dear Newton:

I am aghast when I see how long I have waited to take up our conversation. I hope you can forgive me. I've been waiting for a free and relaxed time and you may guess what things have been preventing that. The last few months have been for me very pressed, partly

---

1. James Agee and Walker Evans's *Let Us Now Praise Famous Men* (1941).

because of added university jobs, partly because an operation this winter ran us into medical and domestic expenses and debts that I have been trying to cope with (vainly!) and partly—and this is more cheering—because I have been taking advantage of some new energy to load up on work just for the fun of having too much to do. But your delightful letter has been on my desk and in my consciousness, actively accreting answers to itself.

I'm terribly pleased that you suggest a collection of essays, for at the moment I'm in negotiation with Norton—that is, I'm waiting to hear from him—about a volume of essays to come out possibly at the beginning of next year.[1] I hesitated about this for some time, partly out of modesty—there is something fairly assertive about "collecting" one's work—and partly out of the feeling that the volume would have no particular point. But one or two friends—there must be at least two for you were one of them—gave me enough encouragement to overcome the modesty (modesty, I suppose, is so nice a virtue exactly because it can be so easily overcome!) and after looking at the essays it seemed to me that there *was* a point after all and that if I did a certain amount of rewriting I could make it appear. The point, the thread, as I see it, is twofold (ignore the metaphorical breakdown) and consists of a consideration of the liberal dilemma and of the place (proper place) of literature in life. If you happened to have read the essay on E. M. Forster I did for the last *Kenyon*, you'll know what I mean by liberal—I mean positivistic, humanistic, Marxist or—oid, reformist, revolutionary, naturalistic, etc.—and also something of what I mean by the dilemma. The dilemma is too complex to state in a sentence or two; but during the last few years I have thought of myself as questioning, as a liberal, a great many of the liberal assumptions which have been unquestioningly accepted by so many, and especially by so many intellectuals. My feeling about the situation is not only rational; I mean it is very personal and passionate. I've lived for a long time by and in the midst of these assumptions and I have strong feelings not only about their bad political and cultural effects but also about their bad personal effects. I've known myself to have been cut off from a great deal by them and I've seen a great many of my friends even more seri-

1. Trilling decided not to proceed with the book at this time; he would publish his first collection of essays, *The Liberal Imagination*, in 1950. See letter of October 3, 1942.

ously deprived and I should say that the chief interest of my writing and thinking for six or seven years is the harm they can do. At the same time, I feel that there is likely to be a kind of turn against liberalism which is likely to go too far and be indiscriminate and destructive and I should like to help stem that by just anterior criticism.

The other part of my intention, to help define the proper place of literature in life, relates to this. Of course, it isn't a matter that criticism itself can settle, but criticism can help. One of the things I feel is that literature has been injured by being made to do more work and of a different kind than is proper and I should like to upset some of the current assumptions that make this possible. When I said something about this matter in an essay on the teaching of literature two years ago, you had some objections, but I hope to make this clearer so that you'll have no cause to object.

If Norton decides to do the book I expect to spend a few months of the summer getting it into shape. I am not particularly eager for him to be its publisher, but I am bound by contract to submit it to him. Indeed, I am almost hopeful that he will refuse, for I don't think he is the publisher for me and I am looking for the ideal publishers who will go along with me on some long-term plans; Norton lacks the quality of continuity—he likes to get in and get out quickly. I have in mind both fiction (hush!) and criticism. Fiction is what I've always had in mind and maybe I'm ready for it now. I have a novel briefly under way, short and rather odd which, if I can keep it going, I'd like to hope will be finished before the summer is out. After that I have the idea for another, longer and more conventional. The idea of another long absorbing book like the Arnold frightens me. Such jobs, I think, take up too much of one's life—it's not a matter of time only. I learned something doing the Arnold: that is, it forced me to live through and really to face certain things as much in myself as in literature and I suppose that I ought to be grateful to the experience. But there was something brutalizing in that kind of work; I find I'm still a little shell-shocked at the idea of another long work, though I suppose no other book would ever again be written under the particular bad circumstances and tensions (personal, political, etc.) of that one and perhaps if the right subject presented itself I'd plunge in again. What I do have in mind, apart from essays, which I more and more like—you get in and you get out fast (in essays a virtue, apparently, in publishers a vice!)—is a book of three long pieces on the romantic poets, three of them—Wordsworth, Keats, and Byron. They might even be little books of English Men of Letters length, *nouvelles* of biography: I have a fondness for the form as I have for the *nouvelle* itself. The reason for the choice of subjects is the interest I spoke about before, the interest in the liberal assumptions. The romantics can give us the situation in purer form, and can allow a discussion of matters which might in their present form be charged with all kinds of partisan implications. The Wordsworth one is closest to me and I believe closest to the present situation.

Looking at the page of your letter in which you talk about the book you are playing with, I see we are parallel lines—and likely to meet and even cross. We have, I think, the same situation in mind, with naturalism central in it. I find and I wonder if you do—this is where we are likely to cross—that while I am committed to naturalism and expect always to be, I find that I operate with a certain suspicion of it. This, I hope, is always an instrument. There is something, I find, in the tone of most naturalism, as it is, though not necessarily as it might be, that has a certain cramping, damping, limiting, fatiguing effect. That, I suppose, is what I mean by the liberal dilemma— nothing much more than this. Certainly what is usually taken to be the opposite of naturalism, religion vague or theological, isn't for me the true corrective for these effects and what is I don't know.

If you get to see the current *Partisan Review,* do look at a piece of mine[1] and see if you agree with some of the things I say about historical as vs. the aesthetic criticism. It's not a complete piece to begin with and it was cut for publication, but think of it as the notes for a future essay. It goes along with you in protest against Empson-Brooks-Tate.[2] They've done good work and I've learned a great deal from them but I wonder if it is they who make me feel lately that though I want to write criticism I *don't* want to read it. (By the way, I *can't* read

---

1. "The Sense of the Past," *Partisan Review* (May 1942); included in *The Liberal Imagination.*
2. William Empson, Cleanth Brooks, and Allen Tate, literary critics associated with the formalist approach known as New Criticism; John Crowe Ransom's book *The New Criticism* was published in 1941.

Burke.[1]) Something in their intention, by the way (their ultimate and unconscious intention, but also their conscious intention perhaps), makes me not trust them. There is something uncomfortably snide about them and, as you say, something restrictive. To take Burke out of his brackets above, I feel of him as of E-B-T that literature shouldn't be so damned much talked about and certainly not in so far off, so portentous a way. This is no doubt a very retrograde view.

[. . .]

Your Yaddo suggestion sounds wonderfully alluring but I'm afraid it's out of possibility. Yaddo and I are not on good terms. This isn't entirely accurate: I like Yaddo and I am on excellent terms with Mr. Slade (is he still president of the Corporation?) but between Mrs. Ames and myself (and my wife) there is, I fear, a coolness. This dates back ten years when I was invited for a generously long summer and my wife for two shorter periods; I left before the time set in my invitation. The circumstances make something of a story, which I won't give you; we thought Mrs. Ames acted very harshly toward one of the guests, an unpleasant and trying but most unfortunate person. Now and then we think that if we had been older our partisanship might have taken a different form—though even then it was not a crude or especially militant partisanship—but we continue to think Mrs. Ames wrong and ourselves right. The difference was never very open and there was never any break between us, only the coolness of profound dissatisfaction with each other. I have often been sorry for sordid practical reasons and now I am sorrier for the better reason that I won't be able to see you up there; it would have been delightful and exciting. But I'll still hope you'll be in town if only briefly. I expect to be here at least until the middle of August.

Meanwhile I hope you'll write again when you get the opportunity. I won't apologize again for not writing sooner. You didn't want me to and if we are to keep in touch we'll have to, as you say, forget that promptness is an essential virtue of letters. But I look forward to hearing.

Yours,

Lionel

---

1. Kenneth Burke (1897–1993), literary critic and theorist.

58. TO JACQUES BARZUN

June 18, 1942[1]
620 West 116th Street

Dear Jacques:

[. . .]

I wish I could cheer you by the news that I am working well, but I am not so, why beat about the bush? That of course is the question I am asking myself daily, for I do little *but* beat about the bush. I am trying to get the preface to my book done; but no go. Still, I do not expect this fit to last long and already I see signs of its lifting. I'm sorry to hear that you are feeling so mean and tired. But you shouldn't take it as the leaden foot of time beating you down; so far as I can make out you take on more work every year and much more than two men can usually do. This you ought really to understand, so that if you find yourself done in at this season you can know that you have a right to the condition and give way to it.

The only interesting thing that has happened to me since we last met is that *Time* magazine offered me its literary editorship. The offer came through the astonishing Whittaker Chambers[2] and his advice was "Don't take it." Of course, I didn't seriously consider it when I learned that it was a full-time job— and a hard one, though I cannot see why it must be—and would mean giving up my university job. The salary that goes with a responsible *Time* job is good and can get to be enormous (this is no doubt because the incidence of nervous breakdowns on the staff is, literally, startling) and there was of course the charm in prospect to which I find I am responsive, perhaps all academics are, of being in something real. I was curiously flattered by the offer and absurdly felt depressed after I had turned it down. Perhaps in some funny way my present uneasiness with work comes from the implications of that incident. By the way, I am in absurdly

---

1. Trilling typed 1924 and corrected the year by hand, adding "(wish-thinking!)."
2. Whittaker Chambers (1901–1961) was a contemporary of Trilling's at Columbia College. In 1942, he was an editor at *Time*, but in the intervening years he had worked underground as a communist spy, before breaking with the party. He would later become notorious for his role in the Alger Hiss case. The character of Gifford Maxim, in Trilling's novel *The Middle of the Journey*, is based on Chambers; see letter of May 22, 1972.

good physical health, nothing delicate about my nerves, only my psyche.

Have we ever discussed the question of whether, since there is Comparative Literature, there must be Superlative Literature or Literature Absolutely. One could project an academic comedy on this interchange:

Professor Dash: I am a member of the Department of Comparative Literature.

Professor Stroke (of a rival institution, looking at his well-manicured nails): Ah! As for us, we only teach the very, very best.

I'm enclosing a reprint or offshoot of my Wordsworth article (What Are Wordsworth? A Semantic Study); as usual your name appears in it. Do you think it ought to be included in the volume? I think not.

By the way, I am not entirely settled on Dickens as the subject for that little book. I'm still open to suggestions if you can conjure any up.

Rest easy and let me have a line from you before you come down.

Yours,

Lionel

59. TO NEWTON ARVIN

October 3, 1942
620 West 116th Street

Dear Newton:

I am appalled by the date of your last letter: it's just two months unanswered. And this isn't really an answer: just a response to the practical matter you raised and an explanation of why I have delayed so long about it.

The book of essays we talked about when we met I've now given up. I begin to feel more and more that the material I had wouldn't make a book—that is, the right book for me to bring out now and feel pleased with. I didn't make the decision on the basis of the value of the essays themselves—that is, not in a mood of self-deprecation but only of "aesthetics" and practicality. The effect of the essays, taken together, would have been diffuse, would not have been useful to the ideas in them and would, therefore, have been of no use to me in any way of the world. It took me a long summer to paddle along to this decision largely because of vanity—a book *is* such a nice thing to have.

So I shall not, after all, be able to avail myself of your kind suggestion that I submit the book to the Yaddo publication committee. But you know how pleased and grateful I am that you made the offer.

Sometime soon I shall write you in response to all the interesting things in your good long letter. Somehow, this year, college starts with pressure and a little confusion for me. But since I have just clinched my decision about the book I wanted you to know at once and, as soon as I could, ask you to forgive my long delay.

Yours,
Lionel

60. TO ALLEN TATE[1]

November 27, 1942

Dear Allen Tate:

It was such a great pleasure to get your letter and I am delighted that you liked the two reviews. Reviews get so quickly lost in the shuffle that it is a wonder anybody bothers doing them (yet somebody must, I suppose) and when they are noticed there is always a special gratification.

Kazin[2] is, as you say, a very clever young man, but he went astray in the chapter in which he dealt with you. I think, really, that he said more than he meant—that he was perhaps working up a case in order to make a mechanical balance between the Marxists on the one hand and the "formalists" on the other hand, the good sound critics lying somewhere between. Indeed, I think that his great fault as a critic is that he is too much inclined to balance: or, rather, balancing. Yet he *is* a good critic and, although you are kind enough to say the contrary, I think I didn't do entire justice to many of his virtues.

---

1. Allen Tate (1899–1979), poet and critic.
2. Alfred Kazin (1915–1998), critic and memoirist. His first book, the literary history *On Native Grounds*, was published in 1942.

Cargill I don't know. Is he awful? Kazin seems to speak of him with some respect. But I shan't seek him out—if he should turn out to be of the Geismar[1] school, I couldn't take him: I find I can take less and less "cultural" criticism, though I myself like to practice it. Indeed, I find I can take less and less criticism—unless it is written out of love or anger or unless it teaches me something new and specific. The whole forward-looking en-masse kind of criticism bores me more and more.

Thank you again for your kind and cheering letter.

With cordial greetings,

Sincerely,

    Lionel Trilling

61. TO JAMES LAUGHLIN[2]

July 22, 1943

620 West 116th Street

Dear Mr. Laughlin:

Today is in theory the publication date of my book. I think you should know some of the facts which I learned today about its condition of publication.

There are no copies in the bookstores. In the University bookstore, which would naturally display and push the book, the buyer had no knowledge of the book whatever—no salesman had ever spoken to her of it, she had received no literature about it. In the newspaper lists of books published today my book is not mentioned, nor are any of the Forster reprints. Review copies have not yet reached the reviewers; they were not sent out until Tuesday (in consequence, I am told, of an insufficient shipment of books from you to Knopf). *The Nation* and *Time*, which happen to know from me when the book was to be published, have been making inquiries about it. I need scarcely tell you that a book which a reviewer receives after its publication date is not likely to be reviewed promptly, possibly not at all, if

---

1. Maxwell Geismar (1909–1979), critic and biographer.
2. James Laughlin (1914–1997), poet and founder of New Directions, the publisher of Trilling's *E. M. Forster* (1943).

other books crowd it in the least. The *Times Book Review* omits reviewing a book if for any reason it cannot review it on time. Fadiman makes a policy of not reviewing books after their week of publication. Any consideration that we get from reviewers of the large-circulation press will now be wholly because of their good nature.

And at best we can expect a straggling in of reviews, instead of the concerted response that is so necessary for a venture like the Forster scheme. You can scarcely revive and build a man's reputation by issuing his books as if it did not matter when and how they came out; the dignity and efficiency which should have attended the publication are entirely lacking.

Now, I understand perfectly that in wartime delays are likely to occur in publication. But it is equally clear that for that very reason the utmost care and the closest supervision are all the more necessary. A delay in publication is not fatal, but a publication such as we have had makes a fiasco. Clearly what should have been done is that the publication should have been postponed until review copies were ready and out: but there was no one here in authority to make such a decision. I am sorry to have to say to you that the publication of a book cannot be directed from across the continent.

I have not said this until now, although I have had cause to say it many times before. Putting this book through the press was attended with difficulties for me that no author contracts for. The manuscript was not edited and styled; I had to call in help to see that this work was properly done on the galleys. The galleys were not read by a professional proofreader; again I had to call in my own help. I have had to be in constant touch with the printer over a multitude of small problems. I have had to answer the inquiries of literary editors who had heard of our Forster venture and wanted to do their best for it. On all sides and on every occasion there were expressions of astonishment at the continued absence of the publisher.

I have made no protest about the work for me which your absence entailed. If you do not undertake to follow the methods of commercial publishers, allowances can be made. But the bad management of publication which results from your absence seems to me to be a failure of responsibility which cannot be condoned. You have no right to feel that your responsibility to a man's work ends with a check to him and another to the printer. The writer undertakes to do his best job for the publisher; and for his part the publisher undertakes to do his best to advance the work; and I do not think you have done your best.

And quite apart from myself, I do not think you have done your best for Forster; our project depended upon the éclat of our publication, and no publication ever had less éclat. In your last letter you speak of advertising, but you speak of it so tentatively and of some time so uncertainly in the future that I am truly dismayed.

You have often implied that the Knopf office was inclined to be uncooperative and inefficient. I have been in constant communication with Mrs. Stegg and I know this not to be true. On the contrary, indeed, the Knopf office has been in every way cooperative and efficient. I am afraid that the blame for the crypto-publishing of the Forster must lie entirely with you.

I am really sorry to have to write to you in this way. As I have said, I should not do so if it were merely a matter of inconvenience to him; but I must naturally very much resent any indifference which injures the career of a work of mine.

Sincerely,

62. TO MORTON DAUWEN ZABEL[1]

August 21, 1943
620 West 116th Street

Dear Morton:

The lateness of this letter is doubly guilty—count one, your letter of three weeks ago; count two, the review. Both of them gave me pleasure which should have been signalized by immediate word, but until a few days ago I was in an entire fog of heat and weariness. Do forgive me.

The review,[2] abstractly speaking, was wholly admirable— "abstractly" I of course mean even supposing I wasn't involved in it. It gave a beautiful sense of Forster's quality as well as his intention;

---

1. Morton Dauwen Zabel (1901–1964), poet, critic, and editor.
2. "A Forster Revival," *The Nation*, August 7, 1943.

and there was great tact in your introduction of Forster's deficiencies. It is so hard to present him fairly—that is, with his deficiencies on his head. Lately, with a little annoyance, I have been writing to friends and distant points explaining that No—I don't think Forster is a Great novelist in the way Tolstoy, Dostoevski, etc., are great novelists. (I cannot be so rude as to point out that [the] book never makes such a claim, and even specifically removes the possibility of the epithet.) I only think, I go on, that he is interesting, perceptive, passionate, right, etc. In a way his position is unique: there are very few novelists (at the moment I can think of no other) to whom one can apply so many fine adjectives and end up with—"and not great." He makes the word a little foolish. I remember that in a letter of some time back you put the matter of his status remarkably well. . . . But all this is an excursus from my admiration of your review, which for an intelligent audience is an ideal introduction to the pleasures of the old boy.

Speaking not abstractly—that is, with all my nice, vulgar, self-regarding feelings involved—I had a wonderful proud time with it, swelling up with self-esteem not only at the praise but at being implicated in such very good criticism. It gave me enormous satisfaction. It can't be good manners for a reviewee to *thank* his reviewer, but what else can he do after so much pleasure?

No doubt you have seen the run of the reviews. There can be no doubt that the book fell into luck. The *Times* piece was pretty soggy what with its dithering about comic matter and comic manner but from the point of view of publicity it helps do the trick: it means that libraries will begin to buy Forster. Fadiman's piece I thought very good for its length and medium; for public purposes it got quite close to the center of Forster. The *Time* piece is, I gather, a story in itself. Its inordinate length has, as *Time* would say, set liberal tongues fussily wagging; and even illiberal eyes pop open with surprise. Phil Rice was one of the few to see that the piece makes my book a Republican campaign document. There is motive somewhere. I must get the detail, but I've seen no one lately with *Time* connections. I know that Nigel Dennis had the assignment and I hear that Whittaker Chambers did the published version. I do not know whether personalities or politics make the chief factor: either being possible.

Up to recently we've had simply intolerable weather; I've never been so conscious of climate or so badly affected by it. It was strange to see people beaming and looking as if a blessing had suddenly dropped on them when it turned cool a few days ago. Summer session ended with the heat and I've been luxuriating in idleness and coolness. For the first time in a long time I'm enjoying doing nothing; I'm often idle but I'm usually unhappy about it. I've read two and a half Eric Ambler novels; the fraction indicates that I found E.A. disappointing, very literate but not ingenious, and too much last-minute violence for solution—all very well for the movies but not for novels. For the Ambler kind of thing Dumas or even Stevenson can't easily be equaled. I've just got hold of Graham Greene's *The Ministry of Fear*. I somehow missed your piece, except the title, and I'm going over to look it up in the library tomorrow.

How do you manage to acquire all your scholarship?—dreadful word: I mean useful information. I let fall a puny parallel of Mr. Elliot and Gilbert Osmond (I am always on the point of calling him Osmond Fraenkel;[1] I suppose the suggestion of Fraenkelstein) and you streak innumerable parallels to that. You ought to do a piece—I know how dull that sounds—on the cruelty-taste theme. I've been thinking lately that we have not written about the nineteenth century in one of the really suggestive ways of writing about a culture, the thematic way. It could tell us so much about the unexpressed assumptions. But this will lead me to much too long a matter, my late disgust with the nineteenth cent. and the sudden revival of interest as I saw how dully I had been thinking about it and a determination to see if I couldn't develop some new feelings and insights. But you are so much the man to shock up the solid worthy intelligences that deal with that time.

I'm looking forward to your visit. Do drop us a line a day or two before you leave so that we can be sure of meeting quickly. Diana sends her greetings with mine.

Sincerely,
Lionel

---

1. Osmond Fraenkel (1888–1983), civil liberties lawyer who defended the Scottsboro Boys.

63. TO ERNEST NAGEL[1]

September 21, 1943

Dear Ernest:

I'm very glad that you got pleasure from the Forster book. It gave me great pleasure that you should have written to tell me.

You do misread, I think, the sentence that sent your eyebrow up. You will see, if you look at the whole passage again, that the "accusation" against intellect, logic, and rationality really *is* a "futile" one—of the same sort as the accusation against romanticism: and here and elsewhere in the book I am at pains to dismiss the accusation against romanticism as being the source of Nazism. The point of the comparison is that the silliness of either accusation may be measured by the silliness of the other.

I would grant that I do allow what might be called a foolish possibility to both accusations—that is, I imply that the foolishness of each may be *understood*. This does not condone either.

To be sure, I do suggest the part in Nazism played by intellect, logic, and rationality. You seem to imply that Nazism is the *expression* of intellect, logic, and rationality, using these words in their honorific sense. But if we do not use the honorific sense of the words, we must see that the Nazis make use of intellect, logic, and rationality as well as of emotion. They brag that they move from premise to conclusion in a very rigorous and precise way, and we see from their actions how right they are in their boast; because we do not like the conclusion or admit the premise does not, it seems to me, allow us to call the progression nonrational or nonlogical: it would not be possible to call what goes on in a Nazi chemical laboratory nonscientific just because we do not like its intention or result. You would seem to be implying, in taking exception to my sentence, that emotions may be either good or bad but that the processes of the intellect are by definition good, and that if they are not good they are not of the intellect.

I should naturally be very much concerned if what amounts to an irony should by many readers be taken in the sense that you have taken it; I hope that I can rely on the tenor of the book to suggest the intended meaning of a sentence that is no doubt awkwardly put.

---

1. Ernest Nagel (1901–1985), philosopher of science and professor at Columbia.

Meanwhile I find myself at present much concerned at your discovering such wide differences with and serious qualifications of what philosophy the book has; and even more by your assumption that I would of course expect—"not be surprised" by—these differences. I wasn't aware that such disagreements were to be taken for granted between us and someday we'll have to talk of them.

Yours,

64. TO JAMES LAUGHLIN

September 25, 1943
620 West 116th Street

Dear Mr. Laughlin:

I am glad that the book is now in the hands of the London agent. I hope that he can soon come to a conclusion with it, for I am very anxious, as I told you, to have an English publication as soon as possible.

The Matthew Arnold had a remarkably good English reception and I should think that there would be no trouble in placing the Forster. Allen and Unwin, the publishers of the Arnold, should be receptive to a new book by me. And if Edward Arnold, Forster's publisher, is not also the publisher of Rose Macaulay's book on Forster, he would seem to be an indicated likelihood too.

My desire for an early English publication prompts me to repeat to you the report that I have heard, via England, that your agent, Pollinger or another, offered Daiches's[1] book at a price so high that it could not be met. I cannot, of course, judge the accuracy of this, but I should not like to see my book meet an impasse of this sort; at the best, the sum that comes from England cannot be large.

I am sorry to have to tell you that your letter, pleasant as its intention certainly was, had the effect, when taken in conjunction with other things, of irritating me a great deal.

I find it irritating, for instance, that you seem not to realize or take very casually the remarkable success the book has had. No work of criticism that I know of in late years has had so wide or so enthusiastic a reception. I have had occasion lately to speak to many publish-

---

1. David Daiches (1912–2005), British literary critic.

ers; all of them were astonished that a book of this sort should have received such a response.

Your lack of understanding of this is implicit in the tone of your letter. The reason for it I can in part understand—you have not seen the reviews. But I do not understand the business methods of a publisher who does not effectively arrange to receive his reviews. I find it not especially important but still ironically indicative that you should have twice asked me to send you the reviews: this is a service which the publisher, through his office, usually supplies the author.

But I think that ultimately your lack of understanding of the book's success is to be charged not to inefficiency but to your being essentially without interest in the project. I am willing to lay myself open to the charge of vanity by pointing out to you that you took no notice of the success until you had occasion to reply to some questions of mine.

Your lack of understanding of the book's situation is made explicit by your apathy about exploiting it. I have no illusions about the number of copies a book like mine can sell, but it seems clear to me that at the moment of its success, while the reviews were still fresh, it should have been advertised. [. . .]

You speak in your letter as though some point had been proved in support of your publishing wisdom by the space the book has received. The good result was not necessarily brought about by the time of publication—my Arnold book was published in the winter and received a press quite as good. Indeed, I can attribute no virtue to the time or the manner in which the book was published—quite the contrary, for review copies did not reach the reviewers until the very day of publication; this resulted, quite according to my expectation, in the book not being reviewed by the daily reviewers. To refer again to the experience of my Arnold, this much longer and far more difficult book was reviewed by the daily as well as the weekly reviewers: they had sufficient time in which to read it before publication day.

You should know too that the reviewers of *Time*, *The Nation*, and *The New Yorker* found it necessary to apply to me for information about the time of publication; if I had not seen to it that books reached them we might have had their reviews too late or, in two cases, not at all.

All this is very much of a piece with the way the book was got through the press. This was done by me alone. I had to deal directly with the press in many telephone conversations. I had to provide, from among my friends, the proofreaders that are properly supplied by the publisher. I also had to provide—and fortunately was able to through the kindness of a friend—the editorial reading that the publisher always provides but which you did not. In this last connection I wish to point out that any proof corrections that are of an editorial nature and that might fairly be expected to have been caught and questioned by an editorial person in the publisher's office must not be charged to me.

I find it dismaying that as yet no books have been sent to Forster. His address could easily have been got from Harcourt Brace, from Knopf—from any number of people. It seems to me that the neglect is discourteous in the extreme. I shall myself undertake to send Forster a copy of the book, though properly it should come from you.

I am truly sorry to find it necessary to write you as I have done, but it seems to me that you do not properly understand, or do not take seriously, the right relation between publisher and author. The interests of the publisher and author are the same. To advance those interests it is the author's part to produce as good a piece of work as he can; this I think I have done. It is the publisher's part to promote the book in every possible legitimate way; his responsibility does not stop with the payment of the printing bill; and his responsibility to any writer who has put a book in his charge is, apart from its largeness, a very serious one.

Very sincerely,

65. TO NEWTON ARVIN

October 24, 1943
620 West 116th Street

Dear Newton:

I must tell you, and I think you would want to know, how much pleasure and profit I received from your review in the *Partisan*.[1]

---

1. "Two Cheers for Forster," *Partisan Review* (September 1943).

Part of the pleasure is simple, even vulgar: I liked the complimentary things you said about me. And beyond that, I feel that the compliments came closer to my best intention than anything anybody has said, and that kind of praise is the only kind that can really touch one below the naive and vulgar liking of just any praise. But still further, and where pleasure and profit meet, I found myself responding with excitement to the question your review raises, partly by implication from Forster, about the adequacy of my critical work. You should know that lately I have had the growing sense that I was committing myself to, as it were, a circle of flexibility, or some such thing which was good but not sufficient for me any longer. This sense your review somehow made clear and explicit, as an external agency so often does to diffuse feelings. (Perhaps it is something for both of us as critics to notice, that without your known and expressed approval of my work, your discriminating dissatisfaction wouldn't have caught me so firmly as it did: I suppose we have to tame a writer's vanity before we can get him to listen!)

I naturally find myself a good deal confused by what, with your help, I have been discovering. To get the qualities that you like in my writing took a long time and an enormous lot of pushing of myself around. To get beyond where I am now is sure to take more time and more pushing around. And the situation around us isn't helpful. Having escaped from a foolish affirmation—I meant the whole dreadful Stalinoid flummery, which I consider one of the most immoral events of intellectual history—I find it terribly hard to find new points of positive attachment. One has to transcend Max Lerner[1] and *PMery*,[2] and Maxwell Geismar and his awful language about having "a positive to your anger," and all the shabby progressivism that is based ultimately, as I believe, on self-pity and self-hatred and contempt for others and on obscured impulses to power, and find a whole new speech, new admirations, and new ways of scorn. I suppose I am too much appalled by the bad qualities of love and hate I find around us, and feel inadequate to try new ways, and so I keep pecking away at what I find. But clearly that isn't enough these days. Perhaps it is

---

1. Max Lerner (1902–1992), liberal writer and journalist.
2. *PM* was a liberal newspaper published in New York City from 1940 to 1948.

something to be aware of the inadequacy and hope that by knowing about it something will be added.

Do you know Rebecca West's big book?[1] I'm inclined to think it pretty great. She says things in it—especially in the explanation of the fauna of her title—that put wonderfully what I feel.

Forgive the self-importance of all this; whether or not you meant to, you stirred me up with your review and I wanted to tell you, and thank you.

Yours,
Lionel

66. TO MELVIN LASKY[2]

February 25, 1944
620 West 116th Street

Dear Melvin:

It was a great pleasure to hear from you, although not—and you will understand, I know, the distinction—a great pleasure to get your letter. "Bad time" or whatever you call what you are having, it sounds unhappy enough. I don't know whether now, after a month—too long—I am writing into the same situation. Very likely not, because one's perceptions, especially of new things, come in bunches; the mind likes a unity of genre and on one day all the women one sees on the street are ugly and another day they are just as consistently pretty; and, as I say, in a new situation this is especially true. But then again it is so very likely that things are still the same, and for that, if it is so, I am truly grieved. I know you must have discounted by now the part that shock must have played in your feelings, the sudden discovery that the mass of people aren't as most literature persists in saying they are. Still, so much of your experience must be a matter of bad luck. A friend of mine has two sons in the army, close to each other in age and training, and one of them has had nothing but happy personal experiences, while the other has had

---

1. *Black Lamb and Grey Falcon* (1941).
2. Melvin Lasky (1920–2004), a former student of Trilling's at Columbia, would go on to become a leading anticommunist intellectual and editor of *Encounter*.

nothing but miserable ones, including being imprisoned by a batty commandant.

But you see what I am doing—trying to digest your experience, ostensibly for you but actually for myself, or trying to put it away somewhere behind as many and as contradictory words as I can. I had better just receive it and let it alone. The only person who can cope with it properly is yourself. Doesn't half the pretentious bad literature of the past decades come from writers trying to digest other people's experiences for them?

From here there is so little to write. You are no doubt following politics better than I am. What I follow I am discouraged by. And for us civilians there is a curious strain developing, a certain dull irritation. We think—at college, say—in terms of the Post War World and the three words are getting to be a weariness. So many of us are living in an event that is not an event—I mean the war. Life is not really touched, just subtly postponed. It makes one—me—very weary and somehow, whatever my intellectual opinions may be, I find it a disquieting thing that life here should go on so much in the appearance of before: or even more so, what with so much more money around. Only very wise soldiers will not be bitter, I am sure; and not even they will escape bitterness about politics.

In life nothing very good is happening. Diana is writing an article for *Harper's* that is a kind of survey of the literary scene: very gloomy she makes it out to be. My book goes very slowly but not without its satisfactions. The situation I spoke of the paragraph just before has its effects on production and they are not to be escaped. *The New Leader*, by the way, patently misses your column. (And I, by the way, missing your envelope with the address on it, will have to send this via *The New Leader*. Let it be a lesson.)

Macdonald's new magazine has got off to a start,[1] but I haven't yet seen it. The *Partisan* has been able to get enough money to ensure another year. So much from that front.

Henry Adams has been my tipple lately, but I haven't got far enough down the bottle yet to know what I will come out thinking—

---

1. Dwight Macdonald (1906–1982), intellectual and critic, launched *Politics* magazine in 1944.

whether my present delicate revulsion, a mild queasiness, will get to be anything coarser. No doubt the *Letters* will do the trick. Still, a very intelligent man.

Do let me hear from you soon. This is conceivably a better letter than the last one, perhaps in the decent category, but not much of a letter at best; and perhaps you are finding that short of personal gossip the writers from home don't make very satisfactory correspondents. Still, a letter can always be a salutation.

Yours,

Lionel

67. TO SAUL ROSENZWEIG[1]

June 30, 1944

Dear Dr. Rosenzweig:

I hope you can forgive my long delay in writing to you. I was recently ill and then had to face the mass of work that had accumulated.

It's good to know that the *Partisan* matter is arranged. I'm afraid I must have made confusion by speaking out of turn. What happened was that someone told me that Philip Rahv[2] was planning to reprint your James article[3] and I took Rahv's intervention for an accomplished fact, and spoke of it so to you.

I read your article with the greatest interest and almost complete agreement. Why no one ever before isolated and dealt with that important autobiographical passage is surely one of the shameful literary mysteries. I've heard reference to some accident that James suffered, but it has always been referred to as if it were a bit of gossip, passed on by oral tradition, not as if it were stated by James himself in print. You handle the matter with great insight and tact and make the thesis perfectly convincing. I suppose it could be objected that you rather limit the evidence by confining yourself to the short stories but I myself feel that the point is *made* and that it could easily be demonstrated over the whole range of James's work. The castration

---

1. Saul Rosenzweig (1907–2004), psychologist and theorist.
2. Philip Rahv (1908–1973) was, with William Phillips (1907–2002), the founder and longtime editor of *Partisan Review*.
3. "The Ghost of Henry James" appeared in the *Journal of Personality* in 1943.

theme surely manifests itself in all the life-death-illness-experience situations which James projects, in all his people who are outside life and want to get in.

The reservations in my agreement with the article refer to your generalization about the artist in relation to neurosis. I have always resisted Edmund Wilson's wound-and-bow theory. It seems to me to suggest that art grows from neurosis and this genesis I reject.[1] I think the artist is no more neurotic than anyone else; I should hasten to add that I think most people are neurotic. But the solid and normal citizens cover their neurotic qualities or have them covered by society, whereas the artist *shows* his neurotic qualities, deals with the unconscious material as best he can. The neurotic quality he has in common with the rest of his society; the artistic power is peculiarly his, and this artistic, shaping, arranging power is precisely rooted in his health, not in his neurosis. The banker, the physician, the professor, the lawyer, and the cabinet minister must hide what the artist shows: but if one were to note them carefully, their minute actions, the things they say, their emotional organization and its relation to reality, I think one would have to conclude that they have the same "wounds" that the artist has. They do not have "bows"—and there is something apt in that figure of the bow as the symbol of the artist. He, like the archer, projects things to a great distance from himself—but they do have other weapons, rather more socially approved ones. They may, of course, have only armor: repression, "front," grave respectability. Or they may have armament more useful to society. But the "wounds" they do have—otherwise would they be able to understand in any degree what the artist is talking about? I suppose one reason society puts the artist in his ambiguous position, and sometimes rejects him wholly, is that society resists (in the psychoanalytical sense) what truth the artist tells about the unconscious, and for the usual reasons.

This puts rather summarily and crudely the objections I have to the wound-and-bow theory. I hope I am not foisting on you what

---

1. Trilling would elaborate on his objection to Wilson and his belief in the fundamental health of the artist in his 1945 essay "Art and Neurosis," included in *The Liberal Imagination*.

I remember of Wilson's formulation of it—at the moment your paper is out of the house, lent to a friend. I want sometime soon to put my view of the matter more precisely and at greater length: I'd be very grateful to know what you think of it.

I've told you how much I enjoyed the paper but I haven't yet thanked you for your kindness in sending it to me.

Sincerely yours,

68. TO ELLIOT COHEN

May 5, 1945
620 West 116th Street

Dear Elliot:

Much as I dislike saying no to anything you would ask of me, I am afraid that I must say no to your flattering invitation to join the board of Contributing Editors of the new magazine.[1]

This answer will not come to you entirely as a surprise. The magazine has naturally made a large part of our conversation for the past months and we have had between us the possibility of my becoming one of the group of contributing editors you planned to organize. And of course you have been aware of the strong doubts I have had from the first about the advisability of my becoming a member of that group. But I am in a way glad that you have put the question to me "formally" because it gives me the occasion to express fully the reasons for my decision. Some of these you already know. Indeed, you probably know or can guess them all. Still, it will be useful for both of us if I set them down in writing.

The first reason—although I would not call it the decisive reason—is personal and practical. During the last year I have had to take into account a new factor in my life as a writer and even as a teacher. The College and the University, after years of letting me benignly alone, have got into the habit of putting me on committees. I suppose people like myself are always flattered by this kind of thing; and then they flatter themselves by discovering that they have a kind of talent

---

1. *Commentary*, a Jewish magazine of opinion, founded in 1945 by the American Jewish Committee. Elliot Cohen was its first editor.

for it. And of course it is often interesting and frequently it is useful—or at least necessary. At a time like this, with so much to do, I can't very well get out from under. But as soon as possible I want to make my escape, for I find that it is materially injuring the kind of work I most want to do. The excitement of opinion and the conflict of personalities stay with me after the meetings are over. Quite apart from the time it demands, this kind of activity takes up, I find, a great deal of *space*. All through this year it has kept me from a great deal of the writing I should have been doing.

In short, I find that the public impulse can be, with me, so absorbing as to be injurious. I have thought a great deal about this, knowing that there is a great deal of cliché about the conflict of the public and the private. I find that with me, at any rate, the antagonism is pretty real. I am pretty sure that I must make a strong effort to avoid the politicalized forms of the intellectual life. It seems to me quite clear that if only because the board of Contributing Editors to which you invite me is bound to be made up of strong, respectable, and antagonistic personalities dealing with highly controversial matters, it would be very unwise for me to join in.

Then there is my reason of principle. It is not wholly a reason of principle—ultimately it has a practical aspect—but it begins as a reason of principle. You know, more than anyone else, what my feelings are about Jewish life. So many of those feelings are negative. Most manifestations of organized Jewish life do not please me. And most do not interest me. Of course I often think about Jews and Jewish problems, and I'm pretty sure I will continue to think about them. With my feelings what they are, I do not think I am a man who should—let alone could—have a quasi-official intellectual position in Jewish life. If I continue to think about Jewish matters, I cannot do so with a quasi-official commitment at my back. When I do think about Jewish matters, it is an advantage to me to feel free to stop thinking about them entirely, even to say that there is no use thinking about them. It isn't likely that I will do the one or say the other, but as an editor of a notable and influential Jewish magazine I could scarcely have the advantage of the freedom.

A great many intellectual problems and projects—more of the latter than the former—have recently begun presenting themselves to me. I think they may be important; at any rate, they are beginning to mean a great deal to me, and when I get around to handling them I do not want to do so in the character of a "Jewish writer" or a "Jewish publicist," which would be, in some part, my identification if my name were on your masthead. Not that a "Jewish writer" or "publicist" could not speak with as much authority or conviction as anyone else, but only that I am sure my character should be a different one.

In brief, given my temperament and my present situation and my plans for the next few years, I know I would harm myself by joining your board of Contributing Editors.

My decision, as you see, is made on very personal grounds. I know I can depend upon you not to see in it an implied stricture on your own decision in regard to the magazine; the tenor of our recent conversations will have made that clear to you. And of course my decision about the board of Contributing Editors has nothing to do with my writing for the magazine. I really think that I am not "rationalizing" when I say that my position as a writer in its pages will be a lot stronger if I appear in my character of uncommitted teacher and writer.

Yours,

69. TO MELVIN LASKY

May 6, 1945
620 West 116th Street

Dear Melvin:

Your letters of Darmstadt and Frankfurt have come in and you may indeed suppose that I read them with enormous interest—and a kind of pleasure, certainly a relief. It is to me very moving to get a human word from the scene itself in the midst of all the newspaper and radio talk. Together with the stories of the great demolitions have come the stories of the atrocity camps, and people are talking a great deal about them, very deeply disturbed, more disturbed, I think, than they are conscious of, yet trying to bring their sense of the thing to consciousness, trying to apply their moral equipment as best they may. I have heard it said, by some people, that the release of the atrocity stories was timed to coincide with the demolition stories as a way of offsetting the guilt for destruction that would be felt. This isn't said to deny the truth of the atrocity stories—indeed, some of those who speak of the "timing" say that the material is rather worse than the press indicates, that much is being held back as indigestible. The sense of guilt that people see coming or already here I do not myself see, nor feel. I do not feel it because, perhaps, I lack imagination but perhaps, to think better of myself, because the word "guilt" lacks imagination—we so often try to deal with new moral facts by analogy merely, with old words. And as for an attitude toward the atrocity-camp stories, that I find very nearly hopeless. When they began coming in, there were days when I wondered why I was so unutterably tired and unable to get anything done—until I sensed that other people were just as tired and just as irritable: there was everything to feel, and nothing to feel except the weary discouragement. This is a very confused paragraph— what it is leading to is that somehow your accounts of what you had seen and said and heard came to lighten the thick confusion, not because you had any solving "ideas" but only because you had a different kind of voice. So much of human affairs goes on by a kind of ghastly ventriloquism of which the radio is simply the mechanical expression— the radio timbre was there before the radio was ever invented.

Last week we had, for a few hours, the false news of the end of the war, and what one felt was how little all the incredible events, the enormous reversal, matched up with the feelings of the bad events of the beginning —the fall of Paris and such things are not equaled in reverse by what is happening now, though nothing in history has the same matter of drama. And it is not only because people are skeptical about the brightness of the future. Apparently success does not equal catastrophe in drama.

From me, personally, there is very little news. I have not been writing very much, partly because of internal difficulties, partly because there have been a great many administrative problems at the university in which I have been involved. I was recently promoted to an associate professorship, but it isn't a rise in the world that can give me much pleasure, although a year or two ago it could have given me some. My inadequate writing doesn't much bother me—except that

I wish that whatever upheavals had to come hadn't come in the middle of several pieces of work. Internal crises are probably necessary, but they ought to choose their times more considerately.

You perhaps did not ever get the news, which I read a couple of weeks after your departure and gift, that Huizinga[1] died. The account of his life in the papers was impressive—I have forgotten the details now, but the effect was a fine one.—By an irony that you will appreciate, I had scheduled myself on a certain Tuesday to lecture on Randolph Bourne,[2] the same Tuesday on which the newspapers carried the announcement of the resignation of Nicholas Murray Butler.[3] I tried, as clearly and as tactfully as possible, to explain the irony to my graduate class, but it was not understood. Indeed, the name of Bourne meant nothing to most of them—they hadn't heard it until I put it on my reading list. He wasn't a really fine mind, Bourne, though he was getting finer as he got older, but he makes the impression of a man who really lived by the intellect, for whom ideas were really realities.

I hope you will keep on sending me your letters—it occurs to me to ask if you might want to permit some of them to appear in print, anonymously, in excerpt. I thought that it might be that *The Nation* might perhaps use passages. Not that one could get much pleasure from seeing one's ideas on Europe in *The Nation*—politically it has become almost invisible: one simply cannot see what it means.

I'll write soon again—meanwhile, good luck and good seeing: you remind me of Josephus. Diana asks me to send her best greetings with mine.

Yours,
    Lionel

_____

1. Johan Huizinga (1872–1945), Dutch historian and cultural critic.
2. Randolph Bourne (1886–1918), radical intellectual and opponent of American participation in World War I.
3. Nicholas Murray Butler (1862–1947), longtime president of Columbia University, was a particular target of Bourne's criticism.

70. TO ELLIOT COHEN

May 18, 1945
620 West 116th Street

Dear Elliot:

I've just read Mr. Saveth's article[1] which I am enclosing. Clearly it is in many ways a very good article—you see at once from the tone of that that I didn't really get pleasure from it. [. . .] What bothers me is that the piece falls into the all too familiar pattern of response to intellectual anti-Semitism: a kind of rigor sets in, a paralysis of the imagination; in order to meet the accusation, the accuser must be destroyed.

I do not think that much is gained by this. Indeed, much is lost. To make out, as Mr. Saveth does, that Henry Adams was a snob, a vestige of a once-powerful class, a man taken in by his own myths, essentially stupid—that is all very well but it does not face the situation. The situation is rather that a very brilliant man with an apocalyptic imagination, a notable historian, a fascinating moralist and observer, a mind of great sensibility—that *such* a personality (and not a lesser one) was an anti-Semite. It seems to me that we must respond to the real situation, not to one that we contrive for our convenience. And the latter, I think, is what Mr. Saveth has done. He deals with Adams's medievalism in a much too literal way—the historical "myth," especially in the nineteenth century, is a common way of dealing with the present problems of social morality; and while I do not believe in submitting docilely to myths, it seems to me necessary to use a more complex criterion in judging them than is here being used: among other things intention must be judged. Even Marx uses the historical myth of medievalism; and it seems to me that a Jew especially must treat historical myths with care, since the rationale of Judaism itself is based on a fairly chancy historical myth.

Another fault of this article seems to me that it serves—of course "objectively" as we used to say—as a kind of implied defense of capitalistic culture. Adams, with his often fanciful historical apparatus

---

1. The article submitted to *Commentary* by Edward Saveth, about Henry Adams, would lead to a dispute between Trilling and Clement Greenberg, then an editor at *Commentary*; see letter of July 11, 1961.

of formulation, was attacking that culture; in raising objections to Adams's laws of phase—rather literal objections—in dismissing Adams's criticism of modern society as the sour grapes of a disinherited snob who did not want to descend into the populist arena, Mr. Saveth seems in effect to be defending modern society, finance capital and all—all the aspects of it that Adams so rightly hated and so brilliantly described. Mr. Saveth dismisses Adams's thermodynamic law and then says, "If there is no immutable law fixing the peak of civilization in the Middle Ages and making all that has transpired since symptomatic of decline, then it follows that civilization of the twentieth century is not inevitably inferior to that of the twelfth." Granting that the use of physical analogies in history is nonsense, granting that the twentieth century is not *inevitably* inferior to the twelfth, is it not possible to conceive of the twentieth as still inferior to the twelfth, not inevitably but according to defined criteria? (I'm of course not at the moment saying that it is.) It seems to me that hidden behind Mr. Saveth's denial of inevitability is a denial of the possibility of cultural judgment (which he probably doesn't really intend but got led into by the nature of his argument) and the implication that the twentieth century is really quite all right.

Well, I mustn't go on, though I have other things I would like to say. I'm of course not interested in defending the good name of Henry Adams, but only a way of criticism. Ultimately that way of criticism has a practical value. The other way encourages in Jews a closed and rigid attitude of mind to intellectual positions that really concern them. We must see, as my old friend used to say, the object as it really is. The immediate object as it really is is a very gifted, learned, brilliant, eccentric, powerful, often malign man who admired many generous things and who hated Jews as the face of capitalism. The general object as it really is is that many notable modern intellects, by no means to be dismissed as injured, frustrated, primitive neurotics, hate Jews. I don't by any means think this is an easy object to deal with; but it must be dealt with; and it cannot be dealt with until we learn to state it accurately.

Yours,

71. TO ALLEN GINSBERG[1]

August 9, 1945
620 West 116th Street

Dear Allen,

I have lately been so preoccupied that I rudely put off reading your new poem until your letter came to spur me to it. I have just read it and I must tell you at once that it affected me very deeply. I have only gone through it twice and I do not yet feel that I have mastered it, but what I have always responded to in your writing (what I more and more think the great thing in all verse) is the voice and its tone, and these, in this new poem, are very impressive, very true (except for here and there, when diction, vocabulary, drags it below itself), and very effective, both in the lyrical parts and in the more, as it were, meditative parts. It is a question with me whether with the same line you should move from unrhymed to rhymed verse—but that is unimportant. There is a good deal of Shelley here—are you aware of it?—the rush of sound and of thought, the delicate clearness of sound together with the relative obscurity of the thought. (Not to mention the quality of the emotion and the imagery.) The opening and closing parts are to me especially effective. If I had you here I might want to raise small objections, matters of taste, such as rhyming "of" which I can never like, failing your presence, I will let my pedagogy go by and simply congratulate you on the performance. I'm going to read the poem again to find further pleasure and perhaps more faults and I'll tell you about both when we meet.

I'm glad you're being happy at the station and I hope things stay good for you. Your mention of Rimbaud crystallized my impulse (a slow one) to know more about him and I am now the next name after yours on the library card of the Starkie biography you so warmly recommended to me. I doubt if he will ever be my "beloved Rimbaud" as he is yours or that I will ever even understand how he can be yours, but if I cannot be affectionate to him I at least need not be ignorant! My present passion is Yeats, who enormously delights me. How can I account for my never having read him before? Is he a friend of yours?

---

1. Allen Ginsberg (1926–1997), poet and counterculture figure, was a student and protégé of Trilling's at Columbia.

What is *Batman*? and how does it make you a regular fellow?

Hart Crane I cannot admire, except for the briefest of moments—the trouble, I think, is the sacerdotal pose (I think that is a phrase of Yeats's wonderful father) the Priest (high)-Poet which to me is very boring. Where is the man's own note, where is his speaking voice?

Send on the sonnets—I'll be glad to see them if you won't expect promptness.

I'll look forward to a visit—better send me a postcard a day or two before, if you can, or phone.

Sincerely,

Lionel Trilling

72. TO ALLEN GINSBERG

September 11, 1945
620 West 116th Street

Dear Allen:

I was very sorry to learn that you had been so ill—the length and energy of your letter suggests to me that you are pretty well recovered and I am glad of that. But pneumonia requires a great deal of good sense about rest and care in the after period and I hope you have it.

I got a great pleasure and instruction from your letter and by a strange and lucky chance, it arrived just when I was at a very difficult place in my novel and in ways that I cannot now explain but that may be apparent when—if ever—you read the book, it helped get rid of the difficulty. All that you say about Rimbaud is illuminating and, I think, true—before your letter came, I had read the Starkie life, and your interpretation is a just one. You will have to understand about me that I am very largely an old-fashioned humanist, and although the humanist tradition sometimes exasperates me to the point of violence, I pretty much stay with it. Involved in Rimbaud's attitudes is an absolutism which is foreign to my nature, and which I combat. On another level, I observe in Rimbaud—it is much more obvious in Baudelaire—the reference to society in an extreme degree, sometimes direct, sometimes inverse: the deep impulse to establishment and "success" and the power of success. The completeness of the rejection of the ordinary social values seems to carry with it an implied acceptance, much too complete. I know this is an easy way of attack, but with R. and B., I think it is fair.

But I mustn't go on—I am running off to the country for a short vacation and I have a hundred things to do before I go.

By the "voice" I mean only something very simple—the tone of the voice in speech. I find it, with people, extraordinarily revelatory of subtleties of character; above all, of what we call "sincerity" or its lack. And in verse I respond to the element of spoken utterance, which is for me more important than metaphor.

Sincerely,

Lionel Trilling

73. TO ERIC BENTLEY[1]

February 14, 1946
620 West 116th Street

Dear Eric:

I will not try to say how sorry I am for having added, by my silence, to the weight of what must have been, no matter how sensible you were about it, an unhappy situation. But perhaps a chronological account of my efforts to write you will at least help make things clear.

Almost immediately upon receiving your note I wrote you a long letter in which I tried to point out what I thought you had done to begin the strained situation between yourself and Margaret Marshall.[2] I referred at length to the letters which you wrote to Miss Marshall following Hook's review of your book.[3] In the course of this present letter of mine, I will tell you how, in my opinion, you were at fault, but for the moment I will only say that you *were* at fault; and from that fault, as I described it in my first unsent letter, I went on to say that I thought the fault had its analogue in certain aspects of your

---

1. Eric Bentley (1916–), theater critic and historian.
2. Margaret Marshall (1900–1974), literary editor of *The Nation* from 1937 to 1953.
3. Sidney Hook's review of Eric Bentley's *A Century of Hero-Worship* appeared in *The Nation*, October 7, 1944.

published work recently. And I concluded with the advice that you write to Margaret Marshall and ask her the reason for the difficulty between you.

But then I kept that letter around for a day, and when I looked at it again, it seemed to me that I had presumed too far. Not that I should not have told you in detail where you went wrong in the letters to Miss Marshall, but that I had no right to carry this opinion, for which you had in a sense asked me, into a comment on your work. Although there's a sizable chunk of years between us, I could not feel that it was a big enough chunk to give me the right to speak with the detestable quality of "frankness" when I was not asked to; and your work, in amount and power, seemed of a maturity that rather neutralized any seniority I might want to claim. And then I could not feel that our relation of friendship, cordial and promising though it has been in our few meetings, was yet enough to allow me the privileges—or put it: the exercise of the duties—of intimacy. So after a good deal of thought about the rights of the matter, I decided to write to you again in another way, speaking only of your letters, not of your work, and ending as before with the advice to write to Margaret Marshall.

But time got the better of me, and before I had the chance to write the new letter, Margaret Marshall told me that you had written your note of inquiry—the very thing I would have suggested—and that she was rejecting your overtures toward a reconciliation. I felt sorry that you had moved without word from me—sorry, that is, that I had so let you down; for although I would have suggested nothing different in a practical way, my explanation might have been of use—and sorry that Miss Marshall was taking the decision she did take about her response to you. I then began to write you again, to urge you not to mind, to let in what light I could upon the situation so that you would be at least in less confusion. But in the very midst of my new letter, I came across your review in the last *Sewanee*. This piece made me very angry—I will give my reasons in a moment—and I did not quite know how to go on with my letter. It now seemed to me clearer than before that there was a connection between the error of your letters and the error of some of your writing: the review was written entirely in that error. It was then that I made so many efforts to tell you what

I felt. The difficulties you will of course see: I did not want to get into a political argument with you, especially one in which I could be easily misunderstood; I was angry, and did not see how I could objectively describe to you a situation which required not only objectivity but disinterestedness and communion. And being angry, I had to be on guard against adding to your feelings about Miss Marshall's letter—for, no matter how sensible we are, rebuffs always have their bad effect—and seeming to be taking sides and heaping coals. And so I again put off writing, or, rather, could not find a satisfactory way of saying what I meant.

So much for the reasons for my long silence. And now I think I had better tell you all I have had on my mind, the substance of all the letters I wrote and did not send.

In all my letters I tried to make it clear to you what was the force of Margaret Marshall's response to the suggestion that you be brought to call on her. It was certainly not intended as a snub or insult to be conveyed to you at second hand. She was, she tells me, distressed that it should have been repeated to you at all, as of course in all decency it should not have been; she had added the injunction, which was disregarded, that you should not be told of her response. She answered as she did because, feeling at the moment tired and low in spirits, she did not want the strain of meeting a person who was antagonistic to her.

I think it is very likely that you will be much surprised at the description of yourself, by Miss Marshall, as a person antagonistic to her. I think you should know that it does not surprise me. When the correspondence about the review of your book in *The Nation* first began, Miss Marshall, knowing that I knew you, consulted me and showed me your letters. My memory of the correspondence is now not very clear, but I well remember that the tone and the seeming intent of your letters disturbed me very much, so far at variance were they from my personal impression of you at our first meeting. The letters were wholly unlike what I would have expected of the man for whom I had had so immediate a liking and admiration. I clung to my personal impression and tried to interpret the letters as a failure in expression. But, as I recall the events, the continuation of this tone made the interpretation difficult, even impossible. But when I next saw you, last year, I again could not reconcile the person with the letters and found it harder than ever to account for the letters.

I am not able to tell you in detail what was so very wrong about the letters, and perhaps you will be content to rely merely on my general impression of them. Of course it is never wise and usually ungraceful to object to reviews. And it is madly *un*wise to object in any other way than by the coldest correction of fact. And it is hopeless to raise the question of *motive*, as I recall you did raise it with Hook's review. More dangerous than any of these is to question even at a distance, or by implication, the motives of the editor who assigns the review, especially of an editor like Miss Marshall in whom a scrupulousness of intellectual and political fairness in the old liberal way is so very notable. The number of available reviewers around any magazine is limited, and an editor, after experience, must believe in the critical integrity of those she selects. You are perhaps not aware that you did bring into question Miss Marshall's motives. But you will surely remember that you did bring into the discussion the question of the discrepancy between the front and the back sections of *The Nation*. I don't know if you see—I hope you didn't then see, but you should have seen—the implications of that act. We all know that there is the discrepancy. It is an anomaly that we must be glad of.

The political section of *The Nation* is controlled by a view that is, to put it simply, committed to Stalinist Russia. Miss Kirchwey would not, I think, admit a bias, but the bias is at least unconsciously there. It is to be seen both in the editorials and in the dispatches. Put it that Stalin's policy is the sacred cow of an often confused editorial policy. But in this policy there is no perfect consistency. Thus Niebuhr, a complex enough mind and deeply critical of Stalinism and Stalinist-liberalism, is very close to *The Nation*. And Miss Marshall, whose views do not by any means coincide with those of the political section, is allowed a perfectly free hand in running her own section. This can be interpreted as greatly to Miss Kirchwey's credit, and I do so interpret it, especially because Miss Marshall has often been under attack, for example, in the *New Masses*, for her divergence from the political attitudes of the front section and even for "Trotskyism." (You yourself, I seem to remember, raised the question of Hook's Trotskyism. In this I may be wrong. In any case, the word has no real meaning in our intellectual life anymore except as a term of abuse for those who do not subscribe to Stalinism, a word that still does have meaning: I cannot think of a single person notable in our intellectual life now who can be accurately described as a Trotskyist.)

What I am leading up to is this: that your appeal to the political section of *The Nation* and to the discrepancy between it and the literary section could only have been interpreted by a person not himself committed to Stalinism as a politically illiberal act, intended to imply that the literary section of *The Nation* should be closed to the free play of opinion by making it conform to the views of the political section. I do not think you would want such a thing to occur; I did not think so when I read the letters; and yet, unless a person were *determined* not to make the interpretation, it would be about the only interpretation possible.

And further: in one of your letters to Miss Marshall I remember a speculation by you about what Miss Kirchwey would think of some aspect or other of the discrepancy I have spoken of, if it were called to her attention. Can you not see that such a remark could only be interpreted as a hint that an appeal over Miss Marshall's head to her chief would bring her a rebuke and weaken or even endanger her position?—that it was nothing less than an affront?

There were one or two other things in the correspondence that pained me, but my memory is dim about them and I don't want to rack it to bring forth the details. The salient elements that made the impression are those I have given. Whatever your intention, you will have to trust to my impression—formed against resistance—that the effect was as I have described it. And you will see that the effect was aggressive in the extreme and personally unfriendly, even inimical, to Miss Marshall.

Here I must say that when I saw you again recently, I could not reconcile you yourself with the writer of the letters and that I much preferred to believe that you were you and not the letters. But you must remember that you and I have a friend in common, and an impulse to friendship with each other, and have had several meetings. Miss Marshall had only a business relation with you—and the letters themselves. She is really a friendly person and accepts offers of friendship easily; so that if your letters hurt and confused her, it is, I think, a comment on your letters.

This is substantially what went into all my unsent letters as my explanation of the beginning of the misunderstanding between you and Miss Marshall.

In the first of my letters I took it upon myself to say something about your work. Your letters to Miss Marshall had failed of their innocent intention, I said, because of a quality that I had lately felt in your published work—I felt, that is, that you were not saying what you really meant because you were saying more than you really meant. I wanted to say that recently I had become aware—not in a formulated way—of a certain unconsideredness of aggression, a kind of anger of judgment, a pushing too hard, an appearance of striking out, and back, at things. A trivial but personally felt example brought the vague awareness of this to formulation. In your article on Strindberg, you spoke of recent literary revivals, among them the Forster revival, and then went on to speak of a snobbery that was an element in their motivation. I read the statement with a personal annoyance at first, for it seemed to me that the Forster revival was remarkably without snobbery—my own book being almost popular in its nature and the novels having been published cheaply and without any attempt at chic. I got rid of the personal annoyance, being assured that you would not want to accuse me of snobbery. But then I passed from the personal annoyance to the intellectual. The search for the new in literature always goes on, I thought, and if there is snobbery in it, in the sense of an impulse to appropriation, then it is a snobbery of a benignant kind, and we all inevitably have it a little. And I was pained for you that you should have felt it necessary to have made the gratuitous blow. I wanted to tell you that intellectual life isn't to be set right by blows of that sort, that it is a waste of ammunition, and bad marksmanship. I wanted to suggest that perhaps you were pushing yourself too hard, working up too much impetus to allow control; that maybe you were undergoing a mood of the moment, or of the year. I wanted to say that whatever the cause, this manner was doing you an injury and an injustice. Your career has been brilliantly successful, I said, and deservedly so, and at this point I think you ought to take stock, most particularly of your manner, asking yourself what you think the intellect can possibly accomplish, in one article or a dozen, that you should, in any one piece, push so violently.

It was this that I thought went rather beyond my rights of directness. My thinking that it did caused me to censor that first letter, and now I wish I had not thought so. In any case, as you see, I have changed my mind—I now think I should be direct or nothing.

And I want to go further. Before I do, I want to prevent a misunderstanding. I know that Margaret Marshall, in refusing a personal reconciliation, made a judgment on your work. I am not, in what I say, undertaking to second her judgment. It is because I have so much confidence in your powers that I am saying what I do.

What I saw in a general way in your work, unformulated until it touched my own vanity, I am afraid I saw very sharply in the Koestler piece. I at first wrote you very angrily about that piece—not, I think, on political grounds alone, but because it so destroyed my interpretation of your letters. You say in effect in the review that distrust or fear or, really, criticism of Russia leads to nothing less than war. I will not draw out all the implications of this. I will only say that it seemed to me that if you meant that, you must also have meant the things in your letters that I did not like and thought you did not mean. But what so much distressed me in that review is not so much your opinions as your method of attack. I suppose I don't have to explain to you that I don't admire Koestler, although I think I see more significance in him than you do. What made me so unhappy about your piece was that you undertook to deal with Koestler not by examining his book but by setting up a group of purely supposititious readers in Greenwich Village whom you lambasted. By doing this you avoided meeting Koestler's charges on Russia, some of them very explicit— and I have not yet seen them refuted or denied—and felt that you had settled his hash by saying that certain Greenwich Village characters are, by their unconsidered criticisms, leading us into war. I say it was not so much your opinions as your method that distressed me. But your opinions distressed me too—they seemed to me to be shared by the same *political* temperament and principles (I mean as against *moral* and *personal* ones) that I saw in the letters. And I am going to say that I don't like them—and fear them.

But the method is the important thing. It is the method of finding *motive*. You find motive for Koestler and you find motive for his readers; you even descend to inventing his readers to ascribe the motive. And this attribution of motive—for something, for anything—is what runs through all the things for which I have blamed you in this letter. And with that motive-attribution goes, quite naturally, a considerable violence of moral condemnation. As a method, it is far beneath you—it is far too personal, it has far too little intellectual validity for a person of your gifts. Of course, the discovery of motives in the large way of, say, Nietzsche does have its validity, but what I am objecting to in your method is not of that kind.

I think you must try to see whether or not I am just in what I have been saying; and if you find that I am, to see what in yourself it is that impels you to the fault.

And I want, since I have assumed an obnoxious role, to give you another piece of advice: that you keep away from the complex literary-political disputes of left-wing New York. You may be right or wrong in your judgments of left-wing politics (I am inclined to think you are wrong) but I am sure that you move pretty much in the dark in the matter of personal and coterie politics. I don't think that these are so entirely unimportant as some people do, but they're certainly not finally important. One is at a distinct advantage in keeping clear of them. I try to keep away, myself, but I have been in their vicinity for so long that I know my way at least around their outskirts. But you are at a distance from them and had best let them alone entirely. They are subtle, complex, and have long and bitter histories. You will only make errors of judgment and fact by trying to deal with them. And I think I should not resist pointing out to you that your interest in them is of a piece with your impulse to attribute motive. They themselves carry on their intellectual disputes all too much by attributing motive and looking for secret reasons, for plots. You made an error in judgment by trying to find the *reason behind* Hook's review of you and his misreading of you, the reason behind Miss Marshall's giving him the book, the reason behind the divergence between the front and the back of *The Nation*. You make the same error in finding the reason behind the interest in Koestler. It's not a good game, certainly not for you.

I have tried to tell you everything I have been thinking in reference to yourself in the past weeks. I can't pretend that this letter, so full of blame of a kind, can give you any pleasure—although I have the hope that you will find some pleasure in my feeling that you will be able to take what I have to say in a simple and direct way, and with a real belief in the friendliness of my intention. Now that I have said so much, there is nothing more of the same sort kept in reserve; you've had the full count of blame—all the rest is the most cordial liking and admiration.

Most sincerely,
Lionel

74. TO ERIC BENTLEY

March 7, 1946
620 West 116th Street

Dear Eric:

You say that you have not worked over my letter page by page but have replied to what you retained of the main impression. Inevitably my letter disturbed you, no doubt hurt you, as I feared it would, and you did what I find myself doing with a disturbing letter, or an especially meaningful one, read it not entirely. But perhaps by now you have gone over it and have seen that some of your understanding of it was wrong. I am going to assume that this is so and not answer *your* letter point by point.

But there are one or two things I must undertake to correct. You say that it was your tone and not your intention that was at fault and you urge this upon me. But that is exactly what I believed. It was my assumption all through my early discussions with Miss Marshall about your letters beginning with the Hook protest: I insisted that something had gone wrong between your intention and your expression.

You explain your intention in the snobbery point in the Strindberg piece—but your explanation is no different from mine. I mentioned that matter as an instance of wrong tone when I had to know that the intention was not aggressive—I know, that is, that you were much at one with me and would not want to attack me even by indirection, or, rather, especially by indirection. If I spoke of my momentary annoyance, it was only to make the point that I realized that your tone had misrepresented your intention and to say that I got over the annoyance.

I did indeed say that I could not interpret the *Sewanee* piece merely as a failure of tone and that it made me question my interpretation of the letters to Miss Marshall. But even there, you will recall, I didn't accuse you of doing a "dirty" thing but only of doing a very wrong one. This time I did not, however, say that it was merely a failure of tone, but rather that it was the result of a wrong intellectual habit which I characterized as motive finding.

I did not think—I don't think I said—that your piece was, as you call it, *insincere*. Again, I thought it *wrong*, in content, method, and tone. Of course to attack Stalinism as a matter of taste is (despite that high-principled statement of Molotov—was it he? or Troyanovsky— on preferences for communism or fascism) trivial. Yet I confess, from my own experience, that I can see how it can be done. I need only put my sense of the inadequacy and badness of the Stalinist personal temperament and sensibility, from my own personal acquaintance with it, into conjunction with my empirical knowledge of the badness of most Stalinist books, my inability to name a good one, and I have what looks very much like a taste. I will not talk of a priori things. I do not insist on the *necessity* of bad Stalinist art, only on the fact. I think I could argue an a priori case—I do argue it in the case of personal temperaments as I meet them about New York: Stalinism must lie, it must do the worst kind of lying, i.e., the advance of the ideal to mask crude power, crude will, and this horrible contradiction I can see in the fore-consciousness of the Stalinists I know—I say "fore-conscious" because it is not unconscious yet not allowed to be fully conscious—and for me it is bound to produce bad art, all the signs of a warped and, to me, hostile sensibility. I do not know Brecht. But the Malraux of *Man's Fate* was a novelist; the Malraux of *Man's Hope* was a high-minded fraud.

You say that ten years ago you were taught that only a communist book could be good. I was taught that too (a little more than ten years ago) but it was the one thing about communism I could not learn. I accepted many of the current communist notions of post-

1931—and lost some years of intellectual growth thereby—but never could believe that a communist book was good. Now I feel free to believe that they are worse than ever.

I do not mean in this particular correspondence of ours to raise a debate with you. But I think it is fair to both of us for you to know that I live with a deep fear of Stalinism at my heart. A usual question at this point which I know you would never ask is: "And not of Fascism?" Yes, of Fascism too, but not so *deep*—in one's fantasies one can imagine going out to fight one's Fascist enemies quite simply; but whenever I fantasy fighting an enemy that has taken all the great hopes and all the great slogans, that has recruited the people who have shared my background and culture and corrupted them, I feel sick. I am willing to say that I think of my intellectual life as a struggle, not energetic enough, against all the blindness and malign obfuscations of the Stalinoid mind of our time.

With this in mind, you will know that if I argue with you on your position, I do not think you are committed to Stalinism. If I thought you were, I would not argue or tell you my feelings. It may be that you are right in your belief that there is an anti-Stalinist orthodoxy which stops thought. I tell you my feelings as directly as I do to suggest that this is not the only attitude of anti-Stalinism. (You see from this how secure I am in your opinion of me!)

To return now to the personal matter. I could never assume of any quarrel that one person was solely active, the other solely passive—a quarrel, God help us, is always a living, growing, symbiotic thing. As feelings go round the personal circle they grow. I don't know when Miss Marshall's abrupt letters began: if after the spring of 1944, they would be in response to your letters, for it was then (as I seem to remember) that she first spoke to me about the correspondence; if before that time, then that is another story and I do not know the reason.

As for what made the acceleration of Miss Marshall's feeling about you between the fall and December of this year, I cannot tell. Annoyance swells for no ascertainable reason at all. You had best set it down as mystery or suppose that the reasons lie in imponderables. If, as would not be unnatural, you ascribe it to the influence of some hostile person, I think you would be wrong. [. . .] Of course, if you exchanged political descriptions of each other and asked political questions, that might be reason enough for accelerating feeling. Perhaps *all* your mistake in the *whole* business is that you attach different intensities to political differences than do the people in New York. People who have a past in the left-wing movement are often extremely bitter about these things. I myself—and I think you will not believe me an ordinarily bitter person—can feel bitterly about them, and I was never deeply involved in an active or institutional way. Yet even I have had experience of chicanery and skullduggery and slander.

Will you leave it to me to decide whether the matter should be opened again with Miss Marshall? I no more than you relish the spectacle of the separation and bitterness. I may want to delay in any move, but I will not let the matter go through neglect.

You say at the end of your letter that I seem to think you bear "all" the responsibility for the unhappy affair. In a way that was not kind of you to say, for it puts me in the position of having been your accuser. I merely undertook to explain to you what to my knowledge you had done to arouse Miss Marshall's anger with you; my explanation was based on what she told me and showed me, and this, in addition to passing it on as information to you, I characterized as justly as I could; but of the living, personal context of what I learned I did not undertake to speak, nor did I try to speculate about it.

And now I think we ought to drop this matter between us. In a sense it has put me into a false position, in the sense that the paragraph above suggests. This was inevitable. It was my knowledge of its inevitability that made me delay my last letter to you so much too long. Now I must ask you to disengage me, if you can, from the feelings you are bound to have about the quarrel. I don't think this will be easy, but you should try. If you recur to what I have said in criticism of you, please try to take it out of the context of its occasion, try to think of it as something I might very likely have said to you personally in a moment of intimacy. I'd be happy if you'd let me know that you can do this.

[. . .]

Yours,

75. TO ERIC BENTLEY

May 12, 1946
620 West 116th Street

Dear Eric:

Without knowing enough about Aragon to speak authoritatively, it seems to me that Greenberg's review is more perceptive than Levin's. I find myself, indeed, rather horrified at Levin's "just" explanation of Aragon's attack on Gide as charitably to be understood as one of Aragon's playboy attitudes. Levin is quite sure that Aragon's defense[s] of the Hitler-Stalin pact are wiped out by his having read the proofs of his present book at Dunkerque. That seems to me a mere willed ignorance of life, let alone of politics.

As for Sartre, I am too entirely ignorant of him to know how to judge Barrett's estimate. But I do not think that the matter, as between us, can be settled by words like "obsession" or "neurosis." Nor, really, do I think it can be settled or advanced by the "plague on both your houses attitudes." You, of course, invoke the plague on both kinds of leftists—I am no longer sure that I am, in any accepted sense of the word, a leftist: put it, not a leftist except ultimately. That is, I certainly have no desire to choose between a Trotskyist of any present complexion and a Stalinist, although I can imagine moving with some Socialist party. I am willing, in the interim, to stand with other anti-Stalinists, keeping my own position clear, because, on the coldest political grounds—the grounds of daily events—and on the furthest cultural, civilizational grounds, I am sure that Stalinism is corrupt and dangerous. What interests me most in it is the death of the spirit which it requires for its success. This death of the spirit is what modern society demands of us all; Stalinism I see not as the opposition to but the projection of modern society, the acceleration of modern bourgeois culture in most of its manifestations. Between the worst examples of bourgeois life and Stalinism there is an odd affinity which will become clearer and clearer—not between all the worst examples but a certain number of them.

I understand your point about power and the fear of it and the tempting attitude of perpetual rebellion. And in many ways I agree with you, although the attitude of the Anarchist and the Impossibilist beguile me; I mean I can like people of the stripe very easily. But if one is willing to admit the reality of power and what it entails and the willingness to take it, one has to be very careful to keep things very clear: I have always cherished the speech of Shaw's Caesar about killing the lion without, in effect, statements, manifestos, and court trials, keeping the action clean and self-preservative. What revolts and disgusts me in the Stalinist grab for power is the hideous involvement of ideals, feelings, social indignations, exhibitions of martyrdom, self-pity. I expect a quantum of injustice in any imperium, I expect contradictions as the price of order—what brings me to the puking point is the fine feelings. And what brings me to the fighting point is the increasingly sure sense that Stalinist power aims at the annihilation of anything that does not contribute to power. There has never been a power ideology that so wished to destroy every human quality that did not add to itself. Formerly power was, as it were, encysted; now it must be inclusive. I have been reading a little Nietzsche again; he seems much to my point.

Did you see my Dreiser piece in *The Nation*?[1] I call that an anti-Stalinist piece. Do you think it is? I call it anti-Stalinist because it is really against emotions that are not felt by the reader or critic, but which the reader or critic thinks he ought to feel for the sake of the power of some idea. We are all engaged in an agreement to diddle ourselves, to fight for things we don't really want because we think they are good for somebody else.

I look forward to seeing your book—when will it come out?

I haven't really had a chance to read *K[enyon] R[eview]*, but from the look of it, it does appear to be better.

It's too bad you missed the Old Vic—we were much beforehand with our tickets and will not see *Henry IV* until two weeks from now. Terribly expensive, but pretty nearly all I enjoy in the theater these days is the Bard.

Yours,

Lionel

---

1. "Dreiser and the Liberal Mind," *The Nation*, April 20, 1946; it would later form part of the essay "Reality in America," in *The Liberal Imagination*.

76. TO R. W. FLINT[1]

June 17, 1946

620 West 116th Street

Dear Mr. Flint:

I have had to wait much too long to answer your letter, which I enjoyed so much, and I'm sure I don't have to expound to you the reason of the delay beyond saying that the end of the college year has been upon me. I know now why they call it Commencement.

I'm delighted that you liked the Dreiser piece, and I agree with almost everything you say in sequence about the writer. Maybe I jib a little at even your restrained notion of responsibility—perhaps not quite reasonably, perhaps only in reaction from all the bad talk about responsibility that you and I dislike. I begin to think that the very use of the word, and the debate about it, suggest something very wrong in our culture. When you and I write to each other we do not think of our "responsibility"—we think only of making ourselves clear, of letting each other know what we really think, for the pleasure of the meeting and because we are two human beings more or less like-minded. We would laugh if either of us suggested that one of us had a responsibility to the other. If we lie or show off, we rather expect that the other will smell it out and so, for the sake of our own well-being and self-respect, we avoid doing such things. We go as "deep" as the subject and the situation require, but we have no sense that we "owe" it to the other to go deeper, or to do anything at all. This seems to me the right, normal situation of the writer (certainly of the critic: the novelist and poet may not have so direct a relation in com-munication) and it carries its own—not morality but something equiv-alent. This is the seed situation of all critical writing. When we break that situation and forget it, we produce all the falsity of tone and of thought that are to be found in modern criticism: modern thinking generally. What the critic with a sense of "responsibility" does is to feel not that he is writing to equals to whom he must not so much *tell* as *act* the truth, but rather he feels that he is writing to inferiors to whom he must tell the right way they ought to feel. This critic, to be sure, does not even assume that if his readers feel as he thinks

---

1. Robert W. Flint (1921–2013), critic and translator.

they should, they will be actually like him but only that they will have taken the *first step* on the way to being like him. The image in the mind of most critics, the image of the act they are performing, is wholly wrong. That is why, when you speak of Montaigne, Goethe, and Emerson, I respond immediately. They so wonderfully refused to be *pious*. They knew how to teach without the odor of stale pedagogicality—because they assumed that their readers were like-minded and their equals: possibly a *little* younger (but not much), probably a little busier with other things and not able to give so much time to thought, but glad to have ideas called to their attention. The truth of Montaigne, Goethe, Emerson follows from this belief in their readers' equality. The writer with the conscious sense of responsibility is the symptom of the mass state—he believes in readers who are less good than he is. He acts like a pedagogue, but actually he is merely the demagogue of mass-state moralism. I'm sure responsibility is nothing if it is not built in and unconscious; also that it must be not to one's readers but to the Good-True-and-Beautiful or the blessed angels or one's ancestral totems; also, that, as used to be said about honor, it mustn't ever be talked about.

The impulse that we see among writers, to have an avowed sense of responsibility, is an aspect, I'm sure, of the modern intellectual's worship of power—and not the old kind of intellectual power, but naked and political power. The "responsibility" is the sop to the conscience: it's what all demagogues and tyrants say they have. Another aspect of this complex is the impulse to believe that the mind is not really important.

All this makes the real critical job what you see it to be. The avowed enemies are easy and one can always get easy credit for attacking them. The subtler enemies are harder and dealing with them is difficult and usually thankless. But ever so much more fun!

I'm afraid I must agree with you that I was a little unjust to Davis. He said so in a decently angry letter and I had to admit a certain measure of injustice, though I tried to avoid it. Perhaps his language in the review was merely unguarded. I suppose I could argue that unguarded language has its own significance but that would be rather straining things. I suppose I got carried away in the heat of combat.

On the question of Matthiessen's[1] belief that there was a falling off in James's moral fervor and perspicacity, I don't agree with you. Matthiessen, in my opinion, reads the later James rather too literally and not in the light of clues that are given in the whole canon. But that makes too difficult a subject to start on.

I'm happy that you liked the last *Partisan* story,[2] the more so because it was less well liked by most people than the one before. I'll be curious to know what you'll think of the two long things I'm working on this summer.

Again, thank you for writing.

Sincerely,

77. TO ERIC BENTLEY

September 15, 1946
620 West 116th Street

Dear Eric:

This isn't exactly a quick answer about your O'Neill piece. Had there been anything to disagree with I would have let you know at once so that you could consider it before publication. But there is nothing; and so, still crowded by work, I've permitted myself to delay.

I don't know quite what to say about the piece in general response to it. This uncertainty has nothing to do with your treatment of it, but with the matter itself. I suppose I could make this comment on your treatment: that I can't quite bring myself to understand why you treated it at all, and how you could treat it so seriously. "Why you treated it at all"—well, of course, it's your *business* to treat it. "How you could treat it so seriously"—I can understand that too, having once some years ago (twice, come to think of it) myself treated O'Neill: one gets involved, one puts one's mind to it with disdain, distaste, and even (so with me) disgust; and having thus submitted, lo! one has treated his work seriously. I remember drawing out, and I think truthfully, though rather gracelessly, a very complex theological movement

---

1. F. O. Matthiessen (1902–1950), scholar and historian of American literature.
2. Trilling's story "The Other Margaret" in *Partisan Review* (Fall 1945).

from beginning to momentary end of his canon. But now, when someone else (you) treats him with the same seriousness I once used, I can't understand why. What comes to me from your I'm sure most accurate account of the play is the dreadful miasma of O'Neill's mind which, even at second hand, sinks my spirits dreadfully. Sinking: he really is a master of the art of bathos. "Derelicts"—good Lord! "Bedrock Bar" etc.—Heaven help us! "Harry Hope" and "Jimmy Tomorrow" and "dreams" and "pipe dreams" and guilty preachers and spectators in the grandstand of life—it all brings back to me the wash of the solemn, frivolous "philosophizing" of the 1920s in America, the kind of thing that used to reach me in college and that I was so ashamed of myself for despising. I never can feel that O'Neill is writing about men—just about the abstracted damp souls of undergraduates. It is not that he cannot "think"—it is that he cannot *touch*: for all that fine "experience" of his young manhood—sea and saloons and sanitariums—the immediacy of life has never reached him. You can see this in his language, that dreadful, dreadful soggy language, which sounds like and has in it the slang of two decades ago. The loss of the sense of touch: it marks more and more of our thought and literature. Even our language to describe it is out of touch: we say "lost contact with." When I reach out to take O'Neill's hand I feel as I had grasped an inflated rubber glove. And simply don't know what he is talking about. Yet matters of guilt and self-deception and one's relations with ultimates, these are things that I like to think about and read about. Take a real theological mind and a real literary mind, like St. Augustine's, and how real all those matters become—how tactile. Life is dreadfully getting away from us. (And especially how I hate it when O'Neill talks about death. Or about *Life*.)

Am I wrong in all this? Am I unperceptive, intolerant, and mean? I'm willing to be corrected. When Maxwell Anderson writes in his high line, I get the same effect and wish he would go back to his earliest simple comedies. Same with Odets. But I cannot see O'Neill's superiority.—I spent an evening with Anderson recently, by the way. Such a nice man. He talked about his Joan of Arc play and I was caught by it—sounds like perhaps the best thing he's ever done. You will be interested in it for many reasons—not the least for what An-

140

derson says he is trying to say about the relation of power and the ideal.—On that matter, I haven't yet read Warren's book.[1] I began it and then retired because of my admiration for the prose, which was too much for the simplicity and low key of the prose I'm trying to keep going for my own book. I thought the prose very fine, though I wondered what its effect would be when long sustained. I said to Warren when I met him here some days ago that I found *Huckleberry Finn* in it—he was startled and I think displeased but to my mind the whole descriptive technique comes from Mark Twain.—I think I shall not wholly like the book when I do read it. I take this prophecy from Diana's account of it to me, not from her view of the political point, where she and I would not be likely to wholly agree, but from her description of the narrative matter. D. was much grieved that she did not like the book better, because she likes Warren so much.

And now I must tell you that I like your own book[2] very much. My response cannot possibly give you the satisfaction you deserve, because the theater does not really draw me. I don't mean that the idea of the theater doesn't draw me—though even there there is perhaps a coolth—but that my experience of the theater leaves me a little indifferent. There are a few theater experiences that are as intense as anything I have felt in art, but their intensity seems to be a function of their fewness. If you understand that about me, you will understand why I take fire from your book when it is literary-critical, not when it is descriptive of the stage and its conditions. I most admire you when you are dealing with ideas that could have appeared in some other medium. That is my limitation, I know. But I spread it here on the record to explain why your handling of Shaw, Wilde, Pirandello, Strindberg, and Sartre aroused my enthusiasm while most of the rest of the book simply evoked my admiration at your skill in handling a subject which I felt was your own, but not mine. This is not to say that the admiration is not real and large—but, as I said, it isn't of the kind that can give you full satisfaction. But there is much else in the book, there are so many opportunities for the literary-critical, that

1. Robert Penn Warren's *All the King's Men* (1946).
2. Eric Bentley's *The Playwright as Thinker* (1946).

I direct your mind and emotions to my response to these opportunities taken. Brecht I am sure will never be my dish: if he was not after your exposition, he never will be.

Is the book selling? I have the impression of its having been received with great pleasure in all kinds of groups.

I am driving on to the end of my little novel,[1] which now will not be so very little after all, and hope to have it done in a matter of days. I'm taking it off with me for a few days of solitude in the country, which will be not technically a vacation but spiritually, if I can write END in football language, a moral vacation.

Jacques and I are junketing to Kenyon for that Anglo-American conference, almost literally for the ride. I can hear one of the English visitors on his return: "And then I went to a place called Kenyon." "*Grand* Canyon?" "No, just a little place, quite small."

Let me hear from you anon and before that give my greetings to Maja.

Yours,
Lionel

78. TO EDMUND WILSON

November 10, 1946
Columbia University

Dear Wilson:

It was nice of you to write to me and I appreciate it very much. But I can't take credit for having gone through anything unpleasant. The trial[2] was absurd and interesting and nothing could have been more amusing than the look on the district attorney's face which showed how much he wished he were anywhere but there. The Hearst press was of course trying to be as gross as possible, but the worst they could get off about me was that I was "unabashed." On the other hand, the *Tribune* story was eminently civilized. And of course all the personal comments that came my way were

---

1. *The Middle of the Journey* (1947).
2. Wilson's book of stories, *Memoirs of Hecate County* (1946), was banned on the grounds of obscenity; Trilling appeared as a witness in defense of the book.

encouraging—everybody sensible naturally thinks the prosecution a bad thing.

It would be nice to see you when you get back. We're both well here, though somehow working too hard—I'm just finished a short-ish novel which started out to be a longish story.

Sincerely,
Lionel Trilling

79. TO ABRAM KARDINER[1]

December 26, 1946
Columbia University

Dear Dr. Kardiner:

A student of mine, Mr. Allen Ginsberg, has applied for admission as a patient to the psychoanalytical clinic at the Medical Center. I understand that the selection of people who are to receive the services of the clinic must necessarily be rigorous and that the chief considerations must of course be medical. Yet I suppose that the social usefulness of prospective patients is taken into account so far as possible and it therefore occurs to me to tell you as a not irrelevant fact about Ginsberg that he is a young man of quite exceptional intellectual gifts. I have been acquainted with him for some years and have been increasingly impressed by his mind, and even when I could not help being aware of how much his thought was being conditioned by his emotional disorder. It seems to me quite likely that a healthy Ginsberg would have a good chance of becoming a person of real intellectual distinction.

It was a pleasure to meet you the other day even though only in passing.

Sincerely yours,

---

1. Abram Kardiner (1891–1981), psychiatrist and Columbia professor.

80. TO RALPH BERKEY[1]

March 15, 1947
620 West 116th Street

Dear Mr. Berkey:

I understand your desire to find out if there is any basis in reality for your wife's continuing concern with me, and you may be sure that if there were the slightest foundation for her feeling I would tell you so honestly. But the fact is that I do not remember her, even as a student. This does not mean that I doubt she *was* a student of mine at Hunter; it simply means that if she was a student of mine, she would have been one of a great many, in no way the object of notice apart from the routine of my teaching duties.

I realize that it was painful for you to write as you did, and I can only be sorry to have to confirm your conclusion that your wife has been creating a fantasy.

Sincerely yours,

81. TO HARRY CARMAN[2]

March 17, 1947
Columbia University

Dear Harry:

I should like you to have a memorandum of our recent conversation about my University salary and status. You will remember that I called on you about ten days ago to ask if you could give me any information about my financial expectations for the next year so that I might the better make my plans for the management of my sabbatical leave. You told me that my salary was to be increased to $6,000; and you added that, if I were to receive an offer from another university, the offer would be met by my promotion to a Professorship. There was no opportunity to comment on this information at the time you gave it to me, for you were then occupied. And so I came in to see you

---

1. Berkey had written to Trilling about his wife, saying that she was fixated on Trilling and believed that he was secretly communicating with her through his published writing.
2. Dean of Columbia University.

again to give you my opinion of it, and this is a summary of the points I made.

The matter of the increase in my salary needs but little space. In a year of considerable movement in the University both in status and in salary, an increase of $500 above the rate of my adjusted salary of this year can scarcely be understood as an act of recognition. If the new statutory scale of salaries has any meaning in reality, I have now been raised to the lowest statutory salary of an Associate Professor.

But the provision which you mentioned—that if I should receive an offer from another university, the offer would be met—requires additional comment. It is much more important to me, and, as I think, to the University itself, for it raises a question of principle for me and a question of principle for the University.

It seems to me that the provision we speak of says in effect that the University considers me to have the qualifications of a Professor of one of its Faculties but it will not give me the rank until I shall be able to confront it with a threat of my leaving the University. Let me draw out for you the consequences of this position. Doing so will involve me in speaking well of myself, which is never becoming, but I will take the burden of that because the considerations I raise will be applicable not merely to my own situation but to the situation of many men of ability throughout the University.

During the last few years I have acquired a considerable prestige in both the academic and the literary world. I have published rather widely and what I have published has been well received both in this country and abroad. And it has been a matter of real satisfaction that, as my name becomes known, it is linked with the University's. But gratifying as this is, it has produced for me an anomalous practical situation. For, naturally, the better I become known and the more I am identified as part of Columbia, the more unlikely it becomes that I will receive the offers from other universities that would serve to advance my career here. It is generally assumed that I am fully recognized by my own University. It happens again and again that I have to deny the assumption that people make that I am a Professor here; this necessity began some years back when I was an Assistant Professor, and now with each year it becomes more difficult to get believed. As you know, the liveliest market time for an academic man is when he is still only promising. When his prestige reaches a certain point, the bidding for him drops considerably. For then his appointment to a new post becomes so much more a matter of university policy. And if he is established in and identified with one of a certain few leading universities—say six or seven, of which Columbia is one—he is likely to be limited in his market to the other universities in this small group, for they are the only ones that can afford him. You know, and it is a matter of record in my own department, that the number of offers that have been made to me in the past has been quite unusually large. They have decreased in number as my reputation has increased and as it has been taken for granted that I am fully recognized at Columbia. The routine bids which might be sufficient to bring about my promotion are not likely to be made to me now—the less likely since a new Columbia salary scale has been so widely publicized. The only thing that I can properly look for is one of the rare major offers which crown rather than advance a man's career.

If we speak of the market, a word is in order about the freedom of the market. You are aware—it has been the subject of several conversations between us—that many offers have been made for me that have never come into my hands. I will not go into this in detail, for I know you understand the situation and share my feelings about it.

But I should point out here that this situation has intensified the anomaly of my position. The refusals that were made for me were accompanied by explanations that I would never leave Columbia, both because I was personally so attached to my own College and University and because Columbia would match any offer that was made. The result is that I have now the reputation—I learn this from all sides—of being unwilling to consider any academic offer at all; and, naturally enough, departments do not open negotiations with a man who, they have been given to understand, is not to be tempted by anything.

All this being so, the methods open to me for getting an offer that would bring about my promotion are not of a very pleasant kind. To attract an academic offer I would obviously have to take steps to contradict the suppositions I have just described—I would have to let it be known that I have not in fact the commitment to the University which I am said to have and actually do have. To attract a nonacademic offer I would have to declare myself to my friends as dissatisfied with the academic profession. I think that either of these declarations would quite promptly have the effect that was intended. But to make either of them without meaning it is something I consider both undignified for me and for our University.

Do not mistake me. I do not think there is anything wrong in allowing the market to be a factor in determining promotion. I have myself, earlier in my career, benefited from competitive bidding. And there is nothing wrong in making use of friends and acquaintances to secure an offer that one will seriously consider accepting. But I do think it is wrong for the market to be institutionalized into a ritual for advancement. And I do think it is wrong to "work" the market by manipulating one's friends, with a view to securing an offer that one has no intention of accepting.

Yet this is the course that the University, in effect, seems to wish to force me to. I have made up my mind that I will not follow it. If I do take steps to let it be known that I am disenchanted with Columbia or with teaching, it will not be because I am trying to manipulate my situation here but because I really mean what I say.

Before confronting the decision forced on me by my situation, I wanted to let you know all that is involved. I cannot honestly say that I am prepared to face an ultimate choice: for the fact is, as you know, that I like to teach and that I especially like to teach at Columbia. At the same time, my devotion now exists side by side with an increasing sense of strain. It seems to me that our good relations require that I tell you so outright.

Yours always,

82. TO RALPH BERKEY

May 14, 1947
620 West 116th Street

Dear Mr. Berkey:

I have consulted with a psychiatrist friend of mine, of course without mentioning any names. His advice confirms my own first feeling in the matter—that just as it would have been wrong for me to write to your wife making believe that I did remember her, just so it would now be wrong for me to write to her in an effort to destroy her delusion. He feels certain that I should have no communication with your wife at all, either directly or by sending you a letter to show her. He suggests that the best thing for you to do at this point is to enlist medical aid in getting your wife to a psychiatrist.

I am sure I need not say again how very sorry I am not to be able to give you more help.

Sincerely yours,

83. TO ALFRED BERNHEIM[1]

June 20, 1947
Columbia University

Dear Mr. Bernheim:

Thank you for sending me the report of the Subcommittee on the Jewish University. I have read it with great interest and I agree with many of its statements. But I prefer not to be one of the signers of the report.

I learn from the report that "the conferees saw no danger, in principle, in the establishment of a Jewish University." With this I quite agree—our country would be in a sad situation indeed were danger to come to a religious or cultural group because it undertook to found a university. Nor do I think it is necessarily wrong from the cultural point of view for a particular group to establish a university in order to bring honor to itself and to protect and perpetuate its particular ideas, emotions, and cultural qualities. I know several such institutions fairly well—they are usually colleges rather than universities— and I respect and like them very much. It is to be noted, of course, that the particular religious tone of these colleges has tended with time to diminish rather than to increase, so that the particular religious aspect of these institutions is a coloration rather than a doctrine. And in the matter of curriculum it is scarcely even a coloration—being in this unlike what is recommended by the Sub-

1. Of the American Jewish Committee. The Subcommittee on the Jewish University was part of the process that would lead to the founding of Brandeis University in 1948.

committee for a Jewish University, for the Subcommittee believes that the curriculum of a Jewish University should "reflect a definite Jewish interest." Yet even if the American Jewish community felt that it wished to go against a tendency that I regard with satisfaction—that is, the tendency of departicularization—I should not necessarily feel that it was wrong. For even though the general movement be away from religious and cultural particularism, I can still understand that one or another group should, for its own reasons, feel the need of particularism at some time in its history, should even feel that the curriculum of its university should "reflect a definite Jewish interest."

But although I can understand such a movement and do not think it wrong a priori, I do not recommend it and do not wish to be identified with it. It would be laborious both for you and for me were I to try to give a full account of my reasons for this decision. But perhaps a single reason will be enough. It seems to me that all institutions of learning that have had an enduring and interesting life have been founded by passionate and positive ideas. The report of the Subcommittee speaks of the projected Jewish University "presenting a positive attitude toward the role of Jewish values in a democratic society." But so far as I can make out—and I think I have a lively awareness of Jewish life—there are now in America no special Jewish values of a large and important sort, such as there have been at earlier times in Jewish history. I am led to believe that, apart from the new intense nationalism which some Jews feel, Jewish life is dominated either by defensiveness and the problems of "adjustment" or, more positively, by the ideas of American sociological liberalism, of which some are admirable and some pretty thin, but of which none are specifically Jewish. I know many Jews of large mind and morality, but I do not know of a single mind in Jewish life that speaks as a Jew and with any intellectual authority in the exposition of Jewish values. It is possible that someday many such minds will appear. If they do, then the establishment of a Jewish University will be called for. I might then not agree with the ideas it would teach, but I would have respect for it and would expect its success.

Sincerely yours,
Lionel Trilling

84. TO RUTH BROWN[1]

June 29, 1947
620 West 116th Street

Dear Miss Brown:

I've always thought that nothing was harder to write than a blurb. Now I think so more than ever, for I've been dealing with the catalog blurb of my book,[2] trying to say why I think that it isn't right for the jacket.

As close as I can come to it, what is wrong is this: that the blurb seems to have been written in a kind of uncertainty and embarrassment. It doesn't present the book as primarily a story to be enjoyed, and then it compensates for this omission by talking about "hot-blooded love-making," of which the book has none at all. It shies away from the seriousness of the book and then compensates with such killing statements as that the reader will find the "main excitement" of the book in an "intellectual search" or that the book is "an excursion into the mind of an adult modern man."

Take the first sentence: "When a distinguished critic undertakes to write a novel . . ." This makes it sound like a stunt: Lawyer Plays Flute. Critic Writes Novel. The word "undertakes" suggests that the remarkable thing is not that he should do it well but that he should do it at all. I think that the phrasing of the sentence comes from the imagined difficulty of having to deal with a novel by a critic and a professor. This shows itself again in the phrase "Written by a knowing student of the craft . . ." Aside from the fact that "knowing" isn't really a complimentary word—implies an unpleasant way of having knowledge—the whole phrase suggests a synthetic, academic performance. And then there is attributed to me "a warm sense of literary values." This isn't anything a novelist ought to have—it is what William Lyon Phelps[3] had. Don't you think the whole difficulty which I detect here could be got rid of—there's really no need nowadays for it to exist at all—by making reference to my short fiction, which has had quite a good reception?

---

1. Of Viking Press.
2. *The Middle of the Journey.*
3. William Lyon Phelps (1865–1943), scholar and popular literary critic.

The phrase about the "excursion into the mind of an adult modern man" suggests that the book is hopeless[ly] internal. Actually it isn't—not more internal than most modern novels, though the internality may be of a different kind. The phrase damns the book. Same with the business about the "intellectual search" being the main excitement of the book.

The story, as I well know, is very difficult to describe. Best, then, not to describe it. Certainly we ought to avoid the characterization of the characters in the manner of the third paragraph. I've talked the thing over with my wife, who, as a reviewer, has had experience of thousands of novel blurbs; she thinks they are of great importance in determining the reviewer's expectations and her feeling about the present one is what mine is; she has especially strong objection to the trick of summarizing the story and taping the characters—says it always makes the impression on her that the publishers do not believe that the characters can be understood, besides falsifying and reducing the characters by anticipating them.

Does this at all make clear why I don't like the blurb? And does it make publishing sense to you? But this is all negative, and in order to suggest the thing more positively, Mrs. Trilling tried her hand at some blurb copy. I won't offer apologies for my own part in sending on this piece of glorification. I'd be very glad if you'd call me up and tell me what you think of it. You'll understand, I'm sure, that it's meant only as a suggestion and by way of practical criticism of the first blurb. Do what you like with it, though I'd be pleased if you'd see your way to using it. What it says in criticism of the first blurb is that the first doesn't claim enough for the book, or doesn't put forth its claims in a firm, confident, and single-minded way. Or perhaps the difference between the two blurbs is that the domestic one takes proper advantage of the fact that I am a writer of already established reputation. This is untoward to have to say, but I think that if it were understood in a simple way, it would bring to an end all the difficulty there's been about writing the blurb for my book.

About the use of Mrs. Trilling's name in the biographical matter: we've had a family conference and have decided that the way you have used it is perfectly all right, quite legitimate biographical information.

Sincerely,

P.S. You would perhaps want to be told, and I forgot to tell you in our telephone conversation the other day, that *Vogue* sent up a photographic crew—one to hold me in talk, one to load the camera, one to snap—to get a picture for a feature in which I'm to figure. It's a piece on writers in the classroom and I think it comes out September or October.

L.T.

85. TO RICHARD CHASE[1]

October 8, 1947
620 West 116th Street

Dear Richard:

All the time I was writing the book I found myself recurring to the idea that you were particularly to be its reader and so you may imagine that your response to it gives me a very particular pleasure and soothes me emotionally. And by your response I don't mean only your estimate, but the way you put your estimate, so very warmly and happily. I'm really very grateful for your letter.

All that you say about the Laskell-Maxim[2] axis I agree with, and have thought of bitterly before. I do not think that Maxim is too large; or, if he is, I am glad of his fault because he ran away with things and grew out of bounds and always came with utter ease—I never had to touch anything he said or did once it was down on paper: and I have the old-fashioned notion, now not honored, that characters ought to run away with things or at least take hold of their fates—Maxim's willfulness I take to be a good omen and a good lesson to me. Laskell, that sneak, he's the trouble—simply not sufficiently detached from his author, nor, on the other hand, sufficiently his author; in the effort to detach him from my own self I somehow sterilized him; and while a certain sterilization is of his character, still it doesn't do him any good. He is the character that often inhabits an early novel; perhaps better than most, perhaps raised a little by Jamesian theory and practice, but not right, not the right kind of person to have in a novel. And I hope never again to have such a one. The hardest thing in the

---

1. Richard V. Chase (1914–1962), literary critic and historian.
2. John Laskell and Gifford Maxim are characters in *The Middle of the Journey*.

book was getting him started right. And you put it with *absolute* precision when you speak of the "appetite and admiration for force" that he might have had: there lies the whole trouble with him, and it was essentially what Diana kept trying to tell me about him. But you will, I know, understand that I am not trying to exculpate myself for this failure if I say that I could not become aware and let myself go on all things, the book having been so difficult and central an event in my emotional life, written out of the strangest adjustment of the will and the unconscious: seeming to get it done at all, to at last clear the way for novels, not this one but all the ones to follow, I had to make some sacrifices, and Laskell is it.

Flint gave me too a postcard verdict of a "superb job." I am eager to see his review. I hope he keeps his enthusiasm through it—I was told that Mark Schorer[1] very much admired the book, but his review (to appear in the *Times B.R.* this Sunday with a libelous picture of me) is ambivalent. These intellectual critics. And these greedy novelists, no better than Italian tenors. Flint has some good sentiments in his letter to *PR*. I share your envy of him.

Give my greetings warmly to Francie. And again accept my gratitude for your letter, and my assurances that my next hero has appetite and admiration for force—I think they'll kill him, poor fellow

Yours,

Lionel

86. TO MORTON DAUWEN ZABEL

October 22, 1947
620 West 116th Street

Dear Morton:

[...]

And now I must tell you of the enormous pleasure I had and continue to have in your review.[2] I think very few people have had the honor and advantage of so fine a piece of praise. I would naturally at the moment of reading it have the full sense of your years of devotion

---

1. Mark Schorer (1908–1977), literary critic and biographer.
2. "The Straight Way Lost," *The Nation*, October 18, 1947.

to critical truth—I would naturally push against that solid fact to test it at the same time that I would pinch myself to see if this was really me. The experimental pinch couldn't tell me much, but there was nothing I could do to budge the rock of your past: so I concluded that you must mean it and that I would have to take myself as seriously as you did and would want me to. One can't properly *thank* a reviewer—yet one can't help being grateful to him for his opinion and effort: and I don't suppose an author could be more grateful than I am to you.

There is much that I would like to talk to you about in your review. I think you are right about the abstraction of the characters, their lack of background, etc. That is in part the result of the book having grown from what was originally to have been a novelette; partly it was lack of skill—not, I think, lack of skill in making characters and giving them backgrounds but rather in finding room for any more about them: the novel, I feel, is too long as it is; but of course the book should have been conceived to accommodate more of the literalness that is for me the very ground of the novel. The only thing that puzzles me is your enumeration of the things that set the teeth on edge: Nancy was supposed to have that dental effect of course, and Emily a little, but I'm unhappy that Susan is with them; although now that I think of it, she did set Laskell's teeth on edge.

So much about the book is not what I should want about another book. Laskell, for instance, so much too much a walking gentleman; the too great concentration; the economy and starkness which you note as making it a particular "type" of novel—this last especially goes against my real grain and in the book I am doing now I hope to get away from it; I think the new job will have greater simplicity, more time and space, more varieties of texture. But beyond all this, beyond any detail of dissatisfaction, I find that I direct toward the book a constant head shaking. I want to forget it—and yet of course I don't, and to remind myself of it in the best possible way I turn back to your review.

In the practical sense your piece is of great value. The reviews have been mixed. William Shirer—is it not strange?—was most enthusiastic in the *Herald Tribune* daily column. Mark Schorer went about and about in the *Times Book Review*, gave fairly generously, and took back much. Lloyd Morris muddily laudatory in the *Tribune Books*. Mayberry very superior and disapproving in *The New Republic*. *Time*—Fitzgerald in the box—very snide. I hear that Wilson "doesn't understand" the book, which is to say, doesn't like it; Lalley reviews it for *The New Yorker* and, I hear, unfavorably. Yet the total impression seems to have been a good one and I have hopes that the book will get around. And in that total impression your piece in full sail gives the book great weight (if you can follow the metaphor). The publishers regarded it with awe and incredulity. (I.e., the review. The book with puzzlement.)

I wanted long ago to write you about your Conrad job[1] but when I had the moment to do so I already knew from Peggy that you had agreed to review my book and it seemed to me that I oughtn't to intrude on you with words of praise, for I think the balance of objectivity in reviewing a friend's work is difficult enough to keep at best. The Conrad volume came to me—are there periods in your life when things move by "psychic" coincidence?—just as I was in the middle of *Under Western Eyes*, which I am reading to see what bearing it had on *The Princess Casamassima*, for which I was writing an introduction. It was my first Conrad since college and I was enthralled by it—not that it is a perfect book but that it is a great one and stunningly relevant. I wondered why Conrad had dropped so below the horizon for me and for almost everyone; a great many answers came to me, none of them cheerful, about the faults of my own thought and feeling or that of our culture. So you see I turned to your volume with an intense readiness for it. It is a really splendid job of appraisal—the introduction I mean—so sound, direct, and serious, seeing all around the very difficult subject; and of course it glows with just the right kind of admiration, which is the most difficult quality of criticism. The selection I couldn't in my ignorance judge, except to approve the inclusion of my almost favorite story in the world—only two or three stand with it—*The Secret Sharer*, which is the one Conrad thing I have reread, and often over the years; and of course the wonderful *Heart of Darkness*. But what was chiefly in my mind was your act of criticism, which gave me such sure pleasure.

---

1. Zabel edited *The Portable Conrad* (1947).

I wish my admiration didn't have to be conveyed in what might look to be an exchange of compliments: I didn't want to wait any longer for a neutral situation to send it. Besides, I don't believe in neutral situations.

[. . .]

Yours,

87. TO ALLEN GINSBERG

October 25, 1947
620 West 116th Street

Dear Allen:

I should have written you before this but I have had a difficult summer and early fall—not only have I been busy but also I've been inefficient in my life, doing things slowly and shying away from correspondence. And no doubt much of the delay in answering your letter was occasioned by its contents. I mean, of course, your protest against the terms of our relationship. I delayed answering not because I found it hard to formulate the answer but because I thought that it might possibly give you pain. Now that it has rested in my mind, however, I have changed that first view of its effect and I believe you will accept it as simply as it is meant. In itself it is really quite simple: it is that I think our relationship is not intended to be the kind you assume in your letter. Its right condition is set by the original connection between us, that of student and teacher, and by the difference in our ages. Having said this, I naturally wonder if I am being merely stuffy; I think not, for I say it from both experience and inclination. I rely on you to understand that I am not saying that the relationship we have is not real, to understand too that I do not believe that the reality of a relationship is determined by its degree merely of intimacy, and that I value highly the relationships that are conditioned by, as it were, function. If you present your life to me in the manner that you have done, I am willing to receive seriously and affectionately what you tell me, but I can do that only as your teacher and older friend; it would be impossible and pointless for me to reciprocate in anything approaching kind.

The novel is out and it is a great relief to have it out. It has been given an importance beyond what I had hoped for it and, really, beyond what I wanted for it, for I have always thought of it, and still do, as rather a small book and a trial run, and I have to remind myself of this. It has been well received by some reviewers, extremely well by others, but the critical reviews which might have established the book to make some money for me have been hostile (*Time*, *The New Yorker*), converting what I suspect to be an ideological dislike into an aesthetic disapproval. But many readers and good ones have liked the book very much and on the whole I am pleased and go on to the next, the question of whether or not I could write a novel being now satisfactorily settled, or at least transformed into the question of whether I can write a second, third, and fourth novel.

I don't want to give a judgment on the verse you sent me in your letter. I think I know what you are after in manner and I think I understand and approve it. I have been wondering for some time how long the clotted metaphor could endure in our taste, recognizing its appositeness to our time what with its implication of thick blood and Macbeth: it has seemed to me that sooner or later we would have to revive the clear organization of the sentence in poetry, the rhetorical unit rather than the merely apperceptive unit of the metaphor, and rely on statement of a simple kind rather than on intensification. Someone, maybe me, will have to look at Wordsworth's sonnets to learn their secret of lyric force. I have in mind something of the same sort in my prose—the result being that people say "well-written," "too well-written" or "enervated." (I mean the prose of my novel.)

Sincerely,
Lionel Trilling

88. TO HYMAN JUSKOWITZ

October 27, 1947
620 West 116th Street

Dear Mr. Juskowitz,

I am horrified to see that three months have passed since the date of your letter. It isn't that I didn't know that I had been delaying unconscionably long in acknowledging your letter—but three months: a quarter of a year! When, after only a month of delay, I began to reply in the summer I put my sin down to heat and fatigue. To that I must now add a general impulse to evade duties and issues—just general unregenerateness. And also a piece of work that up to a couple of weeks ago just would not get finished. But no excuses that I can make can exorcise my sense of having failed in a pedagogical commitment. I hope you can forgive me.

The letter is a good letter. Leaving aside a few lapses of diction—I have the tolerance of the sinful at the moment!—the writing is clear and very good in its tone. I do wish you could find the occasion for frequent—weekly—writing for a good teacher and, even more important, good colleagues. But I liked the relaxation of the manner—as against the rigidity which I found in that other paper of yours—and I hope you cultivate that. I think it is an apparent relaxation that permits real tension in expository prose. The English understand that better than we Americans.

I think we agreed that I wouldn't try to answer your arguments in force—although I think my wish to do so is the real reason for my long delay. But there are one or two things that I do want to say about your position, or approach to a position. Before I do, however, there are two points of correction I must make. One comes from my wife, to whom I showed your letter: she says that she did not accuse Burgum[1] of being too social or socialistic, but of not being openly social and socialistic, of hiding his real interests and intentions under all sorts of technical and aesthetic disguises, as if they were not decent. The other correction is from me and has to do with a detail of your very interesting and really gratifying description of my lecture manner: although, as you guessed, I have learned to cherish the effect in my lectures of an intellectual struggle, and quite on the grounds you suppose, it isn't "pre-arranged" but quite real; I found that a certain kind of insight would often come in a lecture, almost as a direct effect of the audience, and that these didn't come when I was at my desk; since that discovery I've given myself an outline for safety and don't usually follow it. I mention this partly to suggest what you can think of doing when you yourself begin to lecture after more classroom experience.

Without going into the matter to its depths—as someday I should

---

1. Diana Trilling's review of Edwin Berry Burgum's *The Novel and the World's Dilemma* appeared in *The New York Times*, June 1, 1947.

like to do—I think I can best deal with what you say in your letter by taking up one or two sentences.

You ask: "How can a critic (or a magazine like *Partisan Review*) bring the liberal class, and all it stands for to you, closer to the illiberal, disintegrating, yet imaginatively great and powerful art of bourgeois society?" I think that where I disagree with you is in the antithesis you make—on the one hand the honorific liberalism, on the other hand the pejorative bourgeois. I don't mean to quarrel about the words themselves—what I want to make plain is my deep distaste for liberal culture. This is difficult to explain: for I am in accord with most of the liberal ideals of freedom, tolerance, etc. But the tone in which these ideals are uttered depress[es] me endlessly. I find it wholly debased, downright sniveling, usually quite insincere. It sells everything out in human life in order to gain a few things that it can understand as good. It isn't merely that I believe that our liberal culture doesn't produce great art and lacks imagination—it is that I think it produces horrible art and has a hideous imagination. See Steinbeck's *The Wayward Bus* for what I mean about the snivel, the shocking—the really cruel and dead—view of human life: one is not to be taken in by the false heartiness and camaraderie. And this is generally true of all our literature of social idealism, from its centrist generality to its leftist, Stalinist specificity. On the other hand, I am sure that Yeats was a good deal of a son of a bitch and admired a good deal of son of a bitchery, yet I find in him notions of pride, courage, risk, self-assertion, worth—and all in their complexity and dignity—that I want to see in the good society. The largeness and variety of Proust is for me a paradigm of the good society—so too the care with which he sees and the importance he gives to people. And when I come to consider the explicit illiberal ideas of the great modern artists, I am inclined, I confess, to slight them: perhaps illegitimately, but usually I choose to do so, and don't feel harmed and don't think that anyone is likely to be more seducible than I am. So that when you say that "any perceptive reader must conclude from the exhortatory tone [this I question] of this 'decadent' literature that he has here an attitude scarcely congruent with his own," I'm inclined to answer either "What of it?" or "Do him good for a change." But if I do put my mind to a consideration of the illiberal ideas that I find in the modern masters, I can't help wondering if they aren't the direct result—the fault, as we say—of our liberal culture, a conscious recognition of the philistinism of bourgeois liberalism, of the equal or greater philistinism of Russian communism, which has so many affiliations with the bourgeois view of things. We will never, I am sure, have a great literature springing from our bourgeois liberalism, for any man capable of writing greatly is sure to see that really and truly bourgeois liberalism simply does not *want* a great literature, is contrived to deny great literature in its possibility.

Perhaps this shocks you. I think that I have never made this clear to you in our conversation. I always, I suppose, allowed my addiction to the notions of freedom, tolerance, opportunity, and growth to be identified in our talks with political liberalism as it is practiced by *The New Republic, PM*, etc., and never made wholly clear the extent of my despair of the cultural future of political liberalism as we know it now. I don't, I confess, know what organization of politics and thought I want to take its place: and possibly liberalism, if it doesn't get betrayed to the Stalinist Left, may yet for a while serve our political turn: but if it is to be anything culturally it must change itself wholly. Why, we worry over its failure to produce fine art—it hasn't even produced a political writer of even the second class, one with an almost-new political idea!

You speak of the status of art as being singular in our culture and compare it to the merely adjunctive status of art in medieval times. I of course agree with the fact—but this is what, I think, makes art so difficult to produce in our liberal culture. We exaggerate its function, demand of it more than it can ever perform. Liberal culture, quite as much as Russia, gives directives to its artists and expects results. The only results can be mechanical and false. I more and more feel that the subject of art is the absurd, the absurd as the liberal, rational mind judges it, the glorious absurd; and when the liberal mind is willing to recognize the high value of the absurd and is able to judge well among the various absurdities, it will be able to have art; but as I noted in my *Partisan* introduction, it cannot even tolerate the absurd in Freud, it must have a nice clean *rational* unconscious like Horney's, which is contrived to clear out the absurd.

Well, I have gone to much more length than I meant to do; and have got warm into the bargain—not at you, of course, but at the

Situation—and have at best touched the matter only tangentially. I cordially invite you to take the matter up in another letter now that you know my dreadful rate of reply and know that for as much as three months you may seem to have written into a void.

But quite apart from that, I'd be very glad if you'd call me up, as we arranged, to talk about the matter of your dissertation subject.

Sincerely,

89. TO ERIC BENTLEY

November 28, 1947
620 West 116th Street

Dear Eric:

I've delayed too long answering your letter which gave me so much pleasure with its directness and warmth.

First as to the authenticity of Maxim's crime or near crime. I knew a man[1] whom I respected and liked, although having enormous reservations about him, who was high in the CP councils. He once asked me, as Maxim asked Laskell, to receive letters for him. He scarcely concealed that these letters were part of an espionage project. It was later known that he worked here for the GPU and himself at a still later date admitted it. When he broke with the party and the GPU he feared for his life. I will not go into details, nor name names; the story is quite generally known, and there is absolutely no reason to doubt the man. Intimate friends of his are old friends of mine. Then the case of Julia [sic] Poyntz[2] has never been cleared up—the complete disappearance of a woman once high in the party, or in its confidence, although later she broke. There is every reason to believe that the assassin of Carlo Tresca[3] was a Communist: at least there is good reason. The Scottogoggio case is current in which an opponent of Marcantonio[4] was beaten to death; this is not directly connected with the CP but only with that part of

---

1. Whittaker Chambers; see letter of June 18, 1942.
2. Juliet Poyntz (1886–1937) was a leading American communist who disappeared in 1937 after breaking with the Communist Party.
3. Carlo Tresca (1879–1943), Italian American journalist, was murdered in New York City, after antagonizing both the Communist Party and the Mafia.
4. Vito Marcantonio (1902–1954), left-wing congressman representing East Harlem.

the Democratic Party in New York that is dominated by the CP—Marcantonio's district. In Europe there have been many cases of doing away with opponents of the CP. All dissident foreign Communists believe in a simple literal way that they are in danger—in this country I mean. And why should we doubt that a revolutionary party should scruple to assassinate? More idealistic parties than the CP have not hesitated to destroy those whom they considered traitors. Such a course seems almost inevitable in a conspiratorial party. I condemn it in the CP but there are aspects of the CP that I condemn more—I mean the whole mystique and the whole practice of the U.S.S.R. in Europe. Eventually you and I will have to get to the mat about this, for I am always troubled and puzzled by the quick and instinctive way you question all questions raised about the Communists. I must find out from you how you can still feel that they represent any tendency of progress and hope. I would like to do that for my own sake as well as yours, for no doubt my beliefs in the matter have gone too much into assumption, which is not good.

On the matter of *nel mezzo del cammin*—that I *meant* to be a point in time and development. But no doubt there is in addition to *nel m. del c.* a strong quality of via media in the book. The impotence you note is indigenous in this story—the character of Laskell is conceived in it. I can only answer with Dr. Johnson: Impotence, sir, sheer impotence! I simply couldn't then make a character who had an affirmation to offer of a practical sort—for it would have had to be practical. Maybe I won't ever be able to, though I'm trying in My Next. Of course a practical affirmation is too much to ask of any novelist: but I hope at least to get the tone of strength in the next attempt. Maybe that is why tragedy is necessary, not redemption or reeducation, which is always sure to be dim. I think it was that I specifically wanted to avoid tragedy that I petered out in the current job; I thought tragedy would avoid the intellectual issue. But of course I ought just to avoid the intellectual issue and throw the whole damn business into the emotional pot. I'm just not clever enough to escape that way of doing things. Perhaps no one is that clever if he is committed to dealing with things head-on and not by some great device. I can imagine some wonderfully gifted comic writer who sees the sadness and avoids having to say anything explicitly.

I wish I had ten novels out so that this one could find its proper place. I don't think it's merely to avoid responsibility that I myself think of it as if it were a long short story (it began as that) but rather that I express to myself in this way my feeling about its degree of importance and pressure. I didn't mean it to have very much pressure—in a way I think I meant it to be a "light" novel; I find myself much distressed when people don't respond to the comedy and the irony and when they call it a novel of ideas. Actually I think little of the ideas: the ideational conversations were the quickest and easiest to write and needed least revision and I believe that if they are examined closely they will be found to be neither clever nor profound but only suggest the clever and profound. People talk about the book solemnly and speak of "digesting" it or "mulling it over" before they dare give an opinion of it. This is the result of having written a first novel in the m. of the j., which is too late to begin, especially if one starts with the solemn name of a critic.

Which of course doesn't mean that I don't like the book liked and treated seriously, for I set store by it and think it serious. I think you did both—that is, liked it and took it seriously—and that pleases me very much indeed.

[. . .]

Sincerely,

Lionel

90. TO ROBERT WARSHOW[1]

December 13, 1947[2]
620 West 116th Street

Dear Robert:

I thought I made it clear to Elliot Cohen that the publication of your article in the December *Commentary*[3] does not seem to me, as it does to him and no doubt to you, a simple act of intellectual and

---

1. Robert Warshow (1917–1955), editor at *Commentary* and critic, primarily of film.
2. The copy of this letter in Trilling's archive is marked "not sent."
3. "The Legacy of the Thirties," *Commentary*, December 1947, was Warshow's negative review of *The Middle of the Journey*.

editorial integrity. I told Elliot that so far as your essay concerns my book I find it personally offensive—not, certainly, because you express a low opinion of my novel, but because you gratuitously inflate my book for the purpose of your critical tactic, because you choose to set it up in isolation as the very type of modern emotional sterility and artistic impotence, and because the manner in which you do this, whatever you may have intended it to be, has for me clear implications of unfriendliness in its forcing of detail up to and beyond the point of frivolity, its gusto in accumulating evidence and its air of intellectual triumph in drawing conclusions: it is this manner, unbecoming as between persons like ourselves and particularly in the cultural situation that you describe, which most offends me. And it dismays me for the prospect of our cultural life.

I assume that Elliot told you this as the gist of my conversation with him. If he did not and thus let you invite me to write for *Commentary* in ignorance of what I felt, he was at fault in his relation to you. If he did tell you and you then chose to invite me to write for *Commentary* as if nothing had happened between you and me and between *Commentary* and me, then you have either been disingenuous or you have made light of a situation that I take, as I find, with increasing and not with decreasing seriousness.

Since it is for me an essential condition of work that there be a degree of personal sympathy and confidence between myself and the journals for which I write, I should find it impossible as a practical thing to write for a magazine in which my work has been so notably discredited, with so unusual an éclat and with so much editorial sanction. But even if it were a practical possibility for me to write for *Commentary*, your publication of a review by me at this point would make it appear that I condoned your article and its publication. This I have not the slightest wish to do.

Elliot is an old and valued friend and you are a person for whose work I have had much admiration; I have no disposition to let this event attenuate my friendship with Elliot or to become the matter of a grudge between you and me; Elliot has reason to know this and I should like you to know it. But my feeling toward individual persons is not the same as my feeling toward the complex of personalities which produced the event of your article; toward this personal and cultural entity, which, I suppose, is *Commentary*, I have a very hard feeling; and I do not so far find that time and thought lessen it.

Sincerely,

Lionel Trilling

P.S. I think that Elliot should have a copy of this letter and I am sending him one.

L.T.

91. TO ROBERT WARSHOW

December 16, 1947
620 West 116th Street

Dear Robert:

I'm sure that you don't really suppose that I am offended by your essay because it is not, in the sense in which you use the word, "friendly" to my book. And I'm sure that you don't really believe that I would have wished you to disguise your adverse opinion.

At some later time, I think, you will be able to stand back from your essay and see that it is not quite the objective piece of work you now believe it to be.

Had you indeed written of a situation that involves "us all" I should have found no cause for offense. But what reached me as wrong in your piece was your eagerness to exempt yourself from the general fate—it is thus that I read your forcing of detail up to the point of frivolity, your gusto in accumulating evidence, and your air of intellectual triumph in drawing conclusions.

But there is, of course, nothing in the relationship between you and me which permits me to expect you to check the impulses of your ideas and feelings, whatever they may be. My attitude toward your writing the essay is therefore entirely different from my attitude toward *Commentary* publishing it in the circumstances in which it was published. My feeling about Elliot's part in the event I have explained to him as follows: As my friend, as the friend of the book's point of view, and as the kind of editor he is, he should have estimated the weight and tone of what you said and should have seen that it was neither fair nor necessary to let an indictment of modern culture rest on my book or find its conclusive example in my book. Both friendship and criticism would have been equally served by a simple editorial action which would not have compromised integrity in the least or have done any injustice to your views; this would have consisted in the publication of a review of my book as adverse as the reviewer—you or another—thought necessary, followed by the publication of your article sufficiently expanded to include other instances of the tendency you deal with.

Sincerely,

92. TO RICHARD CHASE

February 11, 1948
620 West 116th Street

Dear Richard:

[. . .]

That I have not for so long replied to your long letter in which you write of your relation to me may have told you something that you did not entirely know—that I have my own inarticulacies and rigidities in personal relationships and am often graceless, and no doubt the more because I usually present, as I think, the appearance of a fairly easy communicability. The appearance, if it is indeed there, was hard-won, and worth winning because it helped the reality. But it doesn't always work. I find that I often rear back in the face of affection and praise, no doubt because I like them so much; I think I want to reply in the best possible way and so don't reply in a good way at all, or don't reply. I think this was what happened with your letter—I was very deeply moved by it and so shrank from the effort— but of course there should be no *effort*—to reply to it in its kind. You are right when you speak of a constraint in my dealing with your writing, and I am glad you spoke of it. This is not a response of mine particular to you; I am the same with other friends—even with Jacques after many years of going over his manuscripts and of showing mine to him. This is related, surely, to the other thing. I would call it an inadequacy of *affectionate aggression*. I consider it a grave deficiency in myself and one which has had serious consequences in my life. I suppose it presents itself as an overestimation of the friend's estimation of his own work, an exaggerated sense of the friend's labor of writing and of his stake in the work, of the dreadful power of my negative criticism; no doubt as a fear of his displeasure at my displeasure—if we are to be analytical. As why not?—for I am suddenly aware of how depressed I have been today because Stanley Edgar Hyman,[1] a dull fellow if there ever was one, spoke slightingly of me in an essay of his: I think I must be excessively sensitive to negative criticism and project that into others. And I think there are other reasons too, none of which I like. But as I say, I am glad you wrote of this and from here on out I will let you have it—between the eyes, full in the face, straight, or in whatever other terms of Jamesian violence I can muster, feeling secure that you can take it that way with your faith in yourself of which I have been growingly aware as it has been growing in you. And you, I hope, will reciprocate—it will be good exercise for me.

With your letter just before me urging me to bring out my volume of essays, I this minute had a call from Covici of Viking urging me to bring out the volume for the fall. I don't know what to say—my new novel has been going badly but I just begin to see it again. I don't want to give the time to the revision of the essays that is needed. But maybe I should get free of the compulsion of the novel. Then I'm not sure that I want to publish with Viking, not liking the way they handled my novel. We'll see—maybe I ought to work on both books: maybe my novel has gone so ill because I've been under too little pressure.

[. . .]
Yours,
    Lionel

93. TO EDMUND BERGLER[2]

March 1, 1948
620 West 116th Street

Dear Dr. Bergler:

I have delayed too long in thanking you for having sent me your two papers. I wanted to read them before acknowledging them and until now I have not had the time to do so.

---

1. Stanley Edgar Hyman (1919–1970), literary critic.
2. Edmund Bergler (1899–1962), psychoanalyst and writer.

It seems to me that your paper on writers makes a really important contribution to the psychoanalytical theory of literature—I have in mind your thesis that it is not his unconscious wishes that the artist gives expression to. I do not have the technical equipment which would allow me to presume either to agree or disagree with you when you say that what he does give expression to is his unconscious defense against these wishes and fantasies, although it seems to me that this might well be one of the things he expresses. What I chiefly respond to is your correction of the much too simple assumptions that analysts have hitherto gone on when they have written about literature and authors.

I wish I were able to agree with everything in your very interesting and provocative paper, but very likely you do not expect me to. I have long felt that psychoanalysis has held an inadequate view of literature. Much of this view is expressed in the paper by Brill to which you subscribe—the view that the poet uses "nice" words and is concerned with "beauty," that he subordinates thought to sound, that he does not think at all, etc. And elsewhere in your paper you make the familiar disjunction between fantasy and reality, as if fantasy were not an effective, instrumental element in a culture: every police state knows that it is. It seems to me that Freud in his head-on dealings with literature—not in his tangential ones—made use of many of the assumptions of the commonplace, second-rate literary criticism of the later nineteenth century and that until psychoanalytical writers get beyond these and take a more serious view of literature very little progress will be made.

I imagine that you will scarcely have expected me to accept your typology of the writer. It seems to me that the cases you cite from your clinical experience are chiefly of what Rank (I think it was he) called "half-artists," people who assume the role of the artist for neurotic reasons and even act it out with some degree of unimportant success. The number of cases of writers who give no sign of the masochistic pattern you find would be very large indeed. The half artists are often not the most attractive of people, which might account for the element of animus which I sensed in the portrait of them which you draw. Yet I wonder if you are not too pejorative in your generalization of even these people. If we are to conceive of firmly fixed professional character types, would not an analytical description of any one of them be bound to be grimly unflattering, even, if I may be permitted the example, the psychoanalysts, who so often express and even formulate their affinity with writers?

Sincerely yours,

94. TO DAVID KLEINSTEIN

March 20, 1948
620 West 116th Street

Dear Mr. Kleinstein,

The position which you take in your very courteous letter[1] is, I think, defensible but wrong. It is not a definitive fact about a man that he is a Jew, but it is a relevant fact. It is of course not relevant in all circumstances; and sometimes the introduction of the fact is so irrelevant as to be malign. But it is relevant in our awareness of people —not more but not less relevant than the fact that a person is short or tall, quick in his movements or slow, rich or poor, comes from Atlanta or Bangor. We are all aware of these attributes of a person; they are part of the tone and color of his personality, although they do not necessarily have anything to do with his moral quality. The novelist is likely to be especially aware of them. Dr. Graf would not, as you say he would, be fully described by the other adjectives if the adjective "Jewish" were omitted. A grave, broad, comfortable, mature, and humorless Jew is different from any other kind of man to whom these same adjectives would apply.

You ask what purpose his being Jewish served in the book. I could answer that it helps to suggest the cultural level of certain of the other characters that they, although not Jewish, have a Jewish doctor. But my real reason would not be so definite as that. It is that I "saw" him as Jewish—in the human design of the book it gave pleasure to my imagination to have a Jew in that particular place. Will you forgive me if I say that your implying that every Jew in a work of fiction must have his passport or a raison d'être is an act of inverse social discrimi-

---

1. Kleinstein had written to Trilling complaining about the identification of a minor character in *The Middle of the Journey* as Jewish.

nation. Dr. Graf, a Jew, just walked into my novel, registered as one of the characters, and seemed to feel that he belonged there. You ask what difference it makes whether he is Jewish or not. It makes none—in this connection no more than that he is bald or owns a bulldog.

One does not write novels from a public-relations point of view, but if we speak about the public-relations effects of novels, don't you think it might be very useful to have Jews just walking around in fiction, not certified as good or suffering or significant, but just like everybody else, being present for the same reasons that everybody else is present—because they just work here or live here or happened to walk in?

Sincerely yours,
Lionel Trilling

P.S. I have no personal objection whatever to your sending a copy of your letter to the *Saturday Review of Literature*. But I hope you will not do so, for the chances are all in favor of its being read as an extreme example of the oversensitivity which you disclaim.

95. TO ALLEN GINSBERG

September 14, 1948
620 West 116th Street

Dear Allen,

I am sorry these have gone so long without response from me. But I know you'll forgive me. I won't undertake to speak of them in detail, but assuming that they are pretty much of a piece and a period, I'd say of them that they have a transitional and tentative quality—I have the feeling that you are trying out an idiom that you do not expect to stay with for very long. The tendency is toward lightness and sweetness and this is often very engaging. At the same time, however, I find that things become a little misty and evanescent—the landscape seems rather too subjective, too *wholly* subjective, and indeed, although this is on a quite low level of comment, I found that I was a little thrown off by my sense of the frequency of the first-person pronoun. Which is not to say that I believe the "I" cannot be used effectively—but I a little think that you are using it in a tangential way to both the lyric use and the dramatic use (which eventually are pretty much the same). Seems to me that one gets a deterioration in the force of "I" from the English romantic poets into the Victorians, and there is something a touch Victorian in your use. I think what I wanted as I read was the "I" connected with more objects, more actualities either of feelings or of wit: which is why, I suppose, I liked the business of the automobile in traffic.

Does this make any meaning for you? You know how uncertain and recessive I become when I have to deal with poetry, perhaps especially when it is in manuscript—I'm not to be trusted very far.

I return to Hamilton Hall next week after a not very productive year. Come in to see me.

Sincerely,

L.T.

96. TO JOHN CROWE RANSOM[1]

September 21, 1948
620 West 116th Street

Dear John:

I have had two long letters from Phil[2] which, by their length and thoroughness and eloquence in replying to my comments on the essays, suggest that I may have said more than I meant. I shall reply to Phil, if possible to today, but first I want to resume, to begin all over again, the letter to you I had begun some days back even before I received the essays; this letter had started as a reply to yours in which you asked me to write a piece for the anniversary issue and spoke of plans for next summer.

At the present moment I find myself in an odd state of mind. I should not obtrude my subjectivities on you were they not, so far as

---

1. John Crowe Ransom (1888–1974), poet and critic, editor of *The Kenyon Review*, and founder of the School of Letters, a summer program with which Trilling was affiliated.
2. Philip Rice, managing editor of *The Kenyon Review*.

I can see, wholly concerned with literature; were they not, too, and again so far as I can see, not gloomy and not depressed. I find it hard to explain except as an impatience with myself in the role of critic, which often presents itself as an impatience with literature itself. What a thing to say—what a comical thing!: it is the basis of that joke about Toscanini seeing one of his first violins making the sourest faces all through rehearsal; he pressed for a reason, suggesting that perhaps the man didn't like the way he was conducting the piece and so on and at last he yielded: "Maestro, it's just that I don't like music." But of course it isn't that I don't like literature, it's that I don't like my relation to literature. I don't, I think, like myself in the critical and pedagogic role. I find that I don't any longer have critical detachment. I think of works as attacking me or being my allies—I want to fight back and with them. You've always known me to be ideological; I've never known how ideological I really am: I find myself becoming increasingly a religio-political person, I suppose rather crudely so (but not what is for me the detestable way of Matthiessen). (I don't mean he's detestable.) I say "crudely" because I seem to be alienated from so many of the fine and complex figures of recent art and thought and alienated from their partisans. I find that I am impatient with the canonization of art that has been made by the people who have most to do with literature these days; I have considerable respect for these people, yet I feel some huge discrepancy between their personal being and their evaluation of art. (If you will forgive the personality of my bringing you into this personal record, it is my sense of your difference from them in this respect, my sense of a strong intimacy between your person and your life in art and thought that accounts in great part for the admiration and affection I have for you; these have grown as in the last years I have a better chance to be aware of the intimacy between your person and your life on paper.) Whenever I feel my impatience I become frightened that I am regressing to some sort of terrible philistinism, and yet my bones keep crying out for something else that I am getting or giving.

The other day I put in an appearance to read a paper to the English Institute, the reasonably good quality of which you no doubt know, and came home in the blackest mood about our colleagues; not all of them were of the best, although some of the best were there, and having seen them I felt terribly alienated from the English-teaching profession to which I was once so consciously devoted. Currently I am interviewing candidates for my graduate seminar, and I cannot express to you how puzzled and repelled I am by the young people who come to me because I represent enlightenment and *criticism*. I find I make the most ungenerous ascription of motive to them—I mean unconscious motive, motive in the Nietzschean sense. I try hard to suppress this, but I keep wanting to say to them that they've come to the wrong man, that I have nothing to impart; that I have no "method" and nothing to teach. Two young men who had done well at the Kenyon School were among them and they disturbed me as much as all the others, one by the sense he gave me that he hoped to be safe in the arms of art, the other by his cheerful feeling that he was able to dominate art. Quite apart from my own relation to all these students I had the feeling that we—I mean we critics—had by now become institutionalized: I wonder if you ever get a notion of how established the critical idea has become, not finally established of course, but very largely; two more years of the Kenyon School will, I believe, fix the advance: but now the danger comes that all that was won with difficulty will turn into academic cliché, given back to us by almost all the students who are at all bright. Just as historic scholarship became a device of democratic intellectual life, a method imparted to anyone who wanted to take part in that life, so criticism is likely to become. This, of course, says nothing about the genuine achievements that criticism has made, the achievements that cannot be denigrated by people crowding in on them.

But these last comments do not explain my relation to my pedagogic role. Yet having said they do not, I am not sure. When I think of teaching undergraduates my spirits do not sink: I feel that I am breaking new ground with them, that I almost present them with actualities, with a sense of real consequences. This I can't feel when I deal with professional students.

And then, quite apart from pedagogy, I feel that I must soon be up to something. Perhaps what I am saying is that my unconscious is requiring me to get back to fiction. My novel was, for me, only a very, very moderate success and yet it gives me the only satisfaction I can get out [of] years of writing. And if it isn't fiction, then perhaps it is something else, some new bastard sort of genre I need. At any rate, I find myself in a very odd relation to myself as a critic. You know—I think I once told you—that I never really think of myself as a critic: I always feel that I made myself a critic on a dare to myself at twenty and because I had been such a maundering idiot at college; and now I'm embarrassed and even bewildered when I'm taken seriously!

Well, I express all this badly—hastily and without premeditation. But perhaps as muddled as it is it will explain a few things to you. It will explain the mood out of which I wrote to Phil about the essays. I wrote in a way that was no doubt too strong, too personal, and indeed I was personally troubled by the essays; but if Phil thought I was writing in a hostile or secessionary way about the school he was mistaken, though the error was natural. He is right, and I said something of the sort myself, that students will pick up a posture and a method without enough content to support it. What, for example, Richard Chase does appeals to me enormously, but that is in part because Richard at every moment is making a strong, masculine demand on life and on literature: he has a beast in view, and I suppose students cannot have.

You are not, then, to feel that I am anything but devoted to the school or that my outburst was anything but for the family. I met David Stevens some days back and he spoke of wanting to talk with me about the school; I would not think of confusing his mind with the matters that are now between us.

But feeling as I do, you will understand that, all practical considerations apart, I find it at the moment difficult to think of coming to Kenyon next summer simply because I can't at the moment conceive a course I would like to teach. I think I am honest in saying that I am really trying to do so. The way I am going about it is this: I am making the effort to forget all notions of *genre*, forgetting The Novel, The Long Poem, The Anything, so as to free myself from the possibility of making form or technique paramount. I am trying to find one man of some range whom I would want to deal with in his entirety; or, better, a group of books that I would especially like to deal with, five or six works that please me, perhaps all on one great theme. This is at least for me a possible way and I will try to bring the matter to an issue as soon as possible. As I say, this is apart from practical considerations, which, for me, are not simple.

And what I have so confusedly said in this letter will suggest that it will not be easy for me to say yes—much as I would like to—to your request to contribute to the symposium. I think it proper for me to do so—I had promised myself to do no more criticism this year but I would break my promise for this occasion if I thought I could with reasonable ease do anything at all relevant. But you will guess that, my mood being as complicated and strong as it is, doing anything in criticism isn't easy— and indeed what few little things I have done lately have come very hard—and not likely to fit in small space. But I promise that I will try and I will let you know the prospects.

You—or more likely Coffin—will have probably heard from Barzun. He has not told me the contents of his letter but I think I know that his decision is to beg off from the school. He does, you know, the work of three men and the University burdens him heavily, for he is extraordinarily efficient. He finds that his summers are the only time in which he can work continuously and has learned to work beautifully in those four free months and is right not to surrender them to anything.

Comment as you wish on what I have told you about myself, but don't feel that you must "answer" this letter.

Yours most affectionately,

97. TO RABBI ISIDOR HOFFMAN

March 21, 1949
620 West 116th Street

Dear Rabbi Hoffman:

Thinking about my promise to you to attend the services on the evening of April 1, I have come to realize that the commitment sits with me very uncomfortably. I certainly have no objection to attending synagogue services if an occasion naturally presents itself or if a desire were naturally to arise in me. But to come on a particular evening by prearrangement with a religious counselor of the University takes on the color of a "gesture," which, in the degree that it might be available to any use, however tacit, or liable to be given any significance, would be a quite false gesture for me—for I am not a synagogue goer and cannot properly appear as an example of one.

I am sure you'll understand that I am writing this to you in all personal friendliness but also in careful consideration of the full possible meaning of the situation.

Sincerely yours,
Lionel Trilling

98. TO FREDRIC WARBURG[1]

April 1, 1949
620 West 116th Street

Dear Warburg:

I was delighted to have your letter, not only for itself but also because it makes, as it were, a decisive occasion for my writing you. A letter to you has been in my mind ever since I heard from you at the end of January, but for reasons which will perhaps appear in what I shall say in this letter now, I've postponed and postponed.

It's of course something of a disappointment to me that the book didn't at first go sell up to your firm and sensibly modest expectations for it. I regret that for you as well as for myself. Yet I must tell you that any financial disappointment I might have—and of course I had no glittering financial hopes—is quite swallowed up by my satisfaction at the publication and reception of the book. If the American event had been like the English, I think that you would now be in receipt of or momently expecting another novel from me. I can't tell you how grateful I have been in the last months for the whole English business—your own straightforward presentation of the book and the reception in the press. I thought that the latter, even on the lower levels, had a kind of generosity and responsiveness that did me great good. For the simple fact is that the English response permitted me to feel that I had written a novel and was or could be a novelist. The American press was certainly, one way or another, responsive; but my sense of the situation was that although I might

---

1. Fredric Warburg (1898–1981) of the publisher Secker and Warburg, which published *The Middle of the Journey* in the U.K.

have written an interesting or useful book, I hadn't written a novel, or certainly wasn't what-you-would-call a novelist. On one side this response represented an American suspicion of "intellectuality"; on another side it represented the American hyper-intellectuality—the bright critics carried what I felt to be a most unpretentious, even humble, effort to the empyrean of aesthetics or of ideology and praised or damned accordingly; and as often as not it wasn't the book that was criticized but my position as a critic. All this could provide me with certain satisfactions, but at best they were cold ones, and not of a sort that would urge me forward. I don't of course mean that they deterred me, but they did provide me with a caution. But the English response had the effect of relaxing me, of somehow giving me permission to turn my mind out to free pasture—created a delighted élan about the whole idea of the novel, as a result of which came boldness and a new fertility of conception. The long-projected other novel revived itself into a pattern at once simpler and more daring—the idea that one *can* reach people is indeed most liberating!— and other notions, for *nouvelles*, came tumbling in. Now I live like a horse at the post, straining to get to work.

But here comes the ironic rub. As I see things now, I shan't be free to work as I want for still some months to come. This is due to circumstances resulting in part from material facts not easily to be escaped, in part from internal weakness. The material facts are that my university work has been encroaching sadly on my time. This is a condition to which almost everyone in American universities is subject because of the enormous increase in attendance. Basil Willey was here for a term and was appalled by the pressure on us. In my own case this has been intensified by my becoming, Lord preserve us, a popular professor; partly because I am "literary" the literary students want to work with me, and there are a great many of them. But I have lately been put into a position to make representations to the university about this situation, and I have been given the promise of assistance and substantial relief. I can now expect that next year my situation will be better, and even better the year after. Then in addition to the university situation, I am suffering from something that people tell me about and that I have had to recognize, which is a sort of consolidation in the last year of my literary reputation. This I don't wholly understand, and so far as I do understand it it a little irritates me because almost all that I have done I feel to be provisional and not a reason for a reputation as I conceive it and do indeed want it. But naturally I have awareness enough also to get gratification from it and then to submit to some of the consequences it brings. Vanity masked as responsibility or as the power to do casually what in result takes effort and care lead one—i.e., me—to say yes to friends, or to worthy committees or to a good book that needs an introduction or a review; such a thing as the Kenyon School of English, whose inceptive and controlling body I joined two years ago, now holds me to my promise to give a course this summer, insisting that without me, etc. Money plays some part in my acceptances, but not the definitive part: that, as I now know, is played by the weakness of vanity.

All this my wife has been trying to force me to see for some time but although it was intellectually apparent to me it has only just become a clear, staring emotional fact that I am exhausting all my energies on a piddling, unreal sort of life, all very decent and not without its value but not what I want. So I am working like the devil to discharge all my obligations seriatim by early in the summer and am refusing to take on anything now. I'd better not speak of when you may expect the new book; I'll say only that my determination is in the grain, very deep.

I've written to you personally because I know of your genuine interest; I feel that you should have a full account of the situation and that can only be explained in a quite personal way.

The novel here, for all that I've said about the American as against the English reception, still has, I'm told, a sale, not large but fairly steady, which is of course unusual here with a novel. And there can be no doubt that it has established itself in people's minds, almost as part of their myth of life today. This is naturally very gratifying.

The son,[1] who is now incredibly past eight months, flourishes finely, what with four teeth, a huge appetite, a passion for adventure, great gaiety, and a large interest in people, especially if they are female and pretty. He's been a constant delight to us. My wife is well and, as you have seen, working, but under a good deal of pressure; she has a

---

1. James Trilling, only child of Lionel and Diana Trilling, born 1948.

good nurse for the boy but naturally doesn't want to surrender all his care and of course couldn't even if she would. We are working toward a fairly practicable way of life, though your knowledge of New York will tell you that that isn't easy.

My wife particularly asks me to send her warm greetings to you with mine. We often speak of you with great pleasure.

Sincerely,

99. TO PASCAL COVICI[1]

August 8, 1949
Rayfield, Westport

Dear Pat:

In anything that is written about the book of essays,[2] the following things should figure.

That these essays, although essays chiefly in literature, all point beyond literature, to what we call life itself. Which is not to say that the author believes that literature "teaches" in any simple way, but that inevitably literary tastes and choices have their bearing on life. To paraphrase Péguy's phrase, which I shall perhaps use in the introduction, what begins in the emotions and assumptions of literature issues eventually in politics.

That these essays are written with politics (in the large sense of the word) in mind. A dominant theme in them is that of liberalism. The author, a liberal, conceives it to be the function of the liberal critic to bring into question the assumptions and beliefs of liberalism. If they are not brought into question they become mere comfortable pieties, and liberalism thus loses its power of growth, of meeting new situations; it is thus the more easily attacked. The questioning of liberalism may be thought of as the *unifying* theme of the volume.

That the essays are notable for their variety and catholicity of interest—i.e., subjects from several periods of literature, from history, sociology, and psychoanalysis.

---

1. Pascal "Pat" Covici (1885–1964), Trilling's editor at Viking Press.
2. *The Liberal Imagination* was published by Viking in 1950.

That the essays have appeared over a period of ten years but have all been revised for this volume.

That they are intended for the general reader, not for the literary student alone.

That the author thinks the prose is quite good.

This is, I would think, enough for catalog copy.

I leave it to you to decide whether my critical connections should figure in the catalog piece: Member Advisory Board, *Partisan Review*; Advisory Editor, *Kenyon Review*; Senior Fellow, Kenyon School of English.

Hastily,
Lionel

100. TO JOHN CROWE RANSOM

August 23, 1949
Rayfield, Westport

Dear John:

[...]

And now to the matter of my participation in the School next summer. You will recall that when I wrote to you and Charles in May, I said, although it pained me to say it, that my inability to come this summer must not be construed as implying that I would surely come the summer after. And now I had better say in all definiteness and as early as possible that I cannot come. In 1947 the reason for my inability to be on the ground was an obvious one; and this year my decision was forced by other family matters which didn't, of course, have anything to do with a hesitation to expose the household to the rigors of the Ohio frontier. But during the latter part of this year, and increasingly through the summer, although I have much regretted that I could not be at Kenyon, I have had the growing sense that the decision that was forced upon me was, as some forced decisions are, a fortunate one. I have had to see that I must not mortgage any of my summers to teaching, even to Kenyon School teaching. I shall tell you why I feel that, counting on your friendly sympathy to see the intense cogency of the reasons to me personally, even if you, in your administrative capacity, in your role as the essential creative spirit of the School, feel hostile to them.

For some time now I have been trying to deal with a sizable desperation about my way of life. This had two elements, a sort of bewildered fatigue of mind and spirit and a panicky awareness that I was not getting done the work I had cut out for myself to do. I saw that as I grew older and more established in reputation I was having not more time for my own thought and work but less. It seemed to me that the demands upon me were increasing in amount and intensifying in quality—not only time but nervous and spiritual energy were being taken up by duties that yielded no return. The university made greater demands of me, and of a new sort; and in addition there was literary business of all kinds, most of it fruitless, and then groups, committees, consultations, conferences, calls to help and advise people—I needn't go into the details of the necessities of politeness, friendship, and quasi-public duty which you will know well enough as one of the aspects of our present literary culture. I suppose there are any number of people who can manage this sort of life; and I suppose there are some few people who can manage this sort of life and still be themselves and produce at the top of their bent, but I'm not one of them. I need time and quiet if I'm to get anything done in writing.

Last year the sense of the impossible situation I was getting into began to break upon me, and this year it grew into realization. For a while I thought that my living in New York, together with the particular sort of place I had at Columbia, made up the circumstances chiefly accountable for the rat race. I therefore seriously considered accepting an advantageous academic offer which came to me, thinking that away from the city I would be immune to most of the involvements which one can be drawn into if one is accessible to the demands of a metropolitan literary center; thinking, too, that in a new university, and one where the intellectual life is not so intense and crowded as it is at Columbia, I might make new terms for my teaching, for although I still like some kinds of teaching, I find that the demands made by graduate students with strong professional aims, and the publicness and intellectual competitiveness of graduate teaching, are terribly wearing and not any longer attractive to me. But eventually I decided against making any academic change and undertook to revise and reform from within—for I saw that, although some of the duties of a mature and established life are unavoidable and should not be avoided, there is a form of vanity that accepts more duties than are essential; I also saw that there is a form of cowardice that accepts duties which, exactly because the discharge of them has the aspect of virtue, permit one to escape from other duties which are more difficult to discharge exactly because they are more necessary to one's own life. I had, that is, to see that my busyness was a very good way of avoiding my job of writing, which, I suppose in the degree that it draws me, frightens me and makes me want to dodge it.

And seeing this, I undertook to correct it. On the basis of an offer that had been made to me I was able to talk to the Columbia people about my situation in the university; I had no need to conduct my discussions in terms of rank and I decided not to conduct them in terms of salary—what we talked about was more freedom for my own writing. The administration was most understanding and cooperative, and, beginning next year, my situation will be much improved in point of the amount and kind of work I shall have to do. And in addition to this I have withdrawn from several groups that took my time and attention and have given notice of my intended withdrawal from others. I have pushed to completion all the little odd jobs I had promised to do and have refused to accept anything new and shall continue to do so unless the offer precisely fits my interest of the moment.

The result of this is that for the first time I am beginning to think about my own work with the relaxed concentration it needs. My free summer in the country, the first in a long time, has been a great delight to me and I have worked very well. I have so many plans that I cannot hope to fulfill them for a good many years, but at least I can now think about them without panic and a sense of distracted fatigue.

All this being so, you will understand why I do not want to give up a summer to teaching. I spent this summer preparing a volume of critical essays for publication this fall or winter and my next book is to be a new novel; I hope to have it drafted by the end of the academic year and will need next summer to put it into its final shape— if, of course, I am lucky. Were I planning to write a critical book on a subject that might suit the plans of the Kenyon School it might be possible to think of a course next year as possible and even as an advantage. But my plan being what it is, for me to give a course next year would be fatal to it; for it would mean not only that I would have to sacrifice the summer but also that I would have to give up the spring before, for I should need to conceive a proper subject and devote my attention to its preparation. For me to come to Kenyon next summer means, then, nothing less than that I decide not to write a novel. In the present state of my feeling this is an impossible decision for me to make.

Through all this long explanation of why I cannot come I haven't, you may be sure, lost sight of my having committed myself to coming for one summer of the School's first three—that, indeed, is why the explanation is so long. But I am at the unhappy point where I must weight commitments to choose among them, having involved myself in the immorality of having made too many. There is the commitment to my publisher for several books, now much overdue. There is the implied but strong commitment to Columbia, where certain real sacrifices have been made in order to give me more time for writing—I feel that I should compromise myself were I to, in effect, make use of that time to teach elsewhere. But these commitments are of secondary importance to the one which I feel to my work. It is this that makes the decision for me; and for its sake I am willing to bear the uneasy, the guilty, feeling of going back on my commitment to the school.

You—and Charles too—have been most flattering in making the success of this or that year of the School depend on my being on the ground as one of the teachers. But this is a responsibility which, however gratifying it is that you should conceive it, I can't accept. It doesn't, you'll agree, fit the facts—the success of the School in the past two sessions shows that; the School can't be thought of as depending for its being a going concern on any one man, and if it could, we'd of course better abandon it.

Together with my unhappy feeling at not being able to redeem my promise to the school there goes my unhappiness at your personal disappointment, the latter being much the stronger of the two. This I want to know about, even though there isn't anything I can add to the information. One of the hardest things for me to realize in the revision of my life that I have undertaken is that I must say no to very dear friends whose enterprises I respect and admire; nothing is harder for me to do, and it is literally true that to say no to you is the very hardest of all. I wish I could make you know exactly how hard it is, for then you would understand the force of the imperative that requires it, and you would forgive me the more easily.

There remains to discuss the question of my relation to the School which is raised by my not having participated in any of the three trial years of the School. I think we may have, in our conversations, exaggerated the significance that will be attached to that either by the public or the foundation. Nevertheless, it is a matter that we must consider and settle. Our statement says that one of the three Senior Fellows will be in attendance at each of the sessions and one of the three will not have been. This, rather than any implication of my particular absence, is what we should deal with. But if you do think that my particular absence does carry any bad implication, we can discuss some way of meeting that. The impulse which at first I had when I wrote you in May, to rationalize my inability to carry out my commitment by resigning as Senior Fellow, is obviously not a sound one at all; the very reverse. But we can discuss all this when we meet, which I hope will be soon and which I trust will be, despite my defection, with as much friendly warmth on your part as ever before. Meanwhile I send you my most affectionate greetings and all my good wishes for a restful and happy almost sabbatical.

Always yours,

101. TO DAVID RIESMAN[1]

August 24, 1949
Rayfield, Westport

Dear David,

I've been meaning to write to you for quite a while now, but I spend most of the day at the typewriter and by the time evening comes another séance with it seems beyond possibility. So I've decided to risk illegibility rather than have you wait any longer for word from me about your book.[2]—Well then, I think it's a magnificent book. Nothing I've read in a long time has given me so much pleasure and

---

1. David Riesman (1909–2002), sociologist and cultural critic.
2. *The Lonely Crowd* (1950), which Trilling read in advance of publication.

excitement. My mind goes back, of course, to Tocqueville and you know my extreme admiration of him. The genre is to me new—and I daresay it will be to anyone else, for I can't suppose that sociology usually produces anything of similar kind—but it is absolutely central. I felt all the time I was reading that I was getting now what I used to get or think I was getting from novels, but no novel in years has told me so much as you have—certainly none has turned me back on myself to make me ask what goes on inside. And for all my elaborate defense of the possibility of the novel going on, I begin to think that the novel perhaps can't do it anymore. Between the first and second consignments of your book I read John O'Hara's new novel. I have a good deal of admiration for O'H. and especially for his grasp of social fact. And in the new job he is at great pains to display this grasp in masses of detail. But it has, eventually, no savor of meaning at all, in part because he is working under compulsive necessity to accumulate and exhibit, in part because he, for some internal reason—or perhaps only because he is writing about the past, not his forte— can't connect fact with character—but certainly in part because in my reading of his book your book acted as a question mark.—Of course what contributes to my intensity of response is my sense that you have said outright and at length what in effect I have been fumbling toward in almost all my critical work for some ten years. Lately I have fallen into the trick of saying to people that I was just a nineteenth-century character and couldn't be expected to understand sympathetically what was happening in contemporary high and popular culture, and now I can see that my dull egoistic joke is the truth and that my sniping at the modern character was an attack on other-direction made in the name of the last vestiges of inner direction. I've been revising my essays this summer for a selection to come out soon, and this is surely the gist and burden of them—it is what I have intended by what I've thought of as my attack on liberalism. And it will interest you that in revising an old essay on Fitzgerald this summer, I glossed Fitzgerald's use of the word "aristocracy," by which he meant distinction, responsibility, and heroism, and added this sentence: "He was perhaps the last notable writer to affirm the Romantic fantasy, descended from the Renaissance, of personal ambition and heroism, of life committed to, or thrown away for, some ideal of life. To us it will no doubt come more and more to seem a merely boyish dream; the nature of our society requires the young man to find his distinction through cooperation, subordination, and an expressed piety of social usefulness, and although a few young men have made Fitzgerald into a hero of art, it is likely that even to these admirers the whole nature of his personal fantasy is not comprehensible, for young men find it harder and harder to understand the young heroes of Balzac and Stendhal, they increasingly find reason to blame the boy whose generosity is bound up with his will and finds expression in a large, strict, personal demand upon life."—And the novel that I began some time ago and expect to return to—hoped to begin it again this summer, but the essays take longer than I thought—has for its theme the tragedy of a young man who is the last survivor of the old culture. To this your book is of great help, for I have fussed with the theme and niggled at it and doubted it, supposing it to be personal only, even idiosyncratic, wondering just what largeness and point it had, if any: but you've been able to underwrite its validity for me.—Incidentally, a chapter from an early draft of this novel, done some four or five years ago, appears in the (I think) August *Horizon*; it was published some years back in *Harper's Bazaar* but no one saw it there. I mention it because I think you'll find it relevant to things you say about ideas of work and production. It's called "The Lesson and the Secret"—the idea being the contemporary belief that someone holds, and withholds, the secret that can be imparted for the acquisition of every prestige.

Well, I've done not much more than talk about myself in relation to the book—but what could better tell you about the largeness of my response to what you've done? If I've time at all before you're ready for publication I'd like to read it again to raise questions—this time I read it through at great speed, for the "plot," partly because I more and more thought that was the best way to read it, partly because I have been rather pressed for time, and also for that part of my attention which is exact and editorial. In general, I think the writing is excellent, it being my impression that it gets better as it goes on. I was of course on the lookout for sociological language—I came upon the reprobated (in *PR*) "insightful" but not much else. Still I cannot be sure that this is a correct judgment—I may possibly have surrendered early. [. . .]

But here I am petering out into snippets of observation and what I want to convey now is my general delight and my sense that the book is magnificent. How you've trained yourself to see and conclude! And now my sense of the importance and relevance of the book makes me go back to its manner, to urge you to make it as untechnical and available to the general public as possible.

[. . .]

Yours,

Lionel

102. TO PASCAL COVICI

January 28, 1950

Dear Pat,

Since we talked on Friday I have been thinking about the business of soliciting opinions from critical colleagues and I am writing to tell you that I believe it to be a bad idea.

I don't want to mix into the process of publishing, which of course you understand so much better than I possibly can. You will make your own decision in the matter, with, I know, the best interests of the book in mind. And I am enclosing the list of names I undertook to make for you—use it or not as you see fit. But I should like to give you my reasons against the tactic, which I hope you will consider seriously.

These reasons are only in part personal. I do admit that I don't like solicitations for nice opinions about my work, particularly among people with whom I have professional relations with the usual personal involvements, some close, some formal. It embarrasses me in itself. It embarrasses me the more because I've made something of a principle of not giving prepublication opinions that are solicited of me. And it embarrasses me still more because it is my impression that the business of solicitation isn't usually practiced in the case of the books of critics of standing equivalent to mine. Delicacy has something to do with this, but I believe there is also a practical reason for it. When you publish a volume of critical essays, you aren't quite publishing a book in the ordinary sense, you're in a way presenting a person. To go about asking for confirmation of that person by other persons who aren't any better known or of greater authority than the one you are presenting suggests that your person is in need of confirmation. Certainly this would be true if the person were really preeminent—that is, it would lower and not raise T. S. Eliot's prestige if a lot of other critics were to be got to say that his work is important. And this suggests the fiction that with a book like mine I think it would be wise to employ. I think that what is needed is a firm representation by the publishers themselves which would have the effect of dispensing with the need of accumulating the usual confirming opinions—to create the effect of being above such devices! Of course opinions drawn from reviews or other published comments are something else again.

Do think carefully and with an open mind about this. If you don't find my argument valid and decide to go ahead, please remember that you will be dealing with people who make a profession of measured language and will have all sorts of complicated differences with me and reservations about me, even if they respect my work and like me personally. They won't like being put on the spot, they may even be irritated by it. All this may show in their replies if they make any at all. You may get no enthusiasm whatever. Please don't use any opinions that aren't really firm—I'm still haunted by the advertising use that was made of Kip Fadiman's line about my novel which in effect said that my grammar is good.

Another point: I am making up a list of first-line people and another list of second-line people. The second-line people, for one reason or another, may be more responsive and enthusiastic than the first. It would be very bad if they were in the majority, worse if the quotations were confined to them. This is very important—would you please make it clear to whoever it is who is handling the business? You will be away while it is being worked out; it might be good if you left word that I be consulted if any question arises.

Let me know if you still like the idea of Rebecca West for the *Times* reviewer. If you do, I'll get in touch with Harvey Breit immediately.

Yours,

Lionel

103. TO ALLEN GINSBERG

April 26, 1950
Columbia University

Dear Allen:

It was very good to hear from you and very good to meet you in the subway. If we hadn't met I should have answered your long letter before this, but it seemed to me that we had covered in talking most of the things you had written about with, of course, the exception of the poems. I've read the poems now several times, and I don't quite know what to say about them. I like them. I like their delicacy and their quiet. At the same time, I feel in them a certain lack of force and of dramatic realization. I'm not perfectly sure of this; I should want to read them more times than I have to be sure. But this is my present impression of them; and if it has any accuracy at all, I can understand some of the reasons for the present appearance of the quality I've spoken of—it doesn't seem to me at all a bad sign in development. Of course, it isn't very fruitful in any case to try to deal with poems in writing. Perhaps some time before I close up for the summer, we'll have an opportunity to talk about them. I'd keep them by me for rereading, could I think it possible that in the present rush of dissertations I shall be able to read anything except dissertations: I'd better return them to you for safekeeping.

I do hope that everything goes well with you. Let me know that it does.

Sincerely,
Lionel Trilling

104. TO JACQUES BARZUN

July 11, 1950
Greens Farms

Dear Jacques,

A long silence—forgive it. In the summers, lately, at the beginning, I seem to go into trance, which would be quite all right, I even enjoy it, if it weren't that I always have at that time something to deliver. I try to advance the Keats, now a year overdue, and it moves very slowly, with a sort of ventriloquistic tone. I feel at this point of the year as if I could live forever as a vegetable and I should consider this a perfectly virtuous condition of life if I hadn't met the other academics who in the summer consider vegetation a virtuous inactivity.— I've read a little: Wells, who is around the house, who is in a way the culture of this house, and was much moved by *The Research Magnificent*, which I hadn't ever read before—moved, that is, not by the book itself, but by our history, by our good fortune in having been brought up under that aegis, which we can see the holes in but which is so much better, as aegises go, than any now available to cover the young. How good to have had that sense of personal culture together with the belief that power could be had and the world controlled. Also some Shaw, of whom I was given some of that fine Standard Ed. for my birthday. What prose and what a range! And what a wonderful amenity and benignity! I must find out just when it is that I feel I must turn against him and then admire him enormously up to that point. As a critic he is splendid—very wrong, often unconsidered, but *doing* right all the time. Have you read the essay on Poe in the *Pen Portraits and Reviews*? Very fine.

[. . .]

The Hudson Review carries on its cover the announcement of "L.T. and the New Stoicism"—interesting idea; it turns out not to be an article but a review, remarkably accurate representation, and very *amère*, ending on the religious note. Also *Sewanee* brings out O'Connor's piece, which is well-intentioned but makes me a very dull type. However it helps lay the ground for "L.T., a Reappraisal," "Re-thinking L.T.," and "The Secret Message and Inner Meaning of L.T.," not to mention "T. as Healer."—You're right about Commager[1]— all wrong but quite right in some funny way (i.e., Commager). I liked very much his first chapter—I really think life was like that: it *meant* to be like that when I was a boy, and I find it a pity we've lost even the outward shows.—I've never thanked you for the Moravia. I like him, and though the stories don't quite come off, the second fulfills itself better than the first. I'd pay $157 spot cash to have the original

---

1. Henry Steele Commager (1902–1998), historian. The book discussed here is probably *The American Mind: An Interpretation of American Thought and Character Since the 1880s* (1950).

use of the idea of that gang in the given situation in the first. How much *power* the cultivated thoughtful fiction writer must muster nowadays. The instrument is too big for any but the biggest charge and if he's to get anywhere at all he ought to burst the gun.—Yourself I haven't yet read, haven't the brains. What views do the publishers give you of yourself? Have you yet become the thrall of the French edition?—Di has got over her stomach business, a germ which could eat only farina upon the arrival of our excellent cook. She was quite worn down by it for ten days, but is now cheerful again.—She, i.e., Di, who is filled with pleasurable excitement over the prospect of writing the *Life* piece, and I am full of gratitude at your kindness in helping her become the breadwinner of the family, for I am convinced— determined?—that I shall never again do a useful or profitable day's work or turn another penny—so lazy he wouldn't turn a penny when it was done on one side.—I'm sorry we didn't jibe about your visit here for July—August will surely be more fortunate.

Yours always,
Lionel

105. TO ALLEN GINSBERG

October 20, 1950
Columbia University

Dear Allen:

I'm really terribly sorry that you can't make it on Monday, for I had been looking forward to seeing you. Evenings are never good for me but I know that I can arrange to have lunch with you some Saturday.

The news about the progress of your therapy is really very good and I do hope that it can go on to the new stage you project. The chances are that you will get great benefit from that. I don't know how to respond to your new job—I can't imagine that work in a ribbon factory can be very inspiriting, but there is something fortifying about a considerable pay envelope, especially if some of it is banked for productive leisure in the future.

I won't try to respond to your interesting struggles with the theory of verse. I've been reading Williams lately and have a growing sense of what he is up to. I think I like what he is up to, although sometimes I am wearied and depressed by what he writes, as I was wearied and depressed when I met him last spring, although at the same time I was rather taken by him. Did I ever confess to you that my relation to modern verse is very largely academic and dutiful?—it seldom means as much to me as prose.

Sincerely,

Lionel Trilling

106. TO NORMAN PODHORETZ[1]

May 8, 1951

Dear Norman:

I've been much too long in your debt for a very good letter, a note, and half a postcard. Please forgive me—you'll perhaps have guessed that my life has been more than usually crowded during this past year. When, for a moment, I step out of the university routine, I can't understand just what it is that so consumes and distracts me; and indeed even when I am in it I scarcely know what devours the time and energy—I suppose some sort of self-flattery makes me suppose that my time can only be eaten by large and important beasts and that the smaller ones have no taste or jaws for it. The Graduate School situation has been worse this year than it ever was, to the point where it has become a matter for protest. Perhaps something will be done about it in an official way, but whether or not, I have done something about my own involvement by arranging to put my center back in the college with only one lecture course for graduate students, and no direction of dissertations. The whole of this program won't go into effect until the year after next but I can already feel its good effects, and I look forward to still better ones.

All this will suggest to you that nothing less than the totality of The Modern Situation, the whole of Democratic Culture, has kept me from writing to you as, indeed, it has kept me from writing anything: the year has given me the chance to turn out only one thing, a lecture I gave at Harvard, but no chance to revise it for publication.

---

1. Norman Podhoretz (1930–), a student of Trilling's at Columbia, would become a leading intellectual and longtime editor of *Commentary*.

So many months have gone by since you wrote that I shan't try to "answer" your letter (except to say that in several ways it gave me great pleasure), for by now you and your England and your Cambridge are surely very different from what they were at the beginning and you will not want to be held to your first valuations, happy as they seem to have been. You must write me again to tell me all that has been happening, how your work goes, whom you have met and whom you are working with, and what the gossip is. I will count on you for details of the spiritual life at Cambridge and next year I'll ask specific practical questions, for the English Faculty, which asked me to come over on a Fulbright arrangement for 1951–1952, has very kindly repeated its invitation for 1952–1953, and I think of trying to come, either *en famille* for the year or alone for a shorter time.

But although I shan't reply to your first letter, I do want to reply to your second, that very generous note in which you spoke of the Arnold and postscriptively of your reconsidered feeling about my prose style. I had thought a good deal about your objections after your review appeared,[1] and had I responded to your note at once, I should have said that I was glad you had come around, that upon consideration I had decided that the style was right and your expressed objections of last year wrong. This response would have been part of my involvement with what I have come to feel is the sadomasochistic complex of modern literature which I touched on in the Wordsworth essay of last year and which interests me more and more. What I would have said then about my prose is that there is need for a tone of reasonableness and demonstration, that it was of the greatest importance that we learn to consider that the tone of civil life has its necessity and may even have its "heroic" quality, that we must have a modification of all that is implied by the fierce postures of modern literature. I still think this and I am of course still glad that you have come to feel differently about my prose tone, but with the arrival the last few days of some of the English reviews of my book, I have come to feel that my tone isn't what I had thought it or meant it to be. I have always supposed it had more intensity, irony, and acerbity than the English have been finding in it, and several remarks about its

_____

1. Podhoretz's review of *The Liberal Imagination* in *Scrutiny* (June 1951).

"gentleness" have disturbed me, for I don't think I am gentle in my intellectual judgments, and don't want to be. Possibly the British response is to my willingness to forgive the writer while condemning the idea, but I must also suppose that it is to the style itself—that something is there that I did not mean to be there, or something not there that I meant to be. What I am saying, in short, is that your first judgment now seems to me to have more rightness than I once felt or you now feel. The trouble may be almost only a technical device. Whatever it is, it must be seen to.

Are you still working with Leavis?[1] If you are, find a moment to tell him from me that I now for the first time understand his long pedagogic rage, now that I have been really involved in graduate teaching. (You'll have to explain to him, if you haven't already done so, the difference between Columbia College and the Graduate School.) I now know how angry a man can get at an educational situation, and if I had two lives, I might give one of them, or half of one, to doing something here by way of opposition. I enormously respect Leavis for his frontal attack, but I have decided, failing the second life, not to make it myself. It isn't only that I want to do other things, nor that I dread what doing this would mean (and it would be awful!), but that the whole thing would in the present circumstance be utterly useless. The alternative to the older methods—which don't have here what Leavis has been fighting in England, gentility and snobbery— is understood by faculty and students alike to be "criticism," and I am as much disillusioned by criticism as an academic discipline as I am by scholarship. Nowadays even the scholars here will respect "criticism" and, not knowing what it is, they will accept the pretentious and foolish as what criticism ought to be. And the students who despise scholarship and want to "be critics" or "do their work in criticism," and for my sins attach themselves to me, have very nice sweet minds, but no intellects, no learning, and no knowledge of the issues—their work becomes, almost at best, a display of will, a snatch at status. I've come almost to feel that democratic education ought to declare a moratorium on literature as an academic study. It seems to me that it is no longer an *innocent* study. Perhaps things are still a little better in England than here, perhaps better at other universi-

---

1. F. R. Leavis (1895–1978), combative English literary critic and editor of *Scrutiny*.

ties than here, but we have twelve hundred students in the Department of English of the Graduate Faculties and with that number anything goes—and it's coming to be felt that it's "democratic" and "liberal" to let it go. The College is still ever so much better—from my own private view it is decidedly better because with undergraduates I don't have to produce professional opinions, and then feel that they are subtly modified by my audience, nor that I am being misunderstood and systematized—but the College needs questioning too. I've just, in the midst of writing this, reread your letter, and I find that my heart goes out to the taboo on intellectual talk, to the proscription of literary enthusiasm, at Cambridge. Here it makes for something very bad among the more gifted undergraduates, and only last week I found myself writing to one of your classmates that I could wish we might make games or social finesse competitors with being *bright* as a means of acquiring status. If you are free from the compulsion to acquire that thin admiration that is given to our more articulate A men, then you are fortunate and free. Go punt, go develop a taste in sherry, go wear fine neck cloths, go play football, go bind your books in levant—go do anything that will remind you that man wasn't born to analyze texts or have right opinions, anything to remind you that man was born to be private—that you owe it to the public to be private (this is serious). I intend that this shall be the last word on education I shall ever utter.

Do let me hear about you and about all the surely fine things you've seen, done, and had happen to you.

Give my greetings to Leavis, to Basil Willey, if you ever see him, to Bewley, and to Stanley Mellon.

Yours,

107. TO NORMAN PODHORETZ

November 15, 1951

Dear Norman:

I have had you terribly on my conscience for much too long. I hope you can forgive me—I can't quite forgive myself, for I know how much the *Scrutiny* piece meant to you, and how much my opinion of it also meant, and I should have written to you months ago. That I didn't do so you must understand as being wholly subjective and as having nothing to do with you or the review. You must conceive the much too long delay as being only the result of a skittishness which I had been feeling about the public image of myself. It isn't, as public images go, very large, but for its size it made a considerable amount of quiet trouble for me back in the spring and summer. I found myself shying whenever I saw my name in print, not out of any mere abstract feeling about publicity, but with something like a response to sympathetic magic, or what they tell us some paranoiacs feel about an "influencing machine"—they believe that there is a machine, apparently a representation of a part of their own psyches, which can be manipulated by enemies in such a way as to control their activities. I forget what the explanation of this is, but it's connected with their depersonalization and the split in their personalities. And as the English reviews came in, I found myself in something like their situation. It didn't matter that most of the reviews were very pleasant in their intention. They were all sufficiently off center to be disturbing, to set up an image which wasn't mine and which, I felt, might claim me. With the result that when your review arrived, I could read it only with half an eye and with something less than half a mind. I tried to concentrate on it simply in order to be able to write you, but it was no-go, and my procrastination went on from month to month.

Well, all this nonsense seems to be finished now. I've read the piece with equanimity and care, and it's very fine indeed. Back in the time when I read it with half an eye and half a mind, I had the feeling that perhaps your first piece on the book, for the *Columbia Review*, was in some ways better, considered just as a piece of critical writing—that is, rather more pungent and dialectical. But that isn't the opinion I now have. Naturally, any opinion of mine is in this instance a special one, although you will want it for that very reason; and I can tell you that your way of conceiving the book and presenting it is one of the ways that it gives me pleasure to have it conceived and presented in, and as close to my own way as it could be. These compliments from the *subject* aren't, quite apart from personal feeling, wholly to be dismissed. And then, abstracting myself from the piece as much as I am able, I can see with what relaxation and ease you've learned to move in criticism, yet with no abatement of your characteristic eagerness. This is very fine. [. . .] You've made a really handsome debut, and I, with all my foolish skittishness quite gone, am very struck and pleased that you've made it with me as a subject. In addition, I feel very grateful to you for having put me forth in this very pleasing and reassuring way to the *Scrutiny* audience. In a practical way, you've done me a very material service.

What little I've heard of you—from Mellon—has been most pleasant and gratifying, but I'd like to hear more. Do send me news of yourself.

The year, which suddenly seems to be moving with an intolerable rapidity, promises to be a good one for me. My anticipated withdrawal from the Graduate School next year has already had excellent effects; my load of work has already materially lightened and I feel freer than I have for a long time. I think one reason for this is that I've already shaken off the contentious incubus of American literature and my new course in Wordsworth and Keats has led me to enjoy teaching again. I find myself constantly delighted with all the new things I've found to say about Wordsworth, often extemporaneously and off the top of my head. Someday I must try to find out the deep reasons for my opposite responses to the two subjects, or the two kinds of teaching, one of which seems so grim and tense, the other so light and even gay. The result is that I'm beginning to write again and in a way I rather like.

Give Leavis my greetings when you see him next. And John Rosenberg too.

And do forgive me my almost unforgivable delay in writing.

Sincerely,
Lionel Trilling

108. TO JOHN GAUS

November 26, 1951

Dear Mr. Gaus:

It was very kind of you to write me so pleasantly about my article in *The Reporter*.[1] I'm truly most gratified by your response, and most grateful to you for telling me of it.

I wish I knew what the relation is between the social feelings of

---

1. "Dreiser, Anderson, Lewis, and the Riddle of Society," *The Reporter*, November 13, 1951.

our classic writers and the social feelings of our people. It may be, as you say, that the writers are in this respect out of tune with the people; in that case we are presented with the old problem of "alienation," which, of course, is as much a problem for the people as it is for the writers. I am inclined to think that the a-sociality of the writers is a reflection of something in the people. To be sure, I haven't ever lived in a close and relatively simple community where there is some necessity of social action; urban and suburban and predominantly intellectual communities can't be very typical cases in point. Yet it seems to me that even such communities tell us something, and I get from them a sense—to me sometimes very distressing—of a virtual revulsion from human contact, except of the most formal kind. There is certainly a feeling for some older and more organic form of social life, but as an idyll, and it doesn't in the least lead to such beginnings of true social life—that is, ordinary, easy neighborliness—as are actually possible. I hope your impression is the right one, for mine is so very grim. And what I found in our literature has made me so unhappy in an almost visceral sense that I've had to take a long and perhaps permanent vacation from teaching it!

Again, thank you for your very kind letter.

Sincerely yours,

Lionel Trilling

109. TO NORMAN PODHORETZ

December 3, 1951

Dear Norman:

The pleasure of your letter made me gladder than ever for that day twenty years ago when I picked the basket off the doorstep and found you inside, smiling brightly and ready to explicate the symbolic meaning of the gold sovereigns you clenched in one fist and the coronet that marked your fine linen. How well do I remember your first words— "Not in entire nakedness but trailing clouds of glory do I come from God who is my home." It was necessary, of course, to have you translated, for you then spoke only Hebrew, which was only natural, considering the source you claimed for yourself. Since that time you have never given me a day of trouble. Of how many sons can that be said?

By now you will surely have had my letter which crossed yours. Yet I have some misgivings from the date you used that mine may have gone astray. Let me know if it hasn't reached you—I think I have a carbon.

I don't know Oakeshott,[1] although I want to and have meant to and Eugenio has been after me to. I seem to remember that Eugenio approached *PR* with something *by* Oakeshott and they weren't interested. I'm inclined to think that he's not their sort of man, but I may be wrong. Would be a good thing to do the piece anyway. Perhaps *The American Scholar* would be interested—a good chance it would. Meanwhile tell me more about him.

Very good news about the Synge essay. I've also heard tell of a piece you did on Lawrence to be published. True or garbled?

Admirable idea you should write on Burke for your dissertation. I don't supervise dissertations anymore—I'm going on with my old ones, but I don't take on any new ones and it's pure bliss. But this mustn't stand in your way. Since you won't be ready to choose a subject officially for some time to come, or a director, it may be that I shall then have established my blessed rule of abstinence and can dare to make you an exception. This is not a promise, and you must speak of it to (literally) no one.

I've put your name in at Harvard again for a Junior Fellowship. Chances seem small, but it's worth trying. Have you no claim on the Fulbright—I mean to stay at Cambridge for a doctorate? You've probably heard from Andrew Chiappe that there's little hope for an appointment here in September, although of course we shall keep you in mind.

Delighted with your impressions of Israel. My prophetic soul has long told me as much. We're a damned people, always were. I've ventured to send a copy of your report to Elliot Cohen of *Commentary* thinking he might want an article from you and that you might want to do one. Quite apart from an Israel piece, this would be a good connection for you.

[. . .]

Let me hear from you—your letters are a great satisfaction.

Yours,

---

1. Michael Oakeshott (1901–1990), English philosopher.

110. TO MRS. R. A. HOLZHAUER

December 18, 1951

Dear Mrs. Holzhauer:

So far as I'm entitled to have any opinion at all on the subject, it seems to me that in all respects you're on the right track. "The Other Margaret"[1] is surely the story of Margaret's father rather than of Margaret herself. This, I know, was my conscious intention, and indeed I can't see how the story can be read in any other way. The pathos of the father is much greater than that of the daughter—not only does he suffer for his daughter as well as for himself, but his experience is involved in much larger things than his daughter's is or can be: the awareness of death, for example.

As for the "unessential" elements of this story and the other, there are two things to be said. One is that I don't think they *are* unessential— they are needed for tone and even for idea, the last especially in "The Other Margaret," which is, if anything, too *systematic* a story, too carefully thought out: everything that happens serves as admissible evidence. Also—and this probably refers to "tone"—I think that size and leisure are needed to give authority and weight to the stories. This leads to the other consideration, which is my feeling, perhaps idiosyncratic, although I do not think so, that "economy" is not a virtue and may even be a vice. I don't like stories in which nothing is included except what brings us to the point. Such stories seem to me airless and eventually mechanical. They don't bear rereading and eventually they come to seem to me claustral and depressing. In this regard, you'll be interested to know that "The Other Margaret" began by being much shorter and more "economical"—it was to have begun at the point where Margaret fetches her father a drink. But I found myself being restive in this "tight" conception and loosened it up. I wanted room to move around in, and I wanted room for the reader to move around in—I hate the idea of processing the reader to a conclusion. (This can go too far—*The Middle of the Journey* began as a longish short story, at most a *nouvelle!*)

As for awkwardness of style, that of course is a most delicate matter for the writer himself to speak of. I'm not actually aware that

---

1. Trilling's story "The Other Margaret" first appeared in *Partisan Review* (Fall 1945).

the style is awkward, but I don't think I'd mind if I discovered that it is. Awkwardness is probably a fault, but I should say that it is less a fault than a manifest gracefulness, or a manifest lyricism, or an easy neutrality. I like, in novelists, a certain roughness of texture—and even, I confess, a certain indifference to prose style. I could go on at length about this, but I mustn't. I don't think that the preference is a rationalization by way of defense of my own errors.

Your own involvement with my stories and your friends' resistance to them seems to me perfectly natural. I'm aware of a conscious intention in the few fictions I've written—it's a critical intention, very likely too much so for the soul of what I've done, a "cultural" intention, which is to raise questions about certain ways of feeling and thinking of our liberal, educated, middle class; I've never doubted that this would mean irritating them.

Your letter was interesting and gave me great pleasure. You can imagine that I'll look forward to seeing your essay when it's done.

Sincerely yours,
Lionel Trilling

111. TO WILSON PARKHILL[1]

February 7, 1952

Dear Mr. Parkhill:

I had hoped long before this to thank you for the hospitality of the School and to tell you how much my wife and I enjoyed our visit, but life has been disrupted for me by midyear academic madness, together with the virus of the season running its course through the family. But the School continues to be for us a memorable and even a moving experience about which we still talk. We should especially like you to know the great pleasure we had in your own Latin lesson—the pace, the ease, the communicated enthusiasm made us both wish we could have Latin over again with you as teacher. And the response of the boys showed so clearly how much their training had done for them. Indeed, all the upper grades were splendid in their

---

1. Of the Collegiate School in New York City.

content and in their intellectual and personal tone, exactly the sort of thing we wish for our boy when he is ready for them.

But we did have some questions about the procedure in the earliest grades, all of them having to do with the disciplinary assumption (which, by the way, we didn't find at all in evidence in the upper school). I feel sure you would want me to speak of them since we did have them, and that you'll forgive the inevitable gracelessness of my speaking of them in detail. In the five-year group in particular there were several small incidents that troubled us. While a reading lesson was in progress—and being admirably taught—one of the little boys reached out to toy with a block; he was immediately told that in consequence he might not play with blocks the rest of the morning. Again, one of the youngsters who appeared to have a remarkable endowment of energy, which took, to be sure, the form of bringing himself to the notice of adults, tried to speak some of his ideas to the teacher, whose response was to tell him firmly that she had no time to listen to him. Or again, when the teacher told the children that they were to have a play period, she directed three of them not to play with blocks; this, we understood, was because the three had previously been concentrating on blocks to the exclusion of other activities, but the method of direct prohibition didn't seem the right way to achieve the end in view of getting them to do other things. Then in the six-year-old group which we watched in the gymnasium, two boys began to fight while the class was lined up for tumbling. We thought this could have been handled by separating the two; instead, the teacher sent one to the corner and the other out of the room; the sent-out boy, I must say, seemed very cheerful when we later came on him in the corridor, but the boy in the corner was in tears.

I hope you will not think that in mentioning these incidents, I am taking a stand on the side of infant anarchy. Far from it. It's simply that I don't think such stringency with very small boys is necessary to develop a proper social conformity. I believe that boys ought to have the experience of discipline. The only question is at what age. I think that the chatter of a nine-year-old might well be cut short and that his showing off could be treated drily and even brusquely; with a five-year-old I'd be inclined to move much less directly. I'd be quite strict and even sharp with nine-year-olds who started a battle during gym class, but I think that I'd deal with six-year-olds by separating them and sending them to a different part of the line.

As I speak of these things in isolation they seem to have rather more positiveness and weight than I intend. I confess that I don't quite know how to value them. The questions diminish as the grades advance. And certainly the things we do question don't seem to have had any bad effects as the boys go on. Obviously no dullness in the boys results from the discipline—on the contrary!—and very likely the close unenforced attention of the older boys at all the lessons we saw is connected with their earlier training. So too, probably, is the quiet, self-possessed maturity of their manner, which we found very impressive. In the face of these things our necessary theoretical questions about the lower grades are themselves brought into question.

Perhaps our visits to other schools will help resolve our confusion— Collegiate is still the only school we've seen. We'll let you know, if we may, what happens to our questions in the course of our Wellsian quest. Meanwhile I hope you won't feel that we've violated your generous hospitality by raising them—they don't qualify the great admiration we feel for the School's beautiful seriousness and skillfulness, which were for us a revelation.

Sincerely yours,
Lionel Trilling

112. TO EVELYN KING GILMORE

April 28, 1952

Dear Mrs. Gilmore:

I really can't tell you how much pleasure your splendidly generous letter gave me. If your kind hope for another novel is ever realized, it will be in part your doing. For I think that one of the reasons why I haven't really embarked on a new fiction is that in the reception of the first one no one, or almost no one, saw what you see. It would be fatuous of me to say that the reception of the book wasn't good. It was—in some ways very good. But what people seemed to respond to was what I might call the critical cogency of the book, its general cultural, even political, implications. What I liked about it were the human touches and the humor, for which, in a way, the larger considerations were an excuse. But these were the things that weren't noticed; and their absence was even decried, for the book was frequently called coldly intellectual. But your letter reads the book exactly as I had hoped it would be read, and—I mean this quite literally—it quite revives for me a work that I had come to think was pretty dead. Under your influence I remembered and very much liked things that I had quite forgotten and have been led to think that I'd like to do things like that again. So you see that I have reason to be extremely grateful to you, which I truly am.

Sincerely,

Lionel Trilling

113. TO REBECCA WEST[1]

June 17, 1952

Dear Miss West:

I really haven't wronged you as much as you think, but I have wronged you a little, for which you've repaid me with a very charming letter. I reply to it as late as this because my university work has kept me so busy that I haven't had time until now to look for a copy of your James book—the university library's copy having disappeared—to see how far I actually had wronged you.

You quite mistake the intention of what I say of your book.[2] When I alluded to your "exuberant little study" of James I didn't in the least make the allusion "grimly"—couldn't have done so, because it is a book toward which I have always had the happiest feelings. When I was young it seemed to me the enviable model of the way a young writer should be able and dare to write. And referring to it when I did, when I was so much older and graver than its author, I couldn't possibly have thought of speaking grimly of it, or, indeed, in any way except with a kind of tenderness, which I meant "exuberant little study" to express. I ponder "exuberant" and I can see that perhaps it might be thought a less pleasing adjective than, say, "spirited," which I might have used. Yet exuberant is a nice thing to be at twenty-two,

---

1. Rebecca West (1892–1983), English woman of letters.
2. In Trilling's essay "The Princess Casamassima," in *The Liberal Imagination*.

the book has a lot of brio, I like it for that, and it isn't at all grim of me to observe it.

I wholly wrong you in making you seem to believe that meticulousness is a good quality. My Latin, alas, is of the dimmish New York schools variety, but even if it were Scottish, which I could wish it were, the force of usage might have kept me from ever considering the derivation of the word, for although our dictionaries define it in the sense you meant—but I confess I don't see why, in that sense, you should have applied it to the novel!—still, in actual use with us, it virtually never has the pejorative meaning that Fowler insists on (as I've now discovered). We say "meticulous workmanship" and mean it as praise. And it does seem to me that it is a useful word in that sense, almost as useful as "deprecate" in the wrong sense that everyone uses.

As for the "loyal Fabian" who "could consider it one of the perversities of *The Princess Casamassima* that two of its lower-class characters should say of a third that he had the potentiality of becoming Prime Minister of England," that phrase doesn't, or shouldn't, refer to you at all, but either to some other person I had in mind, whose name got lost in revision, or, more likely, to some suppositious person. For actually you don't refer to Paul Muniment at all. But I confess I don't see how you could suppose that I meant anyone except you, which was careless and clumsy of me.

My having involved you in naturalism follows upon the fun you have with the plot of the story on page 73—my reference to the climate of the naturalistic novel is intended to explain your reference of the book to the tradition of incredible adventure, your seeming to imply that James was being naive, in the face of his sophisticated notions of the novel, in dreaming up an unlikely story. As against that, I wanted only to say, what you say in your letter, that James was dealing with events that at the time everybody would be aware of. The memory of these events was lost to most people between then and the time I wrote, with the result that the nature and intention of the book were misunderstood, and I took your page 73 to be in the denial of the actuality of the circumstances which James was dealing with. And as I read that page again, I must say that I think it's a not unfair inference, although of course your letter shows me that it was mistaken.

I hope I've dispelled the idea that I've expressed anything remotely like the "undisguised contempt" you read in my reference to you. Nothing could be further from possibility, considering the long and great admiration I've had for your work—you are so generous in speaking of your response to my work that I know I can rely on your generosity to take this as a fact and not as a politeness of the occasion. I think I disagree with you on some large matters, as I believed I disagreed with you on this small one, but I can't imagine that the feelings that might ever attend the disagreement could be anything but friendly ones. I hope you believe this. And you can be sure that if my book of essays ever goes into a new edition, I'll not fail to revise the two paragraphs to prevent any possibility of misunderstanding.

Sincerely yours,

114. TO RABBI MAX KADUSHIN[1]

October 6, 1952

Dear Max:

This is a much later response to your book[2] than I had hoped to give you. I read it back at the beginning of August but the summer went faster than it should have, and had more chores than it should have, and ever since our return from the country life has been beating us about the head—lightly, not painfully, but very confusingly—and I have not been able to get anything done when I wanted it done, including this letter.

The first thing I want to say about the book is that I read it with the greatest admiration. I can't judge its scholarship, of course, except by inference, but that is probably an adequate way to judge after all, and I was enormously impressed. The inference I make on the basis of style, which seems to me quite perfect for scholarship. It's a style of complete felicity, the more so because no attention is being paid to felicity, only in getting the thing properly said in the plainest way. There's a striking uncompromisingness in your tone, a sort of

---

1. Max Kadushin (1895–1980), rabbi and scholar, was Trilling's childhood Hebrew teacher.
2. *The Rabbinic Mind* (1952), which helped to inspire Trilling's essay "Wordsworth and the Rabbis," in *The Opposing Self.*

almost military directness and commandingness which quite fasci-
nated me—it seems to me the scholar's tone par excellence, although
one doesn't find it nowadays in scholarly works, or at least not in my
field, but it was pretty common in the nineteenth century. I don't
mean that it is a hard or harsh tone—it certainly is not—but only that
it has a masculine forthrightness which implies the writer's full commitment of opinion and no hedging. This made a very invigorating
experience for me, and not least because it gave me a clearer notion
of you than I have had before.

It was for me a fairly hard book to read, not from sentence to
sentence but in its general impact. Part of the difficulty is of course
my lack of familiarity with your points of reference and the names
for things. The rest is the difficulty of the subject itself, the following
of the translation from one mode of thought into another. At this
point I ought to record a curious phenomenon of my response—that
with so much of what you say about [what] the Rabbis said or meant
I am in very strange accord, but that the Rabbis themselves aroused
any sympathy or fellow feeling very little. The things you ascribe to
them, such as indeterminacy of belief, normal mysticism, the commonplace, and the holy, excited me when I first read the names you
give them, for they seemed to me to sum up the tendency of much of
my own writing. And when I went on to read your exposition of these
phrases I found myself thinking that I must be atavistically determined, so much in sympathy did I feel. I don't know why the Rabbis
themselves, when they appear in their own persons, don't engage me.
This isn't the fault of your presentation of them, and perhaps another
reading of the book will do away with this feeling. At any rate, the
important thing is not this negative emotion, but the positive one
toward the ideas I've mentioned, and toward other things in the book,
such as the relation you expound between the Haggadah and the
Halabah,[1] and what it implies of the possible relation of the intellectual
to the popular culture. These make very fortifying matter for me indeed, and, as I've hinted, it gave me a peculiar pleasure to think that
they are indigenous in the tradition of my ethnic culture and perhaps
reached me directly, as an influence, although I was unconscious of
it, in my rearing. As you know, very little in Jewish religious life speaks

_____

1. *Sic*; properly, "Halakha."

to me, although I think I keep my ears open, but this does speak to me, and I'm glad of that and especially glad that I hear it through you.

I've been doing what I can for the book. Elliot Cohen of *Commentary* was most interested in what I told him of it and has promised to find a really good reviewer for it. I've written to John Crowe Ransom of *The Kenyon Review* to suggest that he himself would find the book of peculiar relevance to his own literary problems, as indeed it is; I've urged that he review it himself, and, failing that, that he find a good man for it. And I've written to Francis Brown of the *Times Book Review* to tell him that it oughtn't to be let go by as too special for review. And if you think that a statement about the book's interest for the educated general reader would be of any help in bringing it to wider notice, I'll be glad to write one.

I imagine you haven't any need for the unbound pages by now, and if that is so I'd like to keep them for rereading. But let me know if you want them back.

It would be good if we can meet sometime soon—I'm likely to be not so tied to my university schedule this year. Meanwhile I send you my warmest congratulations on a really beautiful job.

Yours,

115. TO ALLEN GINSBERG

November 5, 1952
Columbia University

Dear Allen:

The manuscript goes back to you by prepaid express within the next day or two. Let me know if it doesn't reach you in reasonable time.

I don't remember whether or not you told me that the volume is to be published, or if this came to me through someone else, or if I am just making a leap of supposition and hope from Dr. Williams's[1] having written his preface. If it is to be published, you know how glad I am.

As for my response to the volume, you will not, I think, want me to respond in my character of Former Teacher. If I were to do that,

---

1. William Carlos Williams (1883–1963), poet.

I suppose I should come up with something not unlike Dr. Williams's preface. And it would give me pleasure to be able to do that, if that would give you pleasure. But it seems to me that my one virtue as your former teacher has been not to give you the easy response which—I assure you—is so very hard to withhold; and you, for your part, have had the great virtue as a former student, of not expecting the easy and flattering response, and of accepting my reservations very bravely and sometimes with agreement. I have often made these reservations with the warning that I wasn't the best judge for you, that my tastes in poetry were narrow and likely to be doctrinaire, and I have urged you not to heed me. I repeat this warning now when I have to say that I don't respond to the volume. I approve the new plainness of style—although not for Dr. Williams's reasons: my one exchange of opinion with him leads me to believe that his sound instincts are corrupted by his rationalizations (tell him that for me!)—and there are several passages or whole poems that touch me. These generally are the objective representations of misery such as the "old, crippled, dumb people" of the first poem. But the totality of the work doesn't touch me: so far as it does—not very far—I resist it. By which I do not mean that the anguish of the "empty mirror" is not a reality, but that I do not think that it is a thing that ought to occupy us very much. There are other anguishes that are, I believe, more important, more, as it were, to be cultivated. By which—again—I do not mean to set myself up as a connoisseur of anguishes—perish that thought—but only to say that I do not feel that the anguish of the empty mirror is one that I think should be given the countenance of poetry and then of criticism. This is a cultural, an economic-political judgment, as you will understand, not a "human" one. "Humanly speaking," I can recognize the "validity" of the anguish of the holder of the empty mirror, just as I can recognize "validity" of the anguish of the Boss, the Radio Executive, or whatever—they are not so unlike as most people suppose. But speaking critically—which is to say, culturally-politically—I don't respond. And this, I ought to say, isn't only on determination, but on the literary evidence—so far as the empty mirror seeks to persuade or convince, it doesn't tell enough. For what I more fully mean, look at that essay of mine on Sherwood Anderson.

Do forgive me, as you have before, and remember that I think that criticism is the opposition of modes and attitudes to modes and attitudes.

With all good wishes,
Lionel Trilling

116. TO DELMORE SCHWARTZ[1]

December 12, 1952

Dear Delmore:

I must tell you that your letter is very offensive, although I do not think you meant it to be.

Consider, first, that you have felt it necessary to make a personal appeal to me to accept in good part your published expression of a difference with some of my ideas,[2] the ground of your appeal being that you deal with "an important literary matter which transcends personal feelings." And then consider that, having clearly marked out for me the course of my moral and cultural duty, you go on to make a point of expediency by referring to the injury which has been sustained by *Partisan Review*, and by me personally, because of the gossip about the rejection of Blackmur's[3] article on Wilson and me, and also by referring to the embarrassment and humiliation which you have suffered from this gossip—your argument runs: in settling on an attitude toward your article it will be well for me to consider that only by the publication in *Partisan Review* of some strong expression of dissent from my ideas can the reputation of *PR* and of myself be rehabilitated and you relieved of your embarrassment and humiliation.

This in itself is surprising enough; it is astonishing as coming from a man of your sensitivity.

I was not aware that I had the reputation of policing what is

---

1. Delmore Schwartz (1913–1966), poet and fiction writer, was at this time an editor of *Partisan Review*.
2. Schwartz's essay "The Duchess' Red Shoes," in *Partisan Review* (January–February 1953), was a hostile response to Trilling's essay "Manners, Morals, and the Novel," in *The Liberal Imagination*.
3. R. P. Blackmur (1904–1965), literary critic.

written about me. If the essay in which you take issue with me is couched in the ordinarily courteous language of literary debate between people who respect each other—as I should expect it to be—then I should have indeed thought it polite of you in our personal relationship and proper in our *Partisan Review* relationship if you had sent me the page proofs with, perhaps, a note saying that you'd be interested to see what my reply would be. Beyond this nothing more was needed.

But if your essay, in the natural heat of argument, uses a tone that will naturally make me respond with a reciprocal aggressiveness—not necessarily hostility—then you have no right to forestall my emotions and the reply and the tone of the reply that they might give rise to by talk about "an important literary matter which transcends personal feeling."

You offer to tell me of the unpleasant reverberations of the Blackmur affair as they touch me. I have no interest whatever in hearing about them. The gossip, I assure you, is quite local; it has not reached so far as 116th Street, and probably not some distance south of that. And I should think that you have been long enough in the literary life and long enough in the life of *PR* to able to endure the embarrassment, even the humiliation, of attributed motive. Even before my name appeared on the *PR* masthead, I found I was identified with the magazine's policies and made responsible for its errors of judgment and taste, and of course the more so since my name does appear on the masthead; and this, though undeserved, I have found possible to bear with equanimity.

Yet I should like to make a few observations about the Blackmur business.

I did not "request," as you put it, the rejection of the Blackmur piece. And if the impression prevails among the gossips of your acquaintance that I did *request* the rejection of the piece, I am led to conclude that this is the result of bad faith on the part of at least one *Partisan* editor.

That I was consulted about the piece is of course true. It was probably a mistake on the part of the editors to give me the piece to read and on my part to consent to read it. The editors acted more gracefully—although I do *not* think with more of an intimation of friendship—in the similar situation of John Peale Bishop's[1] review of my book on Arnold a good many years ago. (They have in consequence suffered, as I have, some opprobrium in Edmund Wilson's edition of Bishop's prose, but we are all alive and well.) What happened then was that Bishop's adverse review was rejected out of hand and another review written; when I was told of this, after the fact, I protested the action on principled grounds and was told by the editors in a very friendly way that it was none of my business, that the judgment was wholly theirs, that they did not agree with the import of the review, and that they did not consider it a good piece of writing.

But whether properly or not, I *was* consulted in the Blackmur situation, and I think that on the whole any impropriety was mitigated by my being so very closely identified with the magazine and so often consulted about its affairs and sometimes about editorial matters. I assumed that the editors were asking a real question, which is why I decided against being cagey and refusing to be involved; I supposed that they were not asking the question merely to get from me a good-natured dispensation to publish what amounted to a total "attack" on me but that they wanted a considered opinion which had reference not only to myself but also to the magazine. I accepted the awkward situation in the belief, that is, that I was being really asked for help in a difficult situation—I am still inclined to maintain that belief—and I tried to act with a degree of responsibility not less than one of the editors would show. If I did not, and in the nature of the case, could not, act with entire disinterestedness, I did not suppose that the editors themselves were wholly disinterested, for I presumed that they would have a reasonable partisanship with me: but I did not think of myself only. I considered that the piece was not good; had it been good—as good, say, as Blackmur's essential, although polite, dismissal of my book in *Kenyon*—I should not have given the same answer. But I would have given the same answer had the piece not been about me at all but only about Wilson, or about anyone whose work deserved thoughtful treatment, and, in your pages, for one reason or another, polite treatment. I considered too, and mentioned this consideration, what your readers would con-

---

1. John Peale Bishop (1892–1944), poet.

clude about the motives of the editors in publishing a piece which did not merely take issue with me, but attacked me in such essentially personal terms as to be beyond the possibility of reply except in similar terms; a piece, moreover, that was in itself, as this description of it implies, not at all impressive intellectually and therefore not making a categorical intellectual claim on your pages; it seemed to me that its publication could not reflect credit on the feelings of the editors, my connection with *PR* being what it is, Blackmur's connection being what it is, so much less close; whatever Olympian attitude I myself might have taken, your readers would, I assure you, have *gossiped*. I considered, finally, that *PR* was not a literary repository but a magazine willing to make choices and take sides— and consequences.

I find myself now dismayed to learn that the matter is still thought by one of the editors to be an issue. The issue could have been closed, the gossip entirely silenced, by the simple statement that the piece was not good enough and that it dealt inadequately with its subject (with Wilson, of course, no less than with me). It is, after all, not impossible that Blackmur should write badly on occasion, below the standards of Blackmur, below the standards of *PR*. (The piece, let us note, has not yet, to my knowledge, appeared in any of the many journals which would be expected to welcome eagerly almost any piece of Blackmur's.) I think that simplicity and directness and conviction would have dictated this conclusive explanation. If the editors of *PR* did not think the piece an inferior one, then I am much disappointed in their judgment. And if the editors of *PR* cannot *say* that a piece of work by an eminent writer is inferior or not suitable, then I am disappointed by their response to prestige and their inadequate notion of their own authority. In all my years of writing for *PR*, I have never sent the editors an essay or story without having been in doubt how it will be received, and much relieved when it has been accepted. I should be sorry indeed to think that I ought to change this attitude.

Let me in conclusion sum up what I feel about the whole business of adverse criticism of my work in periodicals with which I have any close connection: my critical work is naturally written in order to convince, which is to say that it is there to be disagreed with and contradicted. No question of personality enters here, not even to be, as you say, "transcended." The limits to this are, of course, defined by the cogency and tone of the disagreement. When Will Barrett[1] went after me in a fairly fundamental way, I was sorry that he thought it necessary to reach around Richard Chase to get at me, and of course I thought him foolish for not understanding what I meant and wholly agreeing with it; but I took no slightest offense and enjoyed answering him as hard as I could. And his tone could have been considerably more stringent and less good-natured with me and I should still not have taken offense. But if the piece is not to the point, if it misrepresents me, if its tone is contumacious, then I very simply conclude that hostility is at work and respond in kind—hostility not only on the part of the author but on the part of the editorial management of the magazine that prints the piece. That is because I do not think that literature just happens—any more than you would think it just a cultural phenomenon if your three editorial colleagues decided to accept a dull piece attacking you with animus.

All this should have been obvious to you.

I wish that you would make occasion to read this letter at the next meeting of the editors of *PR*. I enclose for reference a copy of your letter to me.

Sincerely,

117. TO MARY O'NEIL HAWKINS

February 18, 1953

Dear Dr. Hawkins:

I have delayed replying to your letter because I have hesitated to say what I must say before answering your question—that it was not right of you to express any assumption about the relation of my wife's views to my own. My wife and I have been writing under the same surname for a good many years, and our relationship has been pretty generally known, and yet, until you wrote as you did, neither of us has been called on to account for the ideas of the other, not even by implication. For several reasons which will occur to you, we have been very grateful for this.

---

1. William Barrett (1913–1992), philosopher and sometime *Partisan Review* editor.

This said and now quite out of the way, I am glad to make clear the degree of connection between my wife's ideas and my own. Only one of her references to psychoanalysis, that to the relation between the incomes of analysts and their quality of dedication, can be responded to with either agreement or disagreement; I agree with it, and I think that I expressed in my own way the same view in the course of our conversation on the general subject. My wife's other reference can command not agreement but only corroboration—that is, her account of the party of analysts. The event was, I fear, rather more horrendous than she describes it to have been. I should say that in itself it cannot serve as the basis of a generalization about the psychoanalytic profession, but that it may well be taken as symptomatic of a certain phase of the profession at the present time. So, as I understand the "Journal,"[1] my wife took it; and so I took it, and my having taken it so had its effect on what I said, or meant to say, to you when we talked.

I ought to add that what my wife did say about the practice of psychoanalysis expresses only the most superficial part of her criticism—as of mine, which in several respects differs materially from hers.

I do hope that we can soon find another occasion to go into the subject together.

Sincerely yours,
Lionel Trilling

118. TO R. W. FLINT

March 6, 1953

Dear Flint:

I think I ought to say, out of respect for our odd little epistolary relationship, that I am quite unable to understand its recent development. The question of "disciple" and "opponent" is not very real to me; I am surprised that it seems so easily possible to you. My sense of the matter is this, and you can, if you wish, tell me whether or not I describe events correctly. You wrote to say that you thought that Schwartz was right as against me in his *Partisan* essay,[2] and in giving

1. Diana Trilling, "From an Autumn Journal," *Partisan Review* (January–February 1953).
2. Schwartz's essay "The Duchess' Red Shoes"; see page 210.

your reasons, you summarized my attitude to society. I replied by saying that I was rather astonished that you should have read me to the effect of your summary—that I considered my position to be *quite the opposite* of what you seemed to take it to be. To this, which ought to have evoked for you, if not an examination of your understanding of me, at least some degree of astonishment at my long misunderstanding of myself, you replied in a note which said nothing more (and in a rather stubborn way) than that there we were, quite on opposite sides of the fence. My dry response to this, my wonder at how we got there, now brings from you this talk of "disciple" and "opponent." If you want to be an opponent, that's all right—I'm sure that if I have to conceive of my intellectual life in terms of disciples and opponents I couldn't have a nicer opponent than you. And indeed I'm sure that there are more points of disagreement between us than have ever been acknowledged by either. Which will disturb neither of us. All that does disturb me is your refusal to respond to my having questioned your understanding of my intention (and also, perhaps, the brisk alacrity with which you put us on opposite sides of the fence).

Sincerely,

P.S. Why should you think of yourself as a Herbert Read[1] manqué? Isn't a Herbert Read manqué Herbert Read?

119. TO STEVEN MARCUS[2]

March 9, 1953

Dear Steven:

I'll take care of the Fulbright thing—I wrote to Norman, the mischance with Wodlinger may turn out to be useful to you. There's still nothing I can say about the possibility of a job here. The University has moved against the employment of instructors beyond a certain term, but now that the thing has happened that a good many of us wanted, we find that we don't want it, in part for reasons of humanity, in part for

1. Herbert Read (1893–1968), English poet and art critic.
2. Steven Marcus (1928–2018), literary critic and scholar, was Trilling's student at Columbia and went on to become his colleague in the English Department.

reasons of efficiency, and so representations have been made and there may be no changes this year, or none beyond the unforeseen ones.

I feared that anxiety would early invade your year away and now it seems that it has. I'm sorry. Try not to let it spoil too much for you. Something will happen.

I'm glad Rahv wrote to you as he did. Let's think of him as Crawling and Eating Crow. Nothing, as the wise say, succeeds like success.

Both my wife and I were glad to have your word about her "Journal." She was disappointed in what she had done, not thinking it near as good as she wanted it to be, and indeed it was written under the most absurd distractions. But where she expected, at worst, indifference, she faced a storm which in our wildest imaginations we could not have dreamed of. Friends have taken offense on personal and political grounds, usually finding themselves where they were not, and vast numbers of unknowns have taken general offense at the whole thing—they see in the record of disagreements about formative styles and about music and literature the clear evidence of the badness of our marriage (I thought they were perhaps too Darby-and-Joan in the modern manner, and perhaps open to the charge of flattering our relationship), and it is generally said that I am the psychiatric patient! Many people do like it, to be sure, even extremely, but these seem to be readers of relatively modest intellectual pretensions. The rank and file of the militant intellectual proletariat are vociferous. And even Oliver Snyder, who came to see me the other day, was full of reasons why the thing was of a peculiarly special badness. Nothing in my experience has ever so angered me—I don't mean Oliver but the general response. I have had a vision of our culture which consists of abysses opening at my feet. Like Diana, I think the "Journal" isn't as good as she might have made it, though good. But I think, as she does, that it has the virtues you attribute to it, which are considerable, and the negative response to this is, for me, momentous.

Nor was I in the least reassured by the quality of Delmore Schwartz's piece, although I think he made a few telling points. Do you think I should answer it? I'm still of two minds, inclining to yes.

[. . .]

With friendliest greetings to you and Gene,
Sincerely,

120. TO PASCAL COVICI

May 27, 1953
Columbia University

Dear Pat:

I've just finished the galleys of Saul Bellow's novel[1] and I'm delighted with it and enormously impressed. As you know, I went through the manuscript last summer in my search for a chapter for my issue of *Perspectives*,[2] but I read the whole book through again with as much interest and excitement as the first time—indeed, even more. Forgive me if I am so dull as to say that I couldn't put it down and finished it at an ungodly hour in the morning: such is the fact. For some time now I've thought that Saul was the most interesting and promising of the young novelists and the new book quite confirms my earlier opinion. He really does a unique thing—he takes the naturalistic novel, the novel of commonplace, even sordid, fact, and infuses it with poetry and intelligence without in the least betraying the factuality of the fact. I have—although perhaps you won't believe it of me—an addiction to the naturalistic novel, and actually read Farrell with pleasure; but the after-feeling of most naturalistic novels is never for me very pleasant or interesting exactly because they don't have what Saul's book so preeminently does have—put it this way: that with all their presumed commitment to LIFE, they aren't very alive and they don't represent people who are really alive. But it's Saul's gift to see life everywhere. He really believes in the living will. There isn't an inert person in the book, just as there isn't an inert sentence— the prose is really wonderful in its vivacity and energy, in its fusion of the colloquial and the intellectual tradition; it would be remarkable as a tour de force if it weren't so much more than a tour de force, if it weren't, that is, a genuine style.

I know you think I don't know the first thing about publishing, but in spite of this rude and unwarranted opinion of yours, I'd like to give you a piece of advice. Saul's manifest talent and his exigent demands upon it mustn't mislead you into promoting the book as a

---

1. *The Adventures of Augie March* (1953).
2. *Perspectives USA*, an American literary magazine funded by the Ford Foundation for distribution in Europe, was published from 1952 to 1956.

highbrow effort. This will not pay the book the compliment it deserves. It's *not* a highbrow book, not what you publishers are believed to call a "prestige item"—it's a book for many people to enjoy, and if not everybody gets every nuance of it, that doesn't matter: they'll still enjoy it. Proof: our departmental secretary, not a highbrow, returned this letter to me saying, "If you don't have to return those galleys would you give them to me—I just love his writing. I don't know any writer who gives me so much pleasure."

I need scarcely say how much good luck I wish you with it.

Yours,

Lionel

121. TO C. L. R. JAMES[1]

May 29, 1953

Dear Mr. James:

I must ask—again!—your forgiveness for my long silence and for my nonpayment of my just debts. To deal with the latter sin first, I enclose my check for $3—I imagine that even if everybody does remember to pay for the copy of the book he has received, your costs will not be entirely met, and the small excess is to help even if only a very little toward meeting them.

The delay in my reply to your questions about my response to the book[2] you will, I hope, understand to have been chiefly caused by the difficulty of finding time for the decencies of literary correspondence between the exigencies of teaching and writing. But I confess that I might have overcome this difficulty the more easily had I responded more positively to the thesis of your book. I shan't apologize for not going along with you in your interpretation of *Moby-Dick*—I know you don't expect easy or unanimous agreement. And I'm afraid I can't argue the matter with you, although I'll hope to be able to do that sometime—the fact is that I am not at the moment intimate with *Moby-Dick* as I once was and should like to be again. I therefore

---

1. C. L. R. James (1901–1989), historian and Marxist theorist.
2. *Mariners, Renegades, and Castaways: The Story of Herman Melville and the World We Live In* (1953).

can't deal with your thesis in any substantive way, and I concede my deficiency of authority. Yet I do feel that your interpretation can't satisfy me. At least it can't as a central interpretation. I have no doubt it is a *possible* one; and it is acceptable as a subordinate consideration. But it doesn't stand for me as the controlling idea of the book. From what I've said about my present lack of familiarity with the novel, you'll know that I don't have my own special way of reading it. Yet my recollection of the tone and quality of the novel leads me to feel that your way of reading it is reductive. This implies no wish on my part to belittle politics as a subject—nothing could be further from my general feeling or present intention. I do think, however, that the huge complex emotional paraphernalia of the book is directed at something more than the politics you propose. If you want to make politics *part* of what the emotional paraphernalia proposes, I am at one with you; but even then not if you make it the chief part. To take an analogy, *The Castle* certainly has its political aspect, but we do injury to the nature of the book if we isolate and emphasize that. And mind you: I am not saying that a work with as elaborate and moving an emotional paraphernalia as *Moby-Dick*'s might not be directed primarily at politics, but only that *Moby-Dick* is not.

So there you have my disagreement and I hope that someday soon I'll be a better scholar in the book and have a chance to meet you and have it out with you fully. Meanwhile I send my friendliest greetings.

Sincerely yours,
Lionel Trilling

122. TO MADAME DEVETTE HAVEZ[1]

May 29, 1953

Dear Madame Devette Havez:

I hope you can possibly forgive this very late reply to your letter. I am ashamed not to have been more cooperative in a scholarly venture, but I am sure you will understand how the *subject* of such a

---

1. According to Trilling's annotation, Madame Devette Havez was a teacher at a French lycée for girls.

venture must experience a certain diffidence in cooperating in it. And something more than diffidence—for although I might truthfully plead the great press of work of the last year as an excuse for not having written before this, I cannot but suppose that a more decisive reason was my reluctance to write about myself.

And even now this reluctance continues, but I will try to answer your questions as best I can. You ask what I mean by "liberal." This is certainly a most reasonable question, since the word, although I suppose it has some sort of locus of common meaning all over the world, actually means many different things in different countries and in different cultural contexts. It is a word used both in praise and in blame, and I think I use it with both intentions, having reference both to an ideal liberalism and to a false and degenerated liberalism. And I'm sure that before either I have in mind the early liberal meanings of the word—free, generous, enlarging: as we mean it when we speak of a "liberal education." Then I have in mind the great tradition of liberal thought in the nineteenth century, the tradition that stood for freedom and intellect. Here the terminology becomes rather confusing because in England in the nineteenth century the word "liberal" deteriorated and came to be applied chiefly to the Whig followers of Bentham and the Manchester school of political economics and was often thought of as a rather small-minded resistance to all interference by the State. With the result that many of the nineteenth-century writers whom I admire dissociated themselves from what would in their day have been called liberalism. But if you take the best ideas of Bentham—I mean Bentham as he really is, not Bentham as most people represent him—and John Stuart Mill, and Ruskin, and Matthew Arnold, and William Morris, and involve them with the temperament of the English romantic poets, and connect them with Montaigne (this is very important and I don't insist on it merely to make myself clear to a French reader), and much of Rousseau, and much of Stendhal, you will get some notion of the intellectual constellation to which I refer—not a complete idea but a sufficient working notion.

Then you must have in mind the peculiar position of the word "liberal" in American cultural and political life. It has a curious sacrosanctity among people who have any pretensions to education. Of late years it has been linked with the word "progressive." It is meant to imply thoughtfulness, a humane interest in the welfare of others, a degree of commitment to philosophical naturalism, a belief in the possibility of progress by political means, an open mind, the resistance to conservative or reactionary ideas. The typical political manifestation of this was the Roosevelt administration, but of course the manifestations of liberalism were not confined to politics but were to be found in philosophy, literary taste and criticism, theories of education, etc. And I should observe of the liberal mind in its actuality that it was inclined to give to Communism an unreasoned and unintelligent sympathy, sentimental in its first impulse, although often very hard and bitter in its tenacity. And this may suggest to you the sort of cultural error that I have perceived the liberal mind to be likely to fall into.

In short, the word "liberal" may be used to sum up the culture of the middle class of the United States where that middle class made any aspiration to thought and to idealism. I think of the tendency of that culture as on the whole a good thing, but likely to corrupt itself all too easily and I look at it with some fear (as well as irony) because it seems to me that nothing in our time is more dangerous than the corruption of idealism.

Perhaps this will tell you something of the intention of *The Middle of the Journey*, which you can think of as a natural history of the intellectual liberal class as I understand it—its movement to communism, its wish to deny variousness and complexity in life, or, indeed, almost any free emotion, or to admit that life has any depth of mystery (Nancy Croom); or, on the other hand, the movement to a false spirituality (Gifford Maxim).

Your question about what I think is the most important question for the United States nowadays I shall, if you'll permit me, simply evade—too big for me. But if you'll look at the third number of *Profils*, you'll see a piece by me which says something about the situation of the American intellectual class, from which you may be able to draw some more general conclusions.

My book on Matthew Arnold ought to help you with the word "liberal," and also the first chapter of my book on E. M. Forster. But don't make too much of that word in itself or you'll get yourself into historical-semantic difficulties which will obscure all the issues.

Again, forgive the lateness of this reply.

Sincerely yours,

Lionel Trilling

123. TO RICHARD HOWARD[1]

June 3, 1953

Dear Richard Howard:

At this point I can never remember why the university year has been so madly rushed and can scarcely convince myself that it has been so very mad as in fact it was. In the seasonal bedlam I read your letter but hastily, and put it into my correspondence file with the intention of replying to it on some day of peace. Now that that has come (relatively speaking) I can read it again with the amusement it deserves and the awareness of what fun you must be having in your cultural involvement and observation. Perhaps I feel this the more because my own blankness about French culture, after a certain point in the nineteenth century, my almost studied indifference, has lately been breaking down and I find in myself the stirrings of a new curiosity, discovering at the same time that my ability to read French has gone so rusty that I can just about make out the algebraic form of the sentence. Really shocking.

The new interest isn't separable from my continuing sense that in any number of ways French culture is hopeless, and that the Parisian life is of a provinciality beyond help, and this, I gather, you in part feel from your own observation, which has so much more value than my intuition. Still, even in its corruption, the thing glows for me as what we need here—always has, in a way. Having a good deal of the American fear of "civilization" as an idea, I have also the impulse to idealize "civilization" as far as possible, and perhaps especially as against the false-sincere, the fakey nakedness-before-God which is so much the American intellectual pose (vide Delmore Schwartz's essay).

---

1. Richard Howard (1929–), poet and translator, a former student at Columbia.

The new course went delightfully, at least for me, and I had occasion at the end of each term to do what I think I've never done before—thank the class for the good time they had given me! Of the some thirty-five students almost all were interested and responsive, and some were astonishingly gifted, and in a very happy, modest way. This is the first time I've ever given my own course in the College and I found it quite a revelation of pleasure—much more fun than 65–6, the students much more various in mind. The complexity of lines we were able to draw through Austen-Dickens-Lawrence, and then through Wordsworth-Keats-Yeats, was astonishing. I learned a lot and found that my always-threatening disenchantment with teaching was effectually checked for the time being.

I leave in a week or so for the country with the intention of recouping a year of very little writing. I'll look forward to your next report on yourself and Europe. Do you plan to stay another year?

With all my good wishes,

Sincerely,

124. TO FRANCIS STEEGMULLER[1]

July 13, 1953
Bradley Street, Westport, Connecticut

Dear Francis:

This is a call for your scholarly help. In a few days I shall be beginning an essay on *Bouvard and Pécuchet* which is to serve as an introduction to a good translation (Earp and Stonier, published in England a few years ago but now unprocurable) being brought out by New Directions. Jacques Barzun is translating the *Dictionnaire des idées reçues* and it will appear in the same volume, with an introduction by J. Perhaps you have heard of this venture and that the volume is to be offered together with your letters as a dual selection of the Readers' Subscription[2] in January. I find myself fortunate in

---

1. Francis Steegmuller (1906–1994), biographer of Flaubert and scholar of French literature.
2. A subscription book club of which Trilling was an editor, along with Jacques Barzun and W. H. Auden.

being lost in admiration of *B&P*—I knew it was an "important" book when I undertook to write about it, but my memory did not tell me that it was a great book, and as complex and moving as it is. (In general this is a bullish time in Flaubert after a long bearish period in which I admired only *The Sentimental Ed.* I've taken a dim view of *Mme. B.* for a good many years now, but was swept off my feet by a recent rereading.) About *B&P* I think I shall have a good deal to say of an interpretive sort but I want to include something about the history of the book, and although I know in a general sort of way, I'd like to have your help in finding the most authoritative account of its writing and of Flaubert's plans for it. Exhaustiveness isn't necessary: what I want is something solid on which I can base a few informative simple paragraphs. Also, I'd very much like to have references to any letters in which F. speaks in a notable way about the book. If I should quote any of these, I'd naturally like to use your translation—would it be possible for you to let me have a copy, either in a carbon of the MS or in a set of proofs, if these are in existence? Any books you suggest I can have sent from the Columbia library.

I need scarcely say that I'll be ever so grateful for any help you can give me. I shan't hold up my work on the essay to hear from you and I expect to give something like two or three weeks to it (and more may be necessary), so don't feel rushed, although naturally, etc.

How are you and Beatrice? We are recovering some serenity after a most depressing and harassing winter. Diana joins me in affectionate greetings to you both.

Yours,
Lionel

125. TO PASCAL COVICI

September 23, 1953
Columbia University

Dear Pat:

Last spring you asked me to write you a letter about Saul Bellow's book which could be read to your salesmen at their conference. I agreed to do this and did it with enthusiasm, but I made it clear

that my letter was written only for the occasion for which you requested it and that it was not to be used in any other connection. I
even went so far as to ask you not to show it to Saul. I had no slightest doubt that you understood my wish in the matter. Now I find
that the letter has been extensively quoted from in an advertising
leaflet.

I regret this incident more than I shall try to say, but I'll assume it
is the result of some error in your office and we need not discuss it.
I am writing only in order to say that I do not wish the quotation used
in any further advertising.

Sincerely,

Lionel Trilling

But I see this morning that it has been used in an advertisement in
the *Times*.

126. TO PASCAL COVICI

October 12, 1953
Columbia University

Dear Pat:

Just as Saul is wrong about the motives he attributes to Podhoretz,[1]
you are wrong when you bring Podhoretz's competence into question.
I have known Podhoretz for some time, for at Columbia he received
from me a part of what Saul chooses to call his fashionable education, and I have measured him very carefully. I should not think of
treating him as anything but an intellectual equal, and there is no
intellectual matter I would not trust him with.

Podhoretz's opinion of Saul's book is, I suppose, diametrically opposite to that which I have expressed. I think, therefore, that I have
a peculiar right to say that his review is cogent and entirely to be respected, whether or not one agrees with it.

I know from my own experience how personally an author can
take adverse opinion, and I can imagine that a publisher may be so

---

1. Norman Podhoretz's critical review of *The Adventures of Augie March* appeared in
Commentary, October 1953.

involved with a book which does him credit that he takes adverse opinion nearly as personally as the author does. This seems to me as natural and understandable as that there should be differences of opinion in life and literature, and I don't write with the intention of modifying your feeling or Saul's—I write at all only because I don't want to seem to concur by silence in the estimates of Podhoretz which you and Saul express.

    Yours,

      Lionel

127. TO SAUL BELLOW[1]

November 4, 1953

Dear Saul:

It was good to have your letter and to know that you found pleasure in my review of the book. I had a good deal of pleasure in writing it.

Nothing in the book "offended" me, but on this reading, and as I wrote, I had the sense, which before I had never had, that there was an issue between us. A really very important one, and maybe someday we will join it! You mustn't underestimate the doctrinal intention of your book—I mean its cultural, characterological, moral point, whether or not it was consciously made. It's there, and it's important. How important has been borne in upon me by a series of those coincidences which always occur whenever one is seized by an idea: it seems referred to in everything that is said to you. I think I now understand what you say about some of the best young men you know, and their negativism which you doubt my awareness of. I believe I have been aware of it for a very long time, and although only dimly, still with a very great involvement in what it implied; now I think I have a much fuller sense of it, and a much greater understanding. Of this I'm glad, because it gives me the terms, intellectual and dramatic, for something that enormously interests me. I think that the difference between us in our view of what is here implied makes a sounding cultural fact, which we ought to prize and keep ringing.

---

1. Saul Bellow (1915–2005), American novelist, received the Nobel Prize in Literature in 1976.

I get great pleasure from seeing *Augie* on the bestseller list so regularly. I know this no longer means what it used to, alas, but it's something, and it's gratifying, and it bears out my prediction to you that the book would make its way.

With all good wishes,

Sincerely,

128. TO R. W. FLINT

November 6, 1953

Dear Flint:

I've just come again on your good Kipling letter of mid-August, kept in my folder to be answered, and not answered because there are so many good things in it to which I have wanted to respond that a real reply would mean, if not an essay then at least a morning and perhaps an afternoon into the bargain. And now that the term has started this has put itself beyond possibility.

But I did want to say that I'm glad you liked the Kipling essay.[1] If I were writing it now, I should not, I think, have made so much of the "negative aspects"—at any rate, having made as much of them as I did, I've expended my wrath and disappointment and am now ready to move simply and deeply responsive to the good. Of course everybody is beginning to forgive Kipling these days. How useful to know that eventually a writer is forgiven almost everything, if, as Auden says, "he wrote well." Do you know Auden's very good essay on Kipling?

And then I've wanted to make note to you of the part played in taste by boyish experience of literature and the part that *used* to be played in literature by boys. I find myself returning more and more to my boyish literary images, wishing there were more of them, knowing they were definitive in my taste. They were quite conventional, almost Victorian. I shudder to think at the shudders that will be shuddered at my comparing in the essay that will come out in *Partisan*, *Bouvard and Pécuchet* to *Sherlock Holmes*, *Swiss Family Robinson*, and *Tom Sawyer*. And I gather that the whole idea of books for boys and about them is dead, *The Catcher in the Rye*, heaven help us, being its

---

1. "Kipling," in *The Liberal Imagination*.

inheritor. But something ought to be said about the implications of the boy-hero—Tom Brown, Jim Hawkins, Kim, David Balfour, and all the rest, including even the Barbour heroes. They were very happily descended from Wordsworth's boy who shouted to the owls—one of his best things—and they are more important than anyone has yet said. I suppose French culture got rid of them; they're peculiarly English and American.

Well, this has gone on longer than I intended. I send it to Trowbridge Street, not remembering which school you're at, although I think St. Bernard's. It would be pleasant if this year we could meet and lunch together.

Sincerely,

129. TO THE EDITOR OF *THE NEW YORK TIMES*
November 24, 1953

Sir:

The Faculty of Columbia College, Columbia University, recently made a statement on certain questions of academic freedom which have been raised by the congressional investigations. This statement was reported by *The New York Times* in its issue of November 18th. The *Times* report quotes the statement at some length and no exception can be taken to the accuracy of its quotation. But by selecting certain passages for quotation while omitting others of equal importance, the report does not adequately represent the nature of the statement and the intention of the Columbia College faculty in making it.

The statement considers, among other things, the course of conduct which an academic community should properly pursue toward one of its members who, by invoking the privileges of the Fifth Amendment, refuses to testify before a congressional committee. The statement does indeed say, as it was quoted as saying, that "it cannot be made a condition of membership in the teaching profession that a person surrender rights which are guaranteed by the law of the land." But it also says the following: "The Fifth Amendment, to be sure, can scarcely extend its power beyond the courts and the legislative committee room—it cannot prevent inferences being drawn from the actions of those witnesses who claim its privileges. And of the inferences that will inevitably be drawn, some will fairly be that the privileges of the Amendment were invoked for purposes of evasion; some will fairly be that they were invoked by reasons of principle and honor."

In short, it was the intention of the statement not only to say that a refusal to testify must not be automatically condemned but also to say that a refusal to testify must not be automatically condoned. This is the concluding paragraph on the matter of refusal to testify:

"But a decision not to testify or to testify only in a limited way involves complex considerations, both legal and ethical. The principles just expressed are therefore not to be construed as advising or generally approving such action by teachers under investigation. Nor are they to be understood as implying any ethical disapproval of those teachers who take it to be their legal and ethical duty to be wholly responsive to questions that are put to them."

On the basis of the *Times* report, the statement has been interpreted by some readers as a defense of the "right of Communists to teach." The statement does indeed say that "fitness to teach must be tested solely by an individual's actual conduct," and that "membership in an organization, unless it is specifically illegal, should not be thought to constitute sufficient ground for disqualifying a person from continued membership in an academic institution." But it continues as follows: "The specific applications of the general principles of academic freedom are, we recognize, not always easy and simple. At the present time, a crucial question in the discussion of academic freedom is, of course, 'the right of Communists to teach.' We are not concerned to affirm that right; in the same way, were the question a real one, we should not be concerned to affirm the right of Fascists to teach. Although we believe that the civil rights of members of totalitarian groups are to be defended as strenuously as those of anyone, we do not believe that these civil rights include the right of a person to hold a particular academic post when the implied conditions of holding that post have been broken. It is clear to us that membership in Communist organizations almost certainly implies a submission to an intellectual control which is entirely at variance with the principles of academic competence as we understand them. Nevertheless, in the present state of affairs wisdom and prudence suggest that academic freedom is best served if no test of academic fitness be used other than that which we have proposed."

Lionel Trilling

130. TO FRANCIS STEEGMULLER

December 15, 1953
Columbia University

Dear Francis:

I was happy to have your letter and to hear that you liked the *Bouvard* piece.[1] Forgive me this late reply—I've been, as mostly happens, terribly rushed the last weeks.

About the "rejection of culture": I shouldn't want to imply that Flaubert in every way and in every part of his being rejected culture. And certainly there's enough irony and direct satire in the book to require us to be careful about transferring any of its seeming conclusions to Flaubert himself. Still, and giving all due weight to what you say about great writers—incidentally, he does not, as I recall, mock any of the very greatest writers in the literary section: a point I shall have to take account of if ever I should reprint the essay—I still feel that it can be said that he made a rejection of the life in culture, the word being extended almost to the anthropological sense. This, it seems to me, is virtually inevitable in his situation—he must experience this rejection almost by reason of the great store he sets by culture; it is one of the most intense expressions of his "denial of life's goodness." I conceive of it as an aspect of that asceticism and that strange and sometimes inverted idealism (I don't mean in the colloquial sense) that verges on religion, or religiosity (I don't mean this last word pejoratively). He doesn't, of course, reject ideal culture. But doesn't he reject society's culture, which is what we mostly live in?

As for the *Dictionnaire*, I am inclined to agree with you. I wasn't able to collect all the evidence and arguments this summer, although I mean to look further. I am much inclined to agree with Descharmes in the negation. Still, the case apparently can be argued the other

---

1. "Flaubert's Last Testament," *Partisan Review* (November–December 1953).

way, and since the *Dict.* was to appear as part of the enterprise I couldn't, without the highest certainty and authority, deny its propriety there.

The saint business needs a little more development which I hope to give it. I always object to the word "saint" used of uncanonized mortals. This might be better when I refine the idea of the rejection of culture.

The notion of the artistic inferiority of *Little D[orrit]* I will contest to the death.

I'm sorry about Shawn's decision about the review—I should think it would be very much in place in *The New Yorker.*

Yours,
     Lionel

131. TO STEVEN MARCUS

                                      December 15, 1953

Dear Steven:

It was good to hear from you. I take it that it may be some weeks before you will be sending your chapters, so I shan't put off replying to your letter until the MS comes.

I'm of course glad you liked the *Little Dorrit* introduction[1] to the point of feeling that it has preempted your ground—but of course it hasn't, as you will soon see when you come to deal with the book itself. You should, to strengthen your sense of independence when you come to write it, have it in mind that your comments on this book prepared me to respond to its great depth. You'll notice that I avoided dealing with the idea of predestination which you rightly saw as being important and which, I recall, I was inclined to belittle.

The stoicism and stoical Christianity that you perceive of are of the *very* greatest importance. You can't possibly work too hard the idea of *duty* as a dominating idea of the Victorian period. See, at the beginning, what Elinor says to Marianne in *Sense and Sensibility* when Marianne asks her how she was able to be so calm amid all the troubles. I haven't the book at hand, but it's near the end and is

---

1. Reprinted in *The Opposing Self.*

almost the very same speech that Little D. makes. See George Eliot in the garden at Oxford? Cambridge? On God, Immortality, and Duty, of which only the last remains certain. See Bradley's *Ethical Studies*, which is perhaps the summary of the whole Victorian tendency. See Conrad *passim*. *Then* see Saul Bellow, Henry Miller, the Existentialists. Impossible, as I say, to exaggerate the importance of the theme in the light of our response to it.

The impotence theme very important, but you'll have to be very tactful in any use you make of the Ruskin marriage. I mean literary rather than social tact, and I'm not making reference to the sexual aspect of the subject. Mrs. Clennam and the Ruskin parents have certain points in common, but they invert her on the matter of art. Certain points of connection too between the Meagles and the Ruskins—and Daniel Doyce is a Ruskinian idea, no doubt. But, as I say, you must move with great circumspection here.

[. . .]
Sincerely,

132. TO JOHN GILLARD WATSON[1]

December 16, 1953

Dear Mr. Watson:

Please forgive this very late reply to your letter of July—I have been under great pressure of work. Had your letter been less interesting and serious than it is, I should perhaps have answered it sooner, and even now, the pressure of work having abated only a little, I shall force myself to answer it at less than the length it deserves.

"Intellectual" isn't a word that charms me, but it is, in this country at least, rather forced on one. I use it with much of the sense of "intelligentsia" in it, an ugly sense at best; but in the essay to which you refer I had chiefly in mind the group of writers who try to deal seriously with ideas, and with life by means of ideas. I suppose I could define intellectuals in a shifty Aristotelean sort of way by saying that intellectuals are those people whom those of my students who aspire to be intellectuals call intellectuals! The intertribal jealousies as be-

---

1. A student associated with the Oxford Union.

tween our version of the *New Statesman* crowd and the non–*New Statesman* crowd don't matter. And of course the more one uses the word, the uglier it sounds and the less one wants it applied to [oneself]. Maybe we should say *clercs*!

It interests me that you can find parallels in England to the things that I speak of as in process in America. (I'd say that even our advertising, despite what McLuhan says, has of late years been modified—not to the point of being as nearly apologetic as your advertising seems to us: even I feel almost *sorry* for your advertisers and want to buy their products to help them out!) In many ways, of course, you are in much better case than we are. An obvious definitive element for good in your situation is the relative homogeneity of your population. Granting the reality of class differentiation, how much more separative is the ethnic fact. It is only a generation since the Italians have come into political life; they are just now beginning, ever so little, to come into the intellectual life. In New York, to cite an extreme example, we face the problem of a huge influx of Puerto Ricans whose level of culture is quite low. In my boyhood only the very rich or the very snobbish sent their children to any but the public schools, which were, on the whole, fairly good; now it is virtually impossible to expect a child to get any sort of real schooling in them because the Puerto Ricans, scarcely speaking English, have invaded so many neighborhoods: and although the intellectuals sneer at our normal schools and teachers colleges because they teach teachers to "train for citizenship" or talk about "adjustment to society," the plain fact is that this is exactly what is appropriate for the Puerto Rican immigrants. A few weeks ago, while a German scholar was paying me a visit in my university office, we could scarcely hear each other talk because a few thousand of these people, with several bands, were singing hymns and forming a parade in the street beneath my window—my visitor was very disdainful, but I could not help thinking how useful it was that some form of Protestant evangelicism was at work among them to bring them even into ordinary respectability! It will take many generations before they are a part of the central culture. Of course the big cities make a special situation, which nevertheless suggests what the general situation is. Thus, the very *size* of the country makes a problem. You cannot imagine, unless you have lived in a huge country, what an advantage it is to have a political life that seems accessible to the university people and the elite of the working class. It is a specifically political advantage, of course, but what I have in mind is the general cultural advantage.

You say that you find my description of the American situation depressing. I could easily find it so myself if I chose to. I think one makes a conscious choice how one is going to respond. My decision *not* to be depressed by the general situation is based on my feeling that all modern cultures must be unsatisfactory to the people who are conscious of them: maybe that peculiarly modern idea of a "culture" implies dissatisfaction with the object of our consideration. I find myself full of rejections and angers and sorrows and contempts, but now that I am old enough to look back over a significant chunk of cultural life, I don't despair. I recently had to write a chapter for the history of my own college and it was borne in upon me how much had been done over the last fifty years, how strong the development had been.

I'll rely upon you to suppose that I'm not being "defensive" about American culture; if I am defensive of anything at all, it is of the possibilities of modern culture in general: I think we can get nowhere on the cultural pessimism of people like, say, Valéry. Something of my own cultural pessimism on which my optimism (such as it is) is based is expressed in an essay on *Bouvard and Pécuchet* which I published in the last issue of *Partisan Review*.

Well, this hasn't been short at all, but it has been hasty and if it makes nonsense, forgive me.

    Yours sincerely,
      Lionel Trilling

133. TO DAVID RIESMAN

January 4, 1954

Dear Dave:

    [. . .]

The purpose of this letter is to alert you about a situation on *Partisan Review* in which you are involved. In the next issue they will publish a piece of Irving Howe's about the New Conformity.[1] You are a New Conformist, as am I. It is not a vicious piece but it is not in good faith—both of us are misrepresented in it. My own situation is perhaps rather special—this is the second time in a few months that I (a member of their Advisory Board) have been attacked on substantially the same grounds. The essay was proposed by the editors. This fact came out inadvertently—at least no one mentioned it to me when they told me of the piece. Of course, the editors could not have known (as they say) whom Howe would attack: to which my answer has been, did they suppose he was going to attack Arthur Brisbane?[2]

We have here the opening gun of a new group, not perfectly homogeneous but sufficiently so: Howe, Meyer Schapiro, Wright Mills, Norman Mailer who, as you may know, are to publish a magazine;[3] and Mary McCarthy,[4] Dwight Macdonald, Hannah Arendt. In the first group a strong Trotskyist strain. Rahv is responding to these people, feeling, I believe, that they are going to be attractive to the present mood of the intelligentsia. Elliot Cohen, with considerable cogency, believes that they will make an effective appeal to the deep-seated antibourgeois feelings of the comfortable middle class and will gain considerable support. And he and Sidney Hook believe that it is the possible available funds that Rahv is aware of. However that may be, Rahv is troubled by the feelings expressed by Hook and myself as members of the Advisory Board. (William Phillips is troubled by other elements of the incident.) He wants to compromise the situation by printing comments on the piece and no doubt you will be asked to say something. (Let me know if you are *not*.) I have objected to this, saying that I did not think Howe's piece should be given the importance of perhaps two installments of discussion; that I do not want to write briefly in a gang of others with Howe having the last word; that if I wrote at all it would be in a manner of indifference or irony.

---

1. Irving Howe, "This Age of Conformity," *Partisan Review* (January–February 1954).
2. Arthur Brisbane (1864–1936), prominent editorialist for the Hearst newspapers.
3. *Dissent* began publication in 1954.
4. Mary McCarthy (1912–1989), novelist and critic.

Let me know what you think after you've read the article, and what you plan to do.

The business troubles me—not profoundly, you'll understand—but I have no intention of getting involved in the nasty personality politics that are implied. The chances are that I shall soon have to withdraw from my "official" connections with *PR*.

Happy new year,

134. TO FANNIE TRILLING

July 27, 1954
Bradley Street, Westport, Connecticut

Dear Mother:

I want you to have a word of explanation about my part of the financial arrangement now that you are living with Harriet and Rolly. I should have spoken of this before in a definite way, although I did at least indicate it in a general way to you and did speak of it definitely to Harriet.

I plan to send you $60 every month. (This month, however, I am sending only $35, for we are rather pressed for cash at the moment, and the month is a shorter one because of your stay with us through part of it.) I have it in mind that the $60 is to be used to pay for your telephone, your clothes, and any medications that you need. (Should there be any doctor's bills, Harriet will pay them and I will reimburse her for half, as formerly.) The monthly sum from me is to be used to take taxis in order to visit in the city, and so on. The essential purpose of the sum is to allow you to feel as free from any constraint as possible, and you are to use it in the spirit of its purpose. It isn't a great sum to be independent on, but I imagine that you will manage to make out with it—in spite of your extravagant nature! But naturally, if any occasion arises when the sum isn't sufficient, you will let me know.

We are all well and doing nicely. The birthdays were very pleasant. [. . .] Diana seemed particularly happy with her presents, and Jim had, by his request, lobster for his birthday dinner.

We all join in sending love to you and to Harriet, Rolly, and Bill.
Lionel

August 19, 1954

Dear Jacques:

It was good to have your long letter, although I can't say that it cheered me—the image of you in money-angst too exactly matches the image of me in the same box and reinforces the claustrophobia. What a situation, that at our age, and with as much achievement as we have, we should still be in this absurd fret: or, rather, that we should be getting into it more and more. We ought at this time to be working calmly and steadily at only the things that interest and challenge us. Well, I suppose that that has really never been given to any except a few. I think I should mind the whole thing less if the bourgeois life we struggle to maintain had in it some small element of the illusion of vivacity and grace, if we could convince ourselves that just as a life-in-society it had its justifying seductions. But it seems to me increasingly that it hasn't and can't have. I seem always to get low about the look of life in the summer; but this year I have become queasy to the point of nausea, having a consuming sense of the nonentity, hence the ugliness and ungenerosity, of all social groups. And this comes to me most acutely sometimes on the wings of the one thing I used to think must necessarily give me pleasure—I mean "respect." And when I think that it's to ready the children to go into this society that we make so large a part of our effort, I feel grim beyond words.

Such, my dear J., are the reflections that occur to me upon the perusal of your plans to augment your fortune and gain for yourself the establishment in life which befits your rank. And although not of the most cheerful kind, yet to one of your temper of mind.

[. . .]

You will have guessed from your not having yet received the MS of my essays that my summer has not been as forward going as either of us could wish for me, and this has been rather depressing, as, indeed, it has come, in part, from some depression. Nevertheless I have a rather good feeling about the book[1] itself: at least at times it conveys to me the impression of *depth*! Or at least some overtone of

---

1. *The Opposing Self.*

mysteriousness—I find myself puzzled now and then by certain notes. In some strange way I think of it as a more serious book than the *Lib. Im.*, which will probably mean that it will not go down so well as its predecessor. I have a few pages to revise on the last of the essays and introduction to write, so that I can't suppose that I will be ready to send it to you before the first of September. By that time, I imagine, you will have left Cotuit.—It interests me that on all sides now people tell me that they are reading, having bought, the *Lib Im*—these are people of means and some pretensions to culture, but they did not *buy* the book until it cost only 75 cents or until its diminutive size reassured them. There is something very strange in the cultural economy.

[. . .]

Diana finished her piece on the Oppenheimer case[1] against great odds and then, after it was finished and sent, recalled it because she got further along in the record of the hearings, which she had not meant to consider, and discovered that she had quite misconceived the situation. So she is, poor thing, doing the piece over, on the basis of an analysis of the testimony. She has come to the conclusion that the decision is far worse than has yet been said, and what she reports to me of the testimony is complex and fascinating beyond anything I could imagine.

We have two kittens, Paws (male) and Thompson (f)—the latter named so for no discernible reason by Jim. It is dangerous to ask him why he chose this name, for his explanation goes like this: Well, I was sitting on the toilet, and suddenly I felt in my heart that Thompson was the name for that particular cat, and it leaped from my heart to my brain, so I decided Thompson.

Diana joins me in love to you and Mariana.

Yours always,

Lionel

---

1. "The Oppenheimer Case: A Reading of the Testimony," *Partisan Review* (November–December 1954).

136. TO MELVIN SHIMM[1]

August 28, 1954

Dear Mr. Shimm:

I hope you can forgive this late reply to your letter, which I fear must be as inadequate as it is late. I know I could be much drawn to the subject of the symposium you speak of, but I am at the moment so deeply engaged in the completion of a book, and after that I shall have to turn to so many other neglected matters, that I'm afraid I shan't be able to direct my mind to the very interesting matter that occupies you.

I am sincere when I say that I am sorry for this. Last summer I was consulted on a literary obscenity matter and in order to enlighten myself on the present state of the law, I read some of the notable judicial decisions. I was, I'm sorry to have to say, rather sunk by the arguments of the most eminent judges. I am—"naturally," I suppose I ought to say—opposed to the censorship of literature on the grounds of obscenity, but it seems to me that the legal reasoning from the facts was most superficial and precious. Legal friends of mine tell me I should not be disturbed—that the judges are only going through certain necessary motions in order to come out at the right end. But I continued to be disturbed—the whole line of argument seemed so very awkward, and, really, hypocritical. That "dirt for dirt's sake" rule is really nonsense—or unjust; for the educated respectable man's pornography is called "literature" and the under-the-counter purchaser's pornography is called dirt for dirt's sake. The shabbiest sort of thing is called "literature" if it sounds pretentious enough—which the under-the-counter writers have caught on to, and now they supply an elaborate "idea" for each of their frankly pornographic works. (Amazing, by the way, how an "idea" helps pornography do its job!) Similarly the elegance of a revue protects its risqué aspects, the shabbiness of burlesque leaves it open to attack. Undemocratic I calls it.

The only thing that makes me at all lenient with the "liberal" judges is the difficulty I had in an attempt to formulate a standard of judgment.

This reflection on my response to the legal decisions will suggest

---

1. Editor of the journal *Law and Contemporary Problems.*

how much the matter interested me. But alas I can't at this time indulge the interest.

[. . .]

Sincerely yours,
    Lionel Trilling

137. TO BERNARD MALAMUD[1]

November 16, 1954

Dear Mr. Malamud:

I owe you a thousand apologies for not having written to you before this. If I delayed answering your first letter, if was chiefly because, as I must confess, your work wasn't very clear in my mind and I wanted to look it up before replying—from which you will gather that I had in principle no objection to writing in support of your application for a Guggenheim Fellowship. Then when you wrote you were not applying this year, I was in the midst of an impossible situation with a book of my own, and at the very moment when the last days of our bicentennial celebration were demanding all my available time. The result was that I simply gave up all hope of dealing with my correspondence. Please forgive me.

My freedom coincides with the appearance of your story in *Partisan*,[2] and that makes a very happy coincidence for me, because I can write saying that I think your story is a splendid piece of work. I suppose one is—or I am—in a depressed state of mind about literature these days, for I read it not only with delight but *relief*. I think this came from my sense of your commitment to the story itself—I have in mind the idea of creative "innocence," the writer's interest in the fact or the object rather than in his will to be, or his process of being, a writer. I have been turning over in my mind the Chagallian ending: at first I wasn't sure that it was right, but now I think it is. The whole thing is really lovely.

Whenever you *are* ready to apply for a Guggenheim, do get in touch with me again. On the whole, I think Alfred Kazin's advice is

---

1. Bernard Malamud (1914–1986), novelist and short-story writer.
2. "The Magic Barrel," *Partisan Review* (November–December 1954).

sound. My sense of the matter is that the Guggenheim people, who are in most ways quite unpredictable, have at least one criterion that can be perceived, a writer's power of doing continuous work as indicated by at least one published book.

Sincerely yours,
Lionel Trilling

138. TO ELIZABETH AMES

December 29, 1954

Dear Miss Ames:

I am writing to ask whether there would be any possibility of a place at Yaddo, sometime this winter, for James Baldwin, a very gifted young writer of my acquaintance. To say that Mr. Baldwin is one of the best of the young Negro writers would not do him justice, for the category in which that judgment is made is too narrow—he is, in my opinion, one of the best and most promising men of his generation. He has recently returned from several years in Paris and is trying to complete his second novel, which he finds difficult to do amid the confusions of New York. A period of isolation and quiet would be of the greatest help to him. Mr. Baldwin is, I should say, a most charming and attractive person, the best and pleasantest sort of company.

With all my good wishes for the new year,
Sincerely,

139. TO NORMAN PODHORETZ

January 4, 1955

Dear Norman:

It was good to hear from you, and you would have heard from me well before this if I had not devoted December to a virus which, without being anything distinguished in itself, managed to do a considerable job on me. The one moral compensation it brought was hearing my doctor say that I had to put on weight, the first time this has ever been said to me: I had lost seventeen pounds and rather liked the interesting effect. Also I learned, and was scared by, what infirmity of the flesh is, and that one can't overcome debility by willpower. But I'm quite recovered now.

What can I say about your grim and empty situation except that I can imagine it (I think) and that I'm sorry that this had to be your fate? But you won't have a very long time of it, will you? It will be good to have you back again.

I had a call on New Year's Day from Steven. He seems to be un-bowed at Dix, as you were, his experience being, I gather, much like yours. As perhaps you know already, he was down with pneumonia for sixteen days, or, rather, not down but up, kept ambulatory during the whole siege. He seemed in very good shape. He finishes in about two weeks and doesn't yet know what his assignment will be.

There isn't much news of myself to send. Most of the term went to chores, among them getting a new book of essays through the press (the summer went to revision). I don't know what to make of the book and am inclined not to try. The publishers like it and so do some friends who have read it, but I am at the point which I never thought I should reach, of near indifference to it. This, I believe, is a sign of something and I shall be taking thought over the next months when I shall be on leave from teaching. I have to give a few months to mak-ing an anthology for college use from which, so I am told, I should make a good deal of money, which I need; and I hope to use this as a sort of psychic deep freeze or magical sleep. I can't help feeling that criticism, in the way I have up to now conceived of it, is at an end for me, and that I shall have to go on to something more venturesome and elaborate. I feel the sense of something having come to an end as generally pervasive. I was struck when I last saw Steven by his hav-ing said almost exactly what Richard Chase said the day before, that he didn't want to write a review attacking a bad book because he couldn't imagine the audience for whom he was displaying anger and contempt, and also that he didn't want to make the effort to find the language for his emotions, and also that he didn't really want to entertain the emotions, that they gave him no pleasure or satisfaction. I feel as they do, and I suppose it means something that we represent three different "generations." Looking at *Com-mentary*, it seems to me that something has departed from it, that the point, or the irony, of its existence isn't what it was; and the same is true, of course, of *Partisan*. Well, we shall all have to make efforts to move to a higher plane.

Speaking of *Commentary*, did you see the letter against you (and Arnoldian me) from a certain Wasser? When I see you, I'll tell you more about him, now only that he was a graduate student of mine whom I dislike more than any I have ever had. I thought your Faulkner piece was very brilliant, and it certainly was a refreshment in all the cant that has lately been written about Faulkner. Whether or not I wholly agree with your judgment I don't quite know. Perhaps I shall never know—perhaps Faulkner will never really mean much to me one way or the other. But I still suspend my judgment. Not, of course, that I doubt that the new book is impossibly bad.—What happened to the piece at *The New Yorker*? When I spoke to Edith Oliver this summer she said she was pleased with the review.

I wish there were some small gossips to send you, but I've been, as they used to say in the nineteenth century, much out of the world.

Have you had, will you have, a chance to visit England before you come home?

Diana asks me to send her warm good wishes with mine.

Sincerely,

140. TO ETIENNE GILSON[1]

March 18, 1955

Dear Professor Gilson:

Your letter touched and gratified me more than I can say. There isn't, I think, any comment on my work as a literary critic that I would rather have than the one you make, that I am not a literary critic. This doesn't, I need scarcely explain to you, involve any adverse feeling toward literary criticism, or at any rate no large harsh adverse feeling. But I have from time to time approached the realization of what you put so directly, and it has been a secret I have found pleasure in and have taken courage from.

I am enormously caught by what you say about the difference between painting and image making. And you come along with the

---

1. Etienne Gilson (1884–1978), French philosopher.

example of Norman Rockwell at just the moment when I have been thinking that that man has to be dealt with on his own terms, there is no point in going on being snobbish about him. Also I have been trying to cope with my pleasure in the nineteenth-century popular prints, the Currier and Ives sort of thing, which sometimes arouse in me very intense emotions.

For the Rockwell kind of thing in itself, there is, as an actual word in use in art criticism, "illustration." Usually this is used pejoratively, but not always. It comes pretty close to what you mean. But it is of course too limited. If, as I take it, you would include in "iconic art" actual ikons, the word can't do at all.

"Imaging" would be perfectly usable in your context—you will, I'm supposing, set forth to your audience your difficulty in finding a word and you will *try* this one. "Image making" you will want to avoid for the same reason that you would avoid "imagery": they too much suggest the poetic process, the process of metaphor. Even "imaging" carries some overtones of the discussion of poetry. Also, or on the other hand, it has some slight religious connotations—which, of course, may be useful in that they suggest the direct, *intentional* quality of an iconic work. "Picturing" has to me the great advantage of a certain childish connotation: "Picture-book," "See the pretty picture." And "picturing" is exactly what a child does. I should vote for this word, especially if you plan to give a paragraph or two to the explanation of why you chose this in the end rather than "imaging," etc.

You are indeed very kind to think of sending me a copy of your new book. It is not a fair exchange, you are being entirely Trojan in your gift, and I am very grateful, the more because the book headed my list for my summer reading.

It goes without saying that I should be honored to have you quote anything from my book that you might wish.

Let me say again how deep a pleasure your letter gave me and how grateful I am for it.

Sincerely yours,

141. TO MRS. GEOFFREY MADAN

October 24, 1955

Dear Mrs. Madan:

Yours isn't the first challenge I have received to my statement that it isn't possible to like Fanny Price.[1] I, of course, have no settled hostility to her, and I am entirely willing to take heed of the apparently considerable body of testimony to her charm. Of her virtue, even of her rightness, I have never had any doubt, nor have I ever questioned the actuality of the attraction she would have for Henry Crawford.

I'm ashamed to admit that I don't know Logan Pearsall Smith's defense of Fanny, but I mean to be acquainted with it.

Sincerely yours,

Lionel Trilling

142. TO NORMAN PODHORETZ

April 1, 1955

Dear Norman:

I am going to write but briefly, for I seem to be overwhelmed again with work—I'm to give the Freud Birthday lecture in May, which makes a sizable challenge and I'm only just beginning it: but before I withdraw from the world I do want to send you a word.

The death of Bob Warshow was a shattering thing to everyone—I don't know of any death that had the strange *stopping* effect of Bob's. His youth, of course, had something to do with it, but there was more than that. He had a remarkable power of engaging affection, more, even, than I should have supposed, although I had an increasing and very warm affection for him over the past few years; but the shock of his death went even beyond the love people had for him. It seemed to me that many of us—for suddenly there was an "us"—had realized the fact of death almost for the first time.

And then, how strange, how almost shocking it is, that life closes over even so magnificent a thing.

The situation of his little boy is disturbing, and I fear that there

---

1. In his essay on Jane Austen's *Mansfield Park*, in *The Opposing Self*, Trilling wrote, "Nobody, I believe, has ever found it possible to like the heroine of *Mansfield Park*."

is no right person to do anything bold and sensible about it. I have the feeling of Bob's friends that, sweet and good as they are, they haven't the simple reality in action that is needed here.

We saw a fairish amount of Bob this year and last, and everything that he said about his work life has confirmed me in my growing feeling that you must think very carefully about your *Commentary* commitment when you take it up.[1] I actually, and not pretendly, was not disturbed when you made the decision, but the more I think about it the more uneasy I become for you. I think it important enough, you see, to be willing to disturb you, at this distance, and when there is nothing that you can actually do about it. I do not think that you should conceive again the possibility of an academic career, but if not that, then you must not be simple about what will face you at *Commentary*, especially with Bob gone.

My book came out very pleasantly—the publication was full of gratifications. Everybody was very *nice* to me about the book, friends as well as reviewers; the friends for the first time seemed under no strain and showed no self-consciousness. There was a general air of *acceptance*, in which the reviewers seem to have joined. Very nice, as I say, and a little dismaying, for it makes me feel that what everybody is saying is that there is nothing to worry about with me, I'm not going to make any technical *gaffes*, I have a very good mind and quite a prose style, though difficult: and nobody in the least notices *what* I am saying. Misunderstood, you see.

I'm not sure I agree with you about the limitations of criticism as a genre, although to be sure I thought Gilson said the nicest possible thing when he wrote to tell me that I wasn't really a literary critic. At any rate, I feel that one oughtn't underestimate the genre of discourse—one shouldn't, that is, suppose that it necessarily has less energy than fiction. I mean to go on to fiction, as I always mean to, and I'm glad you think of a novel too, but when I speak of a new intensity or a new breadth I don't only mean the difference between fiction and discourse. I think it wrong of us to conceive of fiction as *the* genre of energy to the exclusion of the polemical or contemplative essay.

---

1. Podhoretz began working as an editor at *Commentary* in 1955 and became editor in chief in 1960.

By now the glamour of having been the Soldier of the Month has passed, yet I congratulate you on the distinction. (Were the subscribers able to return you if you weren't satisfactory?)

Let me hear from you and I'll reply as soon as I again emerge. When do you return?

Diana sends her greetings with mine. Jim is quite wonderful these days. He had just got to be very fond of Bob, who a few days before he died brought him a discarded fortress of Paul's, and cannon and soldiers; it was Jim's first experience of someone's dying, and it seemed real but not frightening to him, although of course one never knows about these things with children.

143. TO HERBERT FEINSTEIN[1]

September 20, 1955

Dear Herbert:

I'll see to it that Viking sends Ned Brown a copy of *The Middle of the Journey*, if only to show their interest in the affair. It has always seemed to me that Viking has taken a rather bearish view of this novel, I think for political and cultural reasons that they aren't aware of. The reception of the book in England, which was considerably more enthusiastic than the one it received here, led them to modify somewhat their attitude to it, but only somewhat.

Of course it does seem to me that we are playing in rather bad luck in starting a movie-sale movement at this time, when everybody wants to forget that there is such a thing as the Communist Party or Russia or spies, except that just this morning Burgess and Maclean[2] might have raised the question again in all its splendor. What I mean is that the cultural-political situation of the moment is very similar to that at the time when the novel first appeared.

I shall send you, as soon as I can lay my hands on it, a copy of "Of This Time, of That Place." Here I do think we have a much stronger possibility. Did I tell you that last spring a young man in an advertis-

---

1. A former student of Trilling's, then working at MCA, who had taken an interest in the film possibilities of his fiction.
2. Guy Burgess and Donald Maclean, two members of the Soviet spy ring in England known as the Cambridge Five.

ing agency approached me with a request that I give him permission to dramatize the story for TV? He came back with a script—is this what is called a treatment?—which had some faults that I pointed out but which quite astonished me by the way it brought the story into direct drama visually. I really had not thought that this was possible. The young man, however, has not kept in touch with me—perhaps he was discouraged by a few objections which I made. This summer I mentioned the affair to a TV producer who seemed to take some fire at the possibility of a dramatization. But I believe that at the moment this person is out of a job, so perhaps his response should not be taken too seriously. On the other hand, I also mentioned it to an old acquaintance of mine, William Fitelson, who is, I gather, a very prominent theatrical lawyer here, and he too seemed roused by the idea. So it does seem to me that there is some point in trying to push this along.

I can of course understand why "The Other Margaret" can't be thought of for ethno-cultural reasons.

I take due note of your advice about getting a movie advance on my next novel. Such cupidity had never occurred to me.

Sincerely,
Lionel Trilling

144. TO NATHAN GLAZER[1]

October 5, 1955

Dear Nat:

I should have thanked you and Jason[2] before this for sending us a copy of *Marjorie Morningstar*. An astonishing book. Not the least astonishing part of it is that one *reads* it, and with a kind of curious, hideous interest. Or is it just one of my secret vices that my better nature is overcome by books like this? Leslie Fiedler is right enough in all he says, yet he doesn't take account of the strange awful fascination. But perhaps this *is* a sign of my vice and he's free from it.

---

1. Nathan Glazer (1923–), later an eminent sociologist, was at this time an editor at Doubleday.
2. Jason Epstein (1928–), publisher and editor.

Jason must have been charmed by the picture of Columbia life. Does the author have an unconscious something-or-other about that life? Is Marjorie Morningstar really Marjorie Morningside? Are we to suppose that the Morningside of life, the aurora-dawn, is represented by Herman Wouk (i.e., "Woke," past tense of "wake," what one does in the morning). Very Joycean, very implicative, and I can see the graduate students at work.

Sincerely,

145. TO DON ALBIN

October 10, 1955

Dear Mr. Albin:

The question you ask isn't one that can possibly be answered. You'll forgive me, I'm sure, if I go on to say that it really can't be asked by anyone who means to be a writer. Writing isn't a regular career, like the ancient professions, or even journalism. Financial success, or mere financial existence, hasn't any significant relation with literary talent; or at least no predictable relation—one may write for years without making money and then one may suddenly do very well. The best analogy is with prospecting for precious metals! Liberal ideas in this age of conformity do very well—all publishers have liberal ideas, and so do most reviewers and readers of books. There is only one way to test your ability to make money out of writing—by trying. But there are, I fear, very few young writers who make a living by writing alone.

Sincerely yours,
Lionel Trilling

146. TO IRVING FELDMAN[1]

October 17, 1955

Dear Irving Feldman:

I am sorry to hear that your volume failed to win the Lamont Prize. And of course I'll be happy to write to my man at Farrar, Straus, and Cudahy—it's not Vaudrin, however, but another French name,

---

1. Irving Feldman (1928–), poet, a former student of Trilling's at Columbia.

Giroux.[1] It was to him that I sent your book at Harcourt, but he was then in the midst of the fight which was the occasion of his leaving that firm for Farrar, Straus, and he left the firm without seeing it. He is at present abroad, but I shall write at once anyway and let you know as soon as I hear from him.

I haven't written to you since you told me of your decision to go back to Puerto Rico. I think it was a wise choice. I can't imagine you wanting to spend a great deal of your life there, but the New York situation now seems to me so bad that I think you do well to be out of it. The American situation, generally. My sense of the matter is that this is the time to be alone, there being nothing else one can be. It seems to me that the day of groups and factions for comfort and thought is quite gone by and that this is the time for solitary work. At least I feel that the very last vestige of my life in "circles" is at an end, and I am not sure this is a matter only personal to me or to my generation. I find it harder and harder to suppose that there exists any sort of understanding of what one might say. How much, really, we come to take the political (in the big sense) assumptions for granted! And now it seems that they're finished for the time being. The Geneva mood was indigenous before Geneva.

All that you say about education I agree with, and I can imagine vividly enough what your situation is like. Years ago, when I taught at Hunter College, I used to think that I was in some kind of bad dream, so without normal intelligence, let alone learning, were my colleagues. More and more, even in my own quite good situation, I find that teaching is an unhappy business, harder and harder to justify. I don't always feel this, but very often, and more and more often.

But don't let these things keep you from gorging the honey of life—keep your mind pointed to the sunshine, your marriage, and poetry.

Sincerely yours,

---

1. Robert Giroux (1914–2008), editor and publisher.

147. TO C. WRIGHT MILLS[1]

November 3, 1955

Dear Wright:

In your essay[2] in the Summer issue of *Dissent*, in the footnote on page 207, you say that I have "referred to the Luce publications as examples of high 'intellectual talent.'"

Do you really think that I said any such thing?

I have read over the passage[3] in which I speak of the relation of the Luce publications to intellectual talent. It seems to me that I made it perfectly plain that my remarks about the desire of the Luce publications to employ people of high intellectual talent were not to be understood as a favorable judgment on the intellectual qualities of the Luce publications themselves. It was a matter on which I wished particularly to prevent misunderstanding, and it seems to me that I made my intention unmistakable. But I'd much rather believe that I did not succeed in this than that you willfully, for purposes of polemic, misrepresented what I said.

Sincerely yours,
Lionel Trilling

148. TO C. WRIGHT MILLS

November 22, 1955

Dear Wright:

I was glad to have your letter, and if I've delayed my acknowledgment of it, that is because I've been in and out of the city the last few days and have had no chance to write.

I of course still think that you misinterpreted me, but I don't any longer entertain it as a possibility that you did so by conscious intention. And I am glad of that.

---

1. C. Wright Mills (1916–1962), sociologist and professor at Columbia.
2. "On Knowledge and Power," *Dissent* (Summer 1955).
3. In "The Situation of the American Intellectual at the Present Time," first published as part of the *Partisan Review* symposium "Our Country and Our Culture" (May–June 1952), Trilling wrote, "The Luce periodicals have always been explicit in their desire for the best possible intellectual talent and have been able, by and large, to gratify their wish."

Yet I do think that you were carried away by your *parti pris*, and that you continue to be carried away by it when you explain your reading of what I wrote. You say that you "agree that bright and clever technicians of the word and image abound today, but, really, why use the word 'intellectual talent'? No matter how much it is qualified, 'the point of intellectual virtue' is bound to be taken up." And you add: "About this I am certain that I am not alone."

I must say that you number yourself among some curiously tendentious readers. The word "talent" is a word of very limited import—indeed, it is generally understood to suggest exactly the idea of limitation. It is often used to imply an ability in its potentiality rather than in its realization: that is, a man may still have a talent without doing what is necessary to make himself admirable by it. It quite clearly does *not* convey the idea of virtue. Indeed, the parable from which our word derives (Matt. 25:14–30) says distinctly that one may either put it out at interest and make it increase, or hide it in a hole in the ground, which is a sin.

This being so, it seems to me that there has to be a rather considerable effort of special interpretation to make it appear that my having used the phrase "intellectual talent" necessarily meant the imputation of "intellectual virtue."

Now as to the facts. They are not as you represent them. It is not true that the interest of the Luce publications is confined to what you call "bright and clever technicians of the word and image." *Time* reached out for Irving Howe when he was scarcely known, and engaged him on the basis of his work for other periodicals. Adverse as my opinion of Howe's intellectual performance may often be, I should never think of calling him a bright and clever technician of the word and image—no more than I should apply that description to myself or to my wife: both of us were, at different times, solicited to join the *Time* book-reviewing staff. You have expressed in print and in conversation your admiration of Louis Kronenberger; I share it, although I don't like the book we talked about; and Kronenberger has been for many years an employee of Luce and a most valued one. James Agee was a critic of very high gifts, and a good poet. Robert Fitzgerald is a good poet and a fine classical scholar. I could go on almost indefinitely. Some of the most intelligent people I know are, or have been, in the employ of Luce. The use that has been made of their talents is another question—a question that must loom large indeed in any consideration of our culture. But the facts are as they are.

Then I want to remark on your assertion of the *inevitability* of your interpretation. I am troubled by this because it seems to me to show an intolerance for the usual devices of argument, and, in this far, an impulse to check and limit the uses of the mind. I referred to the Luce publications as an example of the situation I was describing—it should have been clear from what I said about them that I was using them as an *extreme* example. Intellectuals whom you and I are likely to respect do not respect the Luce publications: *therefore* it is the more striking if I point out to them that *even* the Luce publications "desire the best possible intellectual talent." The grammatical or rhetorical device of limiting what is possible or probable by an extreme example is a very simple one, yet it does require for its proper understanding a certain complexity or flexibility of mind which you seem on this occasion to wish to deny—I cannot imagine to what end. Had I said, "Even in the pages of *Dissent* one can frequently find instances of accurate citation of the works of opponents," would you conclude that this was an avowal of my belief in the intellectual virtue of *Dissent*?

But perhaps the acceptance of the extreme example depends upon the reader's judgment of the writer. I know, of course, that you are at odds with my view of American culture, as I am with yours. And perhaps you are at odds with my view of life in general. Yet I think I don't claim too much for my work if I say that its character is such that most people, even those who are antagonistic to my ideas, would not conclude from it that I am the sort of person who would choose the Luce publications as his example of intellectual virtue; if I seemed to them to be doing so, they would find it startling; they would take it to be a notable change in my way of looking at things, not a matter of course. I think I have the right to expect you to know this. It seems to me a *personal* right that I can claim.

I think, too, that you owe it to yourself as well as to me not to sink the disagreement between us to a level where it can be important to neither of us. If you really do believe that I would offer the Luce publications as an example of intellectual virtue, then I am worthy of your satire, but not of your disagreement.

It is in order to preserve the valuable possibility of disagreement between us that I have written at such length to show you something of what your original statement and your defense of it imply.

Now—more briefly, I hope—to the matter of our actual intellectual disagreement, or one particular point in it. You say that the "burden" of my essay is the "rise of the technician and consultant in all areas of modern America." I am not sure that this is a quite accurate description of what I said. The meaning which you give to the words "technician and consultant" is, I gather, a wholly pejorative one. What I had in mind was something at once more neutral and larger. I was trying to refer to the circumstances which require that masses of people work with ideas of some sort and that these people have an intellectual training of some sort. Maybe all people who have this requirement and this training are to be called technicians and consultants—schoolteachers, college teachers, social workers, physicians, laboratory workers, etc. I myself shouldn't use the phrase to describe them, but perhaps it is useful. All these people have considerable schooling and they are all touched with the pride of ideas. I am not sure, as I think I said in the essay, that I like this situation— I'm not a priori charmed by ideology taking the place of principle and honor, as it tends to do in our culture. But ideology carries with it some principle and some honor of its own. And a culture in which ideology is dominant offers an opportunity for the intellectual. The point I tried to make is that the intellectual, by his ignorance of the state of affairs, is missing his opportunity for influence. From the cultural point of view which you express in your essay—a point of view as-it-were aristocratic, and very strict and traditional and ideal—there is nothing to be done with this new class; it is nothing but vulgar and outside the intellectual possibility. I continue to think that this isn't so. I think that a kind of cultural revolution has taken place and that, like the Industrial Revolution, it makes a great deal of mess and vulgarity, but that it also brings with it many possibilities of revision and improvement. The circumstance is fluid, not static.

This, briefly, is my view of the given situation. It may well be that I wrote of it too obliquely, perhaps even, as you say, opaquely. But I am sure that I did not "celebrate" the new technical intelligentsia, although I did speak of the intellectual behavior of certain groups

I had observed as comparing very favorably in seriousness and humility with the intellectual behavior of intellectuals. What I may be said to have "celebrated" was what I took to be the new opportunity for the intellectual, for I believe it to be true that the new intelligentsia are open to education, to the criticism and refinement of ideas. My intention was to say that I thought the intellectual had so far failed in any effect he might have upon the new class—failed because he cultivated his characteristic pathos of powerlessness and isolation and superior personal virtue.

I expressed, I think, a certain optimism about what the intellectual might yet do. This was partly a willed optimism, a way of saying what he *should* do, but not only that, for I did feel some real optimism. If I were writing now I should not express optimism at all. I now think there is very little chance for the American intellectual to be a power in our general life, not in any direct way. It has come to seem to me that the moment arrives in the life of any American intellectual when he elects either torpor or a feckless attitudinizing.

But it would be really good if we could, by our disagreement over many things, convince each other that all is not lost.

Sincerely,

Lionel Trilling

149. TO ALLEN GINSBERG

May 29, 1956

Dear Allen:

I'm afraid I have to tell you that I don't like the poems[1] at all. I hesitate before saying that they seem to me quite dull, for to say of a work which undertakes to be violent and shocking that it is dull is, I am aware, a well-known and all too easy device. But perhaps you will believe that I am being sincere when I say they are dull. They are not like Whitman—they are all prose, all rhetoric, without any music. What I used to like in your poems, whether I thought they were good or bad, was the *voice* I heard in them, true and natural and interest-

---

1. Allen Ginsberg, *Howl and Other Poems* (1956).

ing. There is no real voice here. As for the doctrinal element of the poems, apart from the fact that I of course reject it, it seems to me that I heard it very long ago and that you give it to me in all its orthodoxy, with nothing new added.

    Sincerely yours,
      Lionel Trilling

150. TO EVELYN LONDYN

March 6, 1956

Dear Miss Londyn:

    You raise a very interesting question which I am not able to answer with anything like confidence. But this does occur to me, and it is perhaps too obvious and easy an answer, that the American interest in self-investigation has been given fertile ground by the Protestant tradition. This involves a perpetual examination of the conscience, the research into the inner self, the putting of everything to the question. This tendency is probably fortified by the nature of American society. Where tradition is not strong, where custom is not a strong sanction, the individual falls back on himself, on the determination of motive, of *true* motive, etc. Here Tocqueville might be suggestive to you. In France, of course, tradition and custom are very strong. The sense of society is—or was—very firm. There are ways of behaving that have great authority with the individual. And these ways are so contrived that it is not too difficult to escape from their rigor. Thus, although no doubt it has been much misinterpreted abroad, the sexual life of France has an element of rationalized freedom that is not to be found in England or America. This combination of authority and freedom must have its effect upon the sense of the self. Here the tradition of Molière is much in point—the idea that behavior and manners are of a first importance.

    Add to this that in America, as not in France, the self is something that one feels one can manipulate and augment—can radically change and improve. I have come across the idea in some French writers that Americans cannot bear to be unhappy—hence their recourse to psychoanalysis. I think, too, that in France there may be a greater tolerance of aberrant and eccentric behavior—if one is allowed to relieve the pressures of one's neurotic condition by behavior, one is less inclined to accept the idea of "help" from psychoanalysis, thus less inclined to think of psychoanalysis at all.

And then there is, of course, the long tradition of French moralizing and psychologizing, very great indeed, exerting over intellectuals a great authority of example. If Montaigne and Pascal are in the blood, as it were, perhaps one does not turn so easily to Freud, even though he has much in common with the classic moralists. And the French feeling about mind makes it difficult to respond to the idea of unconscious mind.

I hope these random speculations will at least serve to start your own more systematic ones.

I send you all my good wishes.

Sincerely yours,

Lionel Trilling

151. TO HENRI PEYRE[1]

March 27, 1956

Dear Mr. Peyre,

I have had a letter from Melvin Friedman telling me that in his book certain sentences from an essay of mine appear as part of his own text. He gives an explanation of this and apologizes for it. I have written to Mr. Friedman to say that I assume his use of the sentences was inadvertent, that I do not suppose anything but carelessness is accountable for his failure to put them in quotation marks and to attribute them to their author. To you I will say that I am the more persuaded of this because the essay from which Mr. Friedman takes the sentences is well known: it has been before the public for some sixteen years—I can scarcely believe it!—having been first published in *Kenyon Review* in 1940; it has been frequently reprinted and it is one of the essays of the volume *The Liberal Imagination*, which in its Anchor Books edition has been quite widely circulated. I mention this because it would have been insane for him to have plagiarized from a work which is so little esoteric. And I raise the question of

---

1. Henri Peyre (1901–1988), Yale professor of French literature.

plagiarism because Mr. Friedman writes as if he were under the imputation of having committed it. Is that indeed the case? Or is it that he has thus interpreted a strong reprobation for having been careless in the mechanics of his scholarship?

As for the latter sin, I cannot help being sympathetic to one who has committed it, by reason of my own experience. When my dissertation on Arnold had passed all the academic committees, I was quite sure that it was ready for the printer and was on the point of sending the manuscript off. It was my wife, who is not a scholar, who insisted that I check all quotations by comparison with the original texts, and all dates, etc. This I opposed with considerable force—it seemed to me quite unnecessary, and I was fatigued, and very sick of the book. But wifely insistence prevailed and we spent several weeks of a fiercely hot summer checking quotations and other details. I still shudder over the result—there were literally hundreds of errors, many of them important. Had I published the book in the state in which I thought it was ready and had anyone undertaken to point out the errors that would have appeared, I suppose I should have been forever discredited as a scholar. So I am well aware of how one's notes may become corrupted, how in the passage from a note card to a draft, from a first draft to a second draft, an author's name, or quotation marks may drop out, and, indeed, how a passage meant to be quoted might, by a sequence of errors, come to seem part of one's own thought and composition.

Sincerely yours,
Lionel Trilling

152. TO LOUIS LUBONSKY

November 13, 1956

Dear Mr. Lubonsky:

I am sure that you will understand that yours is a letter that cannot be "answered" but only *acknowledged*. This I do gladly. But there are one or two comments I would make. I see no contradiction between what you call "amassing wealth," what I call making a living, and listening to a Beethoven quartet. It would be quite impossible to listen to Beethoven quartets all day. Maybe that is what some

Beethoven quartets are so sorrowful about. Also I would say that man has never been master of his needs. I suppose that is what is implied by "needs."

Sincerely yours,
Lionel Trilling

153. TO SYLVIA SALMI[1]

November 13, 1956

Dear Sylvia:

There is one picture I do like very much, although it isn't the one you prefer. I've marked it—it's the other one with the hand and cigarette. It has the drawback that the hand hides the lower face, but the general effect is, I think, excellent. We have, I believe, differing theories about pictures—you like the moment and I like the generality—and, so far as I can make out, most good photographers agree with you, so I suppose I am wrong. What I like about the picture I have chosen is its repose. The momentary expressions can all grow out of this—are, as it were, subsumed here. I am sure I often look like the picture you like—amused, ready to joke, a little vulgar!—but I don't think this looks the way I am. The same is so of the others. I have, I believe, a very mobile and changing face, and I haven't the slightest doubt that I appear all these ways. But I don't think that any of them represents the way I look to most people's recollection. Maybe sheer downright lousy vanity dictates this belief. But I do think that theory has something to do with it.

I am surely the Most Difficult Subject Ever, but don't think I am in the least an ungrateful one. Quite the contrary, and I am really very pleased with the shot I do like and shall be delighted to have a print of it.

I do hope we can see you and Herbert before long. Jim has been ill with the grippe for ten days, Diana for five.

Yours,

---

1. Sylvia Salmi (1909–1977), photographer, wife of Herbert Solow, a journalist who had been Trilling's friend since college.

154. TO DIANA TRILLING

December 27, 1956[1]

Dearest:

A page boy knocked to deliver mail that was not mine. I seized upon him to tell him that there was no plug for my electric shaver, and also to say that I needed writing paper. He was *much* concerned over the lack of a plug, looked around, and discovered one in an almost inaccessible place. Again, he was like a character in a moving picture, dead serious, eager (or very ready) to please—chubby-faced, solid, radiating (not the word) self-respect. Such self-respect you never saw. Nor ever heard such an accent—the nice thing about the Cockney accent is that it is used with exactly the same sense of the goodness of the class from which it comes as the genteel or upper-class accent. The plug that was found was a three-prong affair, my contraption a two-prong business. "Tell you what I'll do, sir, I'll see if the house here has the kind that will fit and if not I'll run out and get you one. I'll pay for it myself and bring you the bill and you can pay me when I bring it." Well, that's a good deal of trouble, it's very nice of you. "It's my job, sir"—as a perfectly serious explanation, not as a piety. Returns later to bring paper and to say that the electrician would be up to take care of the situation. I had meanwhile laid out all my English coins and found I had only two sixpence and some copper. It seemed to me that there wasn't enough to tip him with (I am *very* stupid about the money) and so I said I had no silver and would he be around tomorrow? Why, yes, sir, he would be around but there was quite enough here, and with his finger he drew a circle around the two silver sixpences and some copper. I said, pointing to the sixpences, "Do you mean this?" He said, "No, sir, this *and* this," including some copper. I said, "Is that enough?" He said, "Well, it's my job, sir, but if you wish it, *quite* enough." Then he gave me a brief explanation of the money equivalences, and he said, making an elaborate calculation out loud, with much "carrying," "So you see, sir, this is a twentieth of a dollar." This seemed sizable and conclusive—he thought he was being well done by. So did I.

[...]

---

1. Written from London, during Trilling's first visit to Europe.

I think I ought to set it down now while I feel it and before it might happen to change, that I am unbelievably happy being here. I have the sense of saying "I'm in London, I'm in London," and it has the feeling we always hope Jim will have when we give him something special and that maybe he got with his sword. At the moment it is pure and unqualified pleasure; I didn't think I could ever feel it. I keep thinking of what difficulty you may be having, and in the cold economics of the situation I am glad that I am enjoying myself so much—I think quite as much as you would hope.

With all my love—
    Lionel

155. TO DIANA TRILLING

December 30, 1956

Dearest—This is just a reportage letter, but a long one. I'm sending it in two parts.

Friday
    [. . .]
    I went up to change and the Bs taxied me to the Kristols,[1] who have a pleasant flat, very spacious and elegant. (They are unable to get a place of their own and they move from house to house or flat to flat every six months.) Cyril Connolly[2] was there when I arrived, looking miserable and reduced, all his feathers plucked somehow. He was very cordial, but oddly pathetic. I asked him what he was working on and he answered with a genuinely miserable "Please let's not talk about that"—the idea being that he spends so much time reviewing to support himself that, etc. We chatted for a while and then Fred Warburg came and was genuinely friendly and made a date for lunch on Monday. Then the other guests came thick and fast. Each spoke very warmly and intimately until the next introduction was made at which they faded away with none of the Am[erican] em-

---

1. Irving Kristol (1920–2009), editor and intellectual, was at this time editor of *Encounter* in London; married to Gertrude Himmelfarb (1922–), historian.
2. Cyril Connolly (1903–1974), English literary critic.

barrassment about this. They left, when they left, without saying goodbye. Stuart Hampshire,[1] whom I like and who is a very good mind, was most cordial in asking me to put up at All Souls when I come to Oxford, and Isaiah Berlin[2] did the same thing while I was talking with Hampshire. It was not hard or awkward to bring J[acques Barzun] into this. There was an interesting but sad little bit at this moment—Berlin spoke about the Niebuhrs,[3] asked how R[einhold] was, and I said he was better and Urs[ula] looked much happier than last year. B. said, "I like her, yes I do, I like her, despite what everyone says"—and when I expressed surprise at the general opinion, at "despite," he assured me it was so, however much he would not concur, and he put the matter to Hampshire, who said apologetically that he liked R. but not U. Berlin interpreted the general opinion—the English opinion—as holding U. to be too oppressively genteel: in effect, I think, they object to her being English in the old-fashioned way. "I think," Berlin said, "that she is very generous and very intelligent." Mrs. Warburg came and was very cool to me and very attentive to Dwight Macdonald until she discovered that Macdonald was not me, when she became very cool to McD. and very attentive to me: she never attends these functions, but this one she had to come to because F. had said that I must because you were a very particular friend, etc. Very elaborately dressed, the only woman there who was, much black serge, capes, muffs, gloves. She closely resembles—guess who? Correct, except that she is on a more delicate scale: but when they are face to face and you see them in profile, the resemblance is startling. She said she was part Russian and part (is it?) Spanish (or something) but she always marries Englishmen, Fred being her third.

—Stephen Spender[4] very cordial and invited me to lunch on Sunday: and could I do aught but accept? John Lehmann[5] invited me to dinner on Thursday—Spender and Lehmann look more and more

---

1. Stuart Hampshire (1914–2004), English philosopher.
2. Isaiah Berlin (1909–1997), English philosopher.
3. Reinhold Niebuhr (1892–1971), American theologian and intellectual; married to Ursula Niebuhr (1907–1997), English-born theologian.
4. Stephen Spender (1909–1995), English poet.
5. John Lehmann (1907–1987), English man of letters.

babyish—younger than ever as they grow older.—Annan[1] did not come.—Dwight very friendly and rather charming and asked me to a party on New Year's Eve.—I had little chance really to talk to anyone beyond a few sentences, except an odd and interesting young man named David Sylvester[2] who does art and movies for *Encounter*. I drank almost nothing—one martini through the whole evening, partly because the English make martinis in a ghastly way and warm, but chiefly on principle, and I think you would have thought I did well as a guest of honor; I was *most* polite and responsive.

I was introduced, on whatever chance or principle, to none of the relatively few women who attended. I met them by one means or another after the most part of the guests had gone home and the remaining ones stayed to a light supper. Whether this was an English system or the Jewish system of my hosts I do not know—it had something of the effect of social occasions at the Cohens. Gertrude Kristol is intelligent and, I think, nice, but rather meager and uncertain, despite her years here. Irving the same. Dan Bell[3] gives the effect of more personal distinction.

The talk did become general after the supper, but it was friendly and pleasant. We left at about 12:30 and the Feivels drove me to my hotel. (She is a rather interesting woman, South African, and apparently well-to-do. Feivel more recessive than he was in America.) I went for a walk to Piccadilly Circus and got a different sense of London life than I had been getting all day. There you get the raffish, rebellious, rather ugly aspect of the population—some of them very ugly indeed, like characters in Graham Greene's earlier novels, a good many foreigners, Negroes, Cypriotes (the Cypriotes come in great numbers to England, which they are free to do, being British subjects!), etc. A strong dash of Americanism—primitive hot dog stands and Pepsi-Cola stands. None of this attractive [or] good-natured, it seemed to me. On the walk back I saw my first prostitute—she stood quietly on the sidewalk and when I glanced at her she said "How do you do?" in an intense imitation of social elegance, and smiled very socially, and the desperateness of the effort was appalling. I didn't

---

1. Noel Annan (1916–2000), English academic.
2. David Sylvester (1924–2001), English art critic.
3. Daniel Bell (1919–2011), sociologist.

think I would be shocked by a whore's solicitation—but I was, not by the situation, which is so traditional, but by the human actuality of it. The others I saw were quite ghastly—their elaborate dressing and makeup for the role; and as I came into Dover St. a car slowed up and a woman's voice called, very upper-class, "Hello there!" I walked along slowly, thinking that conceivably someone I knew had stopped by to see me, and then, as I came up to the car, I saw that it was two women elaborately dressed, and in white, who asked me if I wanted to go for a ride. Very grim—and apparently a new method here.

Sat.

A very warm day and rather sunny. Went in the morning to St. Paul's. Was rather disappointed by the interior, although the outer shape is really wonderful almost any way you look at it. Inside, it seems grand only when you can sit nearly under the dome. In the crypt I found it hard to know what emotions to have—here Wellington and Nelson are buried and all sorts of heroes and scoundrels, and semi-scoundrels. But more heroes than scoundrels and I found myself resisting. After my second day here I began to understand Lawrence in a new way and that whole English-intellectual tendency to be *agin* and to mock *something*, and the drift toward eccentricity. They allow a good deal more for eccentricity (as we supposed)—they have to: the pressure of established things is really very great, and there is a quality of *trance* about a great many English people. You can understand why people want to burst things open and to be shocking and to talk about *real* feelings—and why so many of them become absorbed again, when they get older, by the established order. It's like H. James said—civilization is very thick here, and so must be its discontents.

From St. Paul's I wandered over to St. Bartholomew-the-Great, the second-oldest church in London—Norman and about half-bombed out. It was very lovely and very cold (in temperature) and I wasn't, somehow, much moved by it. I asked directions in a tobacconist shop of the Charterhouse—which I remembered as being Lamb's and Coleridge's school, which it wasn't, not being Christ's Hospital, although the Charterhouse was a school, which is now in the country—and an old character stepped outside to direct me. As he was doing so along came a little old man, genteelly dressed, carrying a little basket and a walking stick and when he heard the name Charterhouse, he said he was going there and would lead me—I guessed, and I was right, for he soon began to brag about it—that he was one of the "brethren" of the place: it has been since 1611 a foundation for taking care of aged gentlemen, soldiers, naval officers, clergymen, etc. There are now only twenty brothers—"I am one of the brothers," the old man said, very proudly, and he went on to tell me that they had everything of the best and gave me the menu of Xmas dinner. He was eighty, and we talked about N.Y. and how hurried it was, and was it more than two hundred years old, and how there was no more horse traffic, and how expensive it was to live in Piccadilly, although once you could do it for £2 a week, and he said it would be all right for me to look at the court but he had no authority to invite me inside only the Master and the Registrar could give me that permission, and he asked me my name, which puzzled him, and told me his—Lucas—and we said goodbye—I quite naturally lifting my hat to him, as quite naturally I kept calling him "sir": and I could quite understand Thackeray who had gone to the Charterhouse School and had made his Colonel Newcome die as one of the "brothers," having so come down in the world: here was the last vestige of that "simple and innocent gentleman" that the English loved to imagine.

[. . .]

Went then to Spender's for lunch. He lives in St. John's Wood, another semirural suburb, once a great place for love nests, then for artists, now for prosperous or sub-prosperous middle-class people and intellectuals. Houses detached but close together and big shabby green yards. Sp.'s house old (1820-ish) and shabby but very pleasant. His wife away or did not join us. The Macdonalds were there and the Julian Huxleys. Mrs. McD. is very nice and simple, rather gay, late fortyish, pleasant looking. She undertakes to have an effect on Dwight— when he said, on leaving, that we could take a taxi together and I said yes and we would share the fare and he said, as if it were a good and original idea, "Why yes, yes," she said, "Dwight, no, no!" and she must have spoken to him privately on the point because when I got out at my door and offered to pay half, he said, "No, no, wouldn't think of it!" and as if he meant it and was showing off to her how well he could do it. Huxley very affable, and Mrs. H. very charming. She is the Juliet—Juliette?—who, I think, turns up in the Lawrence letters. It was very sweet to see her seeing to it with Spender that her son's book should get a review in *Encounter* (he is an anthropologist of thirty-four). I wondered if we would ever be getting in our literary licks for Jim! She and I got on very happily and she has asked me to supper and an evening on Wednesday when Huxley will be showing some pictures he recently took. I like Huxley, although his political and social ideas are, I think, pretty empty, or wrong.

The meal was not lunch but dinner—excellent melon, roast beef (not good), roast potatoes, peas, salad, a very good lemon custard, cocktails, two wines, brandy, coffee. They employ an Italian cook and a French girl, a student, to help around and take care of the children. There are a boy of eleven and a girl of six, very robust and red-cheeked, very pleasant manners. The boy came in to say hello and left. The girl claimed more privileges and stayed with the guests for quite a while. Spender indulgent with the children but quite firm with them—in general I have the impression that the English are quite as child-centered as we are in Am. I was struck yesterday by the number of fathers walking with smallish boys, often hand in hand.

—At lunch Mary McCarthy was quoted as saying of someone that he was a starry-eyed opportunist, whereupon I denounced the misattribution or plagiarism and affirmed your rights!—

Spender has gone in for art and his walls are heavily hung with examples. Alas I remain anesthetic. He seems to be making a great deal of money—says he is—and thinks of his life as devoted to travel as well as to literature. The Macdonalds on the way home spoke of his virtues as a host, his thoughtfulness and kindness to his guests, but I thought he was singularly abstracted and unresponsive. He seems to me dazed or bemused and to be on the point of breaking into tears, and his voice is in a monotone and terribly dreary.

Must stop now.

But do I get around?

Love,

L.

Kiss Jim for me and tell him I'll write tomorrow. I think I'll get his pistol at the Old Curiosity Shop, but give him no assurances. I've had no word yet—should I have?

156. TO DIANA TRILLING

January 1, 1957[1]
The Atheneum, Pall Mall SW1

Dear Diana,

—for I hope you will allow me to call you that: it is thus that I think of you after the peculiar intimacy of our conversation on the true relation of Church and State over tea yesterday.—So much of what you said has stayed with me in memory. I was particularly struck by what you said about the dangers of complacency. Something of the sort was said to me only the other day by Mr. Arnold. Yet your way of putting it carried a greater force than his, great critic though he is (or as some think him, for I confess that to my taste he is rather too *intellectual*—too, if you will forgive the expression, French). And yet, well as you put the matter, I cannot but feel that we do have reason for pride—not complacency, indeed—in our achievements of the century. Think—for only one example—what the opening of the Suez Canal will mean for England's future and not for England's future alone—what an effect it will have for peace and better understanding as communication grows among mankind!—But we must talk of these things further!

Devotedly,
    Lionel T——

157. TO DIANA TRILLING

January 5, 1957
Paris

Dearest Di,

This morning I went for a long walk to the Cité to see Notre-Dame and Sainte-Chapelle, discovered that I had got my directions mixed and had gone in the opposite direction. So I went to the Louvre

---

1. Trilling dated the letter "January 1, 1867," and wrote accordingly.

instead, there being not time after the walk back for my original intention, and saw the Greek antiquities and also the Galerie d'Apollon of Henry James fame.[1] If you speak to Quentin,[2] tell him the H.J. dream is now clear without a doubt. The Venus de Milo I can live without, and most of the things that have led to the Park art of Paris. This last, as you remember, is devoted to three great subjects— the female rump, which is most lovingly treated; unlikely combats of animals (rhinoceros and lion, lion and crocodile, lion and wild pig, etc.), and transportation—that is, one person carrying another, Aeneas carrying Anchises, but more often, of course, some male mythology carrying some female mythology. The Nike is indeed impressive, and now and then one comes on some tenderly modeled thing, but mostly the fifth century is uninteresting and I had to remember the Elgin Marbles to regain my piety. Tomorrow I'll go to see the *Mona Lisa* and, especially for your sake, the Rubenses. (I have, incidentally, become an enormous walker. I go at a terrific clip and never suffer from pains in the back! Even museums do not tire me!)— Returned to hotel to find N.N.[3] wanting me. Very disconcerting in his appearance, which, as I think I said, is large, gross, and doesn't inspire confidence. Full of the great work the Congress is doing in Vienna for the refugees. At lunch he talked of the rivalry of the various organizations for relief, and I had the impression that you are in a very touchy racket—that it *is* a racket, although a necessary one. We took a taxi to the restaurant where the luncheon was to be held, after a drink here at the hotel. It was a most elaborate lunch, culinarily speaking. It was held in a notable restaurant—I believe the name is Trouant[4] (not sure) and it is known for being the place where the Prix Goncourt dinner is held. The main dish (duck in orange sauce) was presented for my inspection by the waiter, and the manager or owner was also presented to me; he chatted with me in English and told me what an honor, etc.—We had filet of sole with

---

1. The Galerie d'Apollon, a room in the Louvre, is the setting of a nightmare recounted in Henry James's memoir *A Small Boy and Others*; Trilling analyzes the James passage in his essay "The Princess Casamassima," in *The Liberal Imagination*.
2. Quentin Anderson (1912–2003), a colleague in the Columbia English Department.
3. Nicolas Nabokov (1903–1978), secretary-general of the Congress for Cultural Freedom, which sponsored Trilling's visit to Paris.
4. The Paris restaurant Drouant was founded in 1880.

an elaborate sauce, white wine; the duck, red wine; assorted cheeses; fruit; coffee. The food was good, but, alas, did not seem to me different in kind etc. The intellectual quality of the occasion was not good—or put it that the social occasion wasn't well managed. There were some six or so French writers who knew English and America, N.N., a young Am., Hunt, a functionary, and Taverni, another functionary. I sat between a retired lycée professor, Lolou, whose wife had done the good translation of my Flaubert piece, and Manès Sperber.[1] The former not interesting, the latter a very lively character who has a high admiration for your work, of which he spoke at length (your *Partisan* essays and your diary). Across from me sat an attractive and impressive young poet and critic Pierre Emmanuel,[2] who spoke an excellent English, and we had some conversation. I had been told that I would be asked questions about Am. Lit, which sounded grim but reasonable. However, everybody, except Sperber and Emmanuel, acted just as Americans would have acted—they talked among themselves, in French, and quite forgot about me. This was the fault of N.N. and his subordinates. At the end, a little conversation about Am. Politics. At the end I left with Sperber and we went for a walk. It occurred to me right away that I had not been "honored" and that I didn't mind, which was a comfort.—I went for another long walk and reached the Cité this time. I knew it was too late to see Sainte-Chapelle and Notre-Dame properly, or from the inside at all, but I liked the walk along the Quai. I saw Sainte-Chapelle from the outside and actually had a good walk around Notre-Dame in a useful light, studied the portals for a while and saw the inside for a few moments, and shall go back tomorrow.

My feelings about Paris are very complicated, made the more so, I am sure, by the disadvantage of language. Maybe that is why I feel that it is a hostile city—slightly, only. But it delights me too. And in some ways I like the French intellectuals better, as a class, than the English. They want to take themselves seriously, and that is impressive. I was very taken by Merleau-Ponty,[3] whom I met briefly last night

---

1. Manès Sperber (1905–1984), Austrian-French writer.
2. Pierre Emmanuel (1916–1984), French poet.
3. Maurice Merleau-Ponty (1908–1961), French philosopher.

at the concert; I liked also his wife, who is very distinguished in appearance (a "lady") and who is a physician. And there are one or two others who impress me in the same way—Emmanuel among them, who will be in the States this spring and who will come to see us.

The Kaplans immerse themselves in all this life and speak of it very pleasantly, but it is for them rather a spectacle than something they participate in—partly, of course, by reason of their diplomatic position. Tonight I have no engagement and so I ordered a ticket for the Comédie-Française. I shan't understand much, but it's Molière, and I *ought* to have seen it.—Tomorrow I am to dine with the Bowmans of the embassy, Friday the Kaplans are having a dinner party for me. I'll save Saturday for Jacques, Sunday is the cocktail party.—Busy, busy!

With my best love,
Lionel

158. TO DIANA TRILLING

January 15, 1957

Dearest Di,

Arrived from London to find three *marvelous* letters from you. Such a joy to have—not only because there had been four days in Paris without any, but wonderful in themselves. I cannot tell you how happy I am that you have the feelings you have about being alone; it seems to me that this is the best news I have ever had. How much we shall have to learn from this when we are together. For me too the being alone has been a great experience—a curiously *modest* experience—not dramatic—yet quite decisive: it has shown me how little vulnerable I can be to incidental and occasional things, how undisturbed by what would ordinarily bother me a good deal. You speak of your neurosis conspiring with the neurosis of our society; we often speak of your neurosis and mine conspiring; it is not an idle way of speaking. My neurosis may be at work all the time, but it certainly is a different thing when it isn't conspiring with yours, or with that of my society. Of course, that your being alone has given you contentment is a more striking fact than that my being alone has so smoothed me out—in part because you're involved in your habitual society. There is so much to say about this that I scarcely know where to begin: I had better not try, it being already very late.

I didn't in the least think you were aggrieved about an insufficiency of letters—I meant to write jokingly, out of conscious virtue; I was only troubled about the mails.

I left you at the point where I was going off to the party. Pouring rain and great difficulty getting a taxi. Arrived a little late. Party *very* elegant—champagne and scotch whiskey—many writers—all kinds of elegant sandwiches—hot canapés—about, I should say, a hundred people—some distinguished—members of the executive committee and the magazine editors, both groups here for meeting. Chiaromonte[1] (truculent), de Rougemont[2] (just what he was I don't know), Lasky, Kristol, Macdonald. Aron[3] couldn't come but sent his wife, who apologized profusely. The Congress people polite but not effusive to me; I cool, pleasant, reserved. A sizable number of the French people knew my work and were *very* nice about it. Of course a great many did not. [. . .] Again, did not feel *honored*, but again had no emotions about it.

On Monday went to Chartres with Jacques, taking nine o'clock train. Paris at five thirty nearly dark. Frightfully cold in Chartres, inside the cathedral and out. It is, of course, indescribably lovely—the rose windows have haunted me since, the proportions of the columns and the vaulting seemed almost painfully perfect—it was all full of pathos for me of an extreme kind—it seemed so clearly to have nothing to do with God—to be a monument to *order*, perfectly gratuitous.—We had thought we would have to stay until four, that there was no train before, but we found a train at twelve thirty and felt that the cold was too great and our powers of apperception too small to lead us to want to stay longer. We had a sandwich and took the train.—The texture of the stone of the exterior is disturbing—so extremely weathered and pocked—and J. says that the exterior carvings are much darker than he recalls them from his last visit. But it was a wonderful experience—has been with me so clearly since—like that performance of *Richard II*.—Rained hard all afternoon and

---

1. Nicola Chiaromonte (1905–1972), Italian intellectual.
2. Denis de Rougemont (1906–1985), Swiss writer.
3. Raymond Aron (1905–1983), French sociologist and intellectual.

I stayed in and wrote cards. Went to the Régence (Diderot, Napoleon, Stendhal all went here) and had tea and brioche with Sperber—it is really true that you can sit for two hours for just the price of that—no waiter comes near you—young actors and actresses from the Comédie-Française—

What Sperber was after was talk about the relations between the Committee and the Congress.[1] I don't know how much to trust him but I am inclined to take him pretty much at his word. He is unhappy about the hostility between Com. and Cong. and wants to repair the breach. I can't go into it now—much too much detail, but I have it well in mind and shall give it to you in a letter later or when I return. Much of what he said confirms our feeling about the Congress, and he seems to speak our language. He is very intelligent, very perceptive. But the details must wait.

[...]

I loved Paris, for a while I thought it nicer than London. Certainly it is more *beautiful*, but it didn't speak to me in the same way as London—alas maybe because I can't speak to it.

Must stop—

With my best love,
Lionel

159. TO DIANA TRILLING

January 21, 1957
King's College, Cambridge

Dearest Di,

The Oxford trip was quite as good as it could be. I had rather expected that Stuart Hampshire's invitation meant a room and shift for myself, but actually Hampshire was a host of the most assiduous and gracious kind, to the point where I felt almost guilty for the extent to which he devoted himself to me for two and a half days, involving me in the life of the college, taking me around, having people in to

---

1. The Congress for Cultural Freedom, an international anticommunist advocacy organization, was founded in 1950. Diana Trilling played a leading role in its American affiliate, the American Committee for Cultural Freedom.

meet me, etc. And all the fellows of the college were most friendly and cordial—it couldn't have been a more thorough immersion in the life of the place, given the time.—On Friday evening we went to Berlin's for dinner, H., another chap, and the Berlins. Of the house I can say that if you had the wherewithal you would do a home just so, with perhaps the difference that you would have used more English than French furniture, but very maybe not. At any rate, you will know what I mean about the room if I say that it is very casual and a little on the cluttered side, on one wall three Tiepolo drawings, elaborately framed, and so brilliant that you think they *must* be reproductions, but no—and one of them is the finest I have ever seen. Two more elsewhere in the room. A little head of a clown—Daumier. A small, misty scene in a garden—Watteau. On a table a tiny Renoir. Alas, alas, what money can do! And all so indifferent and easy!

[...]

—Left early Monday morning for London and found at the Athenaeum a letter and a phone message from Forster[1] to say that he would have to be away from Cambridge until Wednesday evening. This was dashing, but I set out for Cambridge at twelve nevertheless. Found Forster in, he was not to leave until five. On my arrival I found a most cordial letter from Noel Annan, the new provost, who had been sending me messages by various people and who, as Forster had told me in his note, would be my host. A college guest room had been prepared for me, very pleasant. I spent the afternoon with Forster, who is in very good shape, much more robust than when we saw him eight years ago, and very spirited, and very affectionately cordial to me. He sent his greetings to you very warmly, and you can tell Jim that he asked after him and sent his love.—Forster left for town and I went to evening service at King's College Chapel, which I had previously seen with him. The place is what it is said to be—exquisitely beautiful—and the service of boys' voices charmingly sung, quite lovely under that infinitely high ceiling. I came back to find that Noel Annan was looking for me. He found me and took me to his (magnificent) house for a drink, apologized profusely for being engaged for

---

1. E. M. Forster (1879–1970), English novelist and essayist, was the subject of Trilling's second book.

the evening. He got me a bottle of the College whiskey when I said I had trouble buying some; asked me who I wanted for dinner tomorrow night, brought his wife in, and, when I said I planned to have dinner by myself, took me to the Combination room, introduced me to some of the fellows, and left me. The vice-provost, side-whiskers like Matthew Arnold, took me in charge, led me into the hall, and I had pleasant talk with a young art scholar, a rich British Meyer Schapiro (if you can imagine it) named Jaffe, who works on Rubens; afterward he took me to his rooms with another young man, and we had a good evening, although I had rather looked forward to being alone and quiet. Tomorrow I lunch with Annan, and have dinner with him. Wednesday eve. I have dinner with Lewis, lunch with the Butterfields.—

Tonight I *am* tired and I shall stop now, but I wanted to bring you up to date—even if in skeleton form.

[. . .]

All my love,
Lionel

160. TO WILLIAM FAULKNER[1]

February 18, 1957

Dear Mr. Faulkner:

I have been out of the country for some weeks and so have not been able to answer your letter of January 2.

The "basic three points" which are set forth in the document you enclose with your letter seem to me unexceptionable. But I cannot be in accord with the statement made in the document that "we should free Ezra Pound" when that recommendation is made for the reason which is given. I can believe that an argument might be made for freeing Ezra Pound, but certainly not on the ground that "while the Chairman of this Committee, appointed by the President, was awarded a prize for literature by the Swedish Government and was given a decoration by the French Government, the American Government

---

1. William Faulkner (1897–1962), American novelist, received the Nobel Prize in Literature in 1949.

locks up one of its best poets." This is falsely simple and wholly illogical—to the point of absurdity, if you will forgive my saying so.

Sincerely yours,

Lionel Trilling

161. TO JOHN W. ALDRIDGE[1]

March 6, 1957

Dear Mr. Aldridge:

I am sorry that you have had to wait so long for an answer to your
letter.

Your rebuke—if I may call it that with an entire understanding
of its friendliness—comes home to me. I have more than once thought
that I should have sent you some word after the appearance of *In
Search of Heresy*. The full explanation of why I did not would be something like a chapter of my autobiography. Let me try, however, to at
least outline the reasons.

There is first the sheer matter of the impracticability of my engaging in literary correspondence. I find that it grows ever harder to
keep enough time in my life for work. I don't understand why, with
each year, there seems more to do of an inessential but unavoidable
kind; but so it is. It has become almost impossible for me to read a
book out of simple inclination or curiosity, just for fun; and the
writing situation brings desperation. This being so, I have for some
time made it a point to avoid literary correspondence. A letter about
ideas takes a morning, I find—at least that—and I must not spare
mornings.

But more decisive in my not having written to you is that I have
a principled feeling about not involving myself in controversy about
criticism. I don't think of myself as having a "position." When it is
forced upon me that people do attribute a position to me, I try to keep
the idea of it at bay, willing as much ignorance of the details as I can.
There is, I recognize, a reason for some gratification in people supposing that I do have a "position," but I consider it dangerous for me
to be aware of it, feeling that the awareness would make it harder to

---

1. John W. Aldridge (1922–2007), literary critic.

come at each new book or situation as freshly as I should like. You will recognize this impulse to secrecy, this aversion to talking about one's work, as frequent with creative writers, and perhaps you have seen it in other writers of criticism. I can understand that there is some anomaly in my indulging the impulse, or some evasion of "responsibility"; yet I think I do well to continue.

I am not in the least Olympian about "attacks." I often take them quite personally—I find that they often have a quite personal tone—and can feel angry about them. But I almost never respond to them intellectually, partly because I don't want to, partly because they mostly don't succeed in engaging me. (In general, I do not think of myself as being involved in criticism as a literary institution: I read critical works only infrequently.) I was angry with Delmore Schwartz for his essay—amusedly angry—because I perceived a personal cast in his argument, especially, of course, in his ridiculous misinterpretation and misrepresentation, but I wasn't intellectually involved, except in one small matter where I did think he had caught me out in a careless formulation. I think I did for a while consider answering Schwartz, chiefly out of anger and with the purpose of showing him to be absurd. But then I thought that the one thing one can't debate (especially not in the pages of *Partisan Review*) is *manners*, whatever one means by the word; and that to argue the point I had made about manners and the novel would be to betray the nature of my remark, which was not meant to be an established, ironclad idea, but merely an observation, of sufficient weight, to be sure, but not programmatic, and not really complete in itself.

And here I come full circle to my first reason for not writing. It has seemed to me that in taking up my remark in your *Partisan Review* comment and then in your book, you have dealt with the remark as if it were programmatic and complete in itself. (I haven't either at hand to check this impression now that I present it to you.) That is, if I were to send you word about *In Search of Heresy* and of my gratification that you had so generously come to my defense, I should have had to write at length to set forth the difference between us—as well as to raise the question of whether you were wise to dignify Delmore Schwartz by an answer to an essay that was so bad in tone and idea—and this would have meant a long letter of the kind I avoid, although with some regret. It would, you see, have taken a long letter to tell you why I think that your conception of the part that is played in the novel by an interest in manners is different from mine. I am, you understand, not writing that letter! So I shall not undertake to expound my reasons for discovering the difference between us.

But nothing that I say means that I don't think it deplorable that writers don't talk to each other, and I've already said that I think it deplorable that I didn't get in touch with you about *In Search of Heresy.* I hope you can forgive me.

Sincerely yours,

162. TO RICHARD CHASE

March 21, 1957
35 Claremont Avenue

Dear Richard:

I have read your dialogue[1] and I had better say straight out that, so far as it touches upon me, which of course it does a great deal, it made me angry. I suppose I rather expected it would from what I had heard of it, and perhaps that is why I put off reading it. But the considerable anger which I did feel for a while has now quite passed off. I should like you to believe this, and I should like you to understand that I didn't *undertake* to get rid of it; I wasn't trying to practice forbearance—it just went, quite of itself.

But I owe it to you to say why I was angry. In your dialogue you announce a position for yourself and urge its general rightness and necessity. You go about defining this position by contrasting it with a position which you describe with no little satiric intention and force: a chief part of your ridicule—it quite amounts to that on the page, however you meant it to seem—is the ironic use of phrases which quite obviously come from my work and are intended to indicate it. I make but a small point when I say that it would have

---

1. "Radicalism Today," *Partisan Review* (Winter 1957). Trilling might have seen an allusion to himself in Chase's sarcastic reference to "the moral intelligence," which he equates with "moderation, compromise, countervailing forces, the vital center, the mixed economy—plus the usual cynicism."

been more friendly and courteous to have named me right out as a writer whose point of view you mean to oppose and think others should oppose, rather than to have said this by implication. Aggression—not a very dreadful word in my vocabulary—is always the better for being open and avowed. The course you took inevitably makes your declaration of opposition more personal than you probably intended and as much a matter for gossip as for thought. And the gossip might well be of a particularly unpleasant kind because of the reason you playfully give for your not naming names, even though at that point you are not—as I understand, but not everyone will—talking about me.

Yet this, as I say, is only a relatively small point. The essential reason for my anger—I suppose it is returning as I write! but only momentarily, I think—is the interpretation you make of my position. I of course can't undertake to say here in what particular respects I find you so extravagantly mistaken. It is possible that there will be, or ought to be, an occasion when I should endeavor to do just that. But now I'll only say that I entirely reject the views you impute to me.

It occurs to me to wonder whether, in attributing to me the position you do, you do not really mean to characterize adversely, and to repudiate your own position of a few years ago, and that you confuse mine with yours, for there were surely many points of agreement between us. Certainly some adverse attitude to your own former views must be involved in your present feeling, and I think it would have been more enlightening, more graceful, and (best of all) more interesting, if you had indicated that your former self was one object of the attack you make. But you ought to have it clearly in mind that, although there may have been similarities in the things you and I thought a few years ago, we are two very different temperaments and intellects and the lines of our respective developments were bound to describe very different patterns and, mixing the figure, to have very different resonances; and probably they had essentially different intentions—we each have enough willfulness to make that likely.—I might have been glad to have written the eloquent conclusion to your *Melville* with its praise of community and connection and its warning against the deceptions of liberal moralism and self-righteousness, but it was you and not I who represented Starbuck as being more truly "human" than Ahab, as being the more admirable, the better, man. This is not a judgment I would ever have made, although I found it, when you made it, and even now, interesting and worth thinking about. If it is a judgment you now believe to be wrong, you should not suppose that it was I who made it.

And that's all I have to say, except to add this comment: that this incident of ours points to a sad inadequacy in the lines of communication between us. It is very wrong and strange that I should not have known, except in a vague way, in what direction you have been tending the last few years, and that you should have expressed your radical disagreement with me by implication, and suddenly, and publicly, instead of directly, and over the time in which it was developing, and personally. In this serious failure of communication I hold myself to blame as much as—and, indeed, more than—you.

Yours always,
Lionel

163. TO BRUCE BLIVEN[1]

March 25, 1957

Dear Mr. Bliven:

I am of course sorry that you find my reference to you contemptuous and insulting. I don't think it is either—it is, to be sure, adversely critical, but, as I know from experience, no one can take part in the intellectual life without incurring comment of an adverse kind. I myself cannot get over finding it painful, so I understand something of what you feel, and I am personally sorry that I have caused you pain; but I confess I don't see how the intellectual life can be conducted without adversity.

In my essay on Mr. Wilson[2] I make particular reference to you because of the views you expressed at a staff luncheon which I attended during the literary editorship of George Mayberry. With the exception of the late Isaac Rosenfeld, I don't remember who the other members of the party were. As I recall the occasion, I was in-

---

1. Bruce Bliven (1889–1977) was editor of *The New Republic* from 1930 to 1953.
2. "Edmund Wilson: A Backward Glance" in *A Gathering of Fugitives*.

vited to attend the luncheon and meet you because I had protested
an editorial request to cut a review I had written of a book I considered important. My protest, I suppose, raised questions of principle
and probably spoke of the diminished attention that was being given
to literature in *The New Republic*. Some of the young men on the
staff felt that this was the result of your intention, and wanted me
to discuss the matter with you and urge the contrary view. During
the course of the luncheon the matter came up for extended discussion. I expressed the opinion that, as I say in my essay, "politics
and literature naturally live in a lively interconnection" and that
nothing could be more useful to a liberal political point of view
than the fostering of a strong interest in literature. You professed
yourself—rather impatiently—as being unable to see that this was
so, and said in effect that you thought the political situation was so
very urgent that literature would simply have to take a secondary
place in *The New Republic* for some time to come. It was to this
opinion that I referred when I said in my essay that the idea of the
interconnection between politics and literature was entirely beyond
your comprehension.

In conclusion, let me observe that nowhere in my essay do I
suggest, as you imply that I do, that you had anything to do with
Mr. Wilson's withdrawal from *The New Republic*.

Sincerely yours,
Lionel Trilling

164. TO EDMUND WILSON

April 7, 1957
Columbia University

Dear Edmund,

Glad to see we are still hand in hand. Always a pleasure to me.
Two *general* critics. Two *American* critics. Two critics not *New*—yet,
of course, not *old*. It is pleasant to think that Literary History may
be preparing to receive us together. Pleasant to think that someday
an examination question will read: Name and discuss two general
American critics who are not New Critics but are not Old Critics
either.

Answer: Tilson and Willing!

Just to show how Literary History is made (and how my life is ruled by coincidence, for it came a day or two before your *Crimson*) I enclose a letter from Bruce Bliven (Dear Sir: he calls me) about my traduction of him. Perhaps it will interest you. Whether or not, send it back so that Literary History will not be deprived of a document.

Yours,

Lionel

165. TO MORIKIMI MEGATA

August 27, 1957

Bradley Street, Westport, Connecticut

Dear Mr. Megata:

I have, I fear, waited much too long to respond to your charming and very gratifying letter. I hope you will forgive me for what must seem to you a lack of courtesy—I am sure you will if I tell you that the last months have brought me much more work than I have been able to do and that in consequence my correspondence with everyone has had to suffer.

What you say about the danger to American culture of conformity by "seductiveness" is of course true. But one must not overestimate this danger. For one thing, it has become fashionable for Americans who have any pretensions to intellectual status and to the prestige of liberal opinions to warn against the danger of conformity. One hears the warning on every side, uttered by judges and university presidents, and suchlike people, on every public occasion. The denunciation of conformity has become—we might say—itself an act of conformity! I often wonder whether the people who speak so glibly about nonconformity can really imagine what it is. They speak about it in the abstract, and it sometimes seems as if the only concrete nonconformity they can conceive of is somebody being a Communist!

Then, too, we ought to consider whether it isn't true that every culture has it as one of its characteristics that it tends to impose a very considerable degree of conformity of one kind or another, and that perhaps the greater the culture, the greater the degree of conformity it imposes.

But I think that the word "conformity" is a very misleading one. What I look for as a sign of the vitality of a culture as it makes itself manifest in individuals is a feeling of integrity or dignity which allows them to look at the world with seriousness or with a sense of personal connection with it—with a sense of personal destiny in it. This will no doubt often lead to ideas or deeds that do not conform to accepted standards, but such ideas or deeds will have much more importance than those which arise from a conventional idea of non-conformity. What often troubles me about American culture now is that I do not see enough of the feeling of integrity or dignity to which I refer, not enough of the seriousness and personal connection with the world that alone can give value to the intellectual life; or to any kind of conscious life.

It would be very good if you could come to this country to see for yourself how things are. I do hope that someday that will be possible. If it ever should become so, we will surely meet, and I look forward to that. Meanwhile let me thank you most warmly for the pleasure your letter has given me.

Sincerely yours,

188. TO JOHN WAIN[1]

September 24, 1957
35 Claremont Avenue

Dear Mr. Wain:

It seems to me that your manuscript reproduces in a remarkably accurate way the content and tone of our conversation (which I remember with pleasure).

There are just three emendations that I'd like to propose.

1. I'd be grateful if you could somehow, somewhere, say that I jibbed at the idea of being prescriptive about writing, or that I insisted on treating the prescriptive role with irony. Perhaps the place to do that is on page 4, where you speak of trying to "manoeuvre" me into talking prescriptively. Here you do indeed imply that I tried

---

1. John Wain (1925–1994), English writer, had interviewed Trilling for the *Observer* newspaper.

to evade prescription, but I think I tried harder than your sentence suggests.

2. The one place where you don't represent me accurately is in my first speech on page 3. I thought at the time that you were not really getting the point of my remarks and set this down to a difference in generations and to the difference between the English and the American experience. Rather than the way you put it, my situation ten years ago was this:—I was indeed, as you say, involved with people who stood in defense of progressive and liberal ideas. These people constituted something much more than a "group"—you must remember the ideology of the New Deal, how liberal and progressive it was, how pervasive it was, and then you must have it in mind that there were many people for whom the New Deal ideology was but minimal. The accepted and expected stance of intellectuals at that time, and of people who wished to acquire intellectual (and moral) prestige, was an intransigent liberal-radicalism. These people liked to think of themselves as isolated and beleaguered: they had a very elaborate pathos of their own heroism. Actually they were in many ways very influential. I conceived my role to be that of a critic of the ideology and the sensibility of these people, although counting myself one of them. It seemed to me that the progressive point of view—especially as it was influenced, often unconsciously, by Communism, what here we called Stalinism—was deteriorating into a new philistinism. It was against this that my essays of the period were directed. The preface to *The Liberal Imagination* will give you a fuller statement of this. It will lead you to see why some people speak of me as "antiliberal" and why your statement of my position isn't accurate.

What happened to make me feel "lost" was that the high fervor of the liberal culture abated. Liberalism is endemic among the educated classes of America, but it hasn't at the moment its old high intensity. For example, now that the situation of the Negro has become a matter of government policy, there can be very little intellectual and moral prestige in taking a liberal position on the question—one takes it, of course, but without any sense of doing anything striking in taking it—there's nothing to do *but* take it. (Of course in the South, as I need scarcely say, the situation is very different indeed.) With liberalism no longer fervent, I was deprived of my target. My war was always a cultural rather than a political one.

In the same speech you make me say that "I feel the need to choose a plot that has a direct bearing on public events." I know I said something like that but not quite that. I think I remarked on the fact that a significant number of successful novels do deal with public events or issues. This was by way of making the point that the private life no longer has the same interest to us that it had for Henry James. And I did say that I was drawn to plots that involved large historical considerations. But not what we ordinarily mean by public events or public issues. The sense of things that I should like any novel of mine to suggest is the natural involvement of the fate of private persons in the cultural situation. Again the important word is "culture," used, of course, in its anthropological or sociological meaning. Here I would refer to Lawrence again—to his sense of cultural crisis which goes along with, is part of, his intense response to his individual characters. Dostoevski is another case in point. Or even Tolstoi.

3. On page 7 you say, "If there isn't a sophisticated class . . ." But there *is* one. . . . The point is that it is likely to be isolated or widely dispersed, not continuous or self-perpetuating. And it is far less true with us than with you that people of sophistication—I dislike the word: of education, of cultivation—are to be found in politics, in civil service, etc. (although this state of things is changing).

I don't think that *The New Yorker*'s role is quite so decisive as you make me say, or so active. Rather it is indicative—it *represents* the personal attitudes of the enlightened middle class: very *sweet* attitudes, although rather nerveless and thin.

I hope that these proposals for modification don't make too oppressive a job for you at a busy time.

[. . .]

Sincerely yours,

167. TO DAVID RIESMAN

March 31, 1958

Dear Dave:

I have let too much time go by since your kind letter—you will imagine that this has been because of sizable preoccupation; and to this was added Diana's long and troublesome bout of chicken pox and several trips that I had to make. Nothing about life for the last months has been quiet for us.

I took this Harvard invitation with all seriousness—it was clearly so much more seriously meant than the earlier one—but I have decided not to accept it. The decision has left me feeling rather bleak—I think I need a change in my life and what was suggested by this one was certainly very charming. But I don't have any—except as it were formal and sentimental—doubts about my decision. I think that if I were to summarize all the many considerations that led me to my choice, I would come up with *pride*. Of course I felt very deeply flattered by the offer and no one could have made it with more impressive directness and simplicity than Bundy[1] did. But then I found myself resenting Harvard's power and its impulse to make a concentration of prestige, and a kind of perverse commitment to Columbia's poverty and even to its gracelessness. I felt too that for me to make a radical change in my life at this point—at my age—would constitute a kind of adverse criticism of it; and suddenly I felt an impulse of loyalty to the way I have lived, for all my dissatisfactions with it.

I would not, however, have you think I was quixotic. Actually there was practicality in my choice, for it seemed to me that what I most wanted at this point in my life was a greater measure of privacy. Time certainly seemed of great importance, but privacy yet more. It may have been a mistaken imagination, but I believed that the new job implied a kind of involvement with students that I shrank from. What you tell me of your plans for work with undergraduates is not, I think, only the response of your particular temperament to the implications of the post, but the estimate that a conscientious person is pretty nearly bound to make. The Harvard undergraduate, if I have a true sense of him, is far more conscious of his teachers and makes more demands on them and more personal demands than the Columbia undergraduate ever thinks of doing—it often happens that my students never think of me as particularly a personage at all until they go to Harvard and are quizzed about me by their friends! I can, of course, give what the students would have probably asked for, but

---

1. McGeorge Bundy (1919–1996), at this time dean of the Faculty of Arts and Sciences at Harvard, later national security adviser to Presidents Kennedy and Johnson.

I ought not do so. My preoccupation and my energy have to go into my writing: this I have been feeling more and more, sometimes with a kind of desperation. And of course it isn't the students alone who would have made the situation that I feared, but the colleagues as well—I don't have your confidence that I could control the social circumstances of my intellectual life, and there is a kind of over-awareness of personalities at Harvard that I should not like. All the strong community of the place makes a good academic situation; I respect it and even like it, and I wish that Columbia could have at least some of it. But I think it would harm me.

It might have been possible for me to cope with the adult situation. But the terms of the job, as I understood them, seemed so clearly to suggest intense personal connections that I thought that it would be even more fatiguing—although in a different way—than classroom work. Perhaps if it had been one of the original university professorships that had been offered me, with the emphasis on my work rather than on relation with the undergraduates, I might have made a different choice.

I set forth the first of my reasons to Bundy and he, in a long and extremely pleasant letter, undertakes to say that the fault is his, that he did not present things as they might actually be. Possibly that is so, and possibly my imagination was too timorous. But I don't think so, even though I have, as I say, the misgivings that are natural after so important a decision.

Columbia responded to the possibility of my leaving with a very pleasant dismay and of course undertook to make my situation here a better one. It can't match Harvard in comfort and other things, but it does what it can, and I shall teach less and have more frequent leaves if I want them.

You will suppose that among the things I—we—regret in not making the change is that we will not have you and Evie for neighbors and town-mates. But perhaps with your nearer proximity we will get to see you more often.

Yours always,

168. TO HERBERT FEINSTEIN

August 28, 1958

Dear Herbert:

[. . .]

Now as to your lecture. I like it for its spiritedness, which is of course your constant characteristic. But I am troubled by its length—maybe your audience was patient and even enthralled, but you had better learn now that you can't count on holding people for more than an hour and this means about six thousand words, Everything you said could have been said in that space. Which leads me—not for the first time!—to your diction, to its too many words, to its excessive and particular kind of colloquialism. In an academic situation this may have the effect, for a while, of shocking in a pleasant and amusing way, but in itself it is not good. It is not good in *you*—it inevitably suggests self-depreciation: me, I'm just one of the kids from the corner: surprised, mister, that I know Proust? You don't need this.

As to the content of the lecture, I think you have rather pushed things around to make your point. The sexuality of the Wife of Bath is not really paralleled by any of the Jewish examples you give. *Her* sexuality is very simple, lusty, amoral, comic in its directness, self-justifying in its paganness, and not ugly. The Jewish examples you cite are all ugly. This is suggested by the nature of the suffering of the husbands, which is represented with an addiction to masochism (on the part of the authors) which is to me quite revolting. The fact is that the Jews do not handle sexuality as you—following others—say they do. They are *not* simple about it, they are *not* natural about it and acceptant of it. Irving Howe, dealing with Jewish sexual attitudes and denying that the Jews are puritanical, follows Ludwig Lewisohn[1] and others, but I am sure they misrepresent the case. The antisexual impulse of East European Jews is extreme. They may make a great thing about sexuality as a hygienic measure in marriage—what a people for hygiene, which is always a mask for superstition, which always hides compulsiveness and fear!—but they think that sex is dirty, that all the body is dirty. Instead of Howe,

---

1. Ludwig Lewisohn (1882–1955), American Jewish novelist.

read *Life Is with People*. I think the author's name is Borowski.[1] He turned out to be a Communist agent and murderer, but the book, though sentimental, has a good deal of good stuff about the people of the *stetloch*[2] [*sic*] and it is especially good on the Jewish feelings about the body. (They respect the head and the eyes, nothing else.) Consider the fuss about the *mitzvah*[3] [*sic*]—which is not, as you say in one place, a ritual bath for *bad* women, but for all women—and you will see how disturbed by sex the Jews are, how repelled.

All this may suggest to you that I don't share your enthusiastic admiration for Jewishness as it appears in East European Jewry. No, I don't—I find that each year I regard it with more and more adversity. It has produced some of the best people I have ever known, and some of the people I like best. But I find that I grow less and less sympathetic with almost all manifestations of the culture. (And the late secular literature is erroneously overrated.) Nor do I like the culture any better in its attenuated American forms. I think it has injured all of us dreadfully. Does this shock you?

I think you miss one very simple point in drawing your comparison. Almost any full account of the life of the Jews of East Europe will suggest that in the nineteenth century—and later—they lived lives that were virtually medieval. The status of the scholar, for example. The organization of the yeshivah, the habits and methods of study, all suggest the academic life of medieval times. And this medievalism marks other parts of the culture. Just as much of what we think of as Jewish is not Jewish at all but East European—this is true of food, of manners, of modes of speech and modes of feeling—so much of what we think of as Jewish is medieval. Here the Jewish culture and certain parts of the national cultures are at one. The books about Poland that Virgilia Peterson wrote when she was the princess Sapieha make this quite clear; and what one finds there accords entirely with the life and beliefs of my wife's mother, who was brought

---

1. Mark Zborowski (1908–1990), co-author with Elizabeth Herzog of *Life Is with People* (1952).
2. Properly "shtetlach," plural of "shtetl," a small Jewish town.
3. Properly *mikveh*, a ritual bath.

up in a rural district of Poland. I wish somebody who really knew something would undertake to deal with this at length. But you might start by looking at the *Life Is with People* book.

Sincerely,

169. TO GEOFFREY HELLMAN

October 3, 1958

Dear Mr. Hellman:

This reply to your note comes much too late.[1] I hope that you will put the blame for my delay on housepainters and students and forgive me.

I don't think it is *quite* true that I have written more introductions to literary works than anyone else, although it may be nearly true. But I am sure that you will understand me if I say that even if the estimate is pretty close to the truth, I would prefer that it not be dealt with as a salient or especially interesting fact in my career as a critic. A good many of my most ambitious essays have been written as introductions; with but a few exceptions that I can remember, it has seemed to me that a publisher's invitation to write an introduction to a book presents itself to me as an occasion, a particularly advantageous one, to deal with the book or its author in a large or an intense way, and it is not uncommon for me to publish the essay apart from the book it was written to introduce, in some literary journal. That is, the specifically *introductory* element of my introductions is quite a secondary thing in my mind, whatever may have been in the publisher's mind when he invited me to introduce his book. This being so, I am sure that you will see why I should not want the mere number of my introductions—supposing it to be unique—to be the subject of a Talk of the Town piece. I don't in the least doubt the goodwill with which you would write about me, but with the very best will in the world you couldn't, starting from the point you have in mind, keep from putting me in the uncomfortable position of that poor chap in Boston—his name has slipped me; he was a psychiatrist as

---

1. Hellman, a writer for *The New Yorker*, proposed to profile Trilling in the Talk of the Town section.

well as a poet—who was known for having written *more sonnets than anyone else!*

You will not, I am confident, think that I am being extravagantly sensitive in saying this. I am sorry that I am depriving myself of the pleasure of making your acquaintance—I'll hope that another occasion for that will soon occur.

Sincerely,

170. TO WILLIAM GAMBLE

February 6, 1959

Dear Mr. Gamble:

You will not think it a rebuke but only a statement of principle if I say that in my opinion the subject of a critical essay ought not be consulted, or invited to cooperate in what is to be written about him. Having made my principled position clear, I shall not be so un-friendly—or perhaps so deficient in vanity—as to abide by it in this instance.

I believe that the first work by Freud that I ever read was *Civilization and Its Discontents*. At least this was the first of Freud's works that I read with what might be called critical interest—very likely I had read, or read in, *The Interpretation of Dreams* in the bad translation that was, until recently, the only one available, and I seem to recall that I had read the Clark University Lectures, but maybe not. And of course there were books about Freud, and an atmosphere of knowing about him. I read *Civilization and Its Discontents* in 1930. I was given it for review by *The New Freeman*, which was an attempt to revive the excellent *Freeman*. It will suggest something about the state of Freud's reputation at that time, if you consider that this book was assigned to a young and virtually unknown reviewer. I wrote the review and it was set up and a proof sent to me, but it was never published, for *The New Freeman* suddenly died. I didn't keep a copy of the review but I recall its tenor with perfect distinctness—I characterized the book as ridiculous and even as offensive. I was just then beginning a period of Marxism and any explanation of the human condition by reference to anything else than economic and political injustice seemed to me morally indecent. And the "discontents" that Freud referred to seemed to me absurd and, indeed, really inconceivable.

I don't remember when I changed my opinion of the book and came to think of it as one of the most important books of our time. Very likely this was in 1939 or 1940, when I undertook to read a great deal of Freud for my lecture at Kenyon College which, in a revised form, has appeared as "Freud and Literature."[1] I reread it frequently, for I often assigned it to classes of mine, for one reason or another. But I read it, as a teacher often reads books, in the light of what I had said about it the year before, and very likely, being pressed for time, with an eye to the passages I had marked as especially significant. Last year, however, I read it in a somehow different way (perhaps because I was using a new text!) and so many passages leaped to mind as new and striking that it seemed as if I were reading an almost new book, and I admired it even more than I had done before.

I believe that the only occasion when I devoted a considerable amount of time to reading Freud was the one I have referred to, in 1939 or 1940. At that time I read virtually everything by Freud that has been translated into English, with the exception of the technical papers—my interest, of course, was in Freud's relation to literature and to culture in general, and to ethics.

But as soon as I have spoken of the extent of my reading, it occurs to me that I have never read *Totem and Taboo, The Future of an Illusion*, and *Moses and Monotheism*, serious omissions.

It has long seemed to me that the best introductory work to Freud is the *Introductory Lectures*. Partly because it was one of the books in the Senior Colloquium at Columbia College, a course I gave for many years, I used to know this work especially well. And *Beyond the Pleasure Principle* has always seemed to me a work of peculiar importance.

When I was preparing to write my Freud Anniversary Lecture, I planned to read all of Freud through again. Fortunately for the lecture, I wasn't able to do any reading at all.

Every now and then I read one of the pieces in the five volumes

---

1. In *The Liberal Imagination*.

of the *Collected Papers*, but of recent years I have come to feel that my relation, not to Freud's thought, but to his actual writings has become attenuated, and I have it in mind to spend some time in renewing my acquaintance with his canon, which of course has become the more accessible and attractive with the steady appearance of the volumes of the standard edition. I used to have the idea of writing a short book about Freud as a moralist and I haven't wholly given it up.

I ought to add that although I don't go out of my way to read the psychoanalytical literature, many psychoanalysts send me their papers and I usually read them. I haven't properly informed myself about the so-called ego psychology, which is the most important development of the "orthodox" Freudian line; and I am only just beginning to be aware, at second hand, of existential psychoanalysis. I have a fairly extensive acquaintance among New York psychoanalysts, but this has but little intellectual value—within the limits of my experience, the best of the analysts are not speculative but clinical.

I hope all this has been of some use to you.

Sincerely yours,

Lionel Trilling

171. TO JOHN FAIRBANKS LYNEN

April 17, 1959

Dear Mr. Lynen:

I shall be very glad to have you read the text of my remarks on Mr. Frost at his birthday dinner.[1] But I am afraid that I shall have to ask you to apply to Mr. Stanley Burnshaw of Henry Holt and Company [. . .] for a copy of the manuscript. I am sure that Mr. Burnshaw will make it available to you.

I am glad, too, to give you my personal permission to quote from

---

1. At a dinner in honor of Robert Frost's eighty-fifth birthday, Trilling made a speech in which he referred to Frost as "a terrifying poet," emphasizing the "tragic" side of his work. His remarks sparked a literary controversy after they were reported by J. Donald Adams in *The New York Times Book Review*. "A Speech on Robert Frost: A Cultural Episode" was published in *Partisan Review* (Summer 1959) and appears in *The Moral Obligation to Be Intelligent*.

the text, but you will also need to have Holt's permission, through Mr. Burnshaw. Holt has it in mind to print the speech as a pamphlet later in the year—or did have; the *Times* pundits may have converted them to the idea that it misrepresents their poet.

It will interest me very much to know whether or not you think I spoke justly about Mr. Frost. What I said was largely influenced by my desire to detach his reputation from the Adamses of the world and it may be that I went too far in my reconstruction of Frost's poetic character. Lewis Nichols seems to make it out that Frost was distressed by what I said. I think he was startled but really pleased, and when I met him the next day, he was very jolly with me. His remark about "cruelty" was not as Nichols gives it. After reading "The Road Not Taken," he said, "many people take that poem in the wrong way. It's a cruel poem." Then he thought for a moment and said something like, "I have a good deal more cruelty in me than people know." It seemed to me that this was suggested to him by my having said that he was a "terrifying" poet.

Sincerely yours,
　　Lionel Trilling

172. TO PAUL CARROLL[1]

June 8, 1959

Dear Mr. Carroll:

I had hoped to be able to reply to your letter of May 22, as you requested. But the pressure of dissertations and doctoral examinations was so great in May that I could do scarcely anything else. Perhaps by now my opinion about the "obscenity" of the material published in *Big Table* is of no value to you in your legal defense. But then again it still may have, and in any case I do not wish to seem indifferent to the situation which you describe in your letter.

Let me say, then, that according to any legal definition of obscen-

---

1. Paul Carroll (1926–1996) was the editor of the short-lived magazine *Big Table*, whose first issue, including work by Jack Kerouac and William Burroughs, was impounded by the U.S. Post Office on the grounds of obscenity. The decision was reversed on appeal.

ity that I know of, I can find no obscenity either in the chapters from Mr. Burroughs's novel *Naked Lunch* which you published, or in the fiction "Old Angel Midnight" by Mr. Kerouac.

You may use this letter in any way that you wish. I should like to assure you of my entire support in this matter. I am sure I can count on you not to interpret this as critical approval of the pieces I shall be glad to defend in a legal way!

Sincerely yours,
Lionel Trilling

173. TO STANLEY BURNSHAW[1]

June 8, 1959
Columbia University

Dear Stanley:

This letter follows upon our telephone conversation about the relation of Henry Holt and Company to my speech at the Frost dinner—follows, I am sorry to say, at some distance of time: over the last few weeks I have been not only busy but harried.

I should like you to know that I do not think that Henry Holt and Company are under any obligation, of any kind, to publish the text of my Frost speech. I took the firm's declaration of its intention to bring out the speech as being in some sort a compliment to me, supplementary to its compliment of inviting me to speak at the birthday dinner, and I was pleased and flattered by it. But if reasons of any kind have led the firm to wish to reconsider its intention, it seems to me that they are entirely free to do so.

I say this not without some—what shall I call it?—wryness or dryness. It must naturally seem to me that the firm, by its uneasiness about publication, implies that some credence is to be given to the idea that there is matter in the speech which could be thought offensive to Mr. Frost. This idea is absurd; eventually, when the speech is generally available to judgment, it will make ridiculous whoever has

---

1. Stanley Burnshaw (1906–2005), poet and editor, became friends with Trilling when they worked together, over a period of years, on the anthology *The Experience of Literature* (1967).

held it. And I am naturally wry or dry that Henry Holt and Company should seem to be lending it a sort of tacit assent.

But this does not modify my very clear and simple feeling that the firm is not under any obligation to publish the speech.

Sincerely,
Lionel Trilling

174. TO RABBI ISIDOR HOFFMAN

July 3, 1959
18 Bradley Street, Westport, Connecticut

Dear Rabbi Hoffman:

By an odd chance, your letter came just as I was thinking of writing to you. I have been trying to order my schedule of work for the fall and I have kept in mind your request, made in the spring, that I speak to the Seixas Society.[1] As I recall our conversation, I was to see if there was not some subject of Jewish interest about which I could speak to the society. I am afraid that I must report that, after considerable effort, I can find nothing that I can talk about.

This is not the first time that, to my regret, I have had to say this when you have invited me to speak to the Jewish students. In all probability the incapacity that I report will continue for at least a few years more. I am therefore going to ask you to trust to my goodwill, to let me inform you when I have something to say that will be appropriate to the occasion of my addressing the members of the Seixas Society.

When in the past I have said that I was not able to accept your invitations to speak to the Jewish students, I have felt that you took some degree of offense at my answer. I hope I am wrong in the impression I have had, but if I am right, I should like to urge you to believe that it is my respect for the Jewish tradition that has dictated my refusals of your invitations. I am not learned in that tradition and there is nothing that I might say about it that would conceivably be worth hearing. My own relation to it is private and personal and not susceptible of discussion on a public occasion. You have from time to time suggested that I deal with certain "cultural" subjects and I have

---

1. A Jewish student organization at Columbia University.

tried to see whether I might not be able to do something with one of these, but I have never been able to find them of any real interest. They mostly come down to the Jew in this or that literature, and the day has long gone by when I have been able to find this a matter of much literary importance. I would not deal with these subjects in my writing or teaching—except to touch on them glancingly—and I don't think it right for me to give them an importance to Jewish students that I don't think they have.

It would give me a very considerable pleasure to discover a truly serious subject that would be appropriate for a lecture to the Seixas Society. If I ever do, you can count on my telling you about it and on my asking you to invite me to speak to the Society.

Sincerely yours,

Lionel Trilling

175. TO NORMAN MAILER[1]

July 3, 1959

18 Bradley Street, Westport, Connecticut

Dear Norman:

I am sure you will have supposed that it has not been through neglect or indifference that I have delayed so long my answer to your question about the story.

I have read the story with great interest and with no little admiration. I put the statement of my admiration in that wry, backward, "no little" construction because it is a complicated admiration. It contains all my respect for the vivacity and vigorousness of your writing in itself, and for your skill in narration and in handling the stance of your narrator; and it contains my high respect for your courage in undertaking the theme. When it comes to my response to the story as a whole, I find that this is not really a literary response at all but, rather, a moral response—what I think about is your courage in undertaking the theme and the force of your doctrinal intention. I don't, that

---

1. Norman Mailer (1923–2007), novelist and nonfiction writer, had circulated a letter to fourteen critics asking for their opinion on the advisability of publishing his sexually explicit story "The Time of Her Time."

is, judge what you have written as a work of literature but as a doctrine set forth by literary means. You may find this an adverse criticism of what you have done, but I don't mean it to be and I don't think it really is. I see no reason why literature shouldn't be put at the service of doctrine; on the contrary, indeed, I like to see this done. If you press me to say why I call my response not a literary one, I'd say, I suppose, that I find I don't much care what happens to the people in the story (except, of course, that one is always curious about everyone's sexual fate) but that I was glad to have the report of actuality that the story gives and that I found myself in agreement with some of the ideas it proposes or implies. I could, but I shan't, go on to explain and defend this judgment of mine, perhaps by making reference to some of Lawrence's stories about sexual relations. But let me at least say that I don't think your story has failed, given its elements. Given those elements, I don't think you could have done anything "better" with it or that you could have made it more "successful" in a literary way. It is what it is, and it is all right: admirable for what it is.

So much for aesthetic judgment, which you didn't really ask for.

Now for practical judgment, which must be, of course, a moral judgment as well as a legal one. I think the story *should* be published. I think that there is a considerable chance that it will run into legal trouble. I shall be glad to give you any help in defense that I can.

In saying that I think the story should be published, I am not speaking from a simple—an as it were anarchistic—position about censorship. I don't take the line that the mere idea of censorship is a priori stupid: I think, indeed, that I would undertake its defense in principle. (At least I would as against certain people's superior disgust with the idea.) But I think that there should be no interference with the representation of sexual acts or ideas in fiction of serious import (and I don't mean that the fiction has to be overtly serious, or serious as opposed to gay and funny). Again my position is not simple. I deplore the new tendency to explicitness about sex, I think that it is having all kinds of bad results in feeling and in behavior, but I think that at the present stage of our culture it is necessary and will be necessary for some time to come. Put it that I am in favor of a lot of explicitness for ten, maybe twelve years; then everybody shut up. So I'm with you at least for the next ten, maybe twelve, years.

Does this serve to answer your question? Please don't hesitate to press me further if it doesn't.

I should like to add this: that when I say that I think that the story should be published in your book, I am taking into account your particular position, your particular commitment, what I believe to be your conception of your work and your career. If you were a writer who had just happened to have written an explicitly sexual story as it were simply for literary reasons, I might still urge its publication but with a quite different emphasis and tone. In urging *you* to publish, I have in mind your avowed position as a moralist as well as a novelist. (I hope you don't mind being called a moralist. It is something that I am often called and I am supposed to wince when it happens. But then I am said to be a moralistic moralist—that is, one who moralizes—and you are not.)

Sincerely,

Lionel Trilling

176. TO NORMAN PODHORETZ

August 22, 1959[1]

18 Bradley Street, Westport

Dear Norman.

I liked your piece on Mailer[2] very much indeed. The wonderful energy of its prose is an expression of the energy of its perception and of (what is really a different thing) its sympathy. As I read it, I recurred again and again to the thought of how much good it will do Mailer to know that it is possible for him to be understood with this much seriousness and complication.

I would have written to say this some time back if something had not intervened between your essay and me. And very likely I would have written to you at a greater length of praise if it had not been for the intervention. What happened was that I read the galleys of Mailer's *Advertisements for Myself.* I shall only try to indicate, not say in full, what effect the book had on me. I'll begin by saying that I read it,

---

1. The draft of this letter in Trilling's archive is marked "not sent."
2. "The Embattled Vision," *Partisan Review* (Summer 1959).

at least for some days, with great sympathy and liking, and even enthusiasm. I could never be quite certain whether or not I would have had the same response if I hadn't come to have a slight personal acquaintance with Norman himself and to have had for him a very considerable liking and respect—this, I have often thought, is a good, and serious, and courageous man, and hurray for him. But whether or not the personal judgment had an undue influence on my judgment of the book, I *did* like it. I was pleased by the author's overt ambitiousness, by his effort to make himself defenseless, at the same time that he was always putting up his dukes to defend his masculine honor—I found something most engaging in the open boyish intention of being manly and honorable, and in the connection of these qualities with the life of feeling. But then the grounds of my liking for the book began to give way under me.

If I had more time to make the effort, I would have greater confidence in my ability to explain why my feeling began to change, why, in the end, the book fatigued me and left me feeling irritatedly dissatisfied. Perhaps I can suggest something of my sense of the matter by saying that I came to think that our cultural situation couldn't be properly dealt with by a mind that had this much of Tom Sawyer in it, entrancing as Tom Sawyer can be. You make a point of Mailer's direct and immediate response to culture or to cultural fashion, and this does indeed seem to me to be a notable virtue; you know how much I take to the idea of a man acting out his role on the stage of culture and history. But now that I have put it that way, I wonder if it isn't what is implied by the terms of the metaphor that fatigues and begins to repel me—the "acting out," the "role," the "stage"; the histrionic aspect of our intellectual life bears in upon me and saddens me, more and more. In Mailer's book the personal noise began to bore me, the personality-ism, the pointing to the self. I know it is too cheap and easy a stroke to say that in the very idea of *Advertisements* there is a kind of surrender to the culture Mailer is attacking: I know how it can be said that he is turning the modes of the culture against themselves, etc. But have you ever seen Jack Paar on TV and observed how concerned he is with his truth and sincerity, and with how he figures in the culture, and with how so many of the agents of the culture don't understand him, and misrepresent him, and how within him there is the very kernel of the true, or at least the honest?

This is a harsh comparison to make and I wouldn't think of pursuing it in relation to Mailer—my essential respect for him hasn't diminished: it is only that I think that it will be found that he isn't going about his good intentions in the right way. *His good intentions*: Will it surprise you if I say that what attracts me to him is his disgust with the culture? My own nausea grows daily. But part of it, I more and more know, is revulsion from the people who are most knowing about the right true reasons for disgust. I find myself learning much from them and then being repelled. One reason is suggested (oddly enough) by Harold Rosenberg in the essay in which he deals (unjustly) with you: I have forgotten how he puts the matter. But the effect of what he says is that all the fashionable culture-consciousness goes with a failure of internal actuality and resource. I suppose that I am making a personal, a "quality-of-being" judgment and I suppose it isn't very different from the old judgment I used to make on "the Liberal"—my old sense that all the solemn progressive political moralizing, the ecstatic comfort of *blaming*, was the expression of a great emptiness, and that upon such deficient people no idea of a good social order could be built, perhaps finds its counterpart in my present sense that the new mode of attack on the status quo, justified as it is, has in it the same emptiness at bottom, and that the gnosticism, the quasi-mysticism, the organicism, the apocalypticism, the antirationalism, are all at bottom ways of contriving selves or personalities. That is to say, just as Liberalism was right but not serious, so the new attack on the culture (as against the society) is right but not serious. And I think we are in a very serious situation, a *real* situation, and that it can't be dealt with in the histrionic mode, which, as it seems to me, is the dominant one. It can't be dealt with by attitude and style. I of course know the reason why it *is* being dealt with by attitude and style (which I obviously do myself)—it is perfectly possible, and at times even useful and necessary, to see all of life as ultimately attitude and style. But sometimes a less free and less attractive mode of perception is necessary, a graver and more restrictive mode, which permits us to say "*If* this, *then* this." The thing that has been borne in upon me more and more of late is the acceleration of anti-scientism, to which, at one time or another, we have all paid our respects in the interests of humanism, creativity, and freedom, how this is connected with the idealization of style and attitude, and with an implicit, and not always implicit, denial of "reality"—from which I think some very bad consequences will follow (although perhaps some good ones too). I find myself these days bristling whenever I come across sneers at the mode of thought of science; I begin to think of myself as a rationalist (me!); my old skepticism about Art comes to the fore—I more and more cherish certain stern words of Santayana's (of all people!) about fantasy, and I remember with pleasure that to someone who said something adverse about Freud because of his relatively low esteem of art, I replied that this was one of the most fortifying things about the Old Man.

Do I plan to become the Julien Benda[1] *de nos jours?* No. But out of the incoherences of this letter you will at least draw the impression that I smell a situation, the odor being of gunpowder. Which is one reason why I push hard on my allbedamned book, which goes well but which clearly can never be finished.—We leave here on the fourteenth. Diana joins me in love to you and Midge.[2]

Yours,

Lionel

If you will accept its incoherences, you will not be led to suppose that *all* of the weight of the long paragraph above is intended to fall on N.M.

177. TO EDMUND WILSON

September 2, 1959

18 Bradley Street, Westport, Connecticut

Dear semblable, dear frère:[3]

I am especially glad to have your note because it gives me the occasion to discharge my guilt over having allowed your note of the

---

1. Julien Benda (1867–1956), author of *La trahison des clercs,* a 1927 book that attacked intellectuals for betraying their moral and political responsibilities.
2. Midge Decter (1927–), editor and writer, married to Norman Podhoretz.
3. "Hypocrite lecteur!—mon semblable,—mon frère": line from Baudelaire's poem "To the Reader," quoted in T. S. Eliot's *The Waste Land.*

early spring—or was it actually the winter?—to go unanswered. What happened was that when I came to answer it I found that I had mislaid it together with the little bunch of clippings (including one from *The American Israelite* to modify the exclusive British character of the thing) which showed how far the *semblable-frère* situation had gone. From time to time the thought of it would come to me and I would undertake to answer it, only to feel that surely those clippings must be *somewhere* to be discovered by patience or science or intuition and how much more pointed and authoritative my answer would be with this documentation than without it. So time passed. Forgive me.

The Frost affair was one of the strangest I have ever been involved in. Even very close friends were relieved when they read what I had said, quite as if they were afraid that I had said something really insulting, really shocking, about the old boy. He himself was of two minds about how to take the speech. On the spot he was a little confused, partly because he doesn't hear very well. Then I imagine he was told that he *ought* to feel put out, and did, although not very intensely. When the Holt people told him I was being "attacked," he behaved very well, and early this summer he replied to my having sent him (at his request) the manuscript of the speech shortly after the dinner. His letter was very graceful and very truthful—he said that he had been "taken aback," expecting a "Rotarian" birthday speech and getting serious scrutiny instead, but that he had not been in any way troubled. And when he was interviewed by a reporter from *Newsweek*, he stood up for the speech in a very stalwart way.

I used to be indifferent to Frost as a poet and repelled by him as a person—some years ago, when we were both at Kenyon College, I had to leave the hall when he was talking in his folksy wisdom, doing the kind of semi-malicious clowning that he goes in for. But last year I began to read him again—under the direction of Randall Jarrell's two good essays about him,[1] which select the best of his work—and I found myself deeply moved by a good many of his things, and quite

---

1. Randall Jarrell (1914–1965), poet and critic, wrote about Frost in "Two Essays on Robert Frost," in *Poetry and the Age* (1953).

able to forget the symbol-of-America nonsense. Then I began to forgive him for the way he behaves in public and even to be charmed by the old-elephant aspect of him that you note.

I hope we get a chance to see each other this winter.

Yours in semblance and confraternity,
Lionel

178. TO JAMES ELLISON

November 17, 1959

Dear Mr. Ellison:

There is perhaps something engaging about the action of a young man who addresses himself in angry rudeness to one of his elders, but only when the young man speaks out of his proud sense of his own powers, not when he speaks out of his "need of direction and encouragement." An art does not "improve" because critics undertake to see to its wants. The quality of an art depends only on its practitioners, and the great practitioners of any art have always been far in advance of the critics and have quite properly scorned the tardiness of the critical response to them.

When you put it to me that the novel will improve when someone—myself or another—"is willing to commit himself courageously and selflessly to the future of the novel in the America of our time," you are not thinking like a novelist but like a schoolmaster.

Sincerely yours,
Lionel Trilling

179. TO SAMUEL ASTRACHAN[1]

May 17, 1960

Dear Astrachan:

I am sorry at the news you send me of the two novels, but I am glad that you can write about them so simply. Give the business time. Although heaven alone knows what is to be said and done about the

---

1. Samuel Astrachan (1934–2012), novelist, was a former student of Trilling's at Columbia.

novel these days—almost always my soul curls up after I have gone a few pages in any new novel, and maybe the whole idea repels me. Your concentration camp reading may indeed lead to something. It puts me in mind of my long continuing desire to write a history of the last days of the Warsaw ghetto, really a history—I was distressed by Hersey's assumption that it ought to be and could be a novel.[1] I think that if I could read Yiddish and Polish, I would really try it.

[. . .]

Sincerely,

Lionel Trilling

180. TO URSULA NIEBUHR

January 16, 1961

Dear Ursula:

Please forgive the lateness of my response to your letter. It was chiefly caused by my wanting time to think seriously about your invitation.

If I have won that first forgiveness, I go on to ask for another and larger one. I must say no. I don't for a moment think that you will fail to understand why I give you this answer. I don't think that I have to make a very long explanation, but I do want to make some.

Perhaps the best way I can make it is by taking up your reference to Freud. A few years ago I heard Will Herberg[2] read a paper on Freud's relation to religion. I don't usually admire Herberg, but this time he was very good. He dealt with the usual view of Freud as being only in a negative relation to religion, intellectually rather primitive, and, going behind Freud's overt statements of hostility, proposed the great complexity of his feeling in the matter. I am, in my own degree, in Freud's position. I don't, to be sure, have his conscious hostility to religion—quite the contrary, I should say. But whenever I try to carry my animal feelings up the intellectual path, I reach a point from which I am driven back. And yet whenever I turn to think about

---

1. John Hersey (1914–1993), novelist and journalist, wrote about the Warsaw ghetto in his novel *The Wall* (1950).
2. Will Herberg (1901–1977), sociologist of religion.

the matter that your course addresses itself to, I find that the concepts (and even the language) of religion force themselves upon me. Because all this is so, because I stand in so unremittingly ambivalent a relation to these concepts (and even this language), I have always avoided making statements about "meaning" and "meaning to life," even approximate or tentative ones, although I must suppose that my involvement with the question shows through what I write. It might be that someday I shall want to, or have to, be open and explicit. But that day hasn't come yet. In my wish to please you, I went so far as to think that I might be able to accept your invitation as making an occasion for seeing what could be done in the way of formulation. But the attempt needs so large an effort of precision, and of internal research, and of irony that I should be able to do nothing else for weeks; this isn't practicable, and without that effort I should think of myself as being one of those literary spirituality-mongers who are always turning up at religious symposiums.

Do tell me that you forgive me.

Yours,

181. TO THE NOBEL COMMITTEE OF THE SWEDISH ACADEMY

January 31, 1961

Gentlemen:

I should like to respond to your gratifying invitation to nominate a candidate for the Nobel Prize in Literature for 1961 by naming Robert Frost. This is a name that must have been proposed to you frequently before this and I have no doubt that the details of Mr. Frost's career are known to you, as well as the very high regard in which he is held. I shall content myself with saying that I hold Mr. Frost to be one of the two or three great poets of our time. I take his achievement in poetry to be equal to that of T. S. Eliot.

Sincerely yours,

Lionel Trilling

182. TO HANS ZEISEL[1]

June 26, 1961
2495 Redding Road, Fairfield, Connecticut

Dear Professor Zeisel:

I am sorry that I have been so tardy in coming to your manuscript—I hope that you can forgive me the long delay.

I have read the essay with great interest and admiration, and with considerable, although not entire, agreement. It seems to me that a line of argument that affirms the greatness of *Romeo and Juliet* is inevitably right and that you have drawn your line with great skill. But I can't help feeling that in your attack on the tyranny of the conventional conceptions of tragedy which say that the play is not a true tragedy and therefore not great, you yield too much to the power that even the more liberal and intelligent ideas of tragedy have over our minds. Granting all the moral and aesthetic relevance of Aristotle's prescriptions for the right tragic circumstance, that the tragic sufferer shall not be either wholly bad or perfectly good but should be a good man with a flaw which makes the tragedy possible, I would nevertheless say that we ought to allow the possibility of a significant story which presents the effect of the fortuitous, which allows us to contemplate the fact that mere chance does play a part in life. There are, of course, conditions put upon stories of defeat brought about by the fortuitous; the odds are that most of them are not worthy of contemplation; but some are, and I should say that stories of intense and ill-starred love are likely to be of considerable interest. And it scarcely matters, I think, whether or not we call such stories tragedies. My friend Jacques Barzun has written a very cogent defense of the fortuitous in art; I have forgotten where this appears but I can find out and send you the reference if you are interested.

Your analysis of the character of Romeo is very deft indeed, but I resist your conclusion that his flaw, which makes the tragedy possible and valid, is his impulse to death. This seems to me to have the effect of negating the association of death with very intense love, an association so common as to lead us to say that it is "natural." It seems

---

1. Hans Zeisel (1905–1992), legal scholar.

to be a condition of all love stories great enough to have a legendary quality that the love should be forbidden and that it should end in death. There must be any number of ways of understanding this, including the idea of death as the validation of the passion, suggesting how much is endured for the passion's sake; as the punishment of the passion; as the representation of the intensity of the passion (orgasm as death and also death as orgasm); and perhaps it even represents the nature of the passion: the aggression that would seem to be in it, and the impulse to bring itself to an end at the same time that it wishes to preserve itself (here *Beyond the Pleasure Principle* is relevant).

And then there is just the inability of the human mind to maintain intensity of delight and its propensity to move from delight to dejection or depression—just the other day I was struck again, as I often had been before, by how clear a fact this was to Wordsworth ("Resolution and Independence") and to Keats ("Ode to a Nightingale"). And this suggests that an analogy between the linking of love with death is the linking of art with death. The idea of art seems to propose the idea of death, and art comes to be thought of as an answer—a desperate one—to death, i.e., to time; and this is also true, of course, of love (e.g., Marvell's "To His Coy Mistress").

What I am trying to say, in short, is that for me *R&J* does not gain by being thought of as a tragedy, but it does gain if I think of it as a dramatic poem which celebrates the intensity of love by making us grieve over its extinction by death—or, rather, perhaps, its extinction *in* death *by* life, by, in this instance, chance and society.

Does all this, which I am sure you will understand is not meant to be contentious, make any sense to you?

As for the question of the publication of the essay:—I am sure that you will run into great resistance if you try to get it published as a monograph, unless you are willing to subsidize, at least in part, its publication by a university press. The cost of monograph publication is very high indeed, the returns are very low, and the university presses, generous as they sometimes are, are reluctant to undertake them. You understand, of course, that there is nothing *infra dig* about subsidizing the publication of a monograph; it is frequently done, it is not a form of "vanity publishing" for the scholarly judgment of a university press is not abrogated by the proposal of a subsidy. The only other course I can think of is to make the manuscript somewhat shorter and offer it to a scholarly journal. The one that pops into my head as the most likely is *The Journal of Aesthetics*. But there are of course many others.

I shall return the manuscript to you by mail as soon as I can get to a post office. If you would like to discuss the subject further we can meet on one of your trips to the city when I return in the fall.

Sincerely,

183. TO CLEMENT GREENBERG[1]

June 21, 1961

Dear Clem:

Let me first say that it was a great pleasure to me to have your amiable letter. I have lately thought how seldom our paths cross these days and have regretted that.

Of the several points on which you undertake to correct my memory, the most important is my reference to our heated encounter at Margaret's. You are largely in the right here. It *was* Edward Saveth's article[2] that was the subject of our dispute. I recalled that distinctly and without question as soon as I read your statement of the fact. And so did Diana, who says that in reading my manuscript she had had an unrealized sense of something not quite accurate in my account of the episode. Diana also says that, although you and I were both very angry and although she thought it possible that violence might occur between us, we didn't actually invite each other to "step outside." I disagree with her—you were, as you say, prone to fighting in those days and at the time I was aware that my knowledge of this had the effect on me of licensing an unusual intensity of anger; I have always remembered myself in that episode as being rather captivated by the idea of our coming to blows. But since Diana's recollection is at one with yours, I must consider myself outvoted.

As to whether or not you accused me of Jewish self-hatred, I must

---

1. Clement Greenberg (1909–1994), art critic and intellectual, was an editor at *Commentary* from 1945 to 1957.
2. See letter of May 18, 1945.

continue to think that you did. I certainly was as angry at you as I have ever been at anyone, and I can't imagine what else, in the context of our discussion of Henry Adams's anti-Semitism, could have put me into such a rage. (I should say that the idea of Jewish self-hatred now seems to me to be so complicated a thing that the imputation of it would scarcely be, or would not necessarily be, offensive, and perhaps even then it was the *accusation* more than the imputed emotion that angered me.) I am virtually certain that reference was made to my letter to Elliot—as I recall it, I myself brought it up, citing it as formulating my relation to Jewish life, and that you said something adverse about it.

Where I say that you "quarreled with me" over the letters, I didn't mean to imply that there was a permanent breach between us. By "quarrel" I did indeed intend something more than the force of the word when it is used in the sense of "I quarrel with you over this point," but I didn't have it in mind to say that we remained hostile to each other, although I do think that the episode did make a coolness between us for some time, even though, as I believe, there was always an essential friendliness too.

When the essay[1] appears as the introduction to Bob's book I shall delete the reference to you. Whether or not Bob read the letter, he did feel antagonistic to me on the score of my relation to Jewish life; this is manifest in his review of my novel, where he called me to account for thinking I could represent the nature of American Stalinism without making plain what he thought was its virtually essential Jewish complexion.

I quite understand and wholly respond to the motives of amenity that led you to suggest that the letter of correction to *Commentary* should come from me, and I did try to write one. But I found that to cover all the points and to make all the necessary qualifications that would fairly represent both our recollections could not be done briefly, and that the length to which I had to go gave the letter a tone that I didn't like—I could find no way of preventing length and detail leading to the appearance of egotism. I am reluctant to throw the

---

1. "The Mind of Robert Warshow," *Commentary*, June 1961, was published as the introduction to *The Immediate Experience* (1962), a collection of Warshow's writing.

matter back to you since your inclination is so much the other way, but I am sure that you will be able to write a letter for publication which will make both your corrections and your friendly feelings quite plain, and I will reply in kind, saying where I agree with you and where I do not—I do think that two short letters from both of us will do the job better than one long one from me.

Diana asked me to send you her greetings with mine.

P.S. I have been thinking about your objection to my having characterized Bob as political—or was it politicalized?—and I confess to not seeing its force. It seems to me that in those days we were all political—as I still feel I am—in the sense that we thought that cultural preferences were bound to lead to political choices and even to some degree of political action, and also in the simpler sense that we thought that political partisanship would express itself in cultural preferences and cultural action. I have in mind the *Partisan Review* complex of feelings and conduct in the early days of our association with the magazine and the *Nation* situation in which you and Diana were involved. Bob, of course, was of a younger generation, but I do feel that his writing, and at least some part of his temperament as seen in personal intercourse, were conditioned by the cultural-political situation which we experienced in the 1930s and 1940s and which continued, although with abated intensity, into his time.

184. TO THE EDITOR OF *COMMENTARY*

July 11, 1961

Clement Greenberg is quite right in his recollection of the particular subject that made the occasion of our dispute—it was, as he says, Edward Saveth's article on Henry Adams. I had entirely forgotten this until Mr. Greenberg's mention of it brought it at once and very clearly to mind. But I am as certain as anyone can be in a matter of memory that my letter to Elliot Cohen did have its part in our disagreement. My recollection is that I made the first reference to it and that Mr. Greenberg showed some knowledge of it and commented on it adversely. And I am no less certain that—on the basis either of the letter or of my objections to the way in which Mr. Saveth had dealt with Henry Adams's anti-Semitism—Mr. Greenberg did accuse me of "Jewish self-hatred." The subject of our dispute being what it was, I cannot imagine what else Mr. Greenberg would have said that would have made me as angry as I was. On the question of whether or not we invited each other to step outside for purposes of violence, I must consider myself outvoted, for my wife's recollection agrees with Mr. Greenberg's and not with mine. Nevertheless I can say without any qualification of my certitude that the encounter was far more intense than Mr. Greenberg remembers it to have been; although we were both too sensible to allow the episode to make a permanent breach between us, at the time it took place it was charged with an extreme antagonism.

It was not my intention to describe Mr. Greenberg's relation either to Jewish life or to *Commentary*, although I can see that I may have seemed to do so by implication. What Mr. Greenberg says about the complex terms of his connection with *Commentary* does not differ in essence from what I always, in a general way, conceived them to be. And I am willing to believe that Robert Warshow's relation to the magazine was substantially the same as Mr. Greenberg's—indeed, it seems to me very likely that Mr. Greenberg's account of Warshow's attitude to Jewish life is more accurate than mine. But when Mr. Greenberg says that he took his editorial post on *Commentary* because he needed the job and then says that the job "meant responsibilities to Jewry . . . that had to be taken seriously and literally," he does not go on to realize or remember that the assumption of these responsibilities naturally generated its own ardor, and that this was quite sufficiently intense to lead him, and Robert Warshow in his own way, to take an aggressive stand against my position.

Lionel Trilling

185. TO CLEMENT GREENBERG

July 12, 1961

Dear Clem:

Here is a copy of my letter to *Commentary*. I trust that its tone seems to you as appropriate to the occasion as the tone of your letter seems to me.

I should like to say that it isn't through mere amenity that I say that your description of Bob's attitude to Jewish life is more accurate than mine—I really do think it is. Yet I think you don't recognize, either in Bob's position or in your own, which was perhaps the more complicated of the two, that element of anterior commitment to Jewish life, or to some idea of Jewry, which at the time made it possible for you both to take the *Commentary* jobs, and to accept, as you both so honorably did, their responsibilities. By that time, with my *Menorah Journal* experience—I feared and disliked everything I knew about American Jewish life, and maybe more than that. I remember, for instance, that at about the time we speak of, you wrote a piece—in *PR*, I think—in which you said that the Chassidic Jews constituted the highest form of humanity the world had yet known: some such statement. Although now I would consider it calmly, at the time it aroused me actually to anger. I don't know just what your statement meant to you or just what my anger meant to me, but in that period you had the one and I had the other. Which was, I suppose, enough to make at least a temporary antagonism between us, as between Bob and me.

Sincerely,

Lionel

186. TO JACQUES BARZUN

August 28, 1961
2495 Redding Road, Fairfield

Dear Jacques:

It was a comfort to have your sweet note about my mother's illness. You will be glad to hear that all is now at least serene. After a grim night during which she was attended by a doctor at her literal bedside every moment, she made a quite rapid recovery beginning the next day, and she is now comfortable and in good spirits. We managed to get two very competent nurses and between them they just about cover the day, and the doctor thinks it likely that she will be able to return to Scarsdale by ambulance a few days from now. The medical work in these parts is rather good. The doctor we regularly use is a former student of mine (although unhappily I don't remember him, a fact I blithely ignore); he was not available at the time of the emergency, but the young man who substituted for him behaved splendidly; and *he* said, when I thanked him next morning, that it was an "honor" to have been able to be useful—because he had read me when he was in college!

[. . .]

Yesterday I received a letter inviting me to be the Eastman Professor at Oxford[1]—for 1964! It is something that I am rather drawn to, and so is Di, but I am not sure that I can afford it. I am writing to say that I am interested but that I need more information. The fact that they provide a house, just building, rather scares me—it suggests that maybe I am expected to be a Cultural Center for American students. And other protocol duties propose themselves to my fevered imagination, and I am getting too old, too wise, or too impatient for such things. We will talk about it when we meet.

Diana sends her love with mine.

Yours always,
    Lionel

187. TO QUENTIN ANDERSON

November 7, 1961
Columbia University

Dear Quentin:

I should like you to have a memorandum of a situation in our department which seems to be growing more and more acute—the paucity of the amount of secretarial help we can look to.

[. . .] It is now some years since I have thought it proper to ask our secretary to type my manuscripts, but up to recently I have been able to count on all the help I need with my correspondence. In the last few years I have noticed a gradual increase in difficulty in getting this help because of the ever-growing number of departmental chores that fall on the secretary, and this year I have had so clear a sense of our secretary's crowded working day that I have tried not to call on her for help with my correspondence and have in fact asked

---

1. Trilling accepted the offer and taught at Oxford in 1964–1965.

for very little. This correspondence of mine, as I think you know, is quite large and makes a considerable burden for me—when Mrs. Trosch was with us, she used to be concerned about the number of letters that I answered in a year; the number that sticks in my mind was nine hundred, and that seems too large to be true, although it may be, but I am sure that it wasn't less than six hundred, and since that time the number has undoubtedly increased. This correspondence, as I need scarcely tell you, is all official or quasi-official—I have made a point of not using our secretaries for any letters that were actually personal, although of course the quasi-official often verges on the personal.

My way of dealing with correspondence is to write out my replies in longhand, usually over the weekend, and give them to the secretary, usually on Monday. Up to recently I could count on the whole packet being typed and ready for mailing well before the end of the week and usually in a day or two. But this year I have not been able to rely on this procedure. For example, only last week I gave our secretary two letters which she found impossible to complete until Friday. This is obviously not the effect of any lack of efficiency or goodwill, but, as I say, of the increased amount of departmental detail that a secretary must cope with these days.

I have tried to deal with my own situation by answering as many letters as I could in writing or in my own slapdash typewriting, but in many cases this isn't consistent with the dignity of the department and of the University, nor is it good academic economics to require a university teacher to give this much time and effort to work of this kind.

I have described the situation only in terms of my own experience of it, but other members of the department must be having a similar experience, and it is surely a matter that touches the department as a whole and one that we should take account of at the earliest possible moment.

Yours,

188. TO JAMES LAUGHLIN

September 22, 1961
35 Claremont Avenue

Dear Mr. Laughlin:

I find that I have been resisting the idea of an additional chapter for the Forster book, and upon investigating the reasons for this it has seemed to me that it wasn't merely because I wanted to avoid adding another chore to my life but because I couldn't happily contemplate the job in itself. The book was written in a burst of energy and enthusiasm, very much con amore. I can't recapture my mood of the time—I still admire Forster, of course, but I don't have the fresh, enthusiastic commitment to him that moved the book in the first place. It seems to me that any chapter I might add would be out of the spirit of the book and something of an anticlimax, especially since the work itself—Forster's, that is—although still most attractive, is really of a secondary kind. But I don't think that the book should be issued again without some addition, and it has occurred to me that perhaps the device that Harry Levin[1] used with his *Joyce* might serve our purpose, too—that is, a new preface in which I would say why I was not keeping my promise to you of an additional chapter when one should be needed, explaining the spirit in which the book was written, and perhaps touching upon my sense that I was somewhat disqualified from writing critically about Forster now that I had come to know him personally; I could then go on to give an account of his production since the date of my book, and perhaps speak of him personally. This device would have the advantage for me of making a new occasion, with its own spirit. And my descriptive account of the new work—it really *cannot* be more than descriptive—could be supplemented by your engaging a competent graduate student to bring up to date the list of critical writings about Forster, which has of course greatly increased since My Time. Does this plan appeal to you? If it does, we can try to set a time for my piece to come in—I shan't want to think about it before my present job is off my hands, my white elephant textbook, but I am pretty sure this will be sometime this winter.

Sincerely,

1. Harry Levin (1912–1994), literary scholar.

189. TO JOHN BALPH

April 18, 1962

Dear Mr. Balph:

How can I not be disarmed by your good-tempered letter in answer to my bad-tempered one?

Of course the story was not adequately represented in the dramatic version[1]—a story of inevitable, ironic failure, even betrayal (in some metaphysical sense) was turned into a story of "success." Yet I would defend the version from the full effect of your strictures. It seems to me that it had a degree of decency, even of sweetness, that was exceptional in the medium. At one or two moments I was moved by it. There was also a degree of vulgarity in it—the wife was shocking and the mad mother rattling the door was impossible. And one might remark on other bad things about it. The fact that the response to it was remarkable, that many people have spoken to me of it as more interesting, serious, touching, "adult," than anything they had ever seen on television ought—I really do think—to be taken into account, and yet you are no doubt right, the story was so far from being adequately represented and was near enough to being treacherously dealt with that I can understand that someone might be angry at its treatment, feeling, as you do, that something that they valued had been violated—as I might feel at a tasteless production of some play that I especially admired.

I can only say that I don't have any such feeling. I ask myself if this is a deficiency in me and find that I am willing to suppose it is, for the sake of enlightenment. But I really don't *think* so, any more than I think my impatience with Salinger, White, and Thurber (least with him) to be a deficiency, although I am sometimes surprised by it. I have always disliked these men for a covert self-cherishing and self-pity that I find in their work—it is no accident that they constitute the very essence of *The New Yorker*. I like pride in writers and I very much like it as it expresses itself in the turning down of lucrative offers from the mass media, but I'm not much impressed by pride that bases itself on *New Yorker* security and expresses itself in *New*

---

1. A television adaptation of Trilling's story "Of This Time, of That Place" aired in March 1962.

Yorker disdain of vulgarity. I remember Hemingway's perfect indifference to how his stories were "treated," and this seems to me much to be preferred as an attitude.

I don't by any means, however, think that this settles the matter. I could go on to argue your side of the question, choosing other examples, and certainly I would, if I were trying to be complete, make many modulations in the position that I have been defending. But all I want to say now is that I can't feel troubled over what was done in this instance.

Sincerely,

Lionel Trilling

190. TO DIANA TRILLING

May 4, 1962

Mount Royal Hotel, London

Dearest,

This paper is supposed to free the imagination, or at least the fancy.—I shall try to bring you up to date on my small doings. You can find an aphoristic form for this thought: that the reason travel doesn't broaden the mind is that while it broadens it also narrows— it is simply astonishing how many small concerns there are to occupy the attention. At the end of the day they are forgotten, but the next day brings the same number.—I didn't tell you about dinner with Stuart Hampshire, who, as you have guessed from my last comment on him when I saw him in N.Y., isn't the same man he was five years ago when I knew him at Oxford. It is difficult to know how to describe the change—he has not become feminized but he has lost masculinity; not distressingly, only significantly; or perhaps it is not masculinity that he has lost, but hope and intention. At any rate, the dour, sour (pronounced each according to its own law), resistant person I knew isn't present, and since my expectation of the old qualities is the basis of my interest in him, the meeting was odd, but not at all unpleasant: there is, beyond other considerations, the fact that he is a humane man: he is the kind of person who, after saying all that could be said about Noel Annan, could say: "Beyond other considerations, the fact is that he is a *good* man—he really does good, and he is unenvious—and that is important." So I liked him. Whether or not he is married is impossible to conclude from knowing him. We dined at a restaurant and went on to a pub. He goes every weekend to Oxford, where he still has his fellowship at All Souls, and he never says anything that implies a wife or a home. He invited me down to Oxford to dinner on Saturday night (tomorrow) but I had plans to go to Cambridge on Saturday and also my plane leaves too early on Friday. So I did not accept.—He talked about his family a little—his father was an unsuccessful businessman, much interested in sports; his mother was a successful musical-comedy actress. I suspect the latter circumstance explains his almost erotic feeling for London, where he was brought up. We went after dinner to a pub around the corner. The district, near Sloane Street, is not quite like anything we have, at once respectable and bohemian. I asked him about the people in the pub, all of whom seemed of the same class. He said he thought they were mostly advertising people. I spoke about English social mobility and he said yes, but a little dubiously and went on to speak of the class lines that are still stringent. He said: "I suppose not one of these people went to a really good school," and then he looked around carefully and confirmed himself: "No, not one." (There must have been a hundred people jammed into that pub.) I said: "How can you tell, by their faces?" And he replied with perfect simplicity, "Oh yes." And of course you *can*. Faces and voices and set of the shoulders really do show, and how long it will take before these things don't finally matter is hard to say. But I would guess not long; the new pressure is very great.

Yesterday evening I bathed, changed, and went elegantly out to dinner at the Athenaeum, having first bought a ticket at the hotel for Doris Lessing's play *Play with a Tiger*. The one absolutely sure thing—you *really* can count on it—is going out to dinner in a London twilight in spring: there are so many different centers of elegance or semi-elegance and they are all so quiet and modest. So there I was, walking from the club to the theater in that curious state of empty-minded self-satisfaction such situations induce. The play was not good but by no means bad (you don't mind here if it's not first-rate, not if you're American and $3 for a good seat seems cheap to you) and you would find it most interesting, as I did, while saying it was absurd.

Siobhan McKenna was the heroine, and I do mean heroine, and she was very appealing in a part that could have been only priggish. Well, what was she a heroine about? About woman, and love. Seems she is no longer entirely young, her husband was killed in the war, she has a son of indeterminate age. Seems she is a writer and absolutely hates conformity. Seems, too, that she has a lover whom she loves, a young-younger-American tough boy, sort of intellectual, sort of beat, who goes around laying girls, although he loves, actually, our hero-ine, and has got a very nice American girl, very respectable, from Philadelphia, pregnant. Another man, friend of theirs, although older, is on the same sort of kick, and his wife is miserable. Generalization: Men want freedom, hate love and women, and women suffer, because they want loyalty, stability, true love—and the child who will be the new thing, the Messiah. It was, as an idea, absurd, and yet the play was curiously moving. Perhaps because McKenna had a way of talk-ing very much like you (I mean in manner but she also said, in her better moments, the sort of things you say. Which struck me as odd, my idea of D.L. being what it is), and often of looking like you. I think that in the end she made the young man go back to the girl from Philadelphia, who was, God knows, the prettiest thing that ever came out of Philadelphia, but, as you can imagine, a terrible bore beside McKenna—it was all very unlikely. So that is what it comes down to for this very advanced woman, and after all the passed years, and all the new formulas: marriage and children, but a *true* marriage, and children who will approximate Messiahs (they are all to be sons, by the way, daughters are out). It was, as I say, touching—or did I say moving? And of course I wondered where William was in all this—could he possibly be that former Chicago tough in a big woolly sweater, carrying a knapsack? Could he possibly be that dev-astator of female lives?

[...]

Did you ever have such a long letter in your life? It has taken me all evening.

With my best love,
        Lionel

320

191. TO DIANA TRILLING

May 8, 1962
Jablonna, Warsaw

Dearest Diana,

[. . .]

Today we talked about coexistence in the morning.[1] One knows when a point has been made by the Americans; not when the other side admits anything—it never does—but when it says nothing in answer. This afternoon it was culture and cultural exchange. It was quite dull, mostly given over to the Ford Foundation, and numbers of fellowships etc. I undertook to make a statement which differentiated art, and especially literature, from science, technology, and the social sciences, discussed the nature and function of literature in the modern world, proposed its essentially dissident and dangerous nature, and delicately raised the question of the freedom of literature in the West and here. But I was so delicate that Schaaf, in responding, could ignore my implied question, although he couldn't fail to know what I was saying. So with great amenity and elaborate courtesy I put the question quite explicitly. The answer I received was the affirmation of the free pluralism of opinion in the country, and this was confirmed by the editor of the leading cultural magazine. I had no grounds to press on, so I said I was pleased that things were so good, and so much as they should be. There were offers for me to meet all the dissident elements. My speech, which was quite short and extemporaneous, was generally said to be interesting and eloquent, and it seemed especially to have delighted the Poles by its language—one of them said it was "like a poem," another said that never had he heard sentences so beautifully formed! They are all rather hipped on language. The usual thing is for the child of an intellectual family to learn four languages besides Polish. They begin early with private instruction and go to special language schools. Virtually all the statements at the conference are made in English. Those that are made in Polish are translated into the most superb Oxford English by a young man who had had all his schooling in England and had gone to Oxford and who looks like an English undergraduate.

---

1. Trilling was in Poland for a cultural exchange program.

He introduced me to his mother, who is in charge of arrangements, a rather impressive woman suffering from the fact that her son had just had his first child; she too was a product of Oxford, and she had spent some years in India and had studied Sanskrit and Hindostanee.

You will be gratified to know that I wore my white underwear last night. My tropical worsted suit was the most suitable for the occasion, but it was a chill evening, so I reached a happy average by wearing the thin suit and the heavy underwear.

I sent you a cable today, for I have become concerned over the long delay of mail. But the Poles say that airmail is quite slow, that there are only three planes in a week, and I comfort myself with that.

After supper—the heavy meal at midday—we were taken to a reception at the National Museum, in a bus. The director of the museum received us and then we were taken upstairs to a roomful of Canaletto paintings, of eighteenth-century Warsaw, where wine and cakes were served. Other people of some cultural importance were also invited, about seventy-five of them. I was delighted by the idea of so many Canalettos but wondered why they did not actually delight me as they usually do. Then it turned out that these were by the nephew. The pictures are very precise and on the basis of them the city is being rebuilt. It is a curious undertaking, especially considering the state of the country, but it is certainly rather moving. (Our resident-palace is 85 percent restoration. They are even doing the royal palace all over again!) The director took us through the various collections, which were just being put together after the restoration of the museum and explained in a quite engaging way what was what. It is not a distinguished museum, but the relatively few examples of native art, especially the medieval and the eighteenth century, are interesting. I met Slonimsky,[1] who has been urged upon me by everyone. He is somewhat out of favor, and as I knew, and as he told me, a long poem of his has recently been censored—"confiscated," as he says—but on the other hand, he says that a book of his has just been published and he shrugs his shoulders over the poem. He is a man of seventy-two, very elegant in manner and dress, and talks an excellent English. I am to have tea with him later in the week.

---

1. Probably the poet Antoni Slonimski (1895–1976).

I'll hope to have a cable from you in the morning.
With my dearest love,
    Lionel

192. TO DIANA TRILLING

[May 1962]
Hotel Portoghesi, Rome

I have taken fairly full notes of my impressions and I think I must try
to put them in order, especially following my English impressions. The
thing must be done at length and in a large conspectus. I rather stood
gasping when I came on your mention of Jim's intention of doing a
"philosophical work on the value of religion to combat the mediocrity
of life," for that is exactly what I have been thinking about for the past
two weeks, first in England, then in Poland—not willing to say religion exactly, but something. If one travels in the north, one is inevitably aware of the mediocrity of life, and this is especially true of
Poland—masses of highly developed people in one or another degree,
and nothing to do with their sensitivity and energies. To the Poles
I met I repeated a formulation I had made, that the one thing that
would be met with ruthless repression would be a radical social theory,
perhaps "Marxist," and to this they all responded intensely, as they did
to my saying that unless people were allowed to be serious, were permitted to think of more important things than their careers, accom-
plishments, and acquisitions, there would within ten years be some
terrible form of fascism. I cannot tell you how strongly I felt that life
was being made trivial—or, as Jim says, mediocre—and that this constitutes the gravest political danger. A half day in Rome suggests some
great difference I find it hard to describe, let alone explain, except in
terms that are already too well known—the absolute self-love of these
people is astonishing, they refer to themselves without the interme-
diation of an abstract ideal. And, of course, this is a great relief.
    [. . .]
Love,
    Lionel

May 27, 1962
Minerva Athens Hotel

Dear Jacques,

You were in my mind yesterday at Delphi, where, early in the morning, I had the place virtually to myself. Most of the trip has been, as we say, satisfactory, and, as I think, very useful to my mind, but it has not exactly been joyous, partly because I have been feeling seedy and partly because I have been concerned with "culture," which, as you know, is *very* seedy and usually depressing—only a very little art and only certain kinds of art give pleasure to, or even seem/seems decent to me these days. But Delphi is something else—it quite hit me between wind and water and gave me what old Wm. W. would call joy. And it would you too. The art is negligible, I think, and even the Charioteer isn't more impressive in person than in photographs—when once you get past the idea of him, he is rather a bore. But the nature is quite beyond words, and the conception of the city in this place is partly what makes the nature so magnificent—you forget all the corruption that overtook the town and you really think, as you go through the woods, that you might meet with the old prophetic serpent. It had on me the effect that Chartres had, of something really perfect. My glimpse of Rome—four days, not much more than an actualization of the *idea* of that city, did something to get the chill of Poland out of my system, but Delphi really restored me.

I don't know why Poland had such a severe effect upon me. One sees nothing of the sort that is called "dramatic," nor does one hear of it. But I look back on it as a quite decorous nightmare. Most people do not respond to it in this way, feeling pleased and relieved that the decorum prevails behind the I[ron] C[urtain] and that there is a great degree of tolerance, which is of course all to the good, but I was very hard hit by what goes on behind the presumably good behavior. I shall probably want to write about it, partly because the situation is most relevant to my feelings about "Culture"—which in Poland is, almost consciously, the great substitute for politics, the opium of the intellectuals; and this, need I say, is the death of culture.

I have had numerous twinges of guilt at the idea of you bearing alone the brunt of the Mid-Century,[1] but I have been saved from the development of these starts of conscience by my inability to imagine anyone *doing* anything—I have been feeling for these weeks like some sort of hollow capsule shot into space with all sorts of sensitive gadgets inside it to observe and record things, and no imagination of its own. Actually this sense of detachment has become rather painful and I am truly glad that a week will see the end of it, and me involved in worry, feeling, and work again. But I do have enough integral emotion left to be grateful for the advice, help, and comfort you have been giving Diana, and I shall have more when the whole of the emotional system is working again.

I am eager to see you and shall speak to you next Monday.

Always yours,

Lionel

194. TO NORMAN PODHORETZ

January 5, 1963

Dear Norman:

I like your piece[2] very much indeed. How could I not, my exasperation with the clichés of liberal progressive sentiment being what it is? Against the dreadful liberal-progressive no-feeling, which eventually establishes itself as no-thought and no action, the only antidote is personal testimony of such honesty as yours has. I'm very glad you have given it and I congratulate you on giving it so fully and handsomely and movingly.

It comes hard to me to imagine that anyone could possibly be offended by what you say in the essay and that there could be organizational repercussions of a serious sort. That is one reason why I am writing to you personally and not for publication. Another reason is that, much as I like and admire the piece, and in large measure agree with it, it doesn't *exactly* express my own sense of the Negro problem and of how it may be solved, and if I were to write a letter for

1. The subscription book club of which Trilling and Barzun were editors.
2. Podhoretz's essay "My Negro Problem—and Ours" appeared in *Commentary*, February 1963.

publication in praise of it, I should have to state where I did not wholly agree with you, and this would require considerable time for me to formulate to myself the reasons for the reservations about your position which as yet I am aware of only in a general or instinctive way. But if there should actually be signs of organizational trouble for you, please let me know at once and count on me to do everything I possibly can in your support. Obviously there is much that *can* be done if anyone is malevolently insane enough to make any move against you.

Yours,

195. TO JEFFREY HART[1]

March 25, 1963

Dear Jeff:

Thank you for the E. Wilson and the B. Jonson pieces.

I wish I could respond to them more warmly than I do. As for the Wilson piece, it seems to me that you mistake what Wilson's judgments amount to. I should identify the sum as an old-fashioned (anti-centralizing) liberalism, conditioned by a patrician rearing and a strong infusion of the artist's and the gentleman's anarchism. It is a view of the world that is likely to be ingratiating, and it constitutes Wilson's present charm and value, as a protestant against cruelty, vulgarity, and pretentiousness—in it, liberal individualism combines with the gentleman's abhorrence of bullying to make a personally very attractive way of objecting to ugly governmental or social behavior. But it is also a measure of what in Wilson's criticism is inadequate, at least to me, for I find it lacking in depth and breadth, and energy.

Do you not think that, if you point to Wilson's disgust with the tendencies of the North, you should also make plain his contempt for the society of the South, as shown in his acceptance of Olmsted's view of it? Wilson, I suppose, rather dislikes the very idea of society and is "for" only certain of its occasional fruits—amenity, art, and idealistic and honorable people.

The Jonson piece makes a most acceptable reading of the poem, but it falls within the terms of the objection which I mentioned to

---

1. Jeffrey Hart (1930–), critic and essayist.

you as applying to the group of your essays that I have read—it seems to me that eventually it isn't interesting, or likely to carry conviction, to *say* (and certainly not again and again) that order and high decorum are admirable (as of course they are), and that some people, or classes, or times achieved them, and that the world should learn to admire and achieve them again. And I feel that you leave out of your accounts of the instances of these conditions being achieved all the contradictions and complications that go along with them. If you speak of the Coole Park poems, I think that you ought also to have in mind, as Yeats does, the "violence" and "the bitterness" that are part of the creation of great houses. It is a splendid thing in a house and a family to be able to entertain a king at a moment's notice, but the wherewithal to do that doesn't, like Topsy and a common imagination of cathedrals, societies, and families, just grow.

Isn't it the open secret of all writing about English Society that the established and ordered trace their origins to a vulgar and upstart energy?—that the new, ugly money of the putters-out at ten to one builds the houses that, a couple of generations later, rebuke the latest-come new money with their achievedness? What a *useful* secret to open to the world!—for it helps keep the great houses from being seen as priggish in their rebuke.

In short, it seems to me that what is needed in your praise of the traditional social virtues is a degree of irony.

By the way, I don't think that Wilson's book[1] has been greeted with silence. I seem to recall that it was highly praised in *Partisan*, and at great length, and that William Barrett wrote of it very warmly.

Sincerely,

196. TO NARENDRA PRATAP SINGH

September 29, 1963

Dear Mr. Singh:

I confess I do not see any contradiction between the sentences you quote from my essay. Literature does of course have a part in bringing about social change. I raise some question as to how decisive

---

1. Edmund Wilson's *Patriotic Gore: Studies in the Literature of the American Civil War* (1962).

this part is—literature is clearly not the only agent of social change and it makes its appeal, after all, to a relatively small class. Then, as for the specifically ideational influence of literature, it often happens that a writer's ideas go in one way, but his art has a quite opposite direction, at least in effect. Pound, Eliot, and Yeats held political and social ideas that are to be called reactionary; these ideas had but little influence. But the influence that the art of these men had on the sensibility of their time was a liberating one, serving, I think we may say, the purposes of radical temperaments.

I don't think Shelley was an ineffectual angel,[1] etc. He certainly wasn't immediately effectual in the way that he hoped to be but he contributed much to what we might call the fund of thought and feeling that made it very much harder for men to say that things should stay as they are.

Sincerely yours,
Lionel Trilling

197. TO JOHN KRUMM[2]

October 21, 1963

Dear Chaplain Krumm:

I think I owe you a word explaining why I did not put my name to the "Proposed Statement on Racial Integration." I was quite in accord with all that the statement said up to its last sentence. Not, to be sure, that I think that blame does not attach to the academic community, although of what kind and in what degree need careful discrimination to determine. But "guilt" seems to me a very weighty word indeed, and not to be lightly used. If the idea of guilt is invoked every time a social injustice is considered with a view to correcting it, we shall create a moral atmosphere which is much too heavily charged for the comfort of everyone concerned, including those who suffer from the injustice.

---

1. Matthew Arnold described Shelley as a "beautiful and ineffectual angel, beating in the void his luminous wings in vain."
2. Chaplain at Columbia University.

I should add that several of my colleagues in the English Department share this view with me.

Sincerely yours,

Lionel Trilling

198. TO JACQUELINE KENNEDY

November 10, 1963

Dear Mrs. Kennedy:

A note I have received from Miss Tuckerman dismays me greatly. It replies, in the kindest way, to a letter to which my name was signed asking you for a contribution of money to *Partisan Review*. That this appeal should have been addressed to you seems to me wholly improper and I should like you to know that it was sent quite without my knowledge, in consequence, no doubt, of some office confusion.

But I know that you can be most sympathetic to my embarrassment, having yourself been troubled by your name being put to what you didn't mean to say on the occasion of my having sent you the Lawrence novel! By the way, the reason I never answered your correction of that bit of confusion was that your note was forwarded to me in a packet of letters when I was in Poland and was kept for an unusually extended inspection in the Polish post office and then sent after me to Greece, where it wandered aimlessly for more months. It was so long before it reached me in New York that it seemed a reply could now only be an intrusion. So I can be pleased by the *Partisan Review* awkwardness because, while I am setting this matter straight, I can also belatedly thank you for your sweet thoughtfulness in writing to me as you did.

Sincerely yours,

Lionel Trilling

199. TO C. P. SNOW[1]

November 10, 1963

Dear Charles:

[. . .]

A copy of the *TLS* with your "Second Look" has just reached me and I have as yet had a chance to read you only hurriedly. But I naturally slowed down when you come to me and I should like to speak of your account of my attitude toward modern literature. I don't, I hasten to say, think that you have "misrepresented" me but I do think that there is some inaccuracy of emphasis and that, when the essay appears in book form in the U.S.A., the issue you raise may well be confused by the way in which you describe my position, with the result that all sorts of false hares may be started. For the fact is that many people will be startled by your use of me as the opposite number to Lukács;[2] it is often supposed that I maintain a position of antagonism to modern literature. Thus, Irving Howe recently characterized a new essay of mine as "a full-scale attack on the modernist outlook in thought and literature." Now, I am sure that the essay is no such thing—indeed, I mean it to be ultimately a defense of the modernist outlook. But it is a very *difficult* defense and it contains a considerable amount of adversary matter, and as actual feeling, not as a mere tactic. Although Howe is wrong in his conclusion about the essay, I can understand how he should have concluded as he did.

I should say that I don't think of myself as being either *pro* or *con* in relation to modern literature. I have a good deal of resistance to it, the expression of a stubborn humanistic conservatism; at the same time I am implicated in its enterprise. I speak of this ambivalence not in order to "protest" your account of my position but to make you aware that people here will find it odd that you should choose me as the defender of modern literature; reviewers may either be confused or pretend that they are.

One particular point: the passage you quote from "The Modern

---

1. Charles Percy Snow (1905–1980), English novelist and chemist. Trilling wrote about Snow's concept of "the two cultures" in "Science, Literature, and Culture: A Comment on the Leavis-Snow Controversy," *Commentary*, June 1962, later collected in *Beyond Culture* as "The Leavis-Snow Controversy."
2. György Lukács (1885–1971), Hungarian Marxist literary critic.

Element in Modern Literature"[1] might make it seem that you thought that I approved of what I describe. Actually, as you will remember, the sentences that follow the passage and bring the essay to its end raise the question of what is implied by teaching in our colleges a literature based on an anti-societal doctrine.

In the essay which Howe thinks to be an "all-out attack" on modernism, where the position may be thought of as adversary, it is taken on the ground that modern literature tends to deprecate the sense of social actuality in favor of personal "spiritual" concerns of a "subversive" kind. What I mean to suggest to you is that my sense of the anti-societal in modern literature is pretty overt and that I do not "accept" it without protest. There is thus the similarity between Lukács's position and mine which you note, but the similarity is there to be seen without any special act of discovery!

I should then go on to say that I differ from Lukács in not taking the anti-societal tendency of modern literature at its face value. As you will see from the essay, "The Fate of Pleasure,"[2] which I send you, I conclude by trying to say that this very anti-societal tendency has a political or social intention which may be beneficent and which must be understood.

[. . .]

Sincerely,

200. TO PETER STERN

December 16, 1963

Dear Peter:

I lack my knowledge of history but I can't find any event that was responded to as this one was,[3] with so much actual—physical—grief. It was shattering, and in its commonalty it was awesome. If you can imagine New York radical intellectuals surrendered to sorrow and

---

1. Trilling's essay appeared in *Partisan Review* (January–February 1961) and was later collected in *Beyond Culture* as "On the Teaching of Modern Literature."
2. "The Fate of Pleasure," *Partisan Review* (Summer 1963), later collected in *Beyond Culture*.
3. President John F. Kennedy was assassinated on November 22.

desolation over the loss of a man that, as they wonderingly said, they hadn't had a good word for! Like you, I had had a meeting with him, sufficiently brief but curiously personal, and of course now brilliantly memorable.[1]

[. . .]

Yours,

201. TO ROBERT CLAWSON

December 23, 1963

Dear Mr. Clawson:

It was a great pleasure to have your letter, which, needless to say, interested me very much. But I'm sorry to say that I can't be of much help to you, for the shameful fact is that I haven't yet read *In the Clearing*.[2] And in general I'm not as knowledgeable about Frost as I should be, and as I perhaps seem to be in the light of that birthday speech of mine. Part of my lack of knowledge comes from my unresolved feeling about the poems, and part of that unresolvedness comes from my ambivalence about the man himself. On one of the few occasions when I have met Frost—it was a chance meeting the day after the speech—he was enchanting. But once—at Kenyon, a good many years ago—I had to walk out of the lecture room where he was holding forth, unable to endure his self-reference and his clowning. I think he knew what I had done—at any rate, when we foregathered at the president's house later, he treated me with very witty irony.

It has never been clear to me how Frost took my speech. I have heard conflicting reports; no doubt his feelings responded to what one or another of his friends, of one "side" or another, told him how he ought to feel. His letter to me was generous, but there was, I thought, some touch of troubledness in it. I had the sense that he was a little disturbed by what I said—not that he thought it "rude" but that he had to support the weight of a truth about himself. In the interview with a *Newsweek* reporter, he spoke generously of me and with a stern intention to permit no nonsense about the speech. I remember being

---

1. See letter of February 2, 1964.
2. Collection of poems by Robert Frost published in 1962.

touched by his attitude. My friend Stanley Burnshaw of Henry Holt tells me that he spoke frequently of me and expressed the wish that I come to see him. I have never pressed Burnshaw for the details. You might perhaps learn something from him by asking him directly. I have the impression that Frost had around him people whose annoyance at the speech was extreme and they may well have kept going the uncertainty of his feeling it. I find it rather hard to suppose that his last work was in any way a response to it, but my sense of the unknowability of a poet's ways, and also, I suppose, a natural vanity, prevent me from rejecting the idea wholly!

When I next bring out a volume of essays, I hope within the year, I'll include the Frost speech as printed in *Partisan Review* with an addendum on what I know of Frost's response and an account of how the publication of the speech was received. I think this will be interesting but it won't disclose any "secrets." I do wish I could help you more substantively. When you get your speculations into shape, I'll be interested to read them.

Sincerely yours,
Lionel Trilling

202. TO SAUL BELLOW

December 23, 1963

Dear Saul:

At the last meeting of the Grants Committee of the Institute[1]— the one you couldn't attend—I sat sweet, passive, and acquiescent while our poetry colleagues made their judgments. It seems there are such things as well-made poems. It seems there are such beings as craftsmen. No doubt, no doubt. But by the end of the meeting the sweetness had turned sour, the passivity and acquiescence were converted into irritation and contrariness. It seemed all very well for John Hersey to say that he didn't know anything about poetry and to abdicate his judgment and allow the poets to make their own choices but it began to seem to me that I really did know *something* about poetry

---

1. The National Institute of Arts and Letters, the parent body of the American Academy of Arts and Letters.

and that it was wrong of me to allow my boredom with what most contemporary poetry is to keep me from making my own judgments. What started me up, expectably enough, was a matter of *parti pris*— the shrugging dismissal of my own candidate, Irving Feldman. And so I asked Felicia to send me the work of all the poets who are in the running for grants and began to read them. It seemed to me that our poetry colleagues are talking through their hats. I don't know exactly what claims I would wish to make for Feldman, but as compared with some of the people who have the poetry members' suffrage, he comes out very well indeed. The front-runner of the batch is Gunn: it seems that there is no question in any certified poet's mind but that Gunn is the real thing. But I think Gunn is a neat-minded bore of a craftsman making well-made poem after well-made poem.

This letter has two intentions, one general, one particular. General: to ask you to join me in a caucus to be known as The Prosateurs' Caucus for Seeing Poetry as It Really Is and Then Saying What It Really Is. Particular: to ask you to look again at Irving Feldman's volume to see if you can find merit in it. (I don't remember what opinion you expressed in the letter you sent to the meeting.) If you don't have the volume, I'll arrange to have one sent to you.

All my good wishes for the new year.

Sincerely,

Lionel Trilling

203. TO HAZEL EAGLE

February 2, 1964

Dear Miss Eagle:

Please forgive me for having waited so long to reply to your letter— it has been a busy time for me.

You put your request so delicately that I am sure I can say to you, without extended explanation, that I can respond to it only in a minimal way.

My wife and I were among the guests at the Nobel Prize dinner.[1] When I told the President my name on the receiving line, he stepped

---

1. On April 29, 1962, President Kennedy gave a dinner at the White House to honor Nobel laureates from the Western Hemisphere. It was, he said, "the most extraordi-

back as if in happy surprise, and said "You!" and then added a few words of pleasure at my being present. It was, as you may imagine, a very gratifying moment for me. Mrs. Kennedy chatted with me about a relative of hers—a half sister?—who was at one time a student of mine, apparently in a large class. I told her that I had heard her talked about at a recent visit I had made to Vassar but there was no time for the details she wanted to hear. I rather think that this accounts for the invitation after the party. She and I talked at some length, about Vassar and about D. H. Lawrence. My only conversation with the President, an amusing one, was about what had been said about his wife at her college. He was elaborately ironical when I reported that she was remembered as having been shy.

I have no slightest doubt that you can count on there having been "original sensibility" in the man. No one who met him could doubt this, and those who knew him best seem surest of it.

I think it may be useful to you to have my opinion that, taken as a whole, that Nobel dinner was one of the best parties I have ever attended, of any kind. Some sort of special genius was at work to make people *happy* on an occasion of State!

Sincerely yours,
Lionel Trilling

204. TO NORMAN PODHORETZ

February 15, 1964
35 Claremont Avenue

Dear Norman:

It was good of you to send us a copy of your book.[1] We thank you for it and wish it all good fortune.

As yet I have read only your spirited introduction. I know that when I get on with the book I shall find in it much to discover or remember with pleasure and admiration. But I think that neither truth nor friendship will be served by my passing over in silence the refer-

---

nary collection of talent, of human knowledge, that has ever been gathered together at the White House, with the possible exception of when Thomas Jefferson dined alone."
1. *Doings and Undoings* (1964), a collection of essays.

ence which you make to me in the introduction when you describe your relation to the tendency you call "liberalism revisionism."[1]

Your having grouped me with Sidney Hook, Daniel Bell, and Richard Hofstadter constitutes, as you must surely be aware, what in Stalinist days used to be called an amalgam, a polemical device by which persons of diverse views are represented as being alike, with the effect that the faults or deficiencies of the views of any one of them are imputed to all the persons in the group. To try another example: "American radical thought, as represented by Norman Podhoretz, Maxwell Geismar, Arthur Miller, Allen Ginsberg, and Philip Rahv . . ." It happens that in the amalgam in which you have included me all the other persons have my respect in one or another way or degree. But as I understand myself and them, the consonance of our views and intellectual temperaments is but slight. I shall not try to discriminate among our points of agreement and of difference, contenting myself with saying that a cultural historian who makes the grouping on the basis of our agreement only has propounded a fantasy which can only mislead his readers.

I must go on to remark on the rhetoric in which you set forth your ambivalence toward the group. "It is fashionable in certain quarters," you say, "to dismiss the revisionist liberalism of the 50s . . . as a species of conformist thinking developed by intellectuals who, motivated in part by a genuine horror of Stalinism and in part by an abject failure of critical nerve, took to celebrating the virtues of American society and the values of the middle-class spirit." You do not dissociate yourself from the contemptuous description, which you paraphrase with a gusto that gives no sign of having the intention of irony, except as a degree of reservation is suggested by your having characterized it as "fashionable." And your next sentence can be read only as having the force of a confirmation of the fashionable opinion. "I myself have come more and more to see revisionist liberalism as involving an abdication of the intellectual's proper role as a critic of society." No one could possibly understand the "abdication of the intellectual's proper role as a critic of society" to be anything but another way of saying "a species of conformist thinking developed by

---

1. Podhoretz wrote of "the revisionist liberalism of the '50s—which is associated with names like Lionel Trilling, Sidney Hook, Daniel Bell, and Richard Hofstadter."

intellectuals who, motivated . . . in part by an abject failure of nerve, etc."—no one who reads the judgment of the "liberal revisionists" which you make in your own person can fail to ask by what perversity you believe anything at all that was ever said by these faint hearts and corrupt minds "continues to need saying."

Your ambivalence toward my work is by now an old matter, taken for granted between us. I have hitherto been able to suppose that it was as strong in its positive as in its negative feelings, and I have been able to regard it as a natural and useful element in the development of your thought and even to take a kind of pleasure in it, as making between us an interesting dialectic. The terms in which you choose to set it forth on this occasion are, to put it minimally, a surprise to me.

I will add that I feel that I am exempted from the obligation to consider seriously your characterization of me as an intellectual by the implication of a statement which you make earlier in your introduction. "A literary critic," you say, "ought—or so they tell me—to regard literature as an end in itself; otherwise he has no business being a literary critic." And then, with an air of audacity, you go on to reject that doctrine. Who, I must ask, are "they" who sought to impose it on you? Surely not your teachers either at Columbia College or at Cambridge. I should say that they proposed quite the contrary doctrine to you—although not as needing any special boldness to maintain, for it states what is scarcely a new or radical conception of the critic's function—and that they admired and praised you for your complex understanding and forceful application of it.

Sincerely,

205. TO MARSHALL BEST[1]

March 23, 1964
35 Claremont Avenue

Dear Marshall:

Your letter had the virtue of sending me to look at my contract with Viking, and this has made it necessary for me to reassess my conduct in the unhappy situation that has grown up between us.

I am afraid that when I originally spoke to Pat a few weeks ago,

---

1. Marshall Best (1901–1982), editor at Viking Press.

it was under the impression that my arrangement with the firm was looser than I now see it is; it existed in my mind as the habitual and loosely stipulated continuation of our past connection, and it seemed to me that since the money you had advanced me was by now largely paid off by earnings on books you already had, my further association with you was freely open to negotiation. In fact, it was not alone in my discussion with Pat but also in all dealings with another publisher that this represented my view of my relation with Viking at this time: to the other publisher's question, put in all propriety, about the nature of my tie with Viking, the reply described a situation this open and elastic. Certainly this was the sense of the matter that prompted me to tell Pat, and then you, of the very generous offer that had come to me from another firm and to express my hope that Viking would be able to meet that portion of the financial consideration that I need at this time.

But as I look now at my contract—and I should tell you that in the wish, which I know you must share, to avoid legal entanglements, I have not consulted with a lawyer about it—I recognize that my attitude was not consonant with the position it describes. I therefore have a better understanding of why you reacted as you did. A more proper procedure on my part would surely have been to tell you of the offer that had been made to me and of my pressing need for at least some substantial portion of the sum that another firm was willing to give me; and then to ask you, if such a payment extended you more than you wished, whether you would be willing to release me from my contract with you. By not following this course and by approaching you as I did, I led you, I can well understand, to feel that I was both high-handed and unfriendly, and I am truly sorry for this. I would wish now to apologize for my share, innocent as I hope you will believe it was in its motivation, in creating not only the atmosphere in which we find ourselves but also the poor opinion you must have formed of the other firm.

Even now, however, as I make this apology in the best possible faith and in the hope that it can give us a new and more favorable ground for discussion, I find I must deal with certain impediments to the kind of relationship that I know both you and I believe should properly exist between an author and a publisher. While your earlier response was bound to have been excited by the too-casual assumptions I made, it led you to express attitudes which are not without bearing on the feelings which have grown up in me in recent years—feelings which no doubt contributed, if only unconsciously, to the carelessness with which I moved.

The first of these obstacles is, I think, best summed up in your remarks to me when you evaluated my present behavior in terms of the investment Viking had long made in me and all that the firm had done to "build me up." It is my opinion that, as between us, these cannot be very weighty considerations except as they offend my sense of justice. For you will recall that I came to you after the publication of my first two books, the *Matthew Arnold* and the *E. M. Forster*, by which I had already laid the foundation of my reputation. Authors, I know, are not notable for modesty: I must nevertheless ask you whether you yourself or any fair-minded onlooker could honestly say that it was much of a publishing risk to take on a writer whose earlier publications had won the reception of those two books? I am not aware of any special efforts the firm has made to advance my fortunes as a writer. My sense of the situation is that I have given you three books and that you brought them out in the proper, decent way that is associated with the respected Viking imprint; but I cannot be aware that anything except the existence of the books themselves has made my reputation. As to considerations of money—which is what I take you to have meant when you spoke of investment—I must be conscious both of the fact that you have responded to my request for certain advances in the past in a very pleasant, easy way and that you have not grown rich through me. But I now owe you, as of your last statement, $1,680 in advance of earnings. It is not a sum which suggests to me that the financial risk, as I understand such things, was an extreme one.

Then, too, I feel it necessary to call to your attention now, as I have avoided doing in the past, the fact that I offered you over the years of our relationship no less than four books which you have refused—the new edition of my *Matthew Arnold*, my *Freud and the Crisis of Our Culture*, my *Gathering of Fugitives*, and the trade edition of my forthcoming anthology. I remember with great distinctness the terms in which, through Pat, I proposed the new publication of the *Arnold*—I said that I wanted all my books to appear under the Viking imprint. And so that you will know the kind of relationship which I once thought proper and possible between an author and his publisher, I should like you to consult my letter to Pat of March 23, 1955—it is exactly nine years ago today—to make yourself aware of the terms in which I proposed the little Freud book.

In the history of an association in reference to which you would apparently now counter the undeviating faith and enthusiasm of the publisher to the deficient reliability of the author, where, I must ask, do you place these decisions that Viking made? In each instance the book was felt to have sufficient worth, literary if not always financial, for another publisher to take it eagerly and without my committing to him any further work of mine. And it is my recollection that in the last two of these instances, you not only refused the book but expressed some annoyance over my having introduced the possibility of a competitive situation.

Then, in the light of our present situation, it will be relevant for me to speak of your firm's very casual breaching of a contract with me some years ago. It was when I went to my files the other day for my present contract with you that I came to the agreement you had made with me for a *Portable Keats*, and had it recalled to my memory that, when your firm decided that it after all didn't want the volumes, it simply announced its decision with the entire expectation that I would concur in it, and transferred the advance that had been made for that book to my general advance against further work, with no sentiment of legal or moral obligation to the agreement—an attitude which I condoned by deferring without demur to your practical needs.

Yet again, there is—what is very difficult for me to accept—the minatory and truly humiliating tone in which you tell me how much money you will advance me on what terms. You speak of proof of my reliability being needed, and this, I suppose, is meant to refer to my slowness in producing the books you say you are proud to publish. You are right: I do not produce books as fast as either you or I would like. But do I need to explain to you with your experience of the strange business of authorship, that if there is one attitude on the part of a publisher which is calculated to impede a writer's progress with his work as well as degrade his relationship to his publisher, it is the attitude of reproof which you convey to me, both implicitly and explicitly, in your letter? I will not adduce for you at this point my standing in the literary community as my reason for resentment at being addressed like a delinquent child, ungrateful for the many past favors he has received and not deserving of the continued confidence of his elders. I will only tell you that if, for a good many years now, I have had the sense, which I have tried to put down, that (despite Pat's continuing friendly interest) there has been on the part of the firm a deficiency of respect for my work and me, the impulse by which I suppressed my actual judgment of the situation has now been made impossible.

So here we are. I have formulated my grievances. And these, I fear, are very likely to mobilize counter-grievances on your side, for unhappily this is the way these things always seem to go. Then, in addition, I must reopen the matter of the sum of money that I need—$5,000 now, a sum of which your offer falls short by $1,600, and $2,500 at the beginning of 1965, a sum which you speak of only in a very conditional way. And yet I most sincerely hope that it is still possible for us to effect a viable relationship. And it is in this hope that I explain to you again that the sum I speak of was not hit upon blithely but by most precise calculation of the minimum amount I must leave behind me in America to cover my urgent obligations here, if I am to be free to turn back my attention to writing while I am away. We seem to have two dragons—something that we can call publishing enthusiasm, and money—standing between us. It may still be that you can clear them both out.

Sincerely yours,
Lionel

206. TO ROBERT PAGE[1]

April 3, 1964

Dear Dr. Page:

I have given much thought to the request that your letter makes and I am sorry to have to say that I can't accede to it. I think I under-

---

1. Page, an editor at Ginn and Company, planned to republish Trilling's essay on *Huckleberry Finn*, which appeared in *The Liberal Imagination*, in a school textbook. He had requested Trilling's permission to delete the word "nigger" from quotations in his text.

stand the difficulty you face, but I don't think it is to be solved by the deletion of the offending word. It seems to me that any Negro student who is capable of understanding my essay ought to be presumed to be capable of understanding the ironies that attend the use of the word in Mark Twain's novel and in my account of the book. I feel that to delete the word would be to condescend to the Negro student, and, what is more, to be depriving him, in some sense, of his history. No matter what social advances are made by Negroes, it will be true that, for a good many generations to come, their sense of themselves will include their recollection that they were once oppressed and despised. This is the fact, and it cannot—and should not—be denied; rather, they should bring it, and should be helped to bring it, into a historical understanding of their position. I do not think that the situation of the Negroes is exactly comparable to that of the Jews, and perhaps there was a lack of tact in making *Ivanhoe* and *The Merchant of Venice* assigned high school texts in my day. But I am inclined to think that I am the better for having had to cope with Isaac of York and Shylock as a schoolboy.

Is there any reason why the offensive word—for of course it is in itself offensive, however the context of *Huckleberry Finn* disinfects it—should not be dealt with in a footnote which would explain, among other things, that all ethnic groups in this country are referred to by opprobrious names, which, it might be added, Negroes use as readily as anyone else. I'll be glad to write the note.

It was a great pleasure to hear from you and I was gratified by your recollection of my class—so many years ago!

Sincerely,
Lionel Trilling

207. TO LESLIE FIEDLER[1]

May 17, 1964

Dear Leslie Fiedler:

I'm terribly sorry to blunt a point of yours but I'm afraid that I must do so in the interests of accurate literary history. I did not have

---

1. Leslie Fiedler (1917–2003), literary critic.

Allen Ginsberg in mind when I wrote "Of This Time, of That Place." That, indeed, would have been impossible, as the dates will indicate. I published the story in *Partisan Review* in the issue of January–February 1943; Allen was admitted to Columbia College in July 1943 and, I would suppose, attended his first classes as a freshman in September of that year; I am not quite certain when he was my student, but he was a member of a course usually taken by seniors; I can check the year by digging up my old roll books—I think it was 1946–1947. That I was the author of the story contributed to what interest I had for Allen, and I seem to remember that he identified himself with Tertan, as many literary young men did at the time and have done since. But in point of fact there was nothing in the least like Tertan in Allen's temperament and behavior, or in his prose. We were radically at odds with each other in most things, but I never thought of Allen as anything but my equal in rationality. The actual model for Tertan was a student of a good many years before whose name I still recall; he left college because of a severe and probably hopeless mental condition such as I represent Tertan as having.

I feel sure that you will agree with me that the matter should be set straight. In my opinion, the best way of doing this would be for you to make the correction on the basis of the information I give you. But if you prefer it, I could make the correction, of course quite naturally and uncontentiously. I am sure that a statement by either of us in just one periodical will have the effect of establishing the truth generally enough. The question is, which periodical? I would suggest either *Partisan Review* or *The New York Review of Books*, but you must feel free to make a countersuggestion.

Please give Margaret my warmest greetings and tell her that I have the liveliest and most grateful recollections of her kindness to me when I was in Athens. I'd send my remembrances to the children too if I thought that children ever remembered adults.

Cordially,

Lionel Trilling

208. TO PASCAL COVICI

July 20, 1964
Columbia University

Dear Pat:

I hope we can have lunch together before I leave, but I'm not able to be free for a little time to come, and I did want you to have the word about Saul's book[1] that I said I would give you.

But first I should tell you that it won't be possible for me to review it for the *Times*. As I feared, I am still at work finishing my bedamned anthology[2] before I go, and of course I mustn't allow anything to interfere with that. I am sorry to have to disappoint you—I really do think that I am just the man to do the review; and such was the thought of the new young assistant editor on the *Times*, Erik Wensberg (a former student of mine and very good), who called to ask me to take the assignment; I *wanted* to do the review and I felt unhappy at not being able to.

Not that it would have been an easy piece.

There is something very beautiful about this book, as there is about much that Saul writes, and I found that I was reading it with a kind of personal affection for the writer. I am sure that what makes the ground of my admiration of Saul is his insistence on the possibility of the good life, his refusal of nihilism, and his courage in being explicit about this in the face of powerful fashion. And then there is the splendid freedom and vivacity of his prose.

I read the book in a kind of captivation, for which I found myself often being *grateful*—again, *personally*, as it were. But I must tell you that by the time I began to approach the conclusion, I experienced the foreboding of disappointment, which—I'm afraid I have to tell you—fulfilled itself. Maybe I am hopelessly old-fashioned, but I don't think that a novel can find its proper end in an attitude, an emotional state, a stance. I try to resist this judgment, telling myself that everybody knows that the days of Aristotle are over, but the old prejudice returns. And from my disappointment in the conclusion I find generated some reservation that works backward through the book; it would

---

1. Saul Bellow's *Herzog* (1964).
2. Trilling worked on his anthology *The Experience of Literature* for almost a decade before it was finally published in 1967. See letter of March 19, 1967.

take me too long to formulate how this operates: somehow I feel that so much that I had liked from the beginning is less justified than I had supposed it to be. How much I had liked from the beginning will be suggested if I say that I had this feeling with the sense of great deprivation, which I am still aware of.

Yet I still feel more connection with Saul than with any other novelist writing today, and I think that he is by all odds the most interesting and important writer of fiction that we have. When we do meet, you'll perhaps tell me how you respond to my response.

[. . .]

Yours always,
Lionel

209. TO DANIEL DORON[1]

August 14, 1964

Dear Mr. Doron:

I am sorry that I have had to wait so long to read your essay, sorry too that I have had to read it at a time when I am much pressed by work and distracted by many concerns. But I have at least enough perceptivity left to me to let me see how very gifted the essay is and how interesting. I know that you consider it an important event in your intellectual life, and well you may, one that you are to be heartily congratulated on.

If I speak of a degree of alienation from the subject of the essay that I was aware of, it is not by way of criticism but only for what interest it may have for you. It is that I find myself antagonistic to all ethics of love, and, indeed, to the whole concept—it is perhaps not actually so unitary a thing—of love as it exists nowadays. Nothing—for example—seems more horrible to me in the present racial situation here than James Baldwin's prescription that it be dealt with by love. My feeling is for a much colder word, "respect." This suggests to me all kinds of delightful possibilities, as love does not—on the contrary, indeed.

Don't let this puzzle you—I mean someday to say at length what I mean. And don't, as I say, take it as an adverse comment on your essay, which it certainly is not.

---

1. Daniel Doron (1929–), Israeli writer, had studied with Trilling at Columbia.

It somehow isn't clear to me what you plan to do next year. What-ever it may be, I hope it prospers.

    Sincerely yours,
        Lionel Trilling

210. TO FANNIE TRILLING

October 5, 1964
Balliol College, Oxford

Dear Mother—

Just a brief note—because I am under great pressure to finish my first lecture, which I am to give in a few days—to say that we are nicely settled in Oxford. Everyone is very kind and friendly and we feel very much at home. The town itself is rather disappointing on first acquaintance, after all that one has heard about its beauty, but it slowly grows on one, and I begin to see how people come to love it. Our house proves to be as comfortable as it is pretty. We are looked after by a quite elderly couple who try very hard to please and by an upstairs girl who comes in for an hour every morning to make beds and wash bathroom floors—each of us has a bathroom and there is a third downstairs. So you see that we live in considerable luxury. Indeed, we say every morning when we wake up in our large light bedroom that it is going to be hard—maybe impossible—to come back to our dark apartment. Diana does the cooking but she has to do no other work, and every morning the breakfast table is laid for us. [. . .] However, marketing is rather difficult and Di has to walk a considerable distance for it, and only a few stores deliver. Most of the foods are different from ours and not as good—for some reason which we don't understand, nothing tastes the same as in America. Some things, like bread and eggs (both very good) are cheaper than with us, but on the whole things are by no means cheap.

Jim is well and seems to be enjoying his school thoroughly and to be doing quite well in his work. He came out for his first weekend—a short one—on Saturday and seemed very grown-up and self-possessed.

    With love from us all,
        Lionel

November 4, 1964
Balliol College, Oxford

Dear Norman:

I think that Leslie Farber's piece[1] is good but not so good as you think it. It is surely time that someone began to raise questions about the nature and place of sexuality in our modern lives, and Farber's question is a cogent one. But it seems to me that if Farber says as much as he does, he must say a great deal more, or at least indicate that a great deal more is to be said and suggest the outlines of what this is. Very true that sex has been corrupted by the will, very true that sex, by being made extravagantly conscious, has become scientized and mechanized. But it isn't enough to imply that this is the natural consequence of our commitment to the machine and its efficiency. Thirty years ago that might have seemed an adequate idea; very much less so now. Sex as a means of "health" figures only dimly in the cultural consciousness. If we want to connect it with other cultural phenomena, it seems more relevant to relate it to new impulses of aggression, to drives toward status and autonomy. And very likely Farber would agree, but he does fall back on a rather simplistic [sic] emphasis on "efficiency." I should add that our culture is probably not the first in which one or another form of the dehumanization of sex has appeared, which suggests that the relation to science and the machine is not an essential one. Whether or not such dehumanization has previously made for personal "problems" I can't say. The anxiety manifested in Eastern sexological works suggests that it has.

Then I am rather taken aback by what Farber does with the question of female sexuality. Certainly the modern view on this ought not to constitute a piety, but if it is to be subjected to skepticism, the kind of skepticism that is brought into play ought to be rather more serious than that which Farber uses—a mere speculation that in earlier and better and more natural times the modern notions of female sexuality did not obtain, that they have been imposed upon women, and men, by modern social and political tendencies. My reading of the older literatures does not confirm that view, but I am

---

1. Leslie Farber, "I'm Sorry, Dear," *Commentary*, November 1964.

sure it can be argued: the trouble is that Farber *doesn't* argue it. Science may indeed be the villain of the sexual life—we have all thought so at one time or another—but this doesn't invalidate the rules of evidence; the errors of scientism don't give new rights to arbitrary statement. I feel it to be the more deplorable that Farber is content to stop at mere speculation because of his professional commitment. No doubt the sexual theory of our time would become less exigent if it could be shown that female sexuality is nothing but an artifact of modern culture, that the female orgasm isn't really part of Nature; but the demonstration must make some show of reason—it can't proceed by mere statement. Maybe Will is corrupting but Wish can be deceiving. (Incidentally, I think that Farber might have owned his closeness to Kinsey on this question.)

And then it seems to me that Farber is actually talking about something other than his ostensible subject—he is talking not so much about the bad situation of modern sexuality as about the bad situation of modern marriage, or the bad situation of marital sexuality. Throughout the piece he seems to have only the latter in mind: he speaks of "lovers" but he gives the impression that he means always married lovers, to whom "adultery" presents itself as a natural means of solving or escaping from a sexual difficulty, although a means which is burdensome and unsatisfactory. Maybe a prime element in the modern mishandling of sexuality is the insistence on "basing" marriage on it, or basing it on marriage. Certainly one tendency of our culture—not, clearly, an unopposed one—is toward moralizing sexuality, and socializing it, in a new degree: if we can observe dehumanization, we can also see a new impulse to a perhaps excessive humanization. If this is indeed a mistake, psychoanalysis must bear a considerable responsibility for it (although the impulse to moralize sex extends well beyond psychoanalysis: see D. H. Lawrence) and psychoanalysis ought to examine its doctrine on this matter, a doctrine which is perhaps unavowed but nonetheless strong.

I don't mean to say, of course, that I don't respect what Farber undertook to do and even what he has done. Anyone who brings the modern assumptions and clichés about sex into the range of criticism has done a useful thing, and I am glad that Farber wrote the piece and that you publish it. But with my judgment having in it as much of the adverse as it does have, you'll see that I can't well undertake to write a letter in support of the article, nor would I want to appear in print with anything but a careful response. However, for what it might be worth to you in any quarrel with your Board that may develop, I am enclosing a "hasty note" to you personally and not for publication. You might want to slap it down on the Board table with some such remark as "Here, gentlemen, is the opinion of Dr. Farber's article which is held by that pillar of respectability, the sternest moralist of our age, a fellow of Balliol College, Oxford, an institution which is not less than seven hundred years old, etc. . . ."

Which leads me to say that Oxford is being remarkably pleasant. We are most comfortably set up, and everybody is most agreeable. I think Diana is liking the life even better than I do. I am in that state between being a visitor and a member of a community, no longer chiefly curious and amused, not yet involved, and likely not to be in the year to come; this makes me a little restless at the same time that I enjoy the restfulness of the detachment. The teaching has been a little unsatisfactory so far; I lecture to a pretty large and attentive audience on American literature and get no resonance from my listeners; next term, however, I shall give a "class," which ought to be more my style.

How are things with you and Midge and the family? Is your soma in better shape than it was last year? Did I ever sing you my song, "Oh, the psyche and the soma should be friends"?

Diana joins me in warm greetings to you and Midge.

Lionel

212. TO ALLEN GINSBERG

November 8, 1964
Balliol College, Oxford

Dear Allen:

The address didn't work because you wrote "London" instead of "Oxford."

I'll be happy to support your Guggenheim application, although it often seems to me that my support is the Kiss of Death. Of course no one can do anything against the Poets' Lobby, which seems to me the best-organized political group in the country; I hope, but doubt, that you are in their good books; they work insidiously but infallibly.

It will cheer you to know that a man here told me that his son got into Balliol through your agency, as it were. The boy was—still is—a passionate admirer of yours and when he was set the subject on one of his entrance examination essays, "Who should get the Nobel Prize in Literature?" he proposed you, and then on his oral examination defended the proposal so well that he was admitted.

I did actually know the detail of your having written "Butler has no balls," but Diana didn't. She says it makes an important difference in the story, but I confess I don't understand why.[1]

I wholly agree with your opinion of English poetry now. It's very dim and so is the criticism of it. And I think it will be long before it improves; I like the relation of the English to their language as they speak it, but it isn't of the kind that is likely to yield poetry. And in general I have the sense that everything here conspires to prevent a lively literature. Sometimes I think this is no such bad thing!

We like England, and Oxford is being very sweet to us. Part of the pleasure, of course, is just being *away*: what a happy state.

Diana sends her warm greetings with mine.

Sincerely,
 Lionel

213. TO MARSHALL BEST

November 13, 1964
Balliol College, Oxford

Dear Marshall:

Your letter touched me deeply and made me at once sad and happy. I think that our blowup of the spring, unpleasant as it was at the time, had the effect of bringing us to a clearer awareness of each other and a better understanding; I am glad it took place before Pat died and that he could have satisfaction in this outcome, and grieved

---

1. Diana Trilling tells the story of Ginsberg's graffiti message in his Columbia dorm room, in her essay "The Other Night at Columbia," *Partisan Review* (Spring 1959).

that he isn't here to be an actual part in it, although I think that for both of us he will always be present in it.

You will probably not be wholly surprised if I tell you that the spring date for my book is not possible. I had feared that my first weeks here would be distracting and not exactly conducive to work, but I had not guessed how far distraction would go. For one thing, I found myself, up to a short time ago, radically disoriented by the change of place, and extravagantly fatigued. Both conditions, I suppose, are natural enough. The fatigue presented itself not as the accumulation of a difficult year but of a good many years: this first separation of mine from the routine of a lifetime had the effect of discovering layer upon layer of weariness as I relaxed into a softly smiling heap. And then in a world of strange faces and ways I found it curiously hard to lay my hand on my own personal existence and went around in a sort of daze of amenity which eventually became oppressive. Then my lectures turned out to be much more difficult than I had expected them to be, no doubt the more because of my quasi-comatosity. The attendance began by being quite large and has maintained itself, which it is not supposed to do, and although I lecture only once a week, each occasion makes the demands on me not of a lecture to my class at Columbia, which I handle easily, but of a public lecture in a strange place, needing quite considerable preparation of my formulations. And then Oxford exploded into hospitality, none of it to be escaped. The Eastman Professor — as I have learned to call myself, for that is how I am referred to half the time, written to, and introduced in that way in a community that naturally calls a man by his title rather than by his name—is an institution before he is a person and he must have a reception, and a dinner from the Master of his College, and a dinner from the Vice-Chancellor, after which the Masters and Wardens of other colleges get in their whacks; and then old friends and literary acquaintances take over, and then fellow Fellows of the College undertake to be cordial. Then a stream of correspondence from the now innumerable British and Welsh universities (the Scottish, thank God, are more reserved) asking me to visit and lecture, and the papers, the magazines, the BBC, the American embassy . . . I keep saying no, but the time it takes to say it, without a secretary, is massive.

Nothing about all this is unpleasant. The Oxford people couldn't be nicer or friendlier; even in their official situations they have a kind of simplicity in their friendliness, as in most things, that I find very sympathetic. Diana is perhaps enjoying the life even more than I do; so far all the talk about the Oxford exclusion of women has proved wrong in her case; we are virtually always invited together, even to high tables, and I think it is true that every occasion we have been at has been interesting in one way or another. But, as you may well conclude, the situation isn't conducive to hard work.

However, things begin to quiet down and the word is that the second term is the unsocial and industrious one. More important than that, though, is that I have got into gear again. I begin to know who I am, and I have started to work on my Cambridge lecture, which is, as you know, to be the last piece in my book.[1] As you surmise, the essays will need some revising, although not a great deal, and of course I shall need a strong preface. The lecture is to be delivered in mid-February. I shall be able to send it before then, but I think that a reasonable and feasible date to set for the completed manuscript would be mid-March. I am, I need scarcely say, troubled about the delay, not on my account but on the firm's, for I know you had spring publication strongly in mind.

[...]

Sincerely,

214. TO STANLEY BURNSHAW

December 19, 1964
Balliol College, Oxford

Dear Stanley:

Your letter was extraordinarily generous and kind and it gave me even more comfort than you could have intended. It came at a moment when I was ill and depressed—a bout of influenza, not in itself very dramatic, left me in an extreme state of weakness from which, after more than two weeks, I have not yet wholly recovered: though most of the day my temperature is still quite strikingly below normal, and though I do begin to feel better, I never know when I will be overtaken

---

1. *Beyond Culture.*

by a spell of giddiness or fatigue, or a combination of the two. I can't but suppose that this physical condition is partly based on an emotional one. My mother died two days before Thanksgiving and I must naturally speculate that my state of health is in some degree a response to the event. For a time the most painful aspect of it was the difficulty of making it real. The funeral was held the day after my mother died, and although I had decided with my sister that I should not return if my mother were to die during my year away, this turned out to be one of those failures of the imagination one all too often makes. At the last moment, I tried to make a plane connection, but it wasn't possible to be sure that I would be in time for the funeral, so that I found myself engaged in the "work"—that Freudian word is curiously apposite here—of trying to realize the fact against the tyranny of distance, which has so much more control over the mind than I ever could have conceived, and against the long habituation in expecting the death, not to mention the established rational belief that it had become "better" for my mother that her life be at an end. Things became somewhat easier as I began to get letters from home with the account of the funeral. It meant a good deal to me, I found, that the service was performed by Max Kadushin, who had prepared me for my Bar Mitzvah and who had known and admired my mother, and her father too, and he did the service in the old orthodox way, which has considerable reality in it and which I have always thought necessary as against the genteel euphemisms of the modern Jewish fashion. Diana very wisely said that she thought I ought to say at least one Kaddish, so I called Isaiah Berlin, who has a link with orthodox religion, and he put me in touch with a group of Jewish students who regularly hold services in, of all places, Jesus College; it was an affecting occasion and helpful in a way that I would not have expected. And then as the letters from relatives and friends began to flood in, some from people unheard of for untold years and recalling long distant events, memory did begin to come to the aid of reality. But my relation with my mother had long been one of those American, or American-Jewish, post-Freudian relations, with much of the affection and the piety suppressed in favor of all the devices of separateness and freedom: possibly necessary for me at one time but never handled to my satisfaction in maturity, and, as I have long thought, harmful to me as well as painful to her. I had great admiration for her and always recognized that most of what I might think good in myself came directly from her, but by the same token, most of what I didn't like in myself I conceived of as coming from her too, and resented it, and the tensions of the ambivalence were great; I haven't yet been able to reach any simplicity of feeling, although the need for it is still always asserting itself. I wrote to her frequently from here, telling her all the trivialities of English life, for she delighted in social observation and was proud of having been born and schooled in England and in "knowing" the country, and what I find I most miss at the moment is her being *there* as a point of reference for all those trifling observations.

With so much unfinished in the feelings, I suppose it isn't surprising that the body took over and tried in its inept way to get on with the job in hand.

What with one thing and another, I haven't been able to write those last comments and the introduction, and this naturally sent my state of feeling still lower. So you can see why your letter, with its understanding and forgiving response to my previous long delay, meant so much to me coming when it did.

[. . .]

Jonathan Miller's[1] show is a little better than it began by being, but it is really quite bad. Its effect on me is to alienate me from art and modernity—they seem to make the occasion for such drivvle (drivel?) and such an air of false assurance. I think I especially resent it because it brings a New York tone into our life here. We find it rather wonderful to be with intelligent people who are not New York–cultural. Indeed, and I say this quite seriously, we wonder how we shall endure the situation on our return, and, although an Oxford-Columbia connection doesn't seem possible financially, we continually think, not fancifully, how we can arrange a life that will not be wholly based in New York. I find that I recall the people with a kind of revulsion. Diana feels this even more than I do; she is happy here as she never was in New York. It does seem very late in the post-Jamesian day to say that the English are more civilized than we

1. Jonathan Miller (1934–), performer and director.

are; but they are nicer; they have a better view of what personality consists in; and what actuality is; and they don't make the effect of *buzzing*: I think what I remember with most distaste about New York is a kind of factitious intensity in the people I know.

[. . .]

Yours,

Lionel

215. TO THE NOBEL COMMITTEE OF THE SWEDISH ACADEMY

February 1, 1965

Gentlemen,

On several occasions before this Mr. E. M. Forster must surely have been proposed to you as a candidate for the Nobel Prize for Literature. By now, of course, his best work is behind him and he is of an age at which we can expect but little that is new. For some time in recent years his work came to be less regarded than it once was. To many it seemed to express the moral sensibility of a past time. I myself shared this opinion to some extent despite the enthusiasm I had expressed in my study of Mr. Forster's work. But a recent rereading of the novels and essays has led me back to my old high admiration and to the sense that this body of work has a unique value and relevance for our time. And, if I read the signs aright, many old and new readers are coming to be of this opinion, and more strongly than ever before.

Yours sincerely,

Lionel Trilling

216. TO ALAN MONTEFIORE[1]

March 2, 1965

Dear Alan,

Thank you for letting me see the piece on your grandfather's influence.[2] I read it with great interest and a sad kind of pleasure, for

---

1. Alan Montefiore (1926–), English philosopher.
2. Alan Montefiore's grandfather Claude Montefiore founded the British denomination known as Liberal Judaism in the early twentieth century.

of course it is an elegiac essay, mourning and celebrating something that has died. I don't know when I have seen the question put more simply and with so quiet a lucidity. One has to reach a certain age or to have had a certain experience to understand that the most difficult thing to pass on from one generation to another is a rational faith. My parents tried to do it and failed—with great sensibility they modulated their own unquestioning belief and their ritual to suit the requirements of what they hoped and expected would be an intelligent modern man, with a result which, of course, pained them. What I know of Jewish theology stands in the way of any other, but it engages me less than any other, and the only things that bind me to the tradition are the memories of certain awesome or charming rituals and certain passionate avowals that my father made. Yet the nature of my alienation from Judaism is in large part an irritable response to the unsatisfactoriness—the dimness—of its theological utterances.

[. . .]

Sincerely,

217. TO STANLEY BURNSHAW

November 21, 1965

Dear Stanley:

It's good of you to get exercised over Hoffman's review in *The Nation*.[1] I seem to have put myself into an odd and on the whole useful state of mind about reviews—I am quite aware of a burning core of murderous rage but on the surface I find I am quite undisturbed. Hoffman's was one of three reviews I have had that seemed to me abysmal in their intellectual quality. The other two were Leon Edel's in the *Saturday Review*[2] and George Steiner's in the *Herald Tribune*. Steiner's was the most presentable of the three and full of elegiac respect and sad disappointment. My only reason for *anger* at the writer was a smarmy note from Steiner explaining that the review was

---

1. Trilling's book *Beyond Culture*, published in 1965, was reviewed in *The Nation*'s issue of November 8, 1965, by Frederick J. Hoffman.
2. Leon Edel, "Literature and Life Style," *Saturday Review*, November 6, 1965.

intended to celebrate me. The Hoffman and Edel pieces are quite shocking. Edel takes me to task for not seeing that Yeats despite what I call his "inexhaustible fund of snobbery" was a great poet; he quotes the phrase from a sentence which says that Yeats despite his inexhaustible fund of snobbery is always understood by students, even those who might by their social position be offended by the snobbery, to be a great poet. And he scolds me for praising advertising and taking it as my "cultural ally"! He is a very stupid man, although no one has yet said so, and he has a strong personal antagonism to me, no doubt divining that I know him to be stupid. Hoffman, too, writes out of a manifestly personal animus, the reason for which I think I know. But I shall have other "attacks" that I shall not be able to understand as personally motivated and this seems to me quite in the logic of the situation. For one thing I am in that stage of my career when people naturally say "We've had enough of him." For another thing, I do believe that the new book is a sort of resignation from an old club, with reasons implied. In some way—not in all ways—I rather like the isolate attacked position. A couple of my "radical" friends say that the book is "subversive" in the extreme, but the rest of the radical circle says they are wrong and that I am a hopeless reactionary.

    [   ]

We weren't greatly discommoded by the blackout,[1] being both at home. In the middle of the evening Jim phoned from Exeter, where for some reason light prevailed, not to inquire about our situation but to ask advice about a history paper and a girl. When we said we were short of candles he said that a good way of getting light was to tear up a sheet and dip it in ham fat, and then went on to put his questions, quite as if all the world were aglow.

Diana sends her warm regards with mine to you and Leda.

Yours,

---

1. On November 9, 1965, a blackout left millions without power throughout the northeast United States.

December 4, 1965

Dear Irving:

The mystery of your mislaid letter, with its necessary address, has been solved—it turned up in the folder into which I had put documents and clippings relating to *Beyond Culture*.

I don't remember whether or not I responded to it in any substantive way. Probably not, but if I did a repeated expression of pleasure in it and my gratitude for it can't hurt. You read the book as I had hoped it would be read and you are quite right in seeing its "problem," its "difficulty," the hole it leaves unfilled. I was aware of this when I put the book together and wrote the preface. The concluding sentence had to be "Come now, let us talk together like serious religious men." But this I could not say. There isn't any conceivable actual religious formulation that I can give credence to. And I don't have the power to propose—and probably not fully to conceive—the secular attitudes that arc proximate to the religious position and that might suit me almost as well. At least not, as you say, in criticism.

But it will please you to know that I mean to begin a novel in a few months. It has at least death in it, and fathers, and it engages me more and more deeply and the prospect makes me happy.

The literary world has responded much as you said it might. Some part of my feeling is shame at my people's stupidity (rather touched by malice), some part (less than I should have thought) anger, but mostly (I really do think, although one can never tell with this sort of emotion) a kind of pleasure.

Yours always,

219. TO SAUL STEINBERG[1]

December 4, 1965

Dear Saul Steinberg:

No gift of a book from its author has ever delighted and gratified me so much as yours. It was extraordinarily kind of you to send it and we are more grateful to you than we can say.

---

1. Saul Steinberg (1914–1999), artist and illustrator.

I think I must have seen and admired most of the pictures before, but having them all together made an effect that was new and enormously impressive. The experience of any one picture by itself is of its wit and—what I find I set especial store by these days—its humor, which has always seemed to me unique and deeply engaging. But having all the pictures together makes much more than a sum, and I find that I "read" the volume with the same kind of excitement I still have whenever I go back to one of Balzac's novels. I don't know of anything written today that gives me this particular kind of pleasure. It's a great relief to know that it can still be given, by one means or another, that I can still have it!

Diana tells me that she has a communication to make to you and I enclose it.

Sincerely,

220. TO LEON EDEL[1]

December 4, 1965

Dear Edel:

In your review of my book you make two statements that are quite strikingly in error. It seems to me that there isn't much point in bringing them to the attention of the readers of the *Saturday Review*, but I do think that they should not go unnoted.

You say of me that I "upbraid" Yeats for his "inexhaustible fund of snobbery," and then go on at some little length to say why I am wrong to do what you say I do, your point being that Yeats's social attitudes "did not prevent him from having a transcendent vision."

The sentence from which you quote the phrase which you are at pains to correct occurs on page 168 and reads as follows: "I have yet to meet the student committed to an altruistic politics who is alienated from Stephen Dedalus by that young man's disgust with political idealism, just as I have yet to meet the student from the most disadvantaged background who feels debarred from what Yeats can give him by the poet's slurs upon shopkeepers or by anything else in his inexhaustible fund of snobbery."

---

1. Leon Edel (1907–1997), literary critic and biographer of Henry James.

Earlier in your review you say, "Trilling moreover embraces advertising as a cultural ally." This remarkable statement is quite as far from representing my actual view as what you say I say about Yeats. It summarizes your understanding of two sentences (you quote them) in which I refer to advertising; in their context I think it should be obvious that they do not express my approval of advertising but, rather, my disapproval of certain modes of literary thought and even of literature itself for exaggerating the importance of the choices I am talking about.

I should perhaps say that the description of advertising as a "wonderful and terrible art" is by way of being an irony, and that I think it is possible to express not only a love for literature and a sense of its usefulness but also a dissatisfaction with it, and the belief that it may not only guide us but also mislead us.

Yours sincerely,
Lionel Trilling

221. TO LEON EDEL

January 9, 1966

Dear Leon Edel:

I write to acknowledge your response to my letter.

Snobbery, in one degree or another, is so common a trait of writers that I had come to think of it as but a venial sin, sometimes an amusing one, and now and then even endearing. It must naturally interest me that the biographer of Henry James understands it to be so grave a fault that merely to mention it as characteristic of a writer constitutes a denial of his virtue and value.

Some time ago it began to occur to me that irony was a mode which the ordinarily educated reader could no longer be counted on to comprehend, and lately I have had the sense, in which you confirm me, that it is probably beyond the reach of even very highly trained literary scholars.

Yours sincerely,
Lionel Trilling

222. TO THE NOBEL COMMITTEE OF THE SWEDISH ACADEMY

January 24, 1966

Gentlemen:

I write to nominate W. H. Auden for the Nobel Award for Literature. I need scarcely speak of Mr. Auden's achievements as a poet. These are preeminent. But I should like to remark on Mr. Auden as a cultural figure. He is a critic of great brilliance and percipience. He has served music as a notable librettist and as a collaborator with the remarkable Pro Musica group. Many people, myself among them, think of him as exemplifying all that is best in the conception of civilized life.

Yours sincerely,
Lionel Trilling

223. TO THE EDITORS OF *THE NEW YORK REVIEW OF BOOKS*

October 4, 1966
35 Claremont Avenue

To the Editors:

I would naturally be grieved if I found it possible to credit the news brought by Jonathan Miller that something I wrote played a decisive part in the sad fate of Lenny Bruce.[1] But I fear that in his explanation of how I incurred my unhappy responsibility Dr. Miller has allowed his gift for mordant comedy to get the upper hand of his usually canny sense of cultural fact. By his account, a group of liberals and intellectuals were intent upon making Bruce a martyr to one of their characteristic received ideas, that a free sexuality is the cure for all social ills. In the judgment of these people the most persuasive formulation of their cherished idea had been made by me in an essay on Freud. They communicated the purport of this essay to Bruce, who forthwith allowed himself "to be hanged until he was dead from the yard-arm of this particular ship of fools."

---

1. Jonathan Miller wrote about the death of the comedian Lenny Bruce in "On Lenny Bruce (1926–1966)," *New York Review of Books*, October 6, 1966.

Dr. Miller believes that a commitment to utopian sexuality came easily to Bruce, that quite without prompting from anyone he gave credence to the idea that "if only prudery would relax we could screw our way to peace and prosperity for all." He had no trouble in maintaining the expectation "that in some hypothetical millennium, bigotry and suffering would not be heard for the swishing of the pricks." But although temperamentally disposed to the idea of liberation through sex, Bruce was not ready to suffer martyrdom for it until "he was encouraged to do so by people who were prepared to push a much more sophisticated version of the same argument." This, according to Dr. Miller, was to be found in my essay "Freud and the Crisis of Our Culture." Dr. Miller doubts that the essay itself ever got to Bruce's "immediate attention," but he is certain that Bruce came to know its substance through the agency of people who would stick at nothing in their purpose of making him a martyr, going so far in desperateness that they were "prepared to push" what I had written. In its primitive formulations, the idea that we could screw our way to peace and prosperity had won from Bruce no more than assent; to my "much more sophisticated version of the same argument" he gave his ultimate allegiance. As Dr. Miller sums up the effect of my essay, "Certain intellectuals leaped at its utopian possibilities and then found in Bruce a conveniently self-sacrificing public spokesman on behalf of the doctrine."

Alas, there are no utopian possibilities to be leaped at in my essay. Nor have any intellectuals deceived themselves into thinking that there are—such leaping as they have done has been with hostile intent, upon what they have taken to be the essay's conservative implications. These they discover in the support I give to the continuing emphasis on biology in Freud's thought. Perhaps more than anyone else, I said in effect, Freud had made clear to us the extent to which the human condition is to be understood in terms of culture, yet for him culture was not the only factor in human destiny; there was also biology. The correctness of Freud's position seemed to be confirmed by the developing psychoanalytical theory of child rearing at the time I wrote: I quoted Anna Freud, who said in 1954 that it no longer seemed possible to trace the origin of infantile neuroses to environmental influence; they were now seen as due "to inevitable factors of various kinds." Miss Freud spoke of the new period of psychoanalytic theory as "pessimistic." I said that some comfort might be found in its darkness, that "when we think of the growing power of culture to control us by seduction or coercion, we must be glad and not sorry that some part of our fate comes from outside the culture." And I developed the idea that the biological *given* of man is to some extent intractable to culture. It seems to me quite possible that this idea should be understood as conservative. But my mind boggles at the process by which Dr. Miller came to understand it as a sophisticated version of the utopian belief that we can screw our way to peace and prosperity for all, or even some.

I should like to add that in an essay on Bruce's last trial for obscenity (*Censorship*, Spring 1965) Albert Goldman gives an account of the comedian's conduct that radically qualifies the character Dr. Miller presents in his commemoration. Mr. Goldman tells us that "Bruce broke openly with his distinguished liberal attorney . . . and assumed his own defense, stating that he believed in censorship and did not wish to be exonerated at the cost of weakening the law. The sophisticated public opinion that had championed Bruce in the early course of the trial changed during the muddled last phase to disgust." Many liberal intellectuals had been recruited to testify, or to affirm in the press, that Bruce's performances were not obscene and offensive. Bruce would have none of this. As Mr. Goldman makes plain, he knew that the point of his performances, and their power, lay in their being thought exactly obscene and offensive, in their violation of all (including the liberal) pieties. At least on this one occasion Bruce would seem to have transcended the humble admiration Dr. Miller says he had for liberals and intellectuals.

    Lionel Trilling

224. TO PETER DAVIS[1]

November 14, 1966
35 Claremont Avenue

Dear Mr. Davis,

I hope you can forgive me for having delayed so long in replying to your letter. It came just when I had gone off to the country with a mind quite blank from exhaustion after a desperate push to finish a book that had been with me for years. And then I returned to find that—of course—there were all sorts of things still to be done, and in a rush, before the book was really finished. I don't think this makes an adequate explanation—the letter was of a kind that required an immediate response. And yet, by the same token, it couldn't be answered out of fatigue or in the interstices of intense preoccupation—it was much too moving for that.

For if my essay made your mother more present for you, your letter had the same effect on me, with so much of my own life in attendance on her presence. I am happy that what I wrote did what it did do for you, and grateful to you for the generous way in which you tell me so.

I think that you are largely in the right in what you say about my errors of emphasis, perhaps especially about your mother's relation to Jewishness. The elder Slesingers were a notably acculturated family—the mother, who determined the family style, being more so than the father—and all the children, none of whom "looked" in the least Jewish, made their way into "the world" very easily. There is, of course, the circumstance that Mrs. Slesinger's activity as a social worker was, if I remember correctly, among Jews, and I should say that the family's relation to its Jewishness was not different in kind from that of many other well-established Jewish families that I knew— being Jewish was a felt and in some sort acknowledged circumstance, but not one that was explored with a view to discovering significance in it. My sense of your mother is that her being Jewish was not really

---

1. Peter Davis (1937–), filmmaker and writer, son of the writer Tess Slesinger (1905–1945). Trilling contributed an afterword to a 1966 edition of Slesinger's novel *The Unpossessed*, a roman à clef about the *Menorah Journal* circle, to which they both belonged in the 1920s.

364

important to her, that, indeed in the simplest way, without taking thought and certainly without conflict, she just naturally stepped outside whatever the concept of Jewishness is. It simply was not relevant to her. But for a while, at the time I knew her, she did accept the *mystique* of the group. One reason she did so, I am sure, is that it gave her subjects for her stories, material that recommended itself as actual because observed. (You are of course quite right in supposing that she would have thought her brother Donald's conversion to Episcopalianism both funny and sad. The last time I met Donald was at dinner at the Deanery of St. John the Divine when my friend Pike was Dean;[1] he told me of his ordination and of his practice of psychoanalysis and I thought what a story Tess would have made of the conversation.)

But she certainly never made any avowals, and there was always a discernible detachment in her attitude, even an irony. She was not in the least an ideological person and eventually, I believe, she came to feel that this particular ideology was a kind of bullying, from which she undertook to escape.

If I should ever reprint the essay, as is likely, I shall want to correct the error of emphasis. It resulted, I suppose, from the essay's being my first venture into anything like autobiography—all sorts of things pressed hard to be recalled and some of them, as I can now see, were allowed to bulk larger than they should and throw the picture of your mother a little out of focus.

My own sense of your mother's relation to Communism is, I think, much in accord with yours. Here again the nonideological—even anti-ideological—aspect of her temperament was definitive. She was meant, really, for a traditional society, one that allowed her intellectual life to flourish, one that she could tease, or challenge, into greater animation, or more thought, or more justice. The idea of putting everything, including the instincts, to the question, as intellectual radical groups often do, was repugnant to her, and I would guess that, to the extent that she went along with the Communism of the West Coast, she did so because it was really part of the going culture and something like a tradition; it served to make some of the habitual ground of life, and as such was to be accepted and mocked, a way of

---

1. James Pike (1913–1969), Episcopal bishop and radical theologian.

responding to it which, of course, would be quite in line with that happy, now vanished, Woman-principle I tried to describe.

Perhaps it is there that I should say that you have misread me a little in your understanding of my "merely." I don't think that the subject of men and women is to be condescended to, except as it is dealt with in a doctrinaire way. What I tried to say was that I take the intended subject of the book to have been the dialectic between "nature" and "spirit," of which the relation between men and women is only one aspect, and that it is a fault of the book that this one aspect eventually takes the place of the intended larger subject.

Your mother and I never had a close and easy friendship—it would take a Proustian patience to state the reasons why not—but I've always thought that there we had a particular unexpressed sympathy for each other, and this recollection has been present to me ever since I undertook the essay about her. And the more since I received your very kind letter, for which I am more grateful than I can say.

Sincerely,

225. TO W. J. THORNE

January 7, 1967

Dear Mr. Thorne:

It was very good of you to write to me as you did—your letter touched and gratified me very deeply and I am most grateful for it.

You are of course right in noting that much literature before the twentieth century has grown obscure to students and even to many of their younger teachers. I am inclined to think that this is especially true of nineteenth-century literature. I have the sense that my students are not more distant from the literature of the eighteenth century and earlier than my students were twenty years ago. The distance might be greater than one would wish, but it has not increased. But in the same twenty years the distance between them and the nineteenth century has become ever greater. All the things that I seemed to know instinctively in my boyhood and youth are quite strange to them. And of course it isn't only the nineteenth century that has become strange. Only yesterday, having asked a class of mine to read T. S. Eliot's *The Sacred Wood*, I found that they really couldn't understand anything of the situation out of which Eliot was writing. It was a shock to me, for the book had been of the greatest importance to me when I was in college. But after all, it had first appeared in 1920, forty-seven years ago, nearly half a century, which is a long time in literary culture.

I'm inclined to think that what makes the difficulty is the change in social assumptions. I recently heard that young American professional students of English are thought by their teachers to be maladroit in their chosen field because they really can't understand the whole conception of *class*. Something of the sort, though less extreme, must be happening with the English young—perhaps in time they too, like my students, will have to be instructed that Jane Austen's people do not all belong to "the nobility," or, as my students might say, are not all "nobles."

Yet there is this to be considered, that genius does continue to break through—my students greatly admire Jane Austen, the Brontës, and Dickens, and at least the Thackeray of *Vanity Fair* (not Scott, however!). Or so they did some ten years ago, when I last taught these authors—there has been an acceleration of cultural change within the last decade that may have revised the taste of the young in this respect. After all, I can't any longer *count* on D. H. Lawrence being up their alley!

I sometimes surprise myself by being pleasurably excited by the realization that some author who was once at the very center of my sense of literature means nothing to the young. I don't understand why, but so it is.

Yours sincerely,

226. TO STANLEY BURNSHAW

March 19, 1967
47 Grosvenor Square, London

Dear Stanley:

The truth of existence that you claim for the book[1] was confirmed yesterday by its arrival, not only printed but bound. Like much truth, it did not have a charming effect. Was it the cover that sank my spirits?

---

1. The textbook anthology *The Experience of Literature*.

That awful humanistic head? How sorry I am that I did not pick up the cue of your dislike of it and make a fuss that might have changed the cover design toward dignified simplicity! But when I saw the sketch I was in a daze of completion-emotions and willing to grin in bland acquiescence at anything.—Or was it that I had just heard from Brian Heald that Doubleday had ordered a printing run of no more than 17,500 copies, most of them for the Literary Guild. This did not sustain the impression I had gained that Doubleday was enthusiastic about the book and hopeful of its success. Or do I speak out of ignorance?—And then it suddenly came over me that, from our, i.e., the Holt-Textbook point of view, Doubleday's timing of publication was injurious, that there should have been an interval between the text and the trade publication of a considerable number of months.—And, what with one thing and another, I've got myself thoroughly dejected about the prospects of the book. I'll ask you to comment on these gloomy thoughts of mine so far as they seem to you to be susceptible to practical consideration. But how can I fail to perceive that what I am really suffering from is the result of the dreadful thing having come to its end in completion. Naturally enough, not only holding the physical object in the hand but looking inside it and reading a little here and there has its sinking effects. To read a calm, reasonable, intelligent, but by no means brilliant page cannot fail to raise the question of *why* in the name of everything sensible was my life in bondage to this for so many years? A sweet note from Charles Kaplan tells me that the number of years is ten—I had set a lower figure but Kaplan is of course accurate. My God—it took less time to write *Ulysses*!

Well, all this said, it is nevertheless true that the freedom from the Thing is real and truly very pleasant and there is some satisfaction in having *not* given up on it. I hope never to talk about the book again, but before I send it out of my life, I want to say again what I must often have said in one way or another before, that I am very deeply grateful to you for your part in it—for your forbearance and for the much kindness you showed me in the course of its making.

[. . .]

Always yours,
    Lionel

227. TO STANLEY BURNSHAW

May 31, 1967
47 Grosvenor Square, London

Dear Stanley:

It was kind of you to go to such pains to give me a full account of the fortunes of the Book, and I am touched by your effort to reassure me and grateful for it. I am duly reassured and I am taking your good advice to put my thoughts about it on ice for the summer.

Here we say, what summer? The rain rains and no day goes by without our using the electric fires. But there is always one moment in the day, at least that, and sometimes there are a few, when the marvel of English light gladdens the heart. It is a strange thing: America can be very beautiful but it never has the effect on me that England has, whether in a street or in the country—it never quite welcomes human existence and justifies it. We went to see Penshurst and what Jonson says about it is true of England for us: it is uniquely a place to be dwelt in. And so we go back and forth over the question of whether or not I should retire early and we should come to live out our days here. Eventually something stops me, me more than Diana but her too: it is after all not *ours*. Speaking for myself, it isn't that I feel a stranger, but I never know what it is that I am defending. There may well be something in the Territorial Imperative. And then everything is at a much lower pressure than I like to live, even as I grow older. Or especially as I grow older. Like Yeats said. Now and then I have home thoughts from abroad and have a hankering. But the thought [of] the summer, in some general or technical sense, the word that you and others are signalizing the season by going to the Vineyard or the Cape, which must mean that we are on the last leg of our sojourn, is saddening.

[. . .]

Always yours,
Lionel

228. TO SUSAN SONTAG[1]

October 15, 1967

Dear Susan:

It was good of you to send us a copy of your novel[2] and we thank you for it. You will not be surprised, I fear, if I tell you that I am having trouble with it: you probably know how fixed in the past my taste in novels is. But the purpose of this note is not to say this, rather to tell you how much I admire your *PR* essay on pornography.[3] I don't know when I have read a critical essay that gave me so much pleasure, that seemed to me to do so thoroughly and with so much grace what criticism ought to do. It's a superb job and I congratulate you on it. And Diana wants me to tell you that she too has the greatest admiration for the essay.

Sincerely,

229. TO ISAIAH BERLIN

October 15, 1967

Dear Isaiah:

How good to hear from you! It was only glimpses of you and Aline that we had in our London time, but we miss you very much. New York is being abominable. This opinion, though ours especially, is the common one—almost every reunion has begun with the statement of it by the friends who stayed at home. It has to do with the increasing dirtiness and inconvenience of the city, very much with the Negro situation, and some pervasive sense that everybody else in the intellectual life is behaving badly, with some derogation from good sense, even sanity. Diana and I have fallen into a curious mode of life in which every occasion is experienced not merely in itself but in comparison with what a cognate occasion would be like in England. Last night we heard a *Traviata* which was such a crashing bore, so awkward and spiritless in its sumptuous Cecilbeatonry, and so ill-sung, that we came away in a downright depression, made the worse,

---

1. Susan Sontag (1933–2004), essayist and novelist.
2. *Death Kit* (1967).
3. "The Pornographic Imagination," *Partisan Review* (Spring 1967).

of course, by our recollection of two different Covent Garden performances, not perfect maybe but alive.

Well, you have your own view of the place and I will not interfere
with it. But I do think that something has happened to the American
character, which I once quite admired.

I haven't yet read Bayley's[1] book. So many books. So many books.
So little time. I like Bayley very much and think him very intelligent,
but as a critic he makes me fidget—perhaps because *he* fidgets.
But then I have become impatient with criticism in general and find
it harder and harder to read it. I lately decided that all the books on
Wordsworth I had accumulated were wrong and foolish and that, with
one exception, no one knew what to say about him. I leave you to
guess the name of the exception.

[. . .]

230. TO HAROLD ROSENBERG[2]

November 26, 1967
Columbia University

Dear Harold Rosenberg:

Although I spent the larger part of last year in England, I somehow missed the March issue of *Encounter* and have only recently seen
the copy that had been sent to me here in New York. I would have
read your piece on art and the universities[3] with interest in any event,
but I naturally read it with special interest because it refers to me several times—and with dismay because it represents my position as
being the opposite of yours, although this is not the case. Actually,
indeed, I agree—enthusiastically—with all the points that you make
against the new tendency. In the preface to *Beyond Culture*, from
which you quote, I had meant to express my apprehensions about the
increasingly "liberal," "permissive" attitude of the universities toward
the arts which I see as a way of taking the arts into camp, of institu-
tionalizing them. But I wrote in a mode that was prevailingly ironic

---

1. John Bayley (1925–2015), English literary critic.
2. Harold Rosenberg (1906–1978), intellectual and art critic.
3. "Where to Begin," *Encounter*, March 1967.

rather than direct, and the irony seems to have sadly miscarried. When I said "Dr. Kerr's prophecy is but a reasonable projection into the future of a condition already established," I meant to imply "of an already established condition that ought to be looked at with suspicion." I meant my seeming praise of the sympathetic hospitality of the universities to be understood as a warning that all aspects of life, including the ones that used to be thought wild and liberating, were being taken into the control of the universities and that, as a result, a considerable degree of autonomy was in process of being surrendered.

If I had read your essay on its publication I would have written a letter to *Encounter* to clear up the misunderstanding, taking all due blame for my part in it. Too much time has gone by for that, but I do want to make the position clear to you, especially in view of the possibility that you will someday want to reprint the essay in a collection.

Yours sincerely,
Lionel Trilling

231. TO DOTSON RADER[1]

December 21, 1967

Dear Dotson:

It may well be that if I actually had the experience of the Warhol films I would respond to them more warmly than I did to your account of them. To the remark that people of your age and younger believe them to be true I would make this response: At certain moments of a culture, to certain groups in a culture, intention seems more important than achievement, indeed so very important that achievement comes to seem a negation of it—that which is achieved cannot be intended! A great deal of the art of the 1930s can be understood in this way. No doubt it served its purpose, good or bad; it seemed true, and the truer because its intention was naked. It would be hard for you to imagine how very true it seemed. Its life in truth was very short. Which is certainly not the ultimate condemnation, but it is a thing to be considered.

---

1. Dotson Rader (1942–), writer, had been a student of Trilling's at Columbia.

I of course suppose that when you speak of the deadness and dat-
edness of the Liberal Establishment you intend to make an ad homi-
nem point. I might have been more nearly reached by it if you hadn't
gone on to mere title mongering in saying that it is "all over for the
liberal imagination"—you evidently think that this old phrase of mine
was intended in the way of praise or defense, although the contrary
is so.

I think the lesson I would propose is that to deaden one's awareness of the past is an effectual way of helping to make a cultural revolution, but that if one also undertakes to engage in critical dialectic
about the enterprise, a sense of history is a necessary part of the
armament.

Yours sincerely,
Lionel Trilling

232. TO DOTSON RADER

January 7, 1968

Dear Dotson:

I write only to acknowledge your letter—I can't properly *reply* to
it without writing a book. Which I may yet do.

But in the meantime there are one or two comments I should like
to make. I think I understand *something* of the situation of your generation. After all, age and establishment don't entirely protect one
from the disenchanting elements of the culture. But what I don't understand is the ambiguity of your relation to the old and established.
The accusation of "betrayal" doesn't surprise me. It has often been
made before and I can quite see how it comes to be made. And I can
also comprehend how it happens that there should be a rejection of
the actualities of the social life as it is usually and, so it seems to me,
necessarily conceived—the houses, children, buildings, jobs in institutions that you speak of, and the possibility of there being good
and respected (even rich!) men whose lives end in decent quiet, in
bed. What I don't understand is why you are concerned about the
regard in which you are held by the old and established. Why should it
matter to you whether or not you are "rather unwelcomed"? What
do you want to be welcomed *into*? Why should it matter to you that
you are "a bit disliked" when you deny the validity of the criteria of

those who do the liking and disliking? Or that you sense "boredom" with you?—are you trying to be engaging and interesting to those who have betrayed you?

I find this curious—that you should make a total rejection of a way of life and its personnel and then ask for its approval and "help." I remark on this not to put you down with a debater's point but because it genuinely puzzles me.

I'd like again to recur to history: I suggest that you read Fritz Stern's book *The Politics of Cultural Despair*, for I could not help thinking that your description of the emotions of the young, the vocabulary you use for it, is comparable to what was felt and said by the many German youth groups which, over some decades, prepared the way for the Nazi ideology. Again, I assure you that I am not trying to score points off you but proposing something quite serious.

Sincerely,

233. TO DOTSON RADER

January 21, 1968

Dear Dotson:

I rather think that this particular correspondence ought to come to an end. Your first letter raised overt questions about my honesty, my reply implied a question of yours, and now you return to the charge with another imputation of the same sort. This can lead nowhere. We had better give it up and begin somewhere else.

I should perhaps explain what was not clear in my last letter, that I wasn't pointing to a resemblance between the youth you were describing and the actual developed Nazi movement. What I had in mind were such things as the young people *Wandervogel* movement who cherished their innocence and made a cult of youth and who, without any positive social and political program, nourished the idea—or ideal—of "cultural despair." It was this that made the ground for the ideology of Nazism, which was, we must remember, enormously idealistic, and I more and more find myself thinking that what you describe of our youth has a good chance of leading to a reactionary ideology here.

Sincerely,

234. TO DOTSON RADER

February 27, 1968

Dear Dotson:

I had meant, even before your letter came, to write to you to say that I was sorry that I had lost my temper with you on Thursday afternoon and—again—that I was sorry that I had been forced to miss seeing you the day before.

What you say of yourself in your letter in some way forestalls but also in some way makes the more relevant what I had it in mind to go on to say, that if we are to have any relationship of any kind, it ought to be between two persons and not two institutional representatives. D.R. and L.T. can talk together, but the Spokesman for Dissident Youth and the Spokesman for the Liberal Establishment, once each has taken his appropriate stance and his obligatory attitude, can only exchange hostile platitudes. You and I began better than that when you were a student—the inevitable differences in taste and judgment were, to me at least, interesting and instructive until they became party slogans. I think the time has come for us to give these up and to go back to particularities when we talk.

I'll look to see you on Friday.

Sincerely,

235. TO PAMELA HANSFORD JOHNSON[1]

May 20, 1968

Dear Pamela,

It was very good of you to send us a copy of your new book—we are delighted to have it, thank you for it most warmly, and wish all good things for it. As a physical object it engaged us immediately and wholly by reason of the photograph of you on the jacket: it is, we think, the truest and most engaging photograph of a friend we have ever seen. As a spiritual entity, it has only begun to be known by me, by Diana not at all, because it arrived during the troubles here,[2] which

---

1. Pamela Hansford Johnson (1912–1981), English writer, wife of C. P. Snow.
2. In April 1968, major student protests erupted at Columbia, including an occupation of Hamilton Hall, where Trilling's office was located.

have absorbed and fatigued us utterly. For the first week all the faculty was involved, at least all our friends on the faculty, and in a very immediate way. Then, for some special sin of mine, I was required to be especially involved and I have done nothing else for weeks now. At the moment things are relatively quiet, but there is continued uncertainty and we are not nearly returned to normal. At odd moments at strange hours I have been able to make forays into the book, finding comfort and assurance in its quiet and actuality after noise and several kinds of fantasy, but Diana, who must really read or not at all, hasn't yet made its acquaintance. For days she ran a kind of canteen for the people I brought home or who would drop in at unearthly times, and now she is trying to write about the experience,[1] spending all day at her desk. Everybody over a certain age or level of intelligence experienced the events as a wounding experience. The students seem to have been invigorated by it. To them I find myself in a strange relation—I don't really understand what they feel, or at least why they feel it so much, and I am angry at the disruption they have caused, yet those I have talked with—many—command my respect and even liking. I would find it easier to be simple, but I cannot be.

One blessing: that Jacques was not in the bedeviled and luckless administration.

[. . .]

Ever yours,

236. TO H.-J. LANG[2]

November 7, 1968

Dear Professor Lang:

I trust that the package of Xeroxes I sent a few days ago has reached you safely.

You will no doubt find it useful to know who is who in Mark Van Doren's essay.[3] "A" is Henry Rosenthal, who was my closest friend in

---

1. Diana Trilling's essay "On the Steps of Low Library" would appear in *Commentary*, November 1968.
2. A German academic who planned to write about Trilling.
3. Mark Van Doren (1894–1972), poet and longtime Columbia professor, wrote about

college. The portrait is quite accurate in its suggestion of his ferocity. Rosenthal did become a rabbi, as he had set out to do, but he found that pastoral work went against the grain, and then early in the 1930s he lost his faith, I believe under the influence of Marxism, gave up the rabbinate, took a doctorate in philosophy, and now teaches that subject at Hunter College, one of the colleges of the New York City University. He had, I thought then, literary abilities that amounted to genius, and I think that his story "Inventions," which I sent you, rather confirms that judgment, which was widely shared. For some reason his great gifts left him in early maturity. What little writing of his that I saw after college was not good. I am the friend in the story, rather considerably enhanced as to dandyism. I'm sure I didn't have, or aspire to, that much elegant insouciance. Our respective relations to Judaism did make an issue between us which is pretty accurately represented. The prediction of the end of our friendship came true in the early 1930s. The termination was unilaterally made by Rosenthal.

"B" is Clifton Fadiman. People who did not know him in his youth cannot imagine how brilliant and attractive he was. He was of the most engaging appearance, and infinitely witty. His intelligence was of great strength and range. He thought it important to make money and in those days this belief was in much worse repute than it now is: when he took a job as an editor in a publishing house, he was ashamed and defensive, as his friends thought he ought to be, and when he became the literary critic of *The New Yorker*, he was no less uneasy and his friends were no less supercilious; he did a good job but the size of his salary made his position seem a compromised one. Edmund Wilson, who succeeded him, had no such trouble. After his success with the radio program *Invitation to Learning* and his work for the Book-of-the-Month Club, Fadiman lost touch with the intellectual life of New York, which there was once every reason to think he might dominate. His first wife and my wife were schoolmates and for a good many years after college the two couples were quite close. He now lives in Los Angeles.

"C" is Meyer Schapiro, the art historian, now University Professor

---

Trilling and several other students in a 1927 *Menorah Journal* essay, "Jewish Students I Have Known."

at Columbia. He was even then of an extraordinary erudition—my wife has told me that when she was an art history student at Radcliffe she heard of the wonderful undergraduate at Columbia who was so brilliant and knew so much. Schapiro fulfilled his promise. Although he does not publish much—he has difficulty in writing—he is generally accounted one of the leaders of his field.

"D" is John Gassner, who became professor of dramatic literature at Yale. He died last year. As he grew older, he became broader and his face became redder and he looked *exactly* like a jolly gnome in a fairy-tale illustration. His mind never, I thought, became very interesting.

The erudition that Van Doren ascribes to A, B, C, and D seems to me characteristic of the time—I have never had Columbia students who knew as much as some of my friends did or who took so much pride in knowing. Very likely the European, especially the Jewish European, influence was still at work.

I of course once knew who E and G are, and it makes me sad that I have forgotten. "F" is me. When the article first appeared, I quite resented the portrait, believing that I was both sterner and more spirited than it suggests. But I have come to believe that it catches quite well the impression I made on many at the time.

The Gentile Student, "the best one of them all," is Whittaker Chambers. Van Doren was devoted to Chambers for many years, but after the Hiss case began, his admiration and affection turned to loathing.

I am sure you have discovered that the pieces in *Morningside* signed L.M.T. are by me—it was the convention, not always observed, that the editors should sign contributions with their initials. I gave up the M. (for Mordecai) when *The Menorah Journal* misprinted it as P.—it suddenly dawned upon me that authors might have middle names but not middle initials.

Sincerely,
Lionel Trilling

237. TO D. G. KEHL

April 3, 1969

Dear Professor Kehl:

I am answering your questions as best I can but I cannot agree with your view that modern writers have much to tell teachers of writing about how to help students improve their writing. What you call the current dilemma is by now an old one and it isn't a dilemma of pedagogy but of the culture in general. Writing well—I don't mean writing "creatively"—has to begin as an ideal of the self: it means wanting to be a certain kind of person, the kind of person who sounds a certain way, who has a certain relation to language. If that desire isn't instilled by the general culture—if, that is, the general culture doesn't value that kind of person—no amount of pedagogy will make a student write well.

Yours sincerely,
Lionel Trilling

238. TO JANE KRAMER[1]

May 28, 1969

Dear Miss Kramer:

Thank you for sending me a copy of your book about Allen Ginsberg. I am reading it with interest.

It isn't perfectly clear to me whether the account of Allen's last days at Columbia and his arrest[2] is Allen's own narrative, literally transcribed, or your presentation of the substance and tone of what he told you. In either case remark ought to be made of the errors and omissions it makes.

1. Page 128. I was not "*horrified*," not in italics nor even in roman. I had for some time known from Allen about his association with criminals; I had received the news in an unperturbed way, reserving my expression of adverse feeling for Allen's clichés about criminals

---

1. Jane Kramer (1938–), journalist and longtime *New Yorker* contributor, author of *Allen Ginsberg in America*.
2. In 1949, Allen Ginsberg was arrested after allowing friends to use his apartment to store stolen goods. Thanks in part to Trilling's intervention, Ginsberg was sent to the New York State Psychiatric Institute rather than to jail.

and the criminal life. I rely on this recollection because shortly after the event I came to think I had been wrong, and done Allen a disservice, by not taking a directly moral line about his conduct.

2. Page 128. Allen came to see me *after* his father had chosen a lawyer to defend him. Allen had no confidence in this man, perhaps because he was a bad amateur poet, and the purpose of his visit was to enlist my help in finding another lawyer.

When I took him to see my friend Herbert Wechsler at the Law School, Wechsler did *not* advise him to plead insanity—nothing would have been further from the man's principles and style. What Wechsler said was that Allen had committed a crime and therefore should go to jail. He went on to say that this would do Allen good.

3. Page 129. It was not in the natural course of things that Allen was allowed to plead mental aberration (I'm sure that this and not actual insanity was advanced). Nor was it inevitable that the Columbia Psychiatric Institute, one of the most humane and comfortable mental treatment centers in the country, should be the institution to which he would be sent. The permission to plead mental aberration on condition that Allen undergo treatment for a year was given by the District Attorney responding to the urgent request of the Dean of Columbia College, Harry Carman, who was personally acquainted with him and who, since the District Attorney was a devoted alumnus, could ask it of him in the name of the College. Dean Carman was supported in his efforts to win lenient treatment for Allen by three of Allen's former teachers, Jacques Barzun, Mark Van Doren, and myself. Finding an immediate place in the Psychiatric Institute was by no means easy. The College had to use its influence, to which was added some personal influence that I was able to procure.

These efforts were made out of regard for Allen both as a person and as a student of the College. One of the things I admire in Allen is that he is able to maintain discriminations in his feelings about people, and even institutions, whose principles are different from his, and to be aware of what in their behavior to him is well intended. If his recollection of the incident is actually as it is represented in the book, this admirable ability would seem to have been momentarily in abeyance.

Yours sincerely,
Lionel Trilling

239. TO H.-J. LANG

September 16, 1969

Dear Professor Lang:

I should be unhappy indeed if anything I said by way of express-ing interest in your book had the effect of putting you under the slight-est additional pressure. I would say, what is true enough, that no one could be more understanding than I am, from my own experience, of how one's own work can be interrupted and impeded by public chores, were it not that for me to speak of my "understanding" of your diffi-culties might suggest that you had some responsibility to me as a person, which of course is not in the least the case! I am only a sub-ject, and it is in the nature of being a subject that its treatment is always delayed beyond the expectations of the person who under-takes to treat it. I'll only say, then, that I am sorry that your attention has to be diverted from your literary enterprises. But not wholly sorry, for I can imagine the possibility that the public duties give you some considerable satisfaction. I say this on, again, my own experience. Perhaps I have already told you, what is the case, that the weeks I spent last year dealing with our disorders as a member of the Execu-tive Committee of the Faculty made one of the very happiest times of my life and led to my feeling strangely what I had always felt dimly, that all intellectuals should have occasional experience of the exercise of responsibility in some polity, however small. I think that, after a certain age, a man *needs* this experience. Very likely, when "power" passes from you, you will feel a sense of loss, as I did. I loved the unholy hours, the sleeplessness, the sense of colleagueship, perhaps also the freedom from lonely intellectual work.

The Cox Commission Report[1] I do not regard highly. It proceeds on an excessive [*sic*] simple assumption of cause and effect; I have never been able to believe that the outburst could be explained by particular circumstances. The feeling of many of us here was that the report implicitly advanced the view that we had trouble at Columbia because Columbia was not like Harvard. The trouble at Harvard was not so extensive as at Columbia, and no doubt there are reasons for

---

1. The report of the Columbia committee on the 1968 protests, chaired by Archibald Cox, was published as *The Cox Commission Report: Crisis at Columbia*.

this to be found in some of Harvard's good points, but also in Harvard's geographical and social location. *Up Against the Ivy Wall*, on the other hand, seems to me worthy of considerable admiration. Although written by students, who are almost wholly sympathetic with the rebels, it is fair in spirit and very decent in its tone. I don't at the moment recall any corrections that need to be made—I remember being generally impressed by its accuracy—but I'll take it to Cambridge with me, look through it again, and let you know if I come on any lapses. I had the impression of having been treated on the whole very pleasantly, despite my being a liberal centrist. If you should at some later date use it with reference to me, you might want to be aware of the inadequacy of its index, which does not include all the mentions of my name in the text.

The chances are against the coming year being a quiet one. The student radical-revolutionary movements are well organized, despite the split into two camps, of which you have no doubt heard, and very determined. Whether or not they will be able to activate the mass of students is problematical. Last year, most students seemed to me to be fatigued and wanting quiet.

I agree with you in dissenting from my remark about the event being more hysterical than historical. I don't know what led me to say that—an access of fatigue and discouragement perhaps.

Please don't have any concern about keeping the materials I sent you. I do set some store by the collection of *Post* articles, but I'm sure it is as safe with you as with me.

There will be an article[1] coming out in *Commentary* in which the writer, in the course of a long discussion of Walter Benjamin, institutes an extended comparison between Benjamin and me—very respectful to me but giving B. the better of it, on the ground of B.'s being more overtly Jewish than I am, therefore more attuned to modernity. How does B. stand in the German literary life today? I find him full of good things, but he doesn't really reach me as he seems to have reached his friends and associates.

[...]
Sincerely,
    Lionel Trilling

---

1. Robert Alter, "On Walter Benjamin," *Commentary*, September 1969.

240. TO IRVING FELDMAN

February 5, 1970

Dear Irving:

I'm sorry that we missed each other over the holidays and that you spent them being ill—I do hope you are by now recovered. Actually, I was in New York only briefly, coming in a day before Christmas, leaving the day after New Year's. I gather that you didn't know that I am spending the year here at Harvard, where I am the current Charles Eliot Norton Professor of Poetry. No teaching, but six public lectures to give. They will begin in March, are to be on "Sincerity and Authenticity" (I will not explain: read them when they are published,[1] as they are required to be), and are making some trouble in the composition.

No, I am not going to Oxford in the fall. I was elected to a professorship there but after a long inner debate decided against taking it, the reasons being partly spiritual, largely financial. Columbia has made me a University Professor, which means that I can teach or not as I choose and come and go as I choose. What I will do with this freedom—I mean living-arrangements-wise—I don't yet know. I shall be based in New York until my retirement from the university some four years hence, but whether or not I shall divide the time is still a question. I loathe the city, my wife has even stronger feelings than mine and even more positive ones about grass, a tree, a sight of sky, a house. When I think of how much charm New York once had, I could weep at the change—it's the only great city I know where the faces of the people on the street scare me with the appearance of madness. For a time we thought of settling here in Cambridge, which in general is aesthetically very pleasant, as is still a considerable part of Boston, but we have decided against this, partly because real estate is extravagantly high here, as is the cost of living generally as compared with New York. It may be that London will be our choice; it is still a peculiarly humane town and we do have friends there. Such impossible decisions one has to make!

[. . .]

Yours,

---

1. *Sincerity and Authenticity* was published by Harvard University Press in 1972.

241. TO WILLIAM MORRIS[1]

February 6, 1970

Dear Mr. Morris:

I write to question the definition and derivation of the word "Spackle" as given in the *American Heritage Dictionary*. Has the trademark from which the word is said to have been derived been in existence for as many as fifty years?—for I have been familiar with the word for at least that long. When I first heard it in my childhood—as "spockle" and also as "sparkle"—there was, I am sure, no trademarked preparation for patching plaster; it was quite anonymous. I took the word to be Yiddish, for all the New York housepainters of my childhood were Jewish, and I have for some time supposed that it came from *Spachtel*, the German for spatula, the tool with which the work was done.

I'll take this occasion to say what so many have said before me, what a great pleasure the Dictionary is.

Yours sincerely,
Lionel Trilling

242. TO DONALD LIGHT

October 26, 1970

Dear Mr. Light:

Thank you for your interesting letter.

I of course would not want to say that the "noble" dream has nowadays no vitality whatever. The charm of *Country Life* lies in its ability to make one feel that the old vision is still viable and ever in full force. (*Vogue* and the other periodicals do this less successfully—for me, at any rate—being more committed to modishness and luxe, which must inevitably constitute a denial of "nobility.") And I have no doubt that at least some distinguished form of the old feeling is at work in many aspects of middle-class life. All I would contend is that as a theme for the novel the old vision has no force. That *Herzog* was given a quite ambiguous response would seem to support my view of the depreciation of the vision by the advanced culture. Another case

1. An editor at *The American Heritage Dictionary*.

384

in point, I think, is the settled depreciation of James Gould Cozzens's novels that now prevails. And would we not be hard put to mention any considerable novel of the last decade, or longer, in which the attainment of the "noble" life is represented as a desirable thing and to be taken seriously?

Sincerely,

Lionel Trilling

243. TO DOROTHY HITE CLAYBOURNE

November 5, 1970

Dear Mrs. Claybourne:

I can indeed imagine myself making Kafka's request.[1]

I have often thought about Brod's dilemma and have never been able to conclude that he was anything but right in resolving it as he did. At least he was right from a point of view that might be called practical or "human." I can imagine that a different judgment might proceed from a "metaphysical" point of view. This would refer to the respect due to the authenticity of Kafka's desire for oblivia [sic], to the sanctity of his wish not to exist as an object of consciousness. I think that in Brod's position I would have acted as he did, though with qualms.

Brod's knowledge of the nature and quality of the literary manuscripts does of course bear decisively upon the rightness of his action.

I am rather more hesitant about confirming Brod's preservation of the private papers. But in the event, the private papers being what we now know them to be, I believe he was right.

Yours sincerely,

Lionel Trilling

---

1. Franz Kafka instructed Max Brod, his literary executor, to burn his papers after his death, which Brod refused to do.

244. TO WILLIAM PHILLIPS

December 14, 1971

Dear William:

I'm sorry that I won't be able to contribute to the *PR* Symposium[1]—as usual, my time is mortgaged, this year until at least the end of April.

It would have been fun to have been able to respond to your view of the situation which—as you might suppose—I think is all wrong. So far as I can see, there isn't any hostility to the new: on the contrary, everybody is very nice and kind to the new and hopes it succeeds and secretly wishes it weren't so ghastly boring. Which is to say, everybody takes toward the new the attitude of a devoted headmaster or undergraduate professor, who knows that the future lies with the new and that it must be brought out and encouraged, but who looks elsewhere for his conversation. Here's a bet, say a good lunch: that you can't name me one book in the last five years that has meant something to you, *personally*, as we say, and not as something you rate with an expert's eye. I mean *meant* in the way (I don't demand as much as) *The Waste Land* did, or *A Portrait of the Artist* (I don't demand *Ulysses*), and so on. The new is weekly celebrated in the *Times Book Review*, or at least *received*, but the terms of the welcome by its partisans give the show away: such dull hurrahs. Of course, I've never been a great welcomer of the new—I've never thought I should go hunting for it, rather that it should try to capture me, against my resistance. I'll be pleased to know, and I'll take the information very seriously, who is now working who is likely to overcome my resistance and win my reluctant assent two, three, four, five years from now.

I think we're in one of those bad times when minds lose their tone and make only flaccid noises. Such times have always passed and maybe this one will.

Yours,

---

1. The Summer 1972 issue of *Partisan Review* included a symposium titled "Art, Culture, and Conservatism."

245. TO CYNTHIA OZICK[1]

January 31, 1972

Dear Miss Ozick:

This is just to tell you of my admiration for your essay on Forster.[2] Certainly it is the only significant account of *Maurice* that I have read, but its value isn't merely of a comparative kind.

It might amuse you to know that it wasn't until I had finished my book on Forster that I came to the explicit realization that he was homosexual. I'm not sure whether this was because of a particular obtuseness on my part or because a quarter century ago—more, actually, although it scarcely seems possible!—homosexuality hadn't yet formulated itself as an issue in the culture. When the realization did come, it at first didn't seem of crucial importance, but that view soon began to change, and, as I came to have some slight personal acquaintance with Forster—I had not met him until after the publication of the book—it changed radically.

Sincerely,

246. TO JOHN VOSS

May 8, 1972

Dear Mr. Voss:

Although I was inclined to be in accord with the Emerson-Thoreau Committee's recommendation that the medal this year be awarded to Ezra Pound, thinking that there was magnanimity in it, I can't but respond to the council's rejection of it with understanding and respect. I hope that the scars left by the disagreement won't be conspicuous for long. And if the issue has brought to the fore the question of the Academy's[3] relation to the humanities, it will, I think, have served a good purpose.

If the Academy does plan to give greater attention to humanistic matters, one obvious situation that ought to be looked into is the present state of literature teaching in our colleges and universities. I

---

1. Cynthia Ozick (1928–), novelist and essayist.
2. "Forster as Homosexual," *Commentary*, December 1971.
3. The American Academy of Arts and Sciences.

think it can be taken for granted that within the last few years the relation of students to literature has undergone a radical change. This takes the form which cannot be described as an antagonism to literature but, rather, as a developing insensitivity to it—students seem less and less able to understand its cognitive value or to find that it has the exemplary force it once had. This attitude, which might be thought of as a cultural mutation, is either shared by many of their teachers or has led them to revise their aims and methods in a radical way. The effect of this is increasingly apparent in the diminished morale of graduate study of literature. Just yesterday a friend of mine compared the present status of English literature as an academic subject with the status of the classics at the beginning of this century—at the moment when it had reached its highest point of development, it was rejected by the general culture. (The present decline in the interest in history makes a cognate situation.)

It seems to me that this offers a topic of very great importance which the humanistic members of the Academy ought to take cognizance of, in company with their sociological colleagues.

[. . .]

Sincerely,

    Lionel Trilling

247. TO WILLIAM GOODE

May 15, 1972

Dear Mr. Goode:

I thank you for what you say in compliment to my lecture[1] and no less for your cogent objection to the position I took on the H.E.W. directives. I am the more responsive to these because I have not been easy about my formulations as it [sic] has to do with women. When I come to publish the lecture, I shall try to be more modulated and precise.

I wonder, though, whether your adduction of the academic anti-Semitism which once prevailed is exactly to the point. I, of course, remember it very well and can say how rigorous and unabashed it

---

1. Trilling delivered the inaugural Jefferson Lecture, "Mind in the Modern World," in 1972.

was. But then, almost suddenly, it crumbled and disappeared and now Jewish students are incredulous of its ever having existed. I suppose that my experience of this striking change serves as my model for what I look forward to in the situation of women and ethnic groups.

With my cordial greetings,

Sincerely,

Lionel Trilling

248. TO FREDRIC WARBURG

May 22, 1972

Dear Fred:

What a great pleasure to hear from you! And I am delighted to learn that you are going on with your autobiography and that *The Middle of the Journey* is to have a place in it.

You ask how I came to write the novel and I can best begin to answer by saying that I did not mean to write a novel at all, but only a long short story or *nouvelle*. As I recall it, the story as originally conceived dealt only with Laskell, the Crooms, and Emily and Duck Caldwell and was only tangentially political. But it seemed to need something else, and in response to that need Gifford Maxim, which is to say, Whittaker Chambers, presented himself, together with such political explicitness as he brought, which had to be considerable, for he was the most political man I knew. It was he who gave the novel such largeness of reference as it has and made it as long as it is.

I had had some acquaintance with Chambers at College. He was not a friend of mine, but the friend of friends. He was at an early age a very commanding person, and a first-rate poet, and, it was said, a member of the IWW. In the very early 1930s he was a figure of some importance in the Communist Party, to which for a time Diana and I were drawn. In 1930 and 1931, he "went underground." Among those who knew him, it was thought that he was doing espionage work with reference to army installations. If so, he was the most manifest spy that ever slunk around a corner; he seemed to make a point of looking clandestine and sinister and he solicited his bourgeois friends to act as mail drops. He tried to recruit Diana, but she refused. His connections, it should be said, were with the Russian apparatus, rather than with the American party, to which he had, I gather, a virtually supervisory relation. Not long after this, I should say around 1934 or 1935, he became disaffected from the party and "broke."

In his attempts to "establish an identity," which the novel makes much of, he turned to his old friends, who believed, as I am sure they were right to, that he was in mortal danger. It was at this time that he was taken on as a writer for *Time*, where he soon became a figure of importance.

The novel's representation of Chambers is, within the obvious limits, pretty literal. Naturally, when the Hiss case broke—how many years later was that?—the novel was thought to bear upon it. I had no acquaintance with Alger and Priscilla Hiss, nor had ever heard of them, but Arthur and Nancy Croom, whom I drew from a couple I did know, seemed to be sufficiently like the Hisses in temperament and political disposition to make it appear that I knew all about the Chambers-Hiss relationship, and this false presumption was worked up in several newspaper articles. Which goes to show what a brilliant cultural historian I was! My intentions in writing the novel were not political so much as cultural and moral—I was concerned with the self-deceptions and confusions that followed from the high-minded self-inculpations of the liberal bourgeoisie and its commitment to radical positions.

Does this answer your question adequately? I naturally wonder whether your account of your relation to the book—such a benign one!—will speak of the sour attitude toward it of the Viking people, especially that of Ben Huebsch, of which you once told me.

You will be amused to know that your letter came just two or three days after I had received copies of a new printing of the paperback edition of the novel which Avon got out a couple of years ago. I prevailed upon myself to read part of it, and found it not bad, although not what I would want a novel of mine to be.

You ask if I still think of writing novels and the answer is that I do—if I can get myself to have confidence in the possibility of its transcending the "reasonable" tone of *The Middle of the Journey*, of its taking itself out of my hands and going its own way. I also have it in mind to attempt an autobiographical memoir.

[. . .]

Yours always,

249. TO EDWARD JOSEPH SHOBEN JR.

June 12, 1972

Dear Joe:

I think your speech is simply brilliant in its spiritedness and lucidity and it scares me to death.

You are probably right in your statement of the case. If education is to continue at and beyond the present numerical rate, it pretty surely can't be carried on through instruction in the old discrete disciplines. But I think that when we say this and then go on to the alternatives you propose, which will be more effectual because (in sum) they are directed to the student himself, we are envisaging a desperate state of affairs in which, as if by a mutation in the species, the only things that can be learned are those that bear directly and explicitly—and "supportively"—upon the student's sense of himself. I don't think that this is what the idea of the examined life really means. The alternatives to the old discipline-oriented education all seem to me to involve a flattery of the student, a connivance in his inability or refusal to acknowledge something outside himself, really there and to be deferred to. And this, I should go on to say, is what comes to me from the charming humanity of the book describing Evergreen College, which I continue to read with interest. Maybe this must be the natural response of teachers in a system of mass education, the only way they can respond to the new ambivalence of students, who in effect say: We must learn, we must be privileged to learn, but we will learn only what is virtually Us and does not distress our self-regard.

Am I being unjust? Am I being generational?

Sincerely,

250. TO MRS. R. E. RAWLS

July 12, 1972

Dear Mrs. Rawls:

I shall try to answer the question with which your letter ends. I don't have it in mind to do a new anthology, but there is always the possibility—though not a strong one—that I shall revise *The Experience of Literature*. If I should undertake that job, I would not "plan" to include work by Black writers, just as I did not plan to *exclude* work by Black writers from the present edition. If I found work by Black writers that served the purpose of the anthology, which is to suggest the various forms of literary excellence, I should include it with a special pleasure, which would be, I should add, quite extraneous to my critical purpose. I am sure that the likelihood of my finding excellent work by Black writers is greater now than it was in 1966, when I finished the anthology, for, as we both know, there has been a remarkable burst of Black literary energy over the last few years. But this is not to say that I am certain I would find work by Black writers of a quality equal to that of the work I have included. The likelihood goes the other way. The stories, poems, and plays on which I wrote my commentaries are all, or virtually all, of superlative quality, what we call "great." It is beyond reasonable expectation that Black writers in the relatively short time in which they have been writing should equal the accomplishment of the preeminent writers of the long centuries of Western culture. When I have said this, I'll go on to say that at any moment a Black writer might emerge who will achieve this equality of accomplishment, and after him another, and yet another. Would you not agree with me that this happy event will not come to pass more quickly through the practice of "reassuring" Black writers?

I should add that my anthology didn't undertake to be "representative," to suggest the nature of the "American experience" or the "modern experience." Many anthologies for college students—mine was originally intended for such an audience—do exactly that, and I think you'll find that they make a point of including Black writers. Their purpose is thoroughly good, but it wasn't mine.

I hope you will decide to keep the book. Since the essential part of it isn't mine, you will understand that I am not being immodest when I say that I believe any writer can learn from it.

Sincerely,
Lionel Trilling

251. TO THE EDITOR OF THE *TLS*

October 16, 1972
All Souls College, Oxford

Sir—I am wholly in agreement with the opinion expressed by Jacques Barzun that Leon Edel has radically misinterpreted the letter in which William James refused election to the American Academy of Arts and Letters and has in consequence misrepresented what that document implies of William's feeling for his brother Henry. It is therefore all the more surprising to me that Professor Edel should conscript my support in the reply he makes to Professor Barzun. He quotes a passage from an essay of mine in which I speak about the antagonism which was an element in the relation of the brothers and says of my observations that his own on the same subject are "not at all at variance" with them. But this is by no means the case. Our respective views of the matter are wholly at odds.

In what I said about the fraternal antagonism of William and Henry James I took it for granted that in the relation of any two siblings there is bound to be some degree of rivalry and antagonism. This may, but need not, attenuate or destroy the possibility of their holding each other in true affection. I believe that the affection between William and Henry was strong and remained unbroken. William could be pretty rough in his efforts to make Henry understand that art and Europe were morally inferior to action and America and I have no doubt that Henry must often have been hurt by the judgments which his elder brother passed upon his work; further along in the section of my essay on *The Princess Casamassima* from which Professor Edel quotes I suggest that Henry retaliated upon William by representing him in the character of Paul Muniment. But the famous and significant issue between the brothers surely could not have been fiercely debated through all their mature lives had they not been certain of each other's good faith of affection and regard.

It is, however, exactly Professor Edel's point, made in painstaking detail in the chapter of *The Master* called "The Brothers," that William was strikingly deficient in good faith—that beneath such aggression as was frankly expressed in his knockdown ideological disputes with Henry there lay something far less manly, what Professor Edel calls a "hidden animus" and represents as having its source in envy and as being of such force that it discloses itself with monstrous inappropriateness in a quasi-public document, the letter to the Academy.

Like Professor Barzun, I find this interpretation of the letter inacceptable, and if I may say so, perverse and even absurd. For William to have written that he was encouraged in his decision not to join the Academy "by the fact that my younger and shallower and vainer brother is already in the Academy and that if I were there too, the other families represented might think the James influence too strong" was perhaps not the happiest example of his easy, genial epistolary manner: he is making a cozy, Brahmin-Boston kind of joke which probably doesn't suit the New York, or the generally American, situation. But that anyone could read this sentence in its place in the letter and understand it to be the expression of an animus so powerful that no considerations of decorum and self-respect could prevent its expression is beyond my comprehension.

I would add that William James was by no means the last notable American figure to decide that election to the Academy was an honor he did not wish to accept. Not infrequently the reasons given for refusing membership have been pretty much the same as those James set forth in the part of his letter which was not joking. To the best of my knowledge, none of these persons who declined election had gifted younger brothers already seated in the Academy.

Lionel Trilling

252. TO JACQUES BARZUN

October 31, 1972
All Souls College, Oxford

Dear Jacques:

TLS, as perhaps you have already heard or seen, published my letter promptly and I enclose a montage of the whole correspondence up to this point: it will demonstrate vividly that Edel is surrounded, contained. What his next move will be is, as the experts say, anyone's guess. After reading his chapter on the relation between W. and H. and being dismayed by its mechanical Freudianism and bad reading of the facts, I went on through the whole book and was deeply affected by it, or, rather, by its matter. Edel is not grossly, only subtly, offensive in his relation to this, and I managed to withdraw my gaze from *him* and to let the old Henry, who hasn't been much in my thoughts for a long time, stand forth in all his monumentality and charm. One is led in our bad days to forget how large, how alive, how eager and devoted it was once possible for a man to be.

Have I yet given you my sense of how life orders itself for us here? We live in a flat in a remodeled Victorian house on a quiet street at the beginning of North Oxford, just at the northern edge of the Parks; three bedrooms, a living room, the British equivalent of a modern kitchen. The furniture is Danish modern of the dullest kind, but Diana has done wonders to raise the decor out of its motelity and we are very comfortable. The other tenants, rather excessively bechildered for this day and age, are three All Souls families, two visiting fellows, one new professor of law from Australia. They make pleasant unobtrusive neighbors. In the morning I walk say a mile through or along the Parks to the college, where I have a pleasant small study on the ground floor of a new wing of some ten similar rooms. My window looks out on the Fellows' garden and I have by now overcome my interest in a small fountain just outside and in the birds that on certain set occasions congregate in it. At 12:45 I go into the buttery for a lunch which is served and eaten in great haste. Conversation is rapid, bright, quickly broken off, not to me especially engaging. You probably know the All Souls manner, which I had forgotten, staccato and a little lofty and severe, no harm in it but meant to tell you something about the speaker's intellectual precision. Some of the young men, the prize fellows, are quite astonishing in their competence and assurance. By 1:30, 1:45 at the latest, the coffee room is emptied and I either return to my study or go home. Since we are not official, our way of life is much quieter than it was last time and that is a pleasure. The autumn has so far been very mild and has turned out some of the most brilliant days I can ever remember anywhere. We have dined out a little, lunched out a little, gone a little to the opera—it has been Welsh and splendid—and have found all things gentle and felicitous. The question proposes itself whether we should not retire here.

On one of my first days here I was recognized on the High Street by a Columbia student who undertook to make a tea party for me to meet all the resident Columbians. They came to the number of fourteen or so, most of them quite impressive. But much as I liked them I found myself thinking with satisfaction that I would not for long now have to go on teaching them. Inevitably the satisfaction saddened me.

Our last letter from Jim before his expedition set out into the desert was mailed on October 8. He seems to have found a good deal of pleasure in his weeks in Afghanistan, went a journey into the mountains where he had the gratification of a contretemps with a herd of camels, and communicated to us the sense that he was in high spirits and in a good relation to himself and the world. He told of a menu in Kabul that offered "soupe de jure" and proposed the thought that on alternate days it was probably "soupe de facto," which we thought did him credit.

[. . .]

Yours ever,
    Lionel

253. TO DR. GRACE ABBATE[1]

November 10, 1972
All Souls College, Oxford

Dear Dr. Abbate:

I enclose my check for $1,425 against my account. In doing so I can't simply tell you, as I have often done before, of my gratitude for your most kind patience, although this of course I do feel, but must speak particularly of my especially long delay in making any decisive move toward clearing the outstanding bill. What caused this I don't wholly know. The past year was an exceptionally difficult one, but although its burdens and emergencies seemed from moment to moment to explain my inactivity about the bill despite its being always present to my mind, and did seem to do so until I first sat down to write this letter, I have now to see that external circumstances do not of themselves account for my not having moved toward the discharge of my debt. I won't attempt even an elementary statement of the reasons that now begin to present themselves, for that might lead to fur-

---

1. Trilling's psychoanalyst.

ther delay. I'll only say how deeply I regret what must have seemed an unfeeling silence on my part.

In several ways life goes better than it did. Diana is well recovered from the operation she had last winter for cancer of the uterus; the prognosis we were given was a reassuring one. Our anxiety over Jim's solo tour of the backcountry parts of the Middle East reached a climax last spring when he insisted that he would make it even though for some time it seemed that he could be given none of the necessary shots because the first of them caused what was believed to be a heart stoppage, but this dismaying situation was cleared up and now even our troubled sense that his project was adventuristic and ill-advised— it seemed all too symbolical, a *rite de passage* designed to mark the end of his analysis—has been much quieted by the reassuring tone of his letters, which have been notable for their mature good sense. He is at present in the Afghan desert as a member of a small archaeological expedition of the Smithsonian. There has been no remission of the extreme illness of Diana's sister, which began in the early spring, nor any real progress toward a diagnosis despite all the efforts of the Neurological Institute, but her condition has been grimly stabilized in affectlessness and the certitude that she will always be bedridden; with the agitations of the situation and the need for making practical decisions at an end at least for the time being, we were able to leave Diana's brother in charge and come to spend as much of the year as we might in Oxford, where I have a visiting fellowship at this college. I have no official duties and, after a year of impossible deadlines, no schedules to meet. In general our way of life couldn't be pleasanter.

You will not, I imagine, be wholly surprised that this account of relative external peace turns out to [be] the preface to my telling you that things don't go well within, haven't for some time. Beyond saying that the trouble is a state of detachment or withdrawal or alienation which isn't acutely distressing but in some considerable degree incapacitating I won't try to describe it. It may be that having begun— at the behest, as it were, of this letter—to view it more substantively than I have yet done, I may be able to cope with it at least a little. Whether or not I do, I'll probably be asking for your help in trying to sort things out when I return in September.

You should by now have received two books of mine, the Norton lectures from Harvard and the Jefferson lecture from Viking. The former has already been published here and has been quite warmly received. It will tell you something about my state of feeling if I say that, after a momentary gratification from this public success, I find it disquieting and almost look forward to the American reviews, which are pretty sure to be far less kind than the English ones! The Jefferson lecture, which from the first and with, I think, some objectivity, I found unsatisfactory, is to appear next week in the *TLS* before American publication.

I'll say again how deeply sorry I am for my unconscionable delay in dealing with my bill. I am confident that it will be fully cleared within the next few months.

With all my good wishes,
Sincerely,

254. TO JOHN VAUGHAN

December 15, 1972
All Souls College, Oxford

Dear Mr. Vaughan,

Your questions are all very much to the point and go to confirm my sense that my work is in very good hands. I'll try to answer them as pressure of time will allow—I go off in two or three days for a fortnight in Sicily and confront a desk heavy with correspondence all too long postponed.

Norman Podhoretz is of course quite right in putting me among the "first generation" intellectuals who came from immigrant families, but the category doesn't of itself suggest the actual state of my case. Several circumstances made my background exceptional. One is that my mother, like her mother before her, had been born and schooled in England; she was in her teens when she came to America. The fact of her parents' emigration from England suggests that they were not established economically in that country to a degree that satisfied them but I believe that they were fairly comfortable and that they had undergone the curiously quick and thorough acculturation that seems to be a characteristic effect of England on foreigners. My mother's mind was suffused by the English mythos—among my earliest memories are the things she used to say about Queen Victoria and the royal family, and she set great store by all English things. Something of her early life in London would be suggested by Israel Zangwill's *Children of the Ghetto*, a book of which she was fond. Her mode of speech was very pure, without any trace of a foreign "accent." My father did speak with an accent but with a very precise grammar and rhetoric. He came from a family said to have been intellectually distinguished in Bialystok, Poland, which was also the birthplace of my mother's father, a city in which there was a flourishing Jewish culture. The family name seems to have been Trilling for some generations, and virtually all persons who bear the name trace their origins to Bialystok and give pretty much the same account of an ancestor who was notable as a merchant and scholar and for good works. One makes allowances for Jewish snobbery about lineage, but the legend is established among members of the family later settled in many countries—England, France, Sweden, Finland, South Africa—who, when my name became known, were curious about their connection with me. Whether all the Trillings who appear in the Library of Congress catalog and who wrote in German (some, I seem to recall, in the later years of the nineteenth century) were all Jewish I of course can't tell. I don't know what the origin of the strangely un-Jewish name is but that it *was* un-Jewish made, I have no doubt, a significant fact in my life.

My father had been destined for a scholarly—i.e., rabbinical— career but for reasons of which I am uncertain he emigrated to America when he was fourteen. He became fairly prosperous as a custom tailor but gave up this trade when I was born and became a manufacturer (of men's fur-lined coats), influenced to the change as much by social as by economic considerations. The home, although vexed by financial worry, was firmly and programmatically middle-class. Both parents were devoted not merely to the idea of education as a means of advancement, which was of course characteristic of Jewish immigrants, but also to the idea of "culture," of a life shaped by several kinds of amenity. My first books were from the family bookcase. I still have my mother's set of George Eliot, her favorite writer; she adored *The Mill on the Floss* and identified with Maggie Tulliver. It was seen to that I was supplied with the best children's literature and there were sets of Dickens, Thackeray, and Kipling and the Temple Shakespeare. My copy of *Sartor Resartus* was my father's; I don't think he ever came to terms with it, but he did think he ought to own it. The family religion was orthodox and was taken very seriously, with quite a rich observance, but in a spirit of conscious enlightenment. It says much about the family ethos that Christmas was celebrated at least up to the point of Santa Claus and hanging stockings; a tree was thought to be going too far. I was brought up to think that although being Jewish might make for difficulties, it must never be conceived of as preventing my movement to any part of American life I might choose to enter. It was characteristic of my mother that all her life and especially in her late years she had close friends who were not Jewish. Both parents had a strong explicit feeling for traditional civility, and were remarkably accurate in knowing what constituted it in America. There were periods in my life when I faulted them for this trait but I look back on it now with considerable tenderness as showing something generous and imaginative in their view of life.

I'd yield to the temptation to go into further detail if it weren't that, as I may have told you, I'm attempting an autobiographical memoir and don't want to take the edge off my recollection. But perhaps what I have said will be enough to help you get straight the matter of background.

It was not exactly through choice that I went to Columbia rather than to another college. One reason was financial. By going to Columbia I could live at home and incur only the expense of tuition. (City College, with no expense at all, was out of the question for my parents as being socially inferior, although several of my mother's brothers had gone there and one of them was on the faculty as professor of chemistry.) But even if finances had not been a consideration, my parents would not have consented to my going away from home at the age of sixteen. My three closest friends at high school all went to Yale but this had no weight with my parents, who were even reluctant to allow me to visit New Haven over weekends—for all their acculturation, they thought the world a dangerous place, for me at least; I suppose that much of their apprehensiveness had to do with sexuality.

In 1921, when I entered Columbia, the College was pretty far along toward its Jewish coloration. (There was a piece in *Commentary* sometime within the last year or two which deals with Jewish quotas in the teens and twenties; I think you will find it helpful with the Columbia situation. And do you know John Erskine's[1] autobiography?—it will give you a sense of the more or less upper-class Jewish enclave of earlier years.) A quite large proportion of the student body was Jewish, but "power" was still in the hands of non-Jews—clubs, publications, sports, etc. None of our teachers was Jewish—I was the first Jew to be taken on as an instructor by the English Department (which of course lay under the shadow of the Ludwig Lewisohn "case") with a view to possible promotion; the appointment was consciously made as an "experiment." (What followed makes an interesting story which I shall deal with in its amusing detail in my memoir.) My companions at college were mostly Jewish but I had several warm non-Jewish friends. On the whole, I rather relished the anti-Semitism that could be discerned; I thought of it as making life rather the more interesting and certainly it never gave me any personal pain.

In regard to my relation to my Jewishness at the time, you might want to look at a story called "Inventions" by Henry M. Rosenthal which appeared in *The Menorah Journal* in 1925. Rosenthal was my very closest friend at college; while attending the College, he also attended the Jewish Theological Seminary in preparation for the rabbinate. He had what I have always thought of as nothing less than genius, although a few years later something seems to have happened in his life which kept his extraordinary literary powers from developing. He was ordained as a rabbi, but became disaffected from religion itself and became a professor of philosophy (at Hunter College). When I knew him, he was passionately and obsessively Jewish and the story deals with his relation to me as this was conditioned by *my* feeling about being Jewish. Our relation ended in the early 1930s.

So far as Columbia took the line of liberalism, I experienced it in a diffuse way. Part of the university legend was the reactionary moves that had been made by the President and Trustees against certain members of the faculty during the war, and all intelligent students

---

1. John Erskine (1879–1951), writer, musician, and longtime Columbia professor.

were conscious of this. John Dewey was an admired figure for many of us, and some of my friends attended his lectures; for me he was a revered and shadowy figure, a wise man; I knew nothing of his doctrine and heard him lecture only once, at the insistence of a friend, and found him incomprehensible. (He was notoriously the worst of lecturers.) As a sophomore I took Woodbridge's famous course in the history of philosophy but respectfully found it incomprehensible and almost failed it. Beard and Robinson were already in the past: they were the martyr figures in the legend. Seligmann was for me scarcely a name. As an undergraduate I made no claim to intellect—I was *literary*, that is to say intuitive, perceptive, sensitive, etc. But my circle of friends *was* intellectual and I was thoroughly imbued with the Columbia idea of "intelligence." I can recall virtually no explicit political concern, only a feeling that conservatism was stupid—not intelligent—and the sense that the world was changing, that modernity was upon us. Whittaker Chambers was radical—IWW—but this was thought of as merely an interesting idiosyncrasy.

Your observation of the ambivalence of my intellectual or moral or cultural stance strikes me as accurate and interesting. What might fully account for it probably requires more effort of recollection than at the moment I can give. I think you are quite right in supposing that the liberal-democratic tendency was the mark that Columbia put upon me, a sort of Bertrand Russell view of life (Russell, I recall, was a great name in the college and "A Free Man's Worship" a sacred text). Together with intelligence, "experience" was the great word. A considerable part of my expectation of life was shaped by Wells and Shaw. The conservative tendency is, I feel sure, to be traced to my family and not least to what I think can be called its piety in the good sense of the word. This was rooted, I think it can be said, in religion, even when it manifested itself in specifically social ideals. Thus, the emphasis my parents put on manners was, it has long seemed to me, in accord with the orthodox Jewish insistence on ritually precise behavior. And religion reinforced my curiously vivid consciousness of the past and the authority it had in my imagination—among my earliest recollections are my fantasies about the ancient world which I knew from the myths and tales that were read to me and which I went on to read when I learned how.

Does this set you along the way to reasonable speculation?

You will be pleased to know that *Sincerity and Authenticity* is making something like a success here—I mean that it actually seems to be *selling*; the Oxford bookstores report that they cannot keep it in stock, the first time that anything like this has ever been said about a book of mine. In America, however, it has scarcely been reviewed. By the way, did your copy of it come to you from the Harvard University Press, as I asked that it should? I am, you may suppose, delighted that you can respond to it so warmly.

I send you my warmest good wishes for the new year.

Sincerely,

Lionel Trilling

255. TO DENIS DONOGHUE[1]

December 15, 1972

Dear Denis,

I was delighted to have your letter with its warm response to my Jefferson lecture and its expression of accord, at least up to a point, with the line that it takes. If I did indeed represent mind in exclusively rational (to put it shortly) terms, this was not my intention and doesn't, I would believe, suit with my own mental temperament, which inclines me to give great weight to "imagination, vision, and fiction," although I would guess not as much as would satisfy you. I can well suppose that my emphasis went wrong for several adventitious reasons, but I won't stop to ascertain what these might be but will at once join issue over the strict disjunction which you make, and I would wish not to make, between the two conceptions of mind that you describe. My point is that the activities of mind in the conception of it which is defined by imagination, vision, and fiction are inevitably evaluated by the criteria proposed by the other conception of mind, that which is defined by order, hierarchy, and structure. (I leave out reason as begging the question and tradition as being in this context too particular.) In the discriminations we make between works of art, which are both the outcome and the sustainers of imagination, vision,

---

1. Denis Donoghue (1928–), Irish literary critic.

and fiction, the traits of order, hierarchy, and structure are surely of decisive importance, and I can scarcely suppose you to be saying that, in the interest of immediacy of experience, discriminations ought not to be made. Even in our response to "actual" as opposed to artistic experience they force themselves upon us.

I'll go on to say that in the matter of immediacy of experience I seem to perceive a radical difference between us. I find that I do not make it a desideratum that experience should be in your words, "so dynamic and peremptory that the rift between subject and object is virtually obliterated." I think I actually *like* the rift and cherish it, except maybe on rare awful or enchanting occasions. I might even say that for me it is the subjectivity of subjects and the inviolable objectivity of objects, the me-ness of me and the them-ness of them, that constitutes the interest, the captivating mystery, of existence. And I'd defend this view by considerations of utility—undoubtedly I as subject can be enhanced by the immediacy of my relation with objects, but it is also true that I can be diminished or injured, even destroyed, by them. I must, exactly, know them.

[. . .]

Yours,

Lionel Trilling

256. TO WILLIAM PHILLIPS

January 28, 1973
All Souls College, Oxford

Dear William,

I'm grateful to you for your solicitude in sending the *Wanted* poster.[1] Actually I've known about it for a considerable time—could it be as much as two years? Its contriver is Jonah Raskin,[2] who was once a student of mine at Columbia. He recently published a book (Random) about the treatment of imperialism in English literature[3]

---

1. A mock "Wanted" poster, bearing Trilling's picture and the text "Wanted by FBI: Cultural Imperialist Lionel Trilling. Occupations: Literary cricket, miseducator, intellectual mercenary. Caution: Trilling is a liberal anti-communist; consider dangerous."
2. Jonah Raskin (1942–), writer and scholar.
3. *The Mythology of Imperialism* (1971).

which has a long introduction attacking Eliot, Leavis, and me in what I believe are called intemperate terms. [. . .]—I don't think any action should be taken. The thing does no harm and is probably defeated by its silliness.

It *was* true that I am working on an autobiography but I have suspended it for a while: the tenses are all mixed up but you'll know how to sort them out. Thank you for your interest, but it's *much* too early to think of "showing" it.

Diana sends her love with mine to you and Edna—
Lionel

257. TO CHARLES DEFANTI[1]

June 18, 1973

Dear Professor DeFanti,

I must ask your forgiveness for having so long delayed my reply to your letter.

I can't imagine that Dahlberg[2] will figure in any significant way in my memoir, so my two anecdotes, which aren't, as you will see, of momentous interest, might as well be used by you, if you choose to.

To the best of my recollection I first met Dahlberg in 1929. We were introduced by Clifton Fadiman, who was then an editor at Simon & Schuster. In October of that year my wife and I set up housekeeping in a flat at 1 Bank Street; we had married in June. We both admired *Bottom Dogs* and, as I recall it, were rather engaged by Dahlberg himself, doubtless the more because of his having known D. H. Lawrence. By the autumn or, at the latest, the winter, the sense of catastrophe following the stock-market crash was already very strong and its force was dramatically borne in on us when one day Dahlberg presented himself at our door in what seemed a state of extreme distress: he was unshaven and unwashed and very shabbily dressed and apparently was suffering from exhaustion and hunger. He asked if he might come in to rest and explained that he had been living on the Bowery. My wife of course at once set about making a meal for him, which he ate in silence, and we both undertook to make him

1. Author of a biography of Edward Dahlberg, *The Wages of Expectation* (1978).
2. Edward Dahlberg (1900–1977), novelist.

comfortable and to cheer him as best we could, appalled by the thought that a man of such notable gifts should be so reduced. It was not until the end of the visit, when our concern and sympathy had been fully given, that it emerged that the sojourn on the Bowery had been wholly voluntary and of brief duration and had been undertaken for journalistic purposes—he had been commissioned to do an article on the consequences of the Depression.

Our relationship with Dahlberg continued into the next year. We then had an apartment on upper Claremont Avenue and on Sunday afternoons we used to have large tea parties—this was in the days of Prohibition—which went on to become suppers. Dahlberg came to several of these, accompanied by an enchanting young woman named Sara, who later, I believe, married the artist Kuniyoshi; whether or not she was actually married to Dahlberg I can't now recall. Dahlberg was likely to be rather rude to the other guests and on one occasion he insulted Clifton Fadiman in an overt and elaborate way, engaging in an extended denunciation of Fadiman's character and way of life. My wife interrupted him to say that she could not permit a guest of hers to be spoken to in this fashion and asked him to leave the house. He seemed quite astonished by this but left quietly enough.

So there you are—as I said, the anecdotes are not exactly momentous, but such as they are, you are welcome to them.

Yours sincerely,
Lionel Trilling

258. TO SISTER ESTELLE[1]

November 9, 1973

Dear Sister Estelle:

Auden and I were never actually close friends—although we were associated for a good many years as members of the editorial committee of two book clubs, we didn't see each other apart from work, except by chance. Yet our relation, though not close, was of a good kind—I liked, respected, and wholly trusted him, and friends we had

---

1. A nun who taught at Ohio Dominican College.

in common told me that he held me in similar regard, which was for me a considerable gratification. I felt his death not as a great personal loss but certainly as a significant event in my life. And I couldn't but feel that for his sake it came opportunely. His time at Oxford before he went to Austria in the spring had not been happy. He had become rather demanding, petulant, and eccentric: although, as I think, his work continued to be good, he could not focus his mind on the person he was talking to and fell into anecdote and sententiousness of a compulsively repetitive kind, with the result that people began to be distressed by his company and even his oldest and closest friends found it difficult.

I feel with you about the *Newsweek* reference to his being homosexual. This of course he was—it was a central fact of his life. But I believe he never made an issue of this or dealt with it in an explicit way and it is surely impermissible for anyone to characterize him by reference to it.

It is good to hear that you are hard at work—I hope soon to be in the same happy condition—and I look forward to reading the Dante essay.

I am always made happy when I remember that I figure in your prayers.

Ever affectionately yours,

259. TO NATHANIEL ROSS

January 3, 1974

Dear Nat:

The end of the term has come at last, bringing with it at least enough leisure for me to read your two admirable papers and to write to you about them, even though not at the length and in the detail they deserve.

First as to "Affect as Cognition": It seems to me that this is a remarkably cogent and authoritative statement. A student of literature will inevitably wonder why there was need for it—that is, why the psychoanalytic profession, which for so many years dealt with both affect and cognition, should need to be told that there is a positive and intimate relation between them when literature takes this for granted. Well, perhaps that statement is extreme, but certainly it is true of the literature of romanticism that one of its chief concerns is to assert the close connection between affect and cognition. The classic and definitive instance is the passage in book 2 of Wordsworth's *Prelude* (lines 232–65), in which the poet speaks of the mother's circumambient love as a first circumstance of the infant's cognition. I urge you to look up the passage; it bears significantly on your position. Of course the whole of *The Prelude* is concerned with the question of the relation between affect and cognition—one might say that that is what the poem is *about*. I have never understood why it has figured so little in psychoanalytical writing about creativity, especially because it deals, explicitly and dramatically, with a crisis in the poet's own creative life. Although, as I say, the work as a whole is concerned with the relation between affect and cognition, an especially notable passage is the famous beginning of book 5, which recounts a dream about geometry and literature.

I ought to add that you will find *The Prelude* relevant to and confirmation of what you say about the mystical experience. If you should want to pursue this, I suggest that before going to *The Prelude* itself, you read the first volume of Mary Moorman's biography of Wordsworth (Oxford University Press).

It occurs to me to suggest that somewhere in the paper you ought to speak about what happens to the cognitive powers of children whose affective life is not developed, as in orphanages.

I'll begin what I have to say about "Rivalry with God" by remarking on an error, perhaps in typing—the title of my book is not *The Literary Imagination* but *The Liberal Imagination*. The mistake is repeated in the bibliography. I'll add that I don't think I ought to be characterized as a "creative artist"—there simply hasn't been a large enough body of creative work to justify this. Best refer to me as a critic of literature.

I respond in a positive way to the idea of yours which figures in the paper only in a subordinate way—the idea you set forth in your paper of 1960 and to which in the present paper you refer only in passing. The idea of "rivalry with the product" as a form of inhibition is something that I can recognize, even though dimly and not as finally effective. That is to say, I can be aware of at least a small charge of resentment when a work of mine is praised, the feeling that *it* is getting the attention that I want (and deserve!). I can readily imagine that in some writers this absurd feeling has more force than it has with me.

But I have to say that I am less responsive to the idea that gives the paper its title—"rivalry with God" as a cause of creative inhibition. And [words unclear] as it were in a formal way, grant that it might have force with one creative person or another, it doesn't really command my credence. Perhaps my skepticism about your idea derives from the skepticism I direct to the word "create" as applied to the process of art. Originally the word was used only of God—to create meant to bring something into being out of nothing, ex nihilo, which God alone can—or once could—do. This, of course, is a very different act from that of making, which implies that previously existent materials are shaped into one or another form. The word "poet" means literally "a maker," and the Old English word for "poet" was *makyr*. The word "create" in its various forms was first used of the poet in the nineteenth century at the instance of romantic theories of art which sought to claim for poetry a transcendent importance and for the poet a transcendent status through the imputation of an absolute originality. My own feeling is that the poet, whatever claim he makes for the total originality of his process, damn well knows that he works in a tradition and with what material is given to him by circumstance, both external and internal.

But my resistance to your idea is probably only the failure of a layman's imagination and I tell you of it with all humility before your clinical experience.

I like very much what you say about the "normality" of periods of unproductivity. But no sooner have I said this than I wonder how the writers of an earlier day would have responded to this idea. Has anyone ever gone into the question of when the condition of productive inhibition was first dealt with?

I send you all my good wishes for the new year.
Sincerely,
    Lionel Trilling

260. TO ALAN WALD[1]

June 10, 1974
Columbia University

Dear Mr. Wald:

I'm glad to be able to tell you that I was able to find time to read your manuscript, although perhaps not as precisely as I could wish. In addition, my wife, who, as I say in one of my comments, had a much more intimate and actual involvement with the political activities of the *Menorah Journal* group, has also read it. Her penciled comments begin on page 13; I think you will be able to distinguish her scrawl from mine.

In general I thought the chapter accurate, useful, and interesting. I have this fault to find with chapter 1, that it doesn't give enough—not nearly enough—of the substance and tone of the Jewish situation in the first quarter of the century. To speak of *The Menorah Journal* as a response to Jewish "isolation" isn't nearly enough—you must make the reader aware of the *shame* that young middle-class Jews felt; "self-hatred" was the word that later came into vogue but "shame" is simpler and better. I suggest that you take the lead of some of my statements in my Tess Slesinger article—or wait until I publish my memoirs. It is of great importance that you communicate this situation.

I should like to see a little more done with the political ideology that the group developed but this is difficult—there wasn't much written on this and almost nothing that told the actual personal truth.

I think *The Unpossessed* needs to be treated with more skepticism than you use. Tess Slesinger attenuated all the political feelings she observed. How shall I put it?—perhaps that the whole thing had a more manly or at least masculine tone than she cared to render. And of course, when she wrote the book she was already moving toward Stalinism.

I have noted the need to identify certain people more clearly. Felix Morrow, an odd, interesting character—a "character," very fat, very comical, the son of a delicatessen store keeper and insatiable in

---

1. Alan Wald (1946–), later the author of *The New York Intellectuals* (1987) and other books about the American literary Left.

his appetite—needs clarification. Norman Warren, in many respects the opposite of Morrow, searching restlessly for elegance in every aspect of life, has faded into obscurity and is pretty shadowy on your pages. James Rorty was most interesting and is here too vague; I think he still lives but does not communicate easily; his son[1] is professor of philosophy at Yale.

You will see that I note that there is no mention of Harry Wolfsohn, who survives at Harvard as a sacred object. He meant much to some of us in the old days, as he might well have done, for he is a truly great scholar. Adolph Oko (who looked as Japanese as his name) was another important personage for us. He was librarian of Hebrew Union College in Cincinnati, a scholar of Spinoza, and a great bibliographer. He had a love affair with the wife of a trustee of HUC, married her, gave up his job, and came to live (in luxury) in New York.

I hope all goes well with the progress of your dissertation and that it is happily received by your examiners. I think they can't fail to find it interesting.

Yours sincerely,
Lionel Trilling

261. TO SAUL BELLOW

July 25, 1974
Aspen

Dear Saul:

I have now read your *Harper's* piece[2] and my doing so has not, as you suggest it might, led me to think of you as "silly." The adverse words which occur to me are, I am sorry to have to say, rather graver than that.

You speak of having had "regretful second thoughts" about your essay so far as it refers to me. If I understand you correctly, these thoughts arise from your "remorseful" sense that you have been derelict in your intellectual duty because you did not read the whole of *Sincerity and Authenticity* before dealing with certain ideas of its last

---

1. Richard Rorty (1931–2007), philosopher.
2. "Machines and Storybooks," *Harper's*, August 1974.

chapter. I can assure you that this is not in the least what your offense consists in. The views expressed in the last chapter are coherent with but by no means dependent upon the views expressed in the preceding chapters, and reading the whole book would have done nothing to preserve you from the extravagant error of your treatment of its concluding part.

The simple fact is that you have misrepresented my intention to the extent of exactly inverting it. Let me put it this way: if someone were to say that in Mr. Sammler[1] you had portrayed a voluptuary nihilist who despised England and nursed a secret admiration of Nazism, was gratified by all the manifestations of contemporary culture which deny the traditional pieties, and was incapable of love or solicitude for any fellow being, your purpose would not have been more distorted than are my views in your representation of them.

You begin your strange transaction with my ideas by quoting a passage ("It is the exceptional novelist today, etc.") in which I say in effect that something is happening in our culture which leads to the devaluation of the ancient art of storytelling. I believe that virtually any passably intelligent reader of this passage will recognize that I report this development with regret. Yet although this is my normal expectation, I find it possible to suppose that on infrequent occasions such a reader might fail to perceive any charge of regret in the passage and take it to be a wholly neutral account of a cultural phenomenon. What I am quite unable to imagine is that a reader could conclude that I regard the phenomenon with satisfaction. You announce without qualification that this is exactly what you conclude. And from your conclusion you take license to develop a fantasy in which you envision me in the company of a Mr. Arthur C. Clarke[2] "moving toward 'scientific truth' and the repudiation of art and humanity."

No less outrageous and absurd in its error is what you do with Walter Benjamin's position on the basis of my paraphrase of it. You say of Benjamin that he "objects to storytellers because they had 'an orientation towards practical interests'" and because they "have coun-

---

1. Protagonist of Bellow's novel *Mr. Sammler's Planet* (1970).
2. Arthur C. Clarke (1917–2008), British science fiction writer.

sel to give" and that he held stories in low esteem because they are likely to contain "something useful." No part of this description of Benjamin's position is true. All the characteristics of the art of story-telling which you say explain Benjamin's fancied objection to it are in point of fact the reasons for the love and admiration he gives it and for his thinking that something peculiarly human is lost when the telling of stories is no longer cherished.

There are many things in your essay that ask for extended consideration. For one example, there is the disingenuousness of the process by which you enforce your conclusions about Benjamin and me: your willingness to reason that because Baudelaire was nauseated by the idea of usefulness, it follows that Benjamin is nauseated by stories because they contain "something useful," and that I inevitably share his queasiness, which is also his response, and mine, and that of all members of our modern literary culture, to the Bourgeois, the Child, the Family, etc. There is also the vulgarity of your feigned surprise at my having brought this unknown Benjamin into the discussion of storytelling and your explanation that "intellectuals do refer to one another to strengthen their arguments."

But of course the crucial point is how are your violations of fact and truth to be accounted for? I stand bewildered before the two possibilities of an answer to that question. Each seems as far beyond credence as the other. On the one hand, that you should simply have failed to comprehend what I say and what Benjamin says in my paraphrase of him I can scarcely credit, given your known competence in the reading of texts far more difficult than mine. On the other hand, it is scarcely to be conceived, let alone believed, that you would consciously and deliberately pervert the meaning of what I had written.

Yet in some effectual sense this is precisely what you have done. Something like two years have passed since your essay was first composed to be given as a lecture at the Smithsonian Institution. It is impossible to suppose that in the course of that considerable time there were no occasions when you had reason to doubt whether you had after all dealt fairly and accurately with my views; perhaps some friend to whom you showed your manuscript, or an editor, would have remarked on the discrepancy between what he had always understood the disposition of my mind to be and what you were now saying it was; or perhaps the doubt would have come unprompted, with, say, the thought that, to the best of your knowledge of me, I really hadn't, either in my life or in my work, given any very clear sign of hoping for the end of art as the surest indication that man had achieved maturity and ultra-intelligence. In whatever way the doubt came to you and in whatever form, you decided not to act on it. I must understand this decision to be tantamount to a conscious and deliberate intention *not* to comprehend or present truthfully what I have said.

Sincerely,

262. TO ALAN WALD

November 26, 1974

Dear Mr. Wald:

Eleanor Clark's formulation of the relation of Herbert Solow to my novel is more accurate than yours. Solow can be said to have had "background influence" on the book. He cannot be said to have been "part of the inspiration" of it. That is to say, his relation with Chambers was much closer than mine and from him I learned a few things about Chambers that I might not have known without him. I did, however, have my own relation with Chambers and there were sources of information about him other than Solow. My English publishers are bringing out a new issue of the novel with a historical introduction by me. If you'll remind me to do so, say a month from now, I'll send you a copy of the introduction.

Meyer Schapiro's supposition that "the 'liberals' who had served as a letter drop for Maxim were the Trillings themselves" is quite mistaken.

Quincy Howe's characterization of my wife as "the most concerned Trotskyist extant" is of course sheer nonsense. She never was a Trotskyist—like other of us, she for a time turned to the Trotskyist group but this was out of curiosity rather than conviction and such association as there was continued but for a short time. Here I must very urgently warn you of the pitfalls of that word "Trotskyist"—in general, but most especially as applied to the *Menorah Journal* group. It isn't enough to rely, as you do, upon the use of quotation marks to protect the accuracy of your use of the word. Trotsky was for many of us a more or less sympathetic and engaging figure, but the party that set itself up as representative of his views did not have for us any commanding authority, though doubtless for some it had more attraction than it had for others. What John McDonald says in his letter to you about your use of the word is very sound and I urge you to take it with the utmost seriousness.

Yours sincerely,
Lionel Trilling

263. TO WILLIAM J. McGILL[1]

January 20, 1975

Dear President McGill:

Columbia has been more than generous in the honors it has bestowed upon me and of them all none has moved me so much as the invitation which the Trustees extend to me to receive the degree of doctor of letters, *honoris causa*, at this year's Commencement exercises. For the profound pleasure this gives me I am more grateful than I can easily say.

If, then, I go on to tell you that I have decided not to accept the Trustees' invitation, you will suppose the ground of my decision to be wholly one of principle. This is indeed the case. For some years now I have been confirmed in the opinion that our university's practice of awarding honorary degrees to certain professors upon their retirement, or very shortly after it, is not well advised. My reason for holding this opinion refers to the feelings of the whole body of retired professors, which, I need scarcely say, is very considerable in its numbers.

I think we all understand that for most people retirement from active service in their professions makes a difficult and often even a painful situation. Society urges us to put a good face on it and generally we do. But the likelihood of at least some distress is strong, and in all probability it is especially strong among university people, whose commitment to their work implies an involvement with a community

---

1. President of Columbia University.

and all the emotional ties that this entails. Although one does now and then come across the academic person who thinks of retirement as nothing but a liberation, this is unusual; university people typically respond to their withdrawal from active service with sadness or wryness and a general lowering of morale. Their sense of deprivation is in proportion to the extent to which they have been devoted to the university and have personalized it and regarded it with affection. The separation can't but be a trying experience and those who go through it are bound to be in a highly sensitive state of feeling, one in which they will readily take it to be invidious that, at the moment of separation, one or two of their number should be elected to receive, by way of farewell, the signal distinction of an honorary degree. Those who have not been so honored can scarcely fail to think of this as indicative of an adverse judgment which the university has passed upon them and upon the value of what they have contributed to the university. Among these persons it will be only those of a quite special magnanimity who will not feel slighted and in consequence begin their retirement a little more dispirited than they need be.

Here I should say that I think there are occasions when the awarding of an honorary degree to a retired member of the faculty is not reasonably to be faulted. If someone in retirement should have gone on to do work of a distinguished kind, the university might well wish to celebrate this achievement and could do so, after some passage of time, by means of the award of an honorary degree without the person's former colleagues thinking it anything but appropriate and pleasurable. This, however, is very different in its implications from the practice of annually, or almost that regularly, selecting one or more retiring professors to be honored. It is this practice that I wish to bring into question with the Trustees when I make my decision not to accept their invitation to me to receive an honorary degree at this year's Commencement.

I am confident that they and you yourself will understand that my deciding not to accept the degree in no way interferes with the pleasure and pride I feel in this expression of regard.

Yours sincerely,
Lionel Trilling

264. TO JEROME McGOVERN

February 17, 1975

Dear Mr. McGovern:

Thank you for sending your essay on intelligence as a moral ideal, which I find that I can comment on sooner than I said I could. It seems to me that it raises, with admirable directness, an important and fascinating question, in whose train many other questions follow. Our culture is surely singular in the emphasis it puts upon mental abilities. Schoolchildren—schoolboys—we've doubtless always classed as stupid or clever, but perhaps at no other time has so much weight been given to the distinction and, as you say, so much moral significance, though commonly of a clandestine kind. That this should be so invites endless speculation—a most comprehensive and suggestive account of our contemporary culture could surely be based on a description of this state of affairs and why and how it came about.

Your essay gave me an especial pleasure because I read it just when there had come to my mind the first social generalization I ever made. I was between five and six years old when I took note of the way my family used the word "educated" in praise of certain people and I said to myself in lofty disapproval, "In Olden Times people thought it was good to be honest and brave but now you have to be educated." This seemed to me what I would now call decadent—and no doubt I was right!

Sincerely,
Lionel Trilling

265. TO EMERY NEFF[1]

April 14, 1975

Dear Emery:

It was a great pleasure to me to have your letter, and I am happy to know that you could find interest in my essay about the relation of Whittaker Chambers to my novel.[2]

---

1. See page 89.
2. "Whittaker Chambers and 'The Middle of the Journey,'" *New York Review of Books*, April 17, 1975.

I'm afraid that my experience of Communists doesn't resemble or confirm yours. Things may have been different in an early time, in the days shortly after the revolution—it may then have been possible for people who committed themselves to Communism to have had the sweet naive moral impulses you saw in Philip Loeb and Sydney Kaufman (have I read his name correctly?). Of Zablodowsky I cannot speak—I lost track of him after college and have heard nothing about him since his resignation from the UN secretariat in 1953. But nothing in the moral temper of the Communists I have known has led me to think of them as worthy of being singled out for "respect." Indeed, quite the opposite is so. I of course don't mean to say that their commitment to Communism annihilated all moral sensibility and judgment whatever, but I would say that the closer they came to the actuality of Communism and the more they assented to something that went beyond an ideal and a theory, the closer they came to moral corruption.

I send you my congratulation on your happy and prosperous years of retirement.

Sincerely,

266. TO MORRIS DICKSTEIN[1]

April 28, 1975

Dear Morris:

I shall try to answer your objections to my essay in the order in which you make them.

It was not so much to the avowed Communists of the 1930s and 1940s that I attributed the wish to negate the political life but, rather, to the fellow travelers of Communism. I suppose, however, that my characterization could also be applied to actual Communists.

As to my definition of the political life being a "very special" one, I can't agree with you. Its specialness lies for you in its consisting of such elements as consensus, debate, compromise, and so on. Doubtless this is not the only definition of the political life that can be made—I suppose that all the activities which bear upon the direc-

---

1. Morris Dickstein (1940–), literary critic, a former student of Trilling's.

tion of the polity can be said to constitute the political life. But my definition is the one that is likely to be most salient in consciousness in our culture. I grant that it lies within the possibility of the language to speak of the political life of totalitarian countries, but would you not agree with me in thinking that it sounds odd to speak of a person as being "active in the political life" of Nazi Germany or of Russia? It would be more natural, I think, to describe him as being "a member of the government" or as "a member of the administrative class."

You say that you wonder how much of the political life actually is carried on through consensus, debate, compromise, and so on, and you propose "covert manipulation and influence" as being the real means by which politics is conducted. And you say that in this country—you use the phrase "even in this country" and I confess that in the context I don't comprehend the force of "even"—covert manipulation and influence have "so often been the norm" of the political life. It is doubtless true that in this country, though probably not more than in other countries which have some form of popular political organization, there is a measure of covert manipulation and influence to be discovered. This state of affairs, which I take to be virtually inevitable, qualifies but does not of itself nullify such beneficence as we commonly impute to political systems that proceed by popular participation. I can conceive covert manipulation and influence becoming so pervasive as actually to negate the avowed principles of a popular political system, but the mere presence of covert manipulation and influence does not have this effect.

You seem to imply that the people I characterize adversely refused to accept the political life in my definition of it because my definition is so "very special" as not to have been adequate for them. I must suppose that when you take this position, you do not want me to infer from it that the fellow travelers of Communism, and avowed Communists as well, subscribed to a definition of the political life as consisting in covert manipulation and influence. But if I am right in this supposition, I think you must say what you understand to have been the definition of the political life to which fellow travelers and Communists subscribed.

You say that although I insist that Chambers was an honorable man, I make no judgment about the morality of informing. If indeed I have not done so, at least by implication, I am ready to do so now. I shall not stop to raise the question of whether we can properly equate the concept of honor with what we commonly mean by morality but shall at once remark on the example you offer of perfect honor in situations in which the possibility of informing against others presents itself. You say: "But it strikes me that if there's to be any attribution of honor it must go to a witness like Lillian Hellman,[1] who expressed her perfect willingness to discuss her own beliefs, past and present, but refused to inform on others." I will agree with your judgment that Miss Hellman's position is exemplary so far as it bears upon *beliefs*, and so far as Miss Hellman was able to persuade herself that nothing could be in question except beliefs. But Chambers was not in the position that you conceive Miss Hellman to have been in: he had special knowledge not of mere beliefs of others but of their actions, which were not mere gestures but had actual and measurable consequences. When he himself was a member of the Communist underground, he thought these actions were morally justified. It was for him at least a matter of indifference and perhaps even a satisfaction that the actual consequences of the actions he knew of and took part in might have a serious effect upon the well-being of his own country. When he underwent a change of belief—which, I need scarcely say, is not a dishonorable event in a man's life—it was no longer possible for him to take this position. He now gave his loyalty to his country and could not be indifferent to what might do it harm. This being so, would you say that it was the part of honor for him to keep silent about the acts of espionage against the United States which his former political comrades, some of whom were his friends, persisted in committing? That position has, of course, been taken—E. M. Forster took it, laying it down as an unquestionable rule that one should betray one's country rather than one's friend. I find this reprehensible and contemptible.

I count on you not to misunderstand me if I say that, although I'd be happy to talk with you about your essay on the 1950s, I'd like

---

1. Lillian Hellman (1905–1984), playwright, took the Fifth Amendment when called to testify before the House Un-American Activities Committee in 1952.

to postpone a meeting until after I've completed a historical piece I myself have it in mind to write. I hope to get it finished by the autumn and I'll look forward to seeing you then.

Sincerely,

Lionel Trilling

267. TO STANLEY BURNSHAW

May 1, 1975
35 Claremont Avenue

Dear Stanley:

[. . .]

You are kind to take my literary fortunes into your thoughts and to give me your advice about them. From time to time I've wondered how the two stories, especially "Of This Time, of That Place," might be brought out in a volume of my own, but have never found a way—or not beyond the counsel of perfection which would be to write a few more stories and bring out a volume. To make of them an appendix to the novel doesn't seem quite right. And the notion of a portable L.T., though inevitably it is gratifying, is also uncomfortable—for that I don't have the stature or the configuration. There is also some possibility that a Collected Essays of L.T. will be in the works in a year or two and somehow that seems to be within the range of appropriateness, but not the other. So the problem of what to do with the stories is still unsolved. Maybe there is some advantage in their having no fixed habitation, being always sought after, not to be read until made the object of a devoted quest!

You probably know that I retired from my professorship last year, but I shall go on teaching a few years longer. The thing I got the Guggenheim for is really a sort of autobiographical account of our cultural period, and I have the feeling that, even though I don't mean it to be personal in an intimate way, it may have the effect of liberating me for another shot at a novel; I have the idea for one which just conceivably I'll have the boldness to realize.

And you, what are you doing in the writing way? Your days and your mind can't have been exactly disposed to poetry, but has there been some in spite of everything?

Harold Bloom[1] *is* a Something, isn't he? I keep telling myself that I must discover what he's up to and what it's worth, but maybe this is one of the imperatives I shall after all disobey.

268. TO HENRY F. MAY[2]

May 19, 1975

Dear Professor May:

Thank you for writing to me as you did about the Whittaker Chambers article[3]—your letter gave me great pleasure.

Although I in some degree shared your belief that some courage was needed to publish the piece, it turns out that we were mistaken. I expected a sizable amount of vituperation—including anonymous phone calls!—and actually there was virtually none. Although it may be that *The New York Review of Books* received letters protesting the article, the editors have not forwarded them to me for answer and have decided, I must suppose, not to publish any. The author of one letter for publication sent me a carbon copy of it, very long, very much in the tone of the old days, very primitive in its use of all the Stalinist clichés. The only other letter of objection I received was from a former student and colleague who asked me with sufficient amenity how I justified this or that position I had taken. Although the writer is a literary scholar of quite considerable ability, the naïveté of his views confirms your view, which is also mine, that American intellectuals are not very good at political discrimination.

For the sake of completeness I'll add that a few people were a little distressed at my having attributed to Chambers a "magnanimous intention"—they thought this went a bit too far. In England the publication of the article in the *Times* and the reissue of the novel itself has made, my editor tells me, a sizable stir in the intellectual class; the reviews of the novel itself that I have seen are quite favorable. The English intellectuals have their own political insensibilities, but they at least know that some very engaging members of the upper classes

---

1. Harold Bloom (1930–), literary critic and theorist.
2. Henry F. May (1915–2012), American intellectual and religious historian.
3. See page 417.

did actually work for the Russians. On the other hand, however, a former student of mine now at Oxford tells me that three undergraduates asked him to explain who Whittaker Chambers was! My experience in this country suggests that our young people have no knowledge of the case, or, indeed, of what the nature of the middle-class relation to Communism has been.

But I did think that the commitment of the middle-aged and aging to their old views was more intense than it has shown itself to be in relation to my article. Maybe the explosion is yet to come, the more terrible for its delay!

I'll say again how grateful I am for your letter.

Sincerely,

Lionel Trilling

269. TO JACQUES BARZUN

August 5, 1975
St. Andrews, New Brunswick, Canada

Dear Jacques:

[. . .]

The mention of plans for an earlier departure than planned will doubtless suggest to you that the summer hasn't been a successful one. The weather has been dreadful: thus it must have been in Götterdämmerung; I think we have not had more than two or three bright days since we have been here. This is, I gather, not unique to St. Andrews but is what prevails all along the eastern coast, but I think it comes with special force here in this doubtless pretty but no less doubtless melancholy town. And it comes to underscore and confirm my sense of not being in good form. Chiefly the trouble is of the altitude of the spirits—mine have for the last months been low—but with this goes an osteoarthritic condition, a very [word missing] matter with me but suddenly asserting its authority with a new decisiveness. And then the new cottage to which we have moved after our term at the one at the hotel turns out to be inconvenient and uninviting, what with myriads of quaint American objects all over its walls and shelves. So we have decided to be *positive* and cut our losses and return home about the seventeenth of the month.

Not that nothing good has happened here. I finished a longish essay on Jane Austen[1] (but really more than her) which Diana says is very good and there are moments when I almost believe her. Of course the best part of our time here was having Jim with us for three weeks. He seems in very good shape and has begun to write for publication, we think remarkably well and at least his first editor—at *Commentary*—shares our opinion and has begun to nag him for more reviews. What impressed us even more was that he told Diana exactly what was wrong with the first pages of her book, whereupon she discarded them, began all over again in a new way, and has since begun again to move at a most heartening clip.

I long to hear that you are wholly vegetative and how you go about being so. I think that that information ought not be directed here, where mail comes very slowly, but to Claremont Avenue. If we should change our intention of an early departure, I'll let you know.

Diana joins me in sending dearest love to you and Mariana.

Lionel

270. TO I. BERNARD COHEN[2]

October 31, 1975

Dear Professor Cohen:

Mrs. Trilling has asked me to let you know that unhappily there is still no better news to report of Professor Trilling. She supposes that by now your daughter has told you the diagnosis—an inoperable tumor of the pancreas, rather badly spread. Intensive chemotherapy is for many reasons wholly out of the question but the doctors are still gambling on very mild bearable doses: it should be known in a week or two whether there is any response to them. In the meanwhile his anguish is caused less by physical pain, which can be managed by medication, than by his terrible and always increasing weakness.

Mrs. Trilling is sure you will understand why she feels unable to write all of this to you in her own hand, also how important it is that any non-mandatory use of the telephone be avoided. She thanks you

---

1. "Why We Read Jane Austen" appeared posthumously in *The Last Decade*.
2. I. Bernard Cohen (1914–2003), historian of science, was Trilling's cousin.

warmly for your letter. She says your daughter spoke of Mrs. Cohen being ill and sincerely hopes that by now she is home and well again.

Sincerely,

Laura Palmer
Secretary to Mr. Trilling
Dictated by D.T.

P.S. Jim is of course remaining at home pending developments.[1]

---

1. Lionel Trilling died on November 5, 1975.

ACKNOWLEDGMENTS

The majority of the letters in this volume are found in the Lionel Trilling Papers, in the Rare Book and Manuscript Library at Columbia University. This archive includes twenty-nine boxes of correspondence, both incoming and outgoing. For much of his life, but especially in the 1950s and after, Trilling kept carbon copies of significant typewritten and dictated letters; the archive also contains his original letters to several important correspondents, which were returned and deposited after his death. I am very grateful to the staff of the library for their extensive assistance in navigating the Trilling Papers. Other letters come from the following archives, to whose staff I am indebted:

Newton Arvin Papers, Neilson Library, Smith College
Jacques Barzun Papers, Rare Book and Manuscript Library, Columbia University
Stanley Burnshaw Papers, Harry Ransom Center, University of Texas at Austin
Richard Chase Papers, Rare Book and Manuscript Library, Columbia University
Commentary Magazine Archive, Harry Ransom Center, University of Texas at Austin
Allen Ginsberg Papers, Rare Book and Manuscript Library, Columbia University
Clement Greenberg Papers, Archives of American Art
Sidney Hook Papers, Hoover Institution Archives, Stanford University
Henry Hurwitz Papers, American Jewish Archives
Melvin Lasky Papers, Lasky Center for Transatlantic Studies, Ludwig Maximilian University of Munich
Partisan Review Online, Howard Gotlieb Archival Research Center, Boston University
David Riesman Papers, Harvard University Archives
Harold Rosenberg Papers, Getty Research Institute

427

Meyer Schapiro Papers, Rare Book and Manuscript Library, Columbia University

Francis Steegmuller Papers, Rare Book and Manuscript Library, Columbia University

Allen Tate Papers, Firestone Library, Princeton University

Edmund Wilson Papers, Beinecke Rare Book and Manuscript Library, Yale University

Morton Dauwen Zabel Papers, Newberry Library

Thanks to Abigail Martin for providing me with copies of Trilling's correspondence with her parents, Henry and Rachel Rosenthal. I was fortunate to have research assistance from Terrence Cullen, John Ulrich, Phillip Fry, and Martha Davidson.

The award of a fellowship from the John Simon Guggenheim Foundation was indispensable in allowing me to complete this book. I am grateful to the friends who supported and encouraged the project, including Leon Wieseltier, Andrew Delbanco, Morris Dickstein, Michael Kimmage, and Casey Blake; and to Jeremy Dauber and my other colleagues at Columbia University's Institute for Israel and Jewish Studies. Eric Chinski and Alexander Star of Farrar, Straus and Giroux and Andrew Wylie and Jacqueline Ko of the Wylie Agency made it possible for this book to be published. Finally, I am grateful to James Trilling for entrusting me with the task of editing his father's correspondence.

INDEX

Bloom, Harold, 422
Blum, Léon, 62–63
book clubs: Book-of-the-Month, 377; Mid-Century, 325; Readers' Subscription, 224
Bottom Dogs (Dahlberg), 405
Bourne, Randolph, 118
Bouvard and Pécuchet (Flaubert), 224–25, 228, 231, 235
Bradley, F. H., 233
Brandeis University, 148*n*
Brecht, Bertolt, 132, 142
Breit, Harvey, 188
Brisbane, Arthur, 236
Brod, Max, 385
Brontë sisters, 367
Brooks, Cleanth, 95, 96
Brooks, Van Wyck, 88
Brown, Alan, 61*n*; LT's correspondence with, 61–64
Brown, Francis, 208
Brown, Ned, 248
Brown, Ruth, 150*n*; LT's correspondence with, 150–52
Brown, W. Barrett, 34*n*; LT's correspondence with, 34
Browning, Robert, 8
Bruce, Lenny, 361–63
Bundy, McGeorge, 286, 287
Burgess, Guy, 248
Burgum, Edwin Berry, 158
Burke, Kenneth, 59, 95–96, 199
Burnshaw, Stanley, 293–94, 295*n*, 333; LT's correspondence with, 295–96, 352–57, 367–69, 421–22
Burroughs, William, 294*n*, 295
Butler, Nicholas Murray, 57, 118
Byron, George Gordon, Lord, 87, 95

Caesar and Cleopatra (Shaw), 136
Café de la Régence, 273
Cambridge, Mass., 36, 383
Cambridge Five, 248*n*
Cambridge University, 193, 195, 199, 273–75, 319, 337, 352
Canaletto, 322

Cantwell, Robert, 69
capitalism, 119–20
Cargill, Oscar, 100
Carlyle, Thomas, *Sartor Resartus*, 400
Carman, Harry, 144*n*, 380; LT's correspondence with, 144–47
Carroll, Paul, 294*n*; LT's correspondence with, 294–95
Castle, The (Kafka), 220
Catcher in the Rye, The (Salinger), 228–29
censorship and obscenity, 142–43, 240, 294–95, 298, 363
Century of Hero-Worship, A (Bentley), 123–27, 130, 131
Cervantes, Miguel de, 14, 15
Chagall, Marc, 241
Chambers, Whittaker, 97, 103, 378, 389–90, 402, 414, 419–20, 423; *The Middle of the Journey* and, 161, 389–90, 414, 417
Charterhouse (school), 265–66
Chartres Cathedral, 272, 324
Chase, Richard V., 152*n*, 174, 214, 243; *Herman Melville*, 279–80; LT's correspondence with, 152–53, 166–67, 278–80; "Radicalism Today," 278–80
Chaucer, Geoffrey, 54
Chiappe, Andrew, 199
Chiaromonte, Nicola, 272
Children of the Ghetto (Zangwill), 399
China, 66–67
Civilization and Its Discontents (Freud), 291–92
civil rights, *see* racial issues
Clark, Eleanor, 414
Clarke, Arthur C., 412
Clawson, Robert, LT's correspondence with, 332–33
Claybourne, Dorothy Hite, LT's correspondence with, 385
Clute, Howard M., LT's correspondence with, 41–43
coal miners, 52–53

Cohen, Elliot, 3n, 27–28, 54, 114n, 199, 208, 236; LT's correspondence with, 3, 29–34, 114–16, 119–20, 310, 311; Warshow's article and, 163–66

Cohen, I. Bernard, 424n; LT's correspondence with, 424–25

Coleman, Louis, 55n; LT's correspondence with, 55–56

Coleridge, Samuel Taylor, 15, 58–59, 265; French Revolution and, 58–59; *Table Talk*, 22

Collegiate School, 201–203

Columbia Club, 34

Columbia Review, 196

Columbia University, x, 3, 8–9, 75, 100, 175, 226, 250, 337, 343; Jewish coloration of, 400–401; liberalism and, 401–402; LT as student at, x, 41, 400–402; LT as teacher at, viii, x, 114, 117, 144–47, 177, 181–83, 192, 194–95, 197, 216–17, 292, 351, 354, 378, 383; LT's Harvard invitation and, 286–87; LT's letters written from, 65, 84–85, 87–88, 142–49, 189, 191–92, 208–10, 218–19, 225–27, 231–32, 281–82, 295–96, 314–15, 344–45, 371–72, 410–11; LT's offer of honorary degree from, 415–16; LT's retirement from, 421; LT's salary at, 144–47, 182; Luther invitation and, 56–57; Oxford and, 354, 395–96; Seixas Society at, 296–97; statement on academic freedom, 229–31; student protests at, 375–76, 381–82; Thayer at, 84–85

Commager, Henry Steele, 190

Commentary, viii, 3n, 114–16, 119n, 164, 192n, 199, 208, 226n, 243–44, 247, 309n, 310, 312, 313, 401, 424; "Forster as Homosexual" (Ozick), 387; "I'm Sorry, Dear" (Farber), 347–49; LT's letter to editor of, 311–12; "My Negro Problem—and Ours" (Podhoretz), 325; "On the Steps of Low Library" (D. Trilling),

376n; "On Walter Benjamin" (Alter), 382; "Science, Literature, and Culture: A Comment on the Leavis-Snow Controversy" (Trilling), 330n; Warshow's review of *The Middle of the Journey* in, 163–66

Communism, Communists, 46, 55n, 61, 69, 74, 132–33, 160, 161–62, 248, 282, 284, 418; Chambers and, 97, 161, 389–90, 419–20, 423; and Columbia University statement on academic freedom, 229–31; liberalism and, 222; Slesinger and, 365–66

Communist International (Comintern), 61, 66–67

concentration camps, 116–17

conformity, 282–83, 336; *In Search of Heresy: American Literature in an Age of Conformity* (Aldridge), 276–78; intellectuals and, 336–37; "This Age of Conformity" (Howe), 235–37

Congress for Cultural Freedom, 269n, 273

Connolly, Cyril, 262

Conrad, Joseph, 155, 233

Country Life, 384

Covici, Pascal "Pat," 179n, 337–41; Bellow's *Adventures of Augie March* and, 218–19, 225–27; death of, 350–51; *The Liberal Imagination* and, 167, 179–80, 187–88; LT's correspondence with, 179–80, 187–88, 218–19, 225–27, 344–45

Cowley, Malcolm, 58n, 77; LT's correspondence with, 58–59

Cox, Archibald, 381n

Cox Commission Report, The: Crisis at Columbia, 381–82

Cozzens, James Gould, 385

Crane, Hart, 122

criticism, vii, 94, 95, 100, 106, 137–38, 172–75, 194, 210, 215, 247, 276–77, 281, 337, 371; New Criticism, vii, 95n, 281

culture, ix–x, 85–86, 185, 231,

234–35, 254, 255, 284, 285, 324, 363, 372–74, 399; of conformity, *see* conformity; cultural despair, 374; cultural revolution, 255, 373; Freud and, 362; integrity and dignity and, 283; literature and, 366–67, 388; LT's life and, ix–x; politics and, 85–86, 311, 324; writing and, 379
Currier and Ives, 245
Cutler, Addison T., LT's correspondence with, 56–57

Dahlberg, Edward, 405–406
Daiches, David, 106
Daily Cardinal, The, 9
Daniel Deronda (Eliot), 9
Dante Alighieri, 407
Daumier, Honoré, 51, 274
Davis, Peter, 364n; LT's correspondence with, 364–66
death: art and, 308; love and, 307–308
Death Kit (Sontag), 370
Decter, Midge, 302
Defanti, Charles, 405n; LT's correspondence with, 405–406
Delphi, 324
Dennis, Nigel, 103
Depression, Great, 106
de Rougemont, Denis, 272
Deutsch, Babette, 37
Dewey, John, 66n, 83, 402
Dickens, Charles, 14, 15, 98, 224, 367, 400; *Little Dorrit*, 232–33
Dickstein, Morris, 418n; LT's correspondence with, 418–21
Dictionnaire des idées reçues (Flaubert), 224, 231–32
Diderot, Denis, 273
Dissent, 236, 252, 254
Doings and Undoings (Podhoretz), 335–36
Donoghue, Denis, 403n; LT's correspondence with, 403–404
Doron, Daniel, 345n; LT's correspondence with, 345–46

Dostoevski, Fyodor, 14–15, 103, 285; *The Possessed*, 12
Doubleday, 249n, 368
Doyle, Arthur Conan, *Sherlock Holmes*, 228
"Dreiser, Anderson, Lewis, and the Riddle of Society" (Trilling), 197
Dreiser, Theodore, 136, 137
Drouant, 269
"Duchess' Red Shoes, The" (Schwartz), 210, 215–16
Dumas, Alexandre, 104

Eagle, Hazel, LT's correspondence with, 334–35
Ecclesiastes, 45
Edel, Leon, vii, 359n, 393–95; "Literature and Life Style," 356–57, 359–60; LT's correspondence with, 359–60
Edman, Irwin, 36–37
"Edmund Wilson: A Backward Glance" (Trilling), 280–81
education, 391, 399, 417; literature in, 193–94, 387–88
Edward Arnold (publisher), 106
Eisenberg, Emanuel, 43
Eliot, George, 233, 399; *Daniel Deronda*, 9
Eliot, T. S., 188, 306, 328, 405; *The Sacred Wood*, 10, 366–67; *The Waste Land*, 302n, 386
Ellison, James, LT's correspondence with, 304
"Embattled Vision, The" (Podhoretz), 299
Emerson, Ralph Waldo, 60, 138
Emerson-Thoreau Committee, 387
E. M. Forster (Trilling), 100–103, 105–10, 128, 222, 316, 339
Emma (Austen), ix
Emmanuel, Pierre, 270, 271
Empson, William, 95, 96
Encounter, 110n, 264, 267; "Where to Begin" (Rosenberg), 371–72
Ends and Means (Huxley), 73
Enemy, The, 10

England, 268, 350, 354–55, 369–71; London, 261–68, 273, 318–20, 383, 399; Oxford, 346, 349, 352, 354, 395, 403; Penshurst, 369
English Institute, 172–73
Epstein, Jason, 249–50
Erskine, John, 401
Estelle, Sister, 406n; LT's correspondence with, 406–407
Ethical Studies (Bradley), 233
Evans, Walker, 92n
Existentialists, 233
Experience of Literature, The (Trilling), 295n, 344, 367–69, 391–92
Eyeless in Gaza (Huxley), 64

Fadiman, Clifton "Kip," 17–19, 22, 28, 101, 103, 188; Dahlberg and, 405, 406; in Van Doren's essay, 377
Fadiman, Pauline "Polly," 18
Farber, Leslie, 347–49
Farrar, Straus and Giroux, 250–51
Farrell, James T., 218
fascism, 69, 132, 133, 230, 323
"Fate of Pleasure, The" (Trilling), 331
Faulkner, William, 244, 275n; LT's correspondence with, 275–76
Fay, Alice, LT's correspondence with, 29
Feinstein, Herbert, 248n; LT's correspondence with, 248–49, 288–90
Feldman, Irving, 250n, 334; LT's correspondence with, 250–51, 358, 383
Fiedler, Leslie, 249, 342n; LT's correspondence with, 342–43
Fifth Amendment, 229–30, 420n
Fitelson, William, 249
Fitzgerald, F. Scott, 185–86
Fitzgerald, Robert, 155, 253
Flaubert, Gustave, 224n, 225, 270; *Bouvard and Pécuchet*, 224–25, 228, 231, 235; *Dictionnaire des idées reçues*, 224
"Flaubert's Last Testament" (Trilling), 231

Flint, Robert W., 137n, 153; LT's correspondence with, 137–39, 215–16, 228–29
Flowering of New England, The (Brooks), 88
Ford Foundation, 218n, 321
Forster, E. M., viii, 92, 93, 108, 128, 274, 316, 420; *E. M. Forster* (Trilling), 100–103, 105–10, 128, 222, 316, 339; "Forster as Homosexual" (Ozick), 387; LT's Nobel Prize nomination for, 355; *Maurice*, 387
Fraenkel, Osmond, 104
France, 62, 223; Paris, 268–73; self-examination and, 257–58; in World War II, 85, 117
"France: An Ode" (Coleridge), 58–59
Freeman, The, 37, 291
"Free Man's Worship, A" (Russell), 402
free speech, 56–57
French Revolution, 58–59, 71
Freud, Anna, 362–63
Freud, Sigmund, ix, 69, 160, 168, 258, 291–92, 302, 305, 353, 394; *Beyond the Pleasure Principle*, 292, 308; Bruce and, 361, 362; culture and, 362; "Freud and Literature" (Trilling), 292; *Freud and the Crisis of Our Culture* (Trilling), 339–40, 362
Freud lectures, 246, 292
Friedberg, Charles, 79, 80
Friedman, Melvin, 258–59
"From an Autumn Journal" (D. Trilling), 215, 217
Frost, Robert, 303–304, 332–33; LT's Nobel Prize nomination for, 306; "A Speech on Robert Frost: A Cultural Episode" (Trilling), 293–96, 303, 332–33
Fulbright Program, 193, 199, 216
Future of an Illusion, The (Freud), 292

Galerie d'Apollon, 269
Gamble, William, LT's correspondence with, 291–93

310–12, 342, 388–89, 401; and character of Dr. Graf in *The Middle of the Journey,* 169–70; Chassidic, 313; Columbia and, 400–401; Columbia Club and, 34; *Commentary, see Commentary;* "Jewish Students I Have Known" (Van Doren), 376–78; Liberal Judaism, 355n; LT's lectures on, 53–54; medievalism and, 289; *The Menorah Journal, see Menorah Journal, The; The Rabbinic Mind* (Kadushin), 206–208; Seixas Society, 296–97; self-hatred and, 309–10, 312; sexuality and, 288–89; Slesinger family and, 364–65; Subcommittee on the Jewish University, 148–49; Trilling family and, 399, 400, 402

John Dewey: An Intellectual Portrait (Hook), 83
John Reed Club, 55–56
Johnson, Lyndon B., 286n
Johnson, Marjorie, 10
Johnson, Pamela Hansford, 375n; LT's correspondence with, 375–76
Jonson, Ben, 326–27, 369
Journal of Aesthetics, The, 309
Journal of Personality, 112n
Joyce, James, 10, 46, 47, 54, 250; *James Joyce* (Levin), 316; *A Portrait of the Artist as a Young Man,* 386; *Ulysses,* 368, 386
Judaism, *see* Jews and Judaism
Juskowitz, Hyman, LT's correspondence with, 157–61

Kadushin, Max, 206n, 353; LT's correspondence with, 206–208
Kafka, Franz: Brod and, 385; *The Castle,* 220
Kamenev, Lev, 62n
Kant, Immanuel, 7
Kaplan, Charles, 368
Kardiner, Abram, 143n; LT's letter to, 143

Kaufman, Sydney, 418
Kazin, Alfred, vii, 99, 100, 241–42
Keats, John, viii, 95, 189, 197, 224, 308; *Portable Keats* agreement, 340
Kehl, D. G., 379
Kennedy, Gail, 60
Kennedy, Jacqueline, 335; LT's correspondence with, 329
Kennedy, John F., 286n, 332; assassination of, 331–32; dinner for Nobel laureates given by, 334–35n
Kentucky coal mines, 52–53
Kenyon College, 173, 174, 178, 180–84, 292, 303, 332
Kenyon Review, The, 87, 92, 93, 136, 171n, 180, 208, 212, 258
Kerouac, Jack, 294n, 295
King's College, Cambridge, 273–75
Kinsey Report, viii, 348
Kipling, Rudyard, 228, 400
"Kipling" (Trilling), 228
Kirchwey, Freda, 86–87, 126, 127
Kirov, Sergei, 62
Kleinstein, David, LT's correspondence with, 169–70
Kline, Jerry, 58
Knopf (publisher), 100, 102, 108
Koestler, Arthur, 129–30
Kramer, Jane, 379n; LT's correspondence with, 379–80
Kreisler, Leon, 7
Kreymborg, Alfred, 38–39
Kristol, Gertrude, 262, 264
Kristol, Irving, 262, 272
Kronenberger, Louis, 253
Krumm, John, 328n; LT's correspondence with, 328–29

Lamb, Charles, 265
Lamont, Corliss, 73n; LT's correspondence with, 73–74
Lamont Prize, 250
Lang, H.-J., 376n; LT's correspondence with, 376–78, 381–82

Lasky, Melvin, 110*n*, 272; LT's
correspondence with, 110–12,
116–18
Last Decade, The (Trilling), 424*n*
Laughlin, James, 100*n*; LT's
correspondence with, 100–102,
106–108, 316
Law and Contemporary Problems,
240*n*
Lawrence, D. H., 14, 15, 37, 47, 199,
224, 265, 285, 298, 329, 335, 348,
367, 405
Leavis, F. R., 194, 195, 197, 405
"Leavis-Snow Controversy, The"
(Trilling), 330*n*
Left, *see* liberalism
Lehmann, John, 263–64
Lerner, Max, 109
Lessing, Doris, 319–20
"Lesson and the Secret, The"
(Trilling), 186
Let Us Now Praise Famous Men (Agee
and Evans), 92
Levin, Harry, 135, 316
Levy, Amy, 54
Lewis, Wyndham, 10
Lewisohn, Ludwig, 288, 401
liberal education, 221
Liberal Imagination, The (Trilling),
viii, 93*n*, 182, 239, 284, 408; "Art
and Neurosis," ix, 113*n*; Covici and,
167, 179–80, 187–88; critical
reception of, 193–97; "Freud and
Literature," 292; Friedman and,
258–59; "Huckleberry Finn,"
341–42; "The Immortality Ode,"
88–89; "Kipling," 228; "Manners,
Morals, and the Novel," 210; "The
Princess Casamassima," 204–206,
269*n*, 393; "Reality in America," x,
83*n*, 136*n*; solicitation of opinions
for, 187–88
liberalism, viii, 61, 69, 71, 77, 82,
93–95, 103, 126, 130, 134, 135, 149,
159–60, 250, 281, 282, 301, 326,
373; Bruce and, 361, 363; civil
rights and, 284; Columbia and,

401–402; Communism and, 222;
and LT as "antiliberal," 284;
meaning of, 221–23; *The Middle of
the Journey* and, viii, 222;
progressivism and, 109, 221–22,
284, 325; radicalism and, viii, 284;
revisionism and, 336–37
Liberal Judaism, 355*n*
Life, 191
Life Is with People (Zborowski and
Herzog), 288–90
Light, Donald, LT's correspondence
with, 384–85
Lindbergh, Charles, 9
Linley, William, 15
literary criticism, *see* criticism
Literary Guild, 368
literature, ix–x, 172, 179, 193–95, 360,
366–67; as agent of social change,
327–28; culture and, 366–67, 388;
modern, 330–31; obscenity and
censorship of, 142–43, 240,
294–95, 298, 363; politics and, viii,
77, 179, 220, 281, 327–28;
psychoanalysis and, 168–69;
teaching of, 194–95, 387–88
"Literature and Life Style" (Edel),
356–57, 359–60
Little, Brown (publisher), 75
Little Dorrit (Dickens), 232–33
Littlepage, John D., 73–74
Loeb, Philip, 418
London, 261–68, 273, 318–20, 383,
399
Londyn, Evelyn, LT's correspondence
with, 257–58
Lonely Crowd, The (Riesman),
184–85, 187
love: death and, 307–308; racial issues
and, 345
Low, Sol, 79, 80
Lubonsky, Louis, LT's correspondence
with, 259–60
Luce publications, 252–54
Lucretius, 69
Lukács, György, 330, 331
Luther, Hans, 56–57

Controversy," 330*n*; "The Sense of the Past," 95; *Sincerity and Authenticity*, 383, 403, 411–12; "The Situation of the American Intellectual at the Present Time," 252–56; "A Speech on Robert Frost: A Cultural Episode," 293–96, 303, 332–33; "Whittaker Chambers and 'The Middle of the Journey,'" 417, 422–23; "Why We Read Jane Austen," 424; "Wordsworth and the Rabbis," 206*n*
Trotsky, Leon, 66–68, 415
Trotsky Defense Committee, 66, 73–74
Trotskyism, 61–63, 67, 73, 77, 126–27, 135, 236, 414–15
Troyanovsky, Oleg, 132
Twain, Mark: *Adventures of Huckleberry Finn*, 141, 341–42; *The Adventures of Tom Sawyer*, 228, 300
Two Cultures, The: And a Second Look (Snow), 330
"Two Essays on Robert Frost" (Jarrell), 303

Ulysses (Joyce), 368, 386
Under Western Eyes (Conrad), 155
United Press (UP), 66
universities: literature education at, 387–88; student protests at, 375–76, 381–82
University of Wisconsin, x, 4, 8
Unpossessed, The (Slesinger), 364*n*, 410
Up Against the Ivy Wall (Avorn et al.), 382

Valéry, Paul, 235
Van Doren, Mark, 376–78, 380
Vanity Fair (Thackeray), 367
Varsity, 9
Vaughan, John, LT's correspondence with, 398–403

Viking Press, 150*n*, 167, 179*n*, 248, 337–41, 390, 398
Vogue, 152, 384
Voss, John, LT's correspondence with, 387–88

Wages of Expectation, The (Defanti), 405*n*
Wain, John, 283*n*; LT's correspondence with, 283–85
Wald, Alan, 410*n*; LT's correspondence with, 410–11, 414–15
Wall, The (Hersey), 305*n*
Wandervogel movement, 374
Warburg, Fredric, 176*n*, 262; LT's correspondence with, 176–79, 389–90
Warhol, Andy, 372
Warren, Norman, 411
Warren, Robert Penn, 141
Warsaw: ghetto, 305; Jablonna, 321–23
Warshow, Robert "Bob," 163*n*, 311–13; death of, 246–48; *The Immediate Experience*, 310; LT's correspondence with, 163–66; "The Mind of Robert Warshow" (Trilling), 310
Washington Square (James), 69
Waste Land, The (Eliot), 302*n*, 386
Watson, John Gillard, 233*n*; LT's correspondence with, 233–35
Watteau, Jean-Antoine, 274
Wayward Bus, The (Steinbeck), 159
Wechsler, Herbert, 380
Wellington, Arthur Wellesley, Duke of, 265
Wells, H. G., 190, 402
Wensberg, Erik, 344
West, Rebecca, 110, 188, 204*n*; LT's correspondence with, 204–206
We Went to College, 64
Whalen, Grover, 34*n*; LT's correspondence with, 34–35
"Where to Begin" (Rosenberg), 371–72
White, E. B., 317
Whitman, Walt, 256

A NOTE ABOUT THE AUTHOR

Lionel Trilling (1905–1975) was one of the most important American literary critics of the twentieth century. He taught at Columbia University for five decades and was the author of numerous books, including *The Liberal Imagination* and the novel *The Middle of the Journey.*

A NOTE ABOUT THE EDITOR

Adam Kirsch is a poet and literary critic whose writing has appeared in *The New Yorker, The New York Review of Books,* and other publications. He lives in New York.